Tourism and Heritage Resources in Garhwal Himalaya

An Approach to Planning and Management

S.K. Gupta

Kaveri Books
New Delhi - 110 002

Edition 2017

ISBN-10: 81-7479-056-X
ISBN-13: 978-81-7479-056-9

Published by
Kaveri Books
4832/24, Ansari Road
New Delhi-110002 (India)
Tel: 011-23288140, 23245799
E-mail : info@kaveribooks.com
kaveribooks@gmail.com
Website: www.kaveribooks.com

Typeset at
Delta Book World, New Delhi - 110 002.

PRINTED IN INDIA

Dedicated

to

My Loving Daughter

Suryanshi

PREFACE

Born and brought up in Orissa, let me admit that I knew so little of Garhwal Himalaya, the land of *rishis*, sages, and *ashrams,* which is also traveller's delight and naturalists paradise. My appointment in the Department of Tourism of H.N.B. Garhwal University in 1994 and undertaking this research work provided me an opportunity to explore this beautiful region having rich natural and cultural heritage. The region is rich in natural and cultural resources and includes some of the holiest places of Hindu pilgrimage. The region has vast tourism potential. Keeping in view that tourism has made fast in road into the boundaries of nature and culture, it is high time that region's heritage should be systematically studied and their preservation vis a vis promotion be made within the framework of region's integrated planning so that not only it is saved from fast deterioration from new tourism, but also brought to the lime light for the benefit of both host and guest. The study is aimed at systematic identification and defining the Heritage Tourism Products of the region and to suggest viable strategy to manage and promote it.

Undertaking and accomplishing this work is a herculean task and stands beyond the comprehensive ability of a single hand. Despite of the difficulties involved and the hindrances that have checked the progress, the responsibility undertaken has been fulfilled, with the cooperation received from numerous individuals and institutions. At the out set, therefore, I solemnly perform my pious duty of experessing my deep sense of gratitude to them. To supplement my studies, I was guided by the writings of eminent scholars in the tourism field like Dr. T.V. Singh, Dr. S.C. Bagri, Dr. O.P. Kandari, Edward Inskeep and many other scholars whose name can not be accommodated for want of space. I owe a debt of gratitude to Prof. S.C. Bagri, Director, Centre for Mountain Tourism and Hospitality Studies, HNB Garhwal University, Prof, O.P. Kandari, Chairman, Institute of Tourism and Hotel Management, Bundelkhand University, Prof. D.S. Bhardwaj, Chairman, Department of Tourism, Kurukshetra University, and Prof. S.K. Mushra, IITTM, Bhubaneswar for their kind encouragement and guidance in compiling this work. I also express my sincere thanks to Mr. A.K. Dwiwedi, Dy. Director, Uttranchal Tourism, Dr. D.R. Purohit, Dr. O.P. Gusain, Dr. B.P. Deoli, Dr. M.P.S. Bist and Mr. Sarvesh Uniyal for providing me useful information. I am deeply indebted to my parents who make me able to do his work. I must acknowledge that my wife, Mrs. Poonam Gupta and my father in-law have always been a source of inspiration for me, ever since I started my work.

Last but not the least I also thank Mr. B. Negi and Mr. R. Kaintura for taking special efforts in entering the manuscript in computer and Kaveri Books to publish this book.

—S.K. Gupta

Contents

LIST OF TABLES

LIST OF FIGURES

1

INTRODUCTION

1.1 SCENARIO OF TOURISM

Tourism is an ancient phenomenon-an inherent nomadic urge in man. From the very earliest historical period, travel was a fascination for man. In ancient time pilgrims, traders, and a few scholars and adventures souls had to undertake journey in order to satisfy their respective urges. Records in Brahman, Bible, Homer, Herodotus and Plutarch bear testimony to the early travels of man. Travelling in those times was difficult because of severe constraints of antiquated transport facilities, besides lack of safety and comforts. Thus tourism was limited to wealthy and privileged. The onset of renaissance in Italy during fourteenth century gave a new dimension to travel. The revival of classical literature, art and music made Italy the focus of attention and European centre for culture and humanism. The development of spas in seventeenth century in Europe may be considered as the starting point of modern tourism, which gathered momentum with the subsequent technological and industrial advancements. The industrial revolution brought about major changes in the scale and type of tourism development. The increase in productivity, regular employment and growing urbanisation gave more people the motivation and opportunity to go on holiday. In contrast to the earlier dominance by the wealthy, tourism began to embrace a broader social spectrum. Thus the industrial societies of Europe are responsible for the mass movement. Search for new kind of tourist products led them to discover ever-new destinations. Since tourism is associated with economic gains, the host countries found it necessary to develop facilities. This demand and supply matrix contributed to an organised growth of tourism, which virtually assumed the most dramatic proportions during the twentieth century, particularly after the World War II due to increased mobility. Yet new dimensions were achieved during sixties and seventies. International tourism recorded its highest growth rate of arrivals and receipt during the period of 1960-80.Janez (1982) had estimated an annual growth rate of 8.2% in the international tourist arrivals between 1965 to 1975.While the average annual growth rate was 4.2% between 1980-90{World Tourism Organisation (WTO)}. Talking in terms of total international tourist arrivals, it was recorded at 69 million marks in 1960,which subsequently rose to 160 million in 1970,214 million in 1975, 285 million in 1980, 459 million in 1990 and 663 million in 1999 (WTO). International tourist traffic is expected to grow at a rate of growth of about 4.1% a year over next two decade and will reach one billion tourist arrival by 2010AD and 1.6 billion by the year 2020.The regions which are likely to experience the maximum growth in tourist traffic in the coming years are East Asia/Pacific and South Asia. The tremendous growth in tourism is a direct outcome of economic and social progress, promoted by technological and scientific advancement, higher income, longer leisure time, and demographic and increasingly cheaper and varied tourist plant facilities (Singh 1975). In reality, international tourism, is influenced by wide number of factors such as: supply of facilities, government regulations, disposable income levels, introduction of new technology-particularly communication and transport technology, population changes, explicit and implicit barriers to travel, health of the world economy (income and income distribution), level of international airfares, promotion abroad (Private and Public), international airline and airport capacity and airline routes, political relations, currency devaluation , international inflation, availability of leisure times ,cost of accommodations, food and entertainment. Providing a perspective on future Cam(1969) was categorically worked out various factors leading to an unprecedented growth in tourism. From among them leisure has been considered the primary and most vital motivating factor. Human time can be fragmented more precisely as worktime, biological time, obligated time and free time. The time available solely at the disposal of the individual is the free time. According to the study conducted by the WTO in the member states of European Economic Community, the greatest part of human time is biological time (43.3%) on the annual basis. It is followed by work related time (34.0%), free time (15.7%) and obligated time (7%). The right to rest, leisure, freetime, holidays and leave with pay have been provided in numerous international documents and national constitutions. The legal recognition of right to holidays has led to a new concept of quality of life. Holidays are now being recognised as a time for education, a time of rest and a time for encounters and communication. It is thus basic human necessity rather than an avoidable luxury. The late futurist Herman Kahn (1976) in his book "The Next 200 Years " wrote, "It seems reasonable to assume that by the end of the century tourism will be one of the largest industry in the World, if not the largest." Considering its economic effects, tourism has already emerged as a huge giant. World Travel and Tourism Council (WTTC) studies show that globally Travel and Tourism is now the world's largest export industry, and is expected to more than double in size, in absolute term over the next decade .It is estimated that tourism receipt (US$ 453 billion in 1999) accounts for about 8% of the total world merchandise exports and more than 37% of international trade in services. According to WTTC research the contribution of Travel and Tourism in 1999 was 11.7% directly and indirectly to world GDP .In 1997 Travel and Tourism was expected to provide direct and indirect employment for 255 million people and accounted for 11% of the global workforce. By 2005, the industry job will reach 338 million. In the Gross output/GDP picture North America and the European union are the absolute leader, whereas the South Asia and the China region are the leader of Travel and Tourism employment. In 1995, Travel and Tourism in this region was expected to account for 108 million direct and indirect jobs. It is also interesting to note that it is the fastest growing Travel and Tourism employer in the World, with an expected 84.4% increase over the next decade. The countries include in other pacific (18.3 million jobs) are closely behind at 72.9% growth.

Fig. No-1.1

Percentage Share of World Tourist Arrivals in 1975

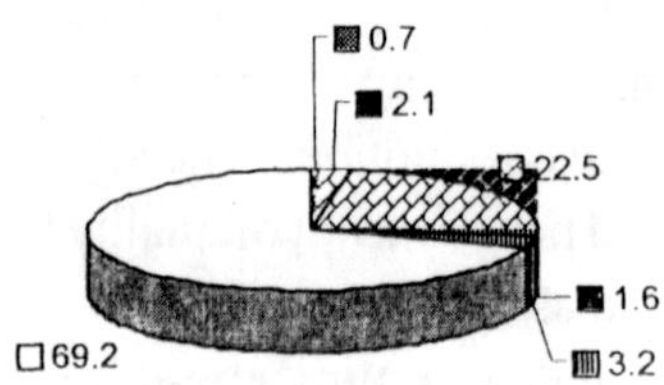

Percentage Share of World Tourism Arrivals in 1999

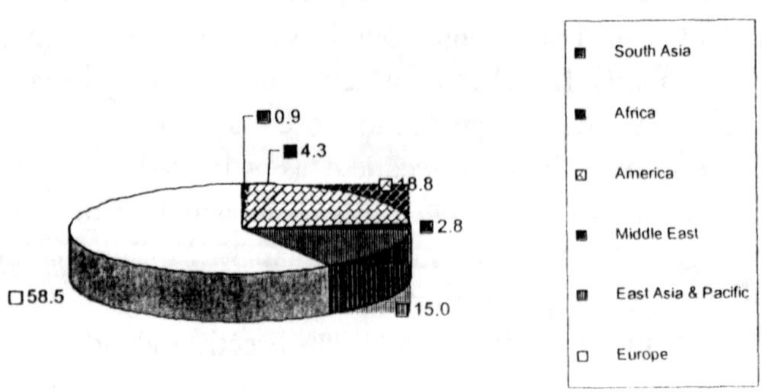

Fig. No-1.2

Percentage Share of World Tourism Receipts in 1975

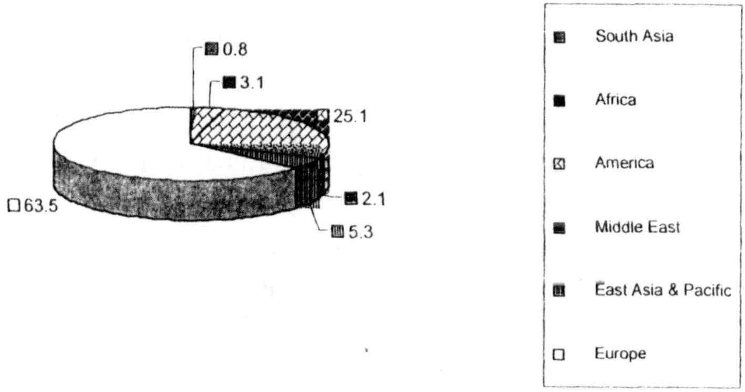

Percentage Share of World Tourism Receipts in 1999

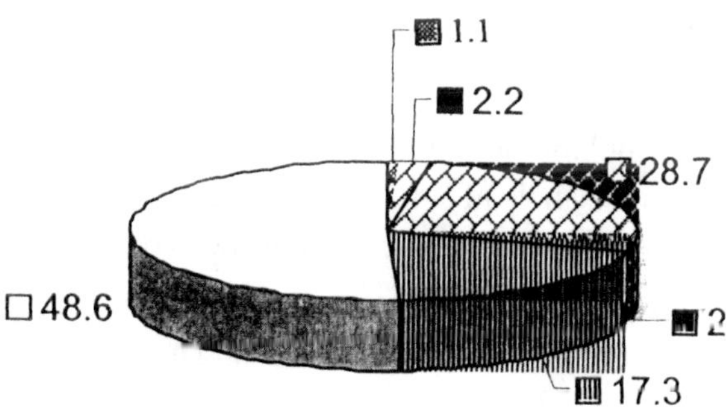

International tourism is growing faster in developing countries both for arrivals and receipts, reflecting a wider redistribution of tourism revenues in favour of the traditional and new emerging tourism destination in the third world (WTO). Virtually tourism has many advantages over other industries, which has promoted many nations of the world to involve themselves in positive action programs. Some of the more beneficial aspects of tourism are detailed below:

i) Tourism initiates harmonic growth in national incomes through on the spot consumption of the goods and the services by tourists. It often blends with other sectors of the economy. The demands of the foreign tourist denote a direct export of goods and services, which helps the countries in overcoming their trade deficits.

ii) Tourism unlike other industries, is much more pervasive in its economic impacts as it represents an injection of external purchasing power in to economy, widely distributed in initial regional impacts; and acting as a stimulus to every sector of economy (Cosgrove and Jackson 1972).

iii) Multiplier of tourism as a whole is higher than the multiplier effect of the other sector of economy, besides having a broader base of productive cycles.

iv) Tourism is highly labour intensive, with a very high employment potential.

v) The implantation of tourism in the areas devoid of other industries, help to correct regional imbalance and combat depopulation of rural and mountainous regions.

vi) Scientifically planned tourism encourages and ensures the protection of vulnerable cultural and natural heritages.

Considering these values and the beneficent role of tourism in fostering social awareness and promoting international goodwill, WTO has declared it as the basic and most desirable human activity deserving praise and encouragement of all people. Significantly, irrespective of the nature and the quality of tourism resources of the developing countries, developed nations have served both as potential tourist market and effective tourist destination. Thus till now almost 78% of the world tourism receipt are taken by European and American Countries (WTO, 1998), leaving behind a small share for the III world. According to WTO in 1998 the developing countries' share was 31% of total International tourist arrivals and 31% of International tourist receipt.

The main reasons behind it have so far been, (I) location of developed countries in the close proximity of potential tourist markets, (II) their clustering, and (III) the advance amenities they provide. However, the developing countries, which virtually need the tourist dollars, are abridging this tourist gap slowly but steadily. The past couple of years have witnessed a gradual diversification of the tourist market and the emergence of the new destinations. The factors responsible for this gradual shift towards the developing countries, is the emergence of special class of tourists and more intra-regional movement. This new class of tourists, tired of the congestion and complexities of modern life is more inclined towards pure nature and heritage resources. Heritage tends to become unique selling points due to their indigenous individuality .The tourist fulfills this recreational needs through close contacts with nature and culture, through activities like mountaineering, rock climbing, trekking, trailing, wild life watching and participation in fairs and festivals. Fortunately, the developing nations including India are still in possession of some unspoiled nature and culture in contrast to the 'built environment' of developed World. Thus the developing countries offer a promise of future market of this growing clientele. Bio-Culturally rich landscape of India makes it a unique tourist destination of Asia. In her natural endowments, she has vast recreational resource reservoirs in her wondrous Himalayas, and beautiful long sea beaches, vast stretches of sands and gregarious tropical forest. In human environment she has a history of over 5000 years and a mosaic of culture and heritage that cover a vast field of human skill, endeavor and perseverance.

Despite of vast potential, India so far has only marginal share of 0.4% of World Tourism movement, and 0.71% in the total expenditure. It lags behind its competitors such as Thailand, Malaysia, Singapore and Indonesia, although it receives a little over the 50% of the total arrivals of South Asia. Lack of infrastructure, comprehensive database and dissipated marketing and promotional efforts are the primary factors effecting India's tourism industry even though it is third largest foreign exchange earner for the country after ready-made garments and gems and jewelry. However, in terms of the net retention ratio, tourism ranks higher, as in the case of gems and jewelry the import content is very high. The foreign exchange earning from tourism during 1998-99 was estimated to be about Rs.12011 crores and the average per capita expenditure of tourist in India was US$ 1337. The rate of growth in foreign exchange earnings from tourism was exceptionally high (23.3% during 1995-96) and is expected to become even higher in the coming year. The most significant feature of tourism industry in India is its capacity to generate large-scale employment opportunities particularly in remote and backward areas. A desirable feature of tourism industry is that it employs a large number of women, both educated & uneducated. In fact women are in large number in hotel, airline services, travel agencies, handicrafts making, cultural activities and other tourism related activities. The direct employment in tourism sector during 1997-98 was about 10 million persons accounting for about 3.4% of the total labour force. The labour capital ratio per million rupees of investment at 1985-86 prices in the hotel and restaurant sector is 89 jobs as against 44.7 jobs in case of agriculture and 12.6 jobs in case of manufacturing industries. The ESCAP study report on " Economic impact of tourism in India" revealed that 1.2 international tourist visits provide employment to one person for a year. Similarly 17 domestic tourists generate employment for one person. By using these employment and projections of tourist traffic, the forecast of direct employment in tourism sector at the end of ninth five-year plan period have been worked out to be 13.00 million.

Now tourism in India is witnessing a steady growth. As revealed by Department of tourism from the base of 16,829 foreign tourists in 1951 when the count was first taken, the number of tourist arrivals reached the half million mark in 1976, one million in 1986, 1.71 million 1990, 2.15 million in 1995 and 2.35 million in 1998. While the decade from 1951 to 1960 recorded the highest rate of growth of 24.7% per year, the next decade from 1961 to 1970 registered a moderate growth rate of 8.6%. Again the decade from 1971 to 80 registered a higher growth rate of 11% per annum and the period from 1981 to 90 registered wide fluctuations in growth rate ranged from 5.6% to 29.1%. While the growth during the period during 1980 to 1985 was almost negligible, the year 1986 registered a remarkable growth of 29%. The tempo in growth was maintained till 1989 with annual increases varying from 6.5 to 7.8% .The year 1990 was however recorded a decline of 0.5% due to various national and international events including Gulf crisis. The average growth rate in the decade from 1981 to 1990 was thus only 5.2%. The period from 1991 to 1995 also registered a moderate growth of about 6%. Recently in India a lot of changes are taking place in various contributing factors for development of tourism. These include: -

i) The process of economic liberalisation and globalisation initiated since July 1991 and the consequent increases in foreign investment in the tourism sector and inflow of business.

ii) The changes that are taking place in the air transportation industry including liberal policy on bilateral agreements, liberalized charter policy, and privatisation of airports and air services.

iii) Greater momentum in the domestic investment in tourism infrastructure.

iv) Greater awareness on the part of State/Union Territory Governments about the real benefits of tourism infrastructure and investment facilitation and

v) Overall developments in the basic infrastructure sectors like airport, air and rail services, special roads and road transport system, telecommunication and power facilities, which are important for the growth of tourism.

The mainstay of tourism is the domestic tourism. The economic growth achieved by the country since independence and the emergence of a large number of urban middle class with disposable income have resulted in the growth of domestic tourism for holiday and sight seeing in the recent past. The economic liberlisation has accelerated the growth of business travel in India. According to the figures available from the state governments, the number of domestic tourists who use paid accommodations is 167 million in 1998. In addition, it is expected that there would be about 150 millions pilgrims tourists who did not use paid accommodations .It is projected that domestic tourist visit would grow at the rate of growth about 9.5% .It implies that the domestic tourist visits are growing at a much faster rate than international tourist arrivals. Tourism offers enormous potentials like economically utilising the natural attractions like landscapes, mountains, beaches, rivers etc.which would otherwise remain either idle or under utilized. The massive Himalayan ranges, being the richest repository of natural and cultural resources is likely to emerge as the most fovourable destinations of domestic as well as the international tourists. Since the Himalayan mountain system cover parts of Pakistan, India, China (Tibet), Nepal and Bhutan, all these country have prepared plans to offer their parts of the Himalayan in a big way, through resources in many cases, is too sensitive and fragile to be put up for touristic sale.

1.2 DEFINITION OF TOURISM, TOURISM INDUSTRY AND TOURIST

The use of the term tourism has led to a range of complex meaning which have become associated with: the movement of people; a sector of the economy; an identifiable industry; services which need to be provided for travelers (Gilbert, 1992). The definition of Tourism is required for study, statistical, legislative and industrial purposes. According to Webster's Dictionary, tour means a journey at which one returns to the starting point, a circular trip usually for business, pleasure or education during which various places are visited and for which an itinerary is usually planned. However, according to the "Oxford English Dictionary" the word 'tourism' first appeared in English in the year 1811 from a Greek word *'tornos'* used for a tool that was round in shape. It is from this word *"tornos"* that the notion of a "round tour" or "package tour" has come which is very much of the essence of tourism. It was as late as 1643 that the term was first used in the sense of going round or travelling from places to places, a journey including visiting a number of places in circuit or sequence embracing the principal places of a country or region. 'Tour' is a Hebrew word. It derives its meaning from the Hebrew term *'torah'*, which means learning, studying and search. A tour represents an attempt by the traveler to discover something about a place he visits. The word 'tourism' consists of all those trades, which together satisfy the various needs of the travelers. Travel may be considered touristic if it satisfies the following condition: -

- Travel must be temporary.
- Travel must be voluntary.
- Travel should not have remunerative employment as its aim.

Definition

There have been a number of attempts to define tourism since the beginning of 20th century. The Ausrian economist, Herman Von Schullard in the year 1910 gave one of the earliest definitions of Tourism. He defined tourism as "the sum total of operations mainly of economic nature, which directly relate to the entry, stay and movement of foreigners inside and outside a certain country, city or region." Professor Hunziker and Krapf in the year 1942 gave more technical definition of Tourism. They stated,

"Tourism is the totality of relationships and phenomena linked with the stay of foreigners in a locality provided they do not settle there to exercise a major, permanent or temporary activity of lucrative nature." Another early definition dating before the Second World War is adopted by an International Association of Scientific Experts in Tourism. It explains, tourism is the sum of phenomena and relationships arising from the travel and stays of non-residents, in so far as they do not lead to permanent residence and is not connected with any earning activity. This definition defines what tourists do and what is done for tourists. The above definitions do not take notice of domestic tourism. Conceptually, tourism distinguishes in particular form the related concept of leisure and recreation on the one hand and from the travel and migration on the other. Tourism in the pure sense is essentially a pleasure activity in which money earned in one's normal domicile is spent in the places visited. It involves a discretionary use of time and money. Technically, tourism represents various types of short-term travel and visits and is variably defined for particular purposes of the journey, its duration and other criteria.

Definition of Tourist

A technical definition of Tourist must clearly define the category of the travel and visits, the time element and the particular situation. It must define the categories of travel and visitors, which are and those which are not included for a particular purpose. The minimum and maximum period in terms of length of stay away from home or in terms of stay at a particular destination may also be established. It must also recognize particular situation, which may obtain for particular purpose and determine whether they are regarded under the purview of tourism. The definition of tourist helps the statician and economist and provides a useful distinction between the residents and the foreign tourists.

Realizing the importance of tourist statistics for further planning and development, a committee of statistical experts of the

League of Nations recommended in 1937 for the first time the definition of International tourist. The definition runs as follows "the term 'tourist' shall, in principle, be interpreted to mean any person traveling for a period of twenty four hours or more in a country other than that in which he usually resides."

In the light of above definition the following persons are considered as Tourist:

- All those persons who are traveling for pleasure and domestic reasons, including health, international meetings, business purposes, and arriving in the course of a sea cruise, even though they may stay less than twenty-four hours.

This definition also specified the persons as non-tourist in the following manner:

- Persons arriving with or without a working contract, to take up an occupation or engage in any business activity in the country.
- Persons coming to establish a residence in the country.
- Residents in a frontier zone and persons domiciled in one country and working in an adjoining country.
- Pupils, students and young persons in boarding establishments and schools.
- Travelers passing through a country without stopping, even if the journey takes more than 24 hours.

Later on, the International Union of Official Travel organizations (IUOTO) resurrected and modified the committee's definition in 1950 by including students on study tours as tourists and by specifying a new type of traveler called an "international excursionist". An excursionist, according to IUOTO guidelines, is an individual traveling for pleasure, who visits another country for less than 24 hours. It also defined transit travelers as those individuals who pass through a country without stopping, regardless of the time they spend in the country or as those individuals who travel through a country in less than 24 hours and make only brief, non-tourism stops. The definition was again revised at the United Nations conference on International Travel and Tourism held in Rome in 1963. The definition used the general term of "Visitor" as describing any person visiting to a country other than that of his usual place of residence, for any reason other than remunerated profession. This definition covers the terms 'Visitor', 'Tourist' and 'Excursionist', which are defined as follows:

VISITOR: Any person visiting to a country other than that of his usual place of residence, for any reason other than remunerated profession.

TOURIST: A visitor making at least a single overnight stay (or a stay of at least 24 hours) in the country visited and the purpose of whose journey can be classified under one of the following headings:

(a) Leisure (recreation, holiday, health, study, religion and sport)

(b) Business, family, mission and meetings.

EXCURSIONIST: A temporary visitor not making an overnight stay (or staying less than 24 hours) in the country visited. An equivalent term for 'Excursionist' is 'Day visitor' and the category may thus include visitors from cruise ships.

This definition objects to include transit passengers as tourists for statistical purposes because they do not legally enter the country. WTO defines a domestic tourist as a traveler visiting a destination in his country of residence for at least 24 hours but less than one year for the purposes of recreation, holidays, sports, business, meetings, conventions, study, visiting friends or relatives, health, mission, work or religion. A domestic excursionist is a visitor traveling in his country of residence for any of the reasons given for tourists, but who stays less than 24 hours at the destination. Recognizing the fact that the development of statistical concept and frame-work for tourism have not kept pace with the changes in nature and significance of tourism world wide WTO again organised an

International Conference on Travel and Tourism Statistics at Ottawa, Canada in June, 1991 to address various issues concerning tourism statistics. The recommendations of the Ottawa Conference were further discussed in the regional seminars and a set of concepts and definitions on Tourism, Forms of Tourism, Traveler, International Traveler, domestic Traveler, Usual Residence, Resident in a country, Resident in a place, Non-Resident, Nationality, Visitor, International visitor, International tourist, International Same Day Visitor, and finally Domestic Visitor were defined clearly. These were considered and approved by the United Nations Statistical Commission in its twenty -seventh session held from 22nd February to 3rd March 1993. The important aspect that was explained in the Tourism definition was the 'usual environment'. The term 'usual environment' is intended to exclude trips within the place of residence, trips to the usual place of work or education and daily shopping and other local day-to-day activities. Secondly, the time factor i.e., inclusion of twelve months duration is intended to exclude long time migration. The common accepted distance to get away from the usual place of environment is fixed around 80 km. The National tourism resource review Commission, USA (1973), recommended that tourist refers to anyone, who travels away from home at least 80 km. (50 miles) one-way for any purpose other than to commute to work, regardless of the duration of the trip. Statistics Canada and tourism Canada use a minimum distance of 80 km for including a respondent in their Canada Travel Survey. But the US Travel Data centre and the US Bureau of census define a visitor as anyone who travels at least 160 km (100 miles) one-way away from home except for purposes of commuting work, and regardless of the length of stay. Australian Bureau of Industry Economics places constrains of the distance on its definition of tourist: A person visiting a location at least 40 kms from his usual place of residence, for a period of at least 24 hours and not exceeding twelve months.

Definitions Followed in India

In relation to the definitions provided by the WTO, those followed in India are different in many cases. A comparison of these definitions is given in the following paragraphs.

An International visitor has been defined as a person holding a foreign passport, visiting the country and the main purpose of whose visit is other than the exercise of an activity remunerated from within the country or establishment of residence in the country.

International Tourist

An international tourist has been defined as a person visiting India on a foreign passport, staying at least twenty-four hours in India and the purpose of whose journey can be classified under one of the following headings:

- Leisure (recreation, holiday, health, study, religion and sport) and
- Business, Family, Mission and Meeting.

The following are not regarded as foreign tourists:

- Persons arriving with or without contract to take up an occupation or engage in activities remunerated from within the country.
- Persons coming to establish residences in the country.
- Nationals of Nepal entering India through land routes along India-Nepal border.
- All foreigners entering India from Bhutan by land and children aged less than three years.

Excursionist

An excursionist is a visitor staying less than twenty-four hours in the country including cruise passengers.

Cruise Passengers

A cruise passenger is a visitor who arrives in the country abroad cruise ships and who does not spend a night in an accommodation establishment in the country.

All the above definitions stipulate that the traveler must hold a foreign passport for inclusion in the category of international visitor. The classification is, thus, based on nationality and not based on place of residence. The implication is that the Indians settled abroad but holding Indian Passport would not be counted as an international visitor when they come to India for recreation, business and other such purposes. However, according to WTO definition, they should have been included as international visitors. The basic reason for this deviation is the assumption that the travelers holding Indian passport will tend to stay with their friends and relatives due to strong family ties and may not entail any demand on tourism infrastructure particularly hotels and restaurants. The magnitude of such travelers and the validity of the above assumption have however, never been assessed. It is, therefore, necessary to have a re-examination of these definitions on an objective basis.

Domestic Tourist

A domestic tourist has been defined as a person who travels within the country to a place other than his usual place of residence and stays at hotels or other accommodation establishments run on commercial basis or in *dharamshalas/sarais/ musafirkhanas/ agarshalas/ choultries* etc., or stays with friends and relatives and uses sightseeing facilities, or pilgrims for a duration of not less than 24 hours or one night and for not more than 6 months at a time for any of the following purposes:

- Pleasure (holiday, leisure, sports etc.)
- Pilgrimage, religious and social functions
- Business, conferences and meetings; and
- Study and health.

Table No.1.1: Official Classification of Travellers

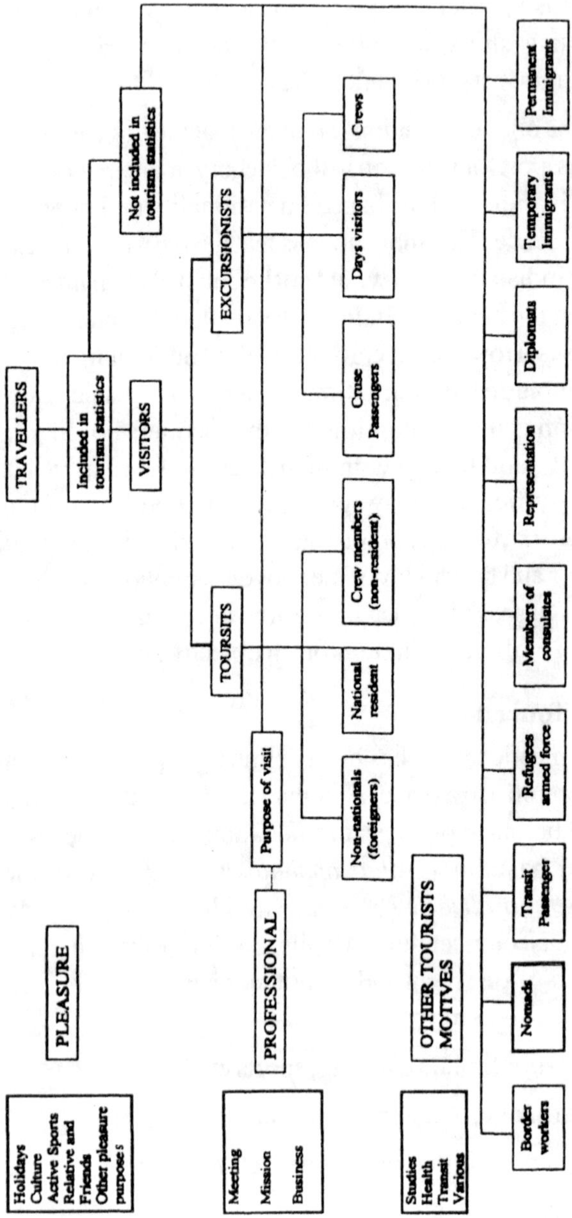

Source: World Tourism Organisation

The following are not regarded as domestic tourists:

- Persons arriving with or without a contract, to take up an occupation or engage in activities remunerated from within the state/centre.
- Persons visiting their home town or native place on leave or a short visit for meeting relations and friends, attending social and religious functions etc. and stay in their own houses or with relatives and friends and not using any sightseeing facilities.
- Foreigners resident in India.

The part of the definition "stays with friends and relatives and uses sightseeing facilities or pilgrimage" is a later addition and is still not used in the collection of statistics due to practical difficulties. The definition of the domestic tourist as followed in India is too restrictive as it makes the use of commercial accommodation as basic criteria. The reason for the restriction is again because of its linkage with the measurement of demand. The working group on domestic tourism constituted by the government in the year 1977 observed that "The definition of a domestic tourist should be related to the planning and provision of tourist infrastructure facilities rather than to serve merely the purpose of collecting such statistics". On the basis of foregoing definitions and interpretation of tourist term the following fundamentals as suggested by Gilbert (1992) can be projected.

1. **Spatial/dynamic:** Tourism involves the movement of people from one location to another outside of the their community. The movement predominantly corresponds with the use of some form of transportation due to the distances covered.

2. **Activity:** People at tourist destinations demand a range of activities, experiences and facilities.

3. **Social:** People enter into a complex system of interacting relationship.

4. **Economic:** Income is generated by the sector of the economy known as the tourism industry.

1.3 TOURISM PRODUCT AND PRODUCT DEVELOPMENT

Kotler's definition of a product is a good example of how a marketing scholar conceptualizes "product": it is "anything that can be offered to a market for attention, acquisition, use, or consumption that might satisfy a want or need. It includes physical objects, services, persons, places, organization, and ideas". Kotler's definition is especially relevant in this context because it makes explicit that products are not just physical objects, but also the stuff-services, persons, places, organizations, and ideas-that constitutes tourism.

Medlik and Middleton (1973) conceptualize tourism products as a bundle of activities, services, and benefits that constitute the entire tourism experience. This bundle consists of five components: destination attractions, destination facilities, accessibility, images, and price. Middleton (1989) also observes that the term "tourist product" is used at two different levels. One is the "specific" level, which is that of a discrete product offered by a single business such as a sightseeing tour or an airline seat. The other is the "total" level, which is the complete experience of the tourist from the time one leaves home to the time one returns. The "total" level is synonymous with the "components model". Jefferson and Lickorish (1988) offer another version of the component model of the tourism product. Observing that "the tourism product needs clear definition" they provide two views: the tourism product is a "collection of physical and service features together with symbolic associations which are expected to fulfill the wants and needs of the buyer" and more succinctly, the tourism product "is a satisfying activity at a desired destination". While the component model has an intuitive appeal, it fails to adequately describe the structure of the tourism product and how that product is produced. Indeed, the diversity of formulations of the component model fails even to lend support to the notion that there is a generic product. A different approach to modeling service products is proposed by Sasser, Olson, and Wyckoff (1978). They argue that the service product consists of three components: facilitating goods, explicit intangibles, and implicit intangibles. For example, the facilitating goods in a restaurant is food, while the explicit intangible is nourishment provided by food and the implicit intangibles are benefits such as service, socializing, ambiance, and/or relaxation.

Normann (1984) presents a simpler model composed of core service and secondary or peripheral services. Drawing from the airline industry, Normann observes that the flight from an origin to a destination is the core service of an airline, while reservations, check-in-flight means, baggage handling, cleaning and servicing the plane, comfort, and the general attitudes of the staff are peripheral services. Lewis and Chambers (1989) propose yet another concept of the tourism product. In their view, tourism products are composed of "goods, environment, and services. They further argue that the product can be viewed on three different levels: the "core product," or that product that the tourist is actually buying; and the "augmented product," which is the combination of core product plus any other value-added features and benefits provided by the supplier. Returning to the restaurant example, the formal product may be a gourmet dinner at a nice restaurant with a friend; the core product is the wine, appetizers, desserts, and coffee purchased by the diners; and the augmented product is the service, candlelight, and the violinist.

These three product levels echo Levitt's (1981) typology of "core product" (the essential service or benefit), "tangible product" (the service actually offered for sale and consumed), and the "augmented product" (the tangible product plus all added-value features). Levitt's typology has been adapted by Kotler (1984) in the context of general marketing and by Middleton (1988) for tourism marketing.

Three conclusions can be drawn from this: first, there is interest in the nature of products generally, and in the nature of services specifically. Second, the structure of services is generally seen as being relatively complex, involving different levels of service. Third, the consumer is recognized as often having some connection to the provision of services.

The Elements of the Tourism Product

The tourism product consists of five elements. These range from the core-the physical plant-to the encapsulating shell of involvement. The progression of elements from the core to the shell is correlated with declining direct management control, increasing consumer involvement, increasing intangibility, and decreasing potential for empirical measurement. The relative importance of each element varies, depending on the specific type of product under consideration, but all tourism products incorporate all five. The success of a product in meeting the needs of tourists is determined by how well each element is designed and integrated with the others. The tourism product is not a simple combination of the five elements, but the result of synergistic interaction among all the components. To borrow a well-worn phrase, the tourism product is more than the sum of its parts. However, to understand the product, the elements need to be separately and objectively identified.

The Physical Plant: The core of any tourism product is the physical plant: a site, natural resource, or facility such as a waterfall, wildlife park, or a resort. It may be either fixed property such as a hotel of Garhwal Mandal Vikas Nigam Limited. The physical plant also refers to conditions of the physical environment such as weather, water quality, crowding, and the condition of the tourism infrastructure. Land, water, buildings, equipment, and infrastructure provide the natural and cultural resources on which any form of tourism is based. Their physical design has a major impact on the consumer's experience. The quality of the physical plant can be assessed by whether the design enhances the user's experience, protects the environment, and makes the product accessible to tourists with a wide range of physical abilities or limitations (Gunn 1977; Mace 1980).

Service: The design and provision of a physical plant, however, is only the beginning. The physical plant requires the input of services to make it useful for tourists. In this context, "service" refers to the performance of specific tasks required to meet the needs of tourists. A hotel needs management, front desk operation, housekeeping, maintenance, and food and beverage provisions to function as a hotel. A tourist bus going to Badrinath needs an escort, driver and conductor and the services of parking personnel to provide transportation. The quality of service can be measured by observing the performance of employees against objective criteria that specify the types and level of technical knowledge an employee must have to perform his/her job.

Hospitality: Quality service, though, is still not sufficient. As Clemmer (1991) has argued, consumers in virtually every field now expect "enhanced service" or "something extra". This expectation of something extra has long been a part of tourism. The distinction between service and hospitality is often difficult to determine in practice, but it is real. For example, while the service of front desk staff refers to the efficient processing of hotel guests, hospitality emerges when this service is performed with a smile, genuine warmth, and the willingness to respond to other needs of the guest such as information on local restaurants. Service at a convention includes meeting room setups, while hospitality provides opportunities to relax and to meet new people or renew old acquaintances. For pleasure travel, hospitality may include a welcoming cocktail party or fresh flowers in the room. Hospitality is more difficult to assess and manage than service because it is more subjective than service. One-way of developing a sense of the level of hospitality delivered by a business is through solicited and unsolicited customer feedback. Hospitality sets the stage and facilitates the addition of the next two elements. These two elements may be the more controversial aspects of this model because they represent the inclusion of the tourist as part of the product. However, the notion of including the customer as part of service delivery is not unique to this model or even to tourism. Normann (1985) has argued that the consumer can be considered as part of the delivery of other service products. However, the inclusion of the tourist as part of product production (not just delivery) is essential if we are to comprehend and accept the notion that tourism is, in a fundamental sense, an experience.

Freedom of Choice: Freedom of choice refers to the necessity that the traveler has some acceptable range of options in order for the experience to be satisfactory. The degree of freedom of choice will vary greatly, depending on whether the travel is for pleasure, business, family matters, or a combination. It varies with the traveler's budget, previous experience, knowledge, and reliance on a travel agent or prepackaged tours. Despite this variation, any satisfactory tourism product must include some elements of choice. The role of freedom of choice is particularly clear in recreational or pleasure travel. Indeed, the concept is well established in the field of leisure studies as an integral part of the leisure experience (Mannell and Bradley 1986). Without the sense that one has permission to play or to choose one's own activities, it is difficult to fully relax or to participate wholeheartedly in recreational activities. Even the most comprehensive, tightly packaged inclusive tour offers choice. The most basic choice, of course, is the freedom to purchase or not. The role of freedom is not limited to pleasure travel. Freedom to choose an airline, an automobile route, a hotel or a restaurant can enhance a business travelers' sense of control and satisfaction with the trip. Even when businesses or agencies restrict their employee's choices of mode of travel or accommodation to preferred suppliers, these suppliers can still enhance customer satisfaction by providing choice of seats, meals, smoking/non-smoking rooms, or other services and facilities to provide some degree of personal choice. Freedom implies not just choice, but also the potential for happy surprises and spontaneity. Spontaneity may range from merely deciding on one's sleeping and waking times to making a last minute decision to get away for a weekend or making a major departure from an itinerary. A number of attractions have recognised the appeal of surprise and spontaneity by deliberately planning for it.

Involvement: A feature of many service products is the fact that customers participate, in some degree, in delivery of services (Boom and Bitner 1981; Fitzsimmons and Sulivan 1982; Normann 1984; Silpakit and Fisk 1985). This is true too, for tourism products. The basis for successful participation by consumers in producing tourism products is the combination of an acceptable physical plant, good service, hospitality, and freedom of choice. These elements set the stage for physical, intellectual, and/or emotional involvement in travel services. For tourism, involvement is not simply physical participation, but a sense of engagement, of focusing on the activity - whether for pleasure or business. Involvement for pleasure travelers means playing or relaxing in a way that is personally satisfying, and feeling sufficiently safe and secure that one can doze poolside, stroll on the beach, or strike up conversation with tourists or locals. It means having access to activities and programs that capture the imagination, interest, and enthusiasm of the potential participant. The sense of involvement causes time to pass without notice, as the tourist explores the world around him, other people, or his own mental and emotional response to the trip. Involvement, combined with freedom of choice, warm hospitality, competent service, and a good physical plant (which includes accessibility, acceptable environmental quality, goodweather, and appropriate numbers of other people) virtually guarantees a quality and satisfying tourist product.

Product Development

Product development is a prerequisite for satisfying tourists' changing demands and insuring the long-term profitability of the industry. Ideally, tourism products meet marketplace demands, are produced cost-efficiently, and are based on the wise use of the cultural and natural resources of a destination. Despite the importance of product development, relatively little work has been done to examine the nature of the generic tourism product.

The term "generic product" refers to the conceptual commodity produced by an industry. For example, the generic products of agriculture are food and fiber; the generic product of the automobile industry is personal transportation. A generic product will take a wide variety of real forms, but each form of the same generic product will provide the same function. In the case of tourism, the function of the generic product is the facilitation of travel and activity of individuals away from their usual home environment. A clear and explicit concept of the product will provide greater precision in discussions related to the nature of tourism and the planning, development, management and delivery of its products. Improved understanding of the structure and functioning of the product also will assist developers, entrepreneurs, and planners in creating more successful products for the marketplace. In the long run, the concept will aid researchers in more accurately measuring, analyzing, and modeling industry performance.

Although few, if any, marketing professionals would challenge the importance of product development, the subject receives much less attention from marketing analysts, planners, and policy makers than do segmentation, consumer behavior, advertising, and promotional strategies. The lack of attention to product development is not unique to tourism. Most service industries also emphasize marketing - that is, selling, advertising, public relations (Culture, 1983:6) over product development. This situation is in marked contrast to manufacturing industries, which devote significant financial resources to research and development to create and refine products for the market. Although product development is contrasted here with marketing, some authors assert that product development is a subset of the marketing concept (Culture 1983; Meidan 1989; Middleton 1989). In practice, though, linking product development with marketing is more academic hope than business reality. Although marketing practice only infrequently addresses product development, the issue of the origin, evolution, and nature of products is not totally ignored by marketing scholars. Haywood (1985) and

Cooper (1992), for example, critique the potential of the product life cycle in tourism market planning. Moutinho (1989) describes a strategy for new product development in tourism.

1.4 HERITAGE TOURISM

The word heritage in its broader meaning is generally associated with the word inheritance; that is something transferred from one generation to another. The 1983 National heritage conference defined heritage as: "That which a past generation has preserved and handed on to the present and which a significant group of population wishes to hand on to the future." The dictionary meaning of heritage is anything that has been transmitted from the past or handed down by tradition. Heritage is defined as the natural, cultural and built environments of an area. Owing to its role as a carrier of historical values from the past, heritage is viewed as part of the cultural tradition of a society. Tourism's fundamental nature is dynamic and its interaction with heritage often results in a reinterpretation of the latter. The eclecticism of heritage is reflected by Printice's (1993) typology of heritage attractions, which comprised the subject- types such as natural history, transport, socio cultural, theme parks, galleries, seaside resorts and regions. Where as this range and diversity is real, a number of distinctions can be made. One such is the distinction between natural heritage, drawing its qualities from the nature, and places, which become heritage sites because of their association with people or events. With respect to tourism, the word heritage has been employed in cultural and natural contexts (Hall and McArthur 1993;Herbert 1989;Yale 1992; Zeppel and Hall 1992). In the cultural arena, heritage can be used to describe material forms such as monuments, historical or architectural remains and artifacts on display in museums; immaterial forms such as philosophy, traditions and art in all their manifestations; the celebration of great events or personalities in history; distinctive way of life, and education as expressed for example, through literature and folklore. In the natural arena, heritage has been used to describe gardens, landscapes, national parks, wilderness areas of scenic beauty, mountains, rivers, islands, and components there of such as flora and fauna. Heritage places include historic buildings or monuments, which bear the distinctive imprint of human history. Their interest may derive from architecture or design, from historical significance, or from combination of these attributes. Heritage places in this sense are linked with people, events, and activities and, in a wider sense, with cultures, societies and economies. A religious site may present a magnificent edifice, which inspires awe; it will also reflect the cultural history of a people and may retain modern religious significance. Natural and people made heritage are not mutually exclusive. A ruined castle has historic interest, but its spectacular setting will add significantly to its role as a heritage attraction. Most of the content of heritage objects, belongings and sites can be viewed as the tangible remains of some past period but all are transformed by the subjective gaze of their viewers, into something which is personal and particular. Interpretation plays a part in this process of transformation.

Rather than just being peripheral or added attraction, heritage is increasingly becoming major catalysts for the whole travel experience. Fortunately a fairly large number of persons visit heritage sites and many World Heritage sites are major tourism destinations. It includes the place and the parks of Versailles (France), the old city of Dubrovnik (Yugoslavia), kaukadu National park (Australia) and Pyramid of Egypt (Cheah 1983). Individual heritage sites such as Eiffel Tower in Paris and Shakespear's birthplace at Stratford-upon-Avon in England, provide the motivation for the people to visit the country in the first place (Miller, 1989). The world heritage sites selected by UNESCO in India include, the Ajanta and Ellora Caves;the Agra Fort, the Taj Mahal and Fatehpur Sikri in Agra; the Sun temple in Konark; the group of monuments at Mahabalipurum; the Kaziranga National park; the Manas wildlife sanctuary; the Keoladeo National Park; Churches and Convents of Goa; the Khajuraho group of monuments; the group of monuments at Hampi; group of monuments at Pattadakal; Elephanta Caves; Brihadeswara

Temple in Tanjavur; the Sundarbans National park; the Nandadevi Biosphere Reserve in Uttaranchal; the stupas at Sanchi; Qutab minar and Humayun's Tomb in New Delhi. Heritage tourism, based on history tends to be education-oriented and includes guided tours of buildings, monuments and ruins, dramatic sound and light performances and re-enactment of historically significant occasion. Heritage tourism also includes local cultural traditions. Added to architecture, archaeology and natural sites, are family patterns, religious practices and the subtleties of refined traditions that combine in various ways to make up what we describe as heritage of a country (Collin, 1983). The community heritage embraces folkloric traditions, arts and crafts, ethno history (ways of life), social customs and cultural celebrations. Heritage Tourism is thus a broad field of specialty travel including many special interest aspects of tourism ranging from examination of the physical remains of the past and natural landscapes to the experience of local cultural traditions. In heritage tourism, heritage hotel, reflects one of the few concepts, being gifted to international tourism by India. The architecture and grandeur of these historic buildings reveal the rich tradition and culture of the region. Such magical is the grandeur of these buildings that tourist is hypnotized and finds himself in the glorious past of the "Raj Days".

Heritage tourism represents a growing market segment for both domestic and international tourism and can be viewed as being a type of special interest tourism market. Heritage tourism is rapidly becoming integrated in to the mainstream tourism industry in certain destinations. It is being developed to offset the effects of the economic restructuring and provides rationale for urban redevelopment to establish new tourism markets. It boosts the cultural image and raises the tourist profile of the regions with their enduring visitor appeal and moveability. Heritage tourism often creates a source of community pride that helps to ease resentment towards visitors and to prevent displacement of resident's business. Heritage attractions are therefore being increasingly promoted as essential parts of tourism experience in many countries and regions.

Heritage Management: It is a new concept that has developed alongside the growth of a new industry, the heritage industry. There are three main aspects to 'heritage' in the context of planning and conservation. Preservation involves the retention, in largely unchanged form, of sites or objects of major cultural significance. Conservation encompasses the idea that some form of restoration should be undertaken to bring old buildings and sites in to suitable modern use. Exploitation recognizes the value of heritage sites particularly for tourism and recreation, and encompasses the development of existing sites and new sites. Heritage sites are in the center of the struggle between the potentially conflicting aspirations of conservation and tourism. Good heritage management with a major focus on heritage interpretation and presentation ensures that one complements the other.

The central challenge in linking heritage and tourism lies in the reconstructing past in the present through interpretation. Interpretation is not only a description of physical facts and tangible elements: it moves into realms of spiritual truth, emotional response, deeper meaning and understanding. Meaning lies in the observer or participant (i.e. the tourist) rather than as some objective quality inherent in the object itself. Heritage requires more than preservation: its significance should be conveyed to the visitor, leading to an enriched understanding in the context of the present. Creative interpreters of heritage encourage visitors to create their own mental space by traveling to the past to complete the heritage reconstruction. Interpretation can create valuable outcome both for the interpreters and visitors. For visitors, these outcomes include greater appreciation, awareness, understanding, self-fulfillment and enjoyment. For those responsible for interpretation, the positive results include many of those outcomes enjoyed by visitors as well as increases in patronage and improvements in visitor flow. So interpretation is an integral part of marketing, managing and planning heritage tourism (Herbert, 1989). Heritage resources are converted in to products through an assembly process involving interpretation and packaging. These are not merely the bringing together of a given set of resources but a means of selecting and transforming resources. Selection, interpretation and packaging involve a series of choices about which product is being produced and, thus, which resources are to be used and in which ways. The end product, various heritage tourism packages, has specific meaning, which is not synonymous with the existing one. It is a product defined by, and intended to be consumed by defined market. Thus, quite different products intended for quite different markets can be created from the same sets of environmental resources by varying the assembly process and specially interpretation. If the product is market defined then quite different markets can thus create quite different products from the same environment, which are then sold to different consumers at the same physical locations.

In developing countries, many of the heritage structures such as buildings, archaeological sites, ancient town, museums and so forth are found in the middle of living communities such as cities, towns or villages. Local people interact with these structures directly as they go about their everyday lives. There is a need to recognize the inter dependencies that exist between the community and the heritage structure or area. Local people, as an integral part of the "heritage locus", can contribute vitality to an area and there by assist in the maintenance of an atmosphere conducive to tourism (Ashworth and Tunbridge 1990, Schulz, 1980). In developing country the development of heritage tourism involves not only reconstructing the past; it is also part of restructuring the economy. However, relationships between heritage tourism and local people involve more than jobs and incomes. They include questions of land ownership, competition between the old and the new and changing lifestyles with variations in the types and extent of adjustments that are made (Dogan 1989, HSWG, 1991). Heritage tourism also has to deal with politically sensitive questions such as what to preserve from the former era, property rights, and the interaction between the tourists and host communities with their different social structures and expectations that can lead to misunderstandings and even conflicts. In addition to these issues, there are often more intricate problems to deal with, including community relocation and questions of compensation for substantial numbers of people. Developing countries including India and especially Garhwal region face the challenge of limited funding resources and inadequate institutional capabilities. For these countries, heritage tourism raises more than planning and management problems: they are fundamentally the problems of development.

Before the middle of the 19th century, few travelers visited the Himalayas except explorers, traders or pilgrims. This situation changed with the establishment of British rule in India and the development of the summer resorts. The tremendous growth in mountaineering (and subsequently trekking) tourism dates from the 1950, stimulated by the conquest of Everest by Sir Edmund Hilary and Sherpa Tenzing in 1953. *Tirtha Yatra* is the earliest form of trekking tourism in Garhwal Himalaya when thousands of Pilgrims, since time immemorial, have been attracted to the numerous holy places of Garhwal region (Bagri, 1994). Nestling in the hills of the Himalaya is the El-Dora do Garhwal, the land of *rishis*, sages, and *ashrams*, which is also traveler's delight and naturalists paradise. Encompassing scenic locales along the Himalayan range, Garhwal is redolent with mythology and includes some of the holiest places of Hindu pilgrimage. Hence since ancient time pilgrims in great number visited this region due to location of most sacred places like Badrinath, Kedarnath, Gangotri and Yamunotri and Sikh Gurudwara at Hemkund Lokpal, Origin of holy rivers like the Ganga and Yamuna and holy mountains like Nanda Devi, Gangotri Peak. The Natural beauty of the majestic Himalaya, Wildlife, peace and tranquility of the region have attracted people from far and wide. The parks and sanctuaries of Garhwal Himalaya are the rich depository of natural resources viz. Wildlife, forests, meadows, water bodies, mountain peaks and glaciers. Some of the resources are also dotted with important historical and religious sites and the tribal settlements. The driving force to visit this region has been to experience the rich, unique natural and cultural heritage of this region.

Within the Garhwal region, the pattern of tourism development has been varied, although certain problems are common to almost all destinations. These include environmental pressures, rapid population growth and in-migration to urban centers associated with uncontrolled tourism expansion. The intensity of problems produced by tourism development is related to three factors; the duration of tourism development, government and private sector policies and the type of tourism that has been encouraged. Today's visitor is likely to be a special interest traveler although adventure and cultural tourism are major motivations. Visitors to this region are often seeking "life-enhancing" travel experiences where contact with other cultures is used to gain a sense of personal achievement and satisfaction. Many visitors travel with adventure tour companies and have a constant need for new regions and new tourism products. However in this region domestic tourism remains significant, and pilgrimage still represents a major motivation.

1.5 GARHWAL: An Indroduction

Garhwal is administratively, comprised of six districts of erstwhile U.P. Himalaya* (now the new state Uttaranchal)- Chamoli, Rudraprayag, Pauri, Uttarkashi, Tehri and Dehradun. The region lies almost centrally in the long sweep of Himalaya between co-ordinates of 29°27' to 30°33' N latitudes and 77°48' to 80°06' E longitudes. Its estimated area is 30090 sq.Km, which is more than a half (54%) of the Uttaranchal and about 7.01% of the total Indian

---

* Garhwal along with Kumaon division constitutes the entire erstwhile U.P Himalaya, or the Uttarakhand covering an area of 51,112 km^2.Now it is the major part of newly created Uttaranchal State with area 55,845 sq.km.

Himalaya**. Historically, the region has the long prestigious background, well documented in the pauranic literature*** . Ever since the pauranic times, it has been a religious sanctuary of the Hindus, and thus the most favored pilgrim zone. The land is closely associated with legendary heroes of the Ramayana and Mahabharata epics that have left their imprints in the names of many places, the devotional lives of the people and even on the social customs and cultural activities like Pandav dances.

1.5.1 History

The recorded history of the vedas tells us indirectly about this land. The vedas are associated with the *Aryans* whose first arrival in the sub-continent took place about the middle of the 2nd millennium BC. In the first millennium B.C., the *Khasas* (off shoot of the Indo-Aryans) constituted one of the predominating tribes of the region migrating from Central Asian steppes first into northwestern Mountainous tract, then infiltrating in to the north-east from Kashmir to Kangra and Garhwal to Kumaon. *Puranas* and the *Mahabharat* mention the names of some tribal groups like the *Khasas, Kiratas, Rajaya Kiratas* and *Nagas* who were flourished in this part of the Himalaya.

In the Mauryan period during the time of Ashoka, Garhwal was out of the limits of his empire. The Rock Edicts at Kalsi (Dehra

---

** The Himalaya is spread over a total length of about 2,200 km measured along the chord of the arc and nearly 2,400km measured along the arc itself. The width of the Himalaya varies from 325 to 425 km. The actual Himalaya range commences from Nanga Parvat(8126m) in the northwest, and passes through Kashmir, Pakistan, Himanchal Pradesh, Garhwal, Kumaon, Nepal, Sikkim, part of North Bengal, Bhutan and Arunanchal Pradesh and ends at Namche Barwa(7828m) in the East. From west to east, the Himalaya is divided into Punjab Himalaya, Nepal and Assam Himalaya.

*** During different phases of history the study area has had different identities viz. ***Utterkeru, Himawant, Uttar Panchal, Tangoni, Suvarna Bhumi, Manaskhand and Kedarkhand.***

Dun) suggest that Ashoka's political hegemony might have bordered the area. Culturally Mauryan remains from the region are not lacking as found from the various excavations such as Ranihat, Moradhwaj, Bharat Mandir (Rishikesh) and Panduwala (Near Hardwar), (Nautiyal and Khanduri, 1972). The history of Garhwal after the Mauryan period is known in lesser measure. In the middle of the second Century B.C. there was again a great tribal upsurgence in Central Asia. The Indo-Greeks, *Sakas* and the *Kushans* ruled over the greater part of north India. But in Garhwal the discovery of the tribal coins gives the instances of the existence of local feudatory rulers of tribal dynasties like the*Kunindas, Yaudheyas, Malvas, Arjunayanas* etc. under the *Kushans*, from 2nd Century BC to 3rd Century AD. Regarding the Gupta period, from the Allahabad pillar inscription of Samudragupta, it can be told that during the reign of Samudragupta the region of Uttarakhand was under his empire, probably as one of the frontier kingdoms, which paid taxes, obeyed orders and rendered obeisance in person to the imperial power. The post-Gupta history of the region is also not very clear. On the basis of inscriptions at Gopeswar Trident, the Barahat Trident and the Lakhamandal, we come to know the emergence of several smaller dynasties of the Post-Gupta period like the *Nagas*, the *Yadavas* and the *Pauravas*.These dynasties began their political career as the fudatories to the imperial Guptas, but not long after, they declared their independence. During the period of Harshavardhan (c AD 606-647), one of the greatest kings of ancient India, the Uttarakhand region was ruled by several dynasties and lost its unity. And in this situation Harshavardhan probably succeeded in acquiring kingdom of the region. After the Harsha a greater part of the higher Himalaya of Garhwal was under the Tibetan rule. The relics of the Tibetan Buddhism scattered in the border of Garhwal, particularly at Nala, Okhimath and at several other places support this. The relations between Tholingmuth (Tibet) and the Badrinath Shrine had probably originated during this period (Nautiyal, 1969). In the beginning of the eighth Century AD the regions of Uttarakhand was under the influence of kings Yasovarman and Lalitaditya. The dynastic history of Uttarakhand is available only after the close of the 7th Century AD. Prominent dynasties in the region during the 7th-8th Centuries were:

(i) The Kingdom of Bhillang

(ii) The Kingdom of Chandpurgarh

(iii) The Katyuri dynasty

The Bhillang kingdom was named after river Bhillangana and extended up to the remote regions of Bhagirathi, Alaknanda and Vishnu Ganga. The kingdom of Bhillang became powerless after the advent of Ajaypal (AD 1500-1537) of Garhwal dynasty. The kingdom of Chandpurgarh was situated in the upper Alaknanda valley. Chandpurgarh fort is 15 km. east of Karnaprayag near Adibadri and it is associated with the kings of Garhwal. Kanakpal was the founder of Garhwal dynasty. Recorded history indicates the Katyuris (*Suryanbanshis*) to have ruled Garhwal amongst others from ninth to the eleventh century and having formed the first dynasty of rulers. This dynasty had left some records of its achievements in the form of inscriptions and temple architecture, which are well scattered all over the Uttarakhand. *Katyuri* dynasty had derived its name from *Karttikeyapura*, the then capital city. The Katyuri dynasty (850-1050 AD) declined from the extreme cruelty and oppression of the rulers in the later years. The kingdom broke up and the pretty chieftains set up their own principalities with forts (garhs) and ruled their areas. The name Garhwal is of recent origin, coined during the early sixteenth century, when Ajaypal (1500-1549 AD), the first ruler of Panwar dynasty for the first time united the then existing smaller *Garhis* (tiny fortress kingdoms) in unified Garhwal. From time immemorial *Garhwali* and *Kumaoni* rulers had been fighting with each other. The boarder areas were so distributed by constant warfare that the agricultural fields were abandoned and gradually turned to wastelands and forests. During 1640, Prithvi Sah was the king of Garhwal and he was succeeded by the Maidni Sah and there after by the Fateh Sah or Fateh Singh who in 1692 AD led a memorable raid from Dehradun to Saharanpur. Fateh Sah extended his power into Tibet. Dhalip Sah succeeded Fateh Sah in 1717 and during the reigns of Fateh Sah and his son Pradip Sah, Garhwal became very prosperous. In 1772 his son Lalit Sah succeeded him. He also helped religious temples through his donations of lands. He neglected Dehradun where the *Mahant* of the Sikh temple became supreme. For many years Deharadun became the happy hunting grounds of *Gujar* and *Sikh* marauders.

In 1801,a Maratha invasion of Garhwal wrought much destruction and paved the way for the Gorkhali invasion. 1803 was a year remarkable for the great and successful efforts of the Thapa party of Nepal to invade Garhwal. Raja Pradhuman sah, the ruler of Garhwal fled at first, then he assembled forces, but died in battle in Dehradun in January 1804. Amar Singh Thapa ruled Kumaon and invaded Garhwal in 1804 and this continued till 1815. However the day of reckoning came for the Gorkhas soon after their defeats at the hands of the Britishers in 1815. Sudarshan Sah in 1811, after his escape, promised Major Hearsey to grant him Dehradun should he procure the restoration of his territory occupied by Gorkhas. The British officially waged war against him in 1814. At the termination of the war Sudershan Sah was handed over the portions of Garhwal situated to the west of Alaknanda and the *parganah* of Rawain lying between Alaknanda and the Bhagirathi rivers.

Thus in 1815, the region again witnessed a major cleavage, when half of it (present Pauri, Rudraprayag, Chamoli and Dehradun), came under the sway of Britishers and the Sudershan Sah set up his new capital at Tehri with Tehri and Uttarkashi districts in hands. With the independence of India in 1947, British Garhwal automatically became a part of free India and the native state of Tehri was also amalgamated.

1.5.2 Ethnicity

The fabric of cultural landscape of the Garhwal himalaya is woven with the multi tribal racial elements of culture. Longways back the region was settled by various tribes or races like the *kols*, the *Kirats* and the *Arayans*. Geo economic forces landed different tribes or races on different geographical locations. The struggle for existence in the rugged and inhospitable terrain was punctuated by adjustments and adaptations among the tribes or races.

The high valleys (2400m-3600m) bordering on Tibet are inhabited by the Mongoloids races whose nomadic infiltration into the south has contributed to the yellow infusion among the descendants of the Indo-Arayan or the Mediterranians. The *Bhotias* are of mixed *Tibentan* origin.The aboriginal (represented by the *Koltas, Doms*, and other Artisan castes) and many of the latter had received Indo-Arayan blood through mixed marriages. The *dom* and the *Koltas* are correctly supposed to be the remnants of the original inhabitants. The *Rajputs* with the *Brahmins* constitute the apex of the social ladder. Both belong to the same ethnic stock and are similar in origin and share similar culture. However the ancient inhabitants of the Garhwal were the *Kols* (*Mundas*) who lived in the Himalayan forests right from the food gathering and the hunting stage (Dabral 1965). A Mongoloid tribe named *Kirat* entered the Himalayan region from the east. They pushed the *Kols* into more inaccessible areas. The second major wave of pastoral migrants came from the west through the Himalayan ranges and was *Khassa*. They pushed the *Kiratas* into higher and inaccessible valleys in the north where they get intermixed with the Tibetans and are represented by *Jad, Marcha* and *Tolcha Bhotias*. A few of them found shelter in the *Terai* and *Bhabar*, where they got intermixed with other races and are represented by *Bhokas* and the *Mahars*. Mazumdar holds almost similar opinion about the racial structure of Garhwal. At present we have three important racial strains. The highest altitude are represented as the Tibetians and other Mongoloid people, the central belt is composed of a tall fair race represented by *Khas Rajputs* and *Khas-Brahmins*, the *Bhats*, and a comparatively dark aboriginal type represented by the Doms; a generic name used to include all artisan castes like the *Kolis* and the *Koltas*. The last belt is of *Brahmins* and *Rajputs* of Jaunsar

Bawar claim decent from the Pandavas of Mahabharata whose monuments exist at Lakhamandal and other adjoining region. During the Medieval period, a number of Rajput princes with their loyal followers penetrated into the valley of Himalayas to escape the atrocities of the Muslim invaders. They founded small colonies in isolated valleys. Thus there is curious mixture of different ethnological groups who came in from different directions and settled here permanently.

1.5.3 Physical Set-up

The area has a remarkable heterogeneity in its entire natural and cultural environment. This is evidenced by a variety of the land forms, viz., snow peaks; black mountain; steep escarpment; deep gorges; hanging valleys; glaciers and lakes; numerous streams and swifter, cascading, falling, foaming river; lush green meadows; and vast forested tracts. Broadly speaking, the entire region barring a narrow strip of *Terai- Bhabar* and duns, is largely a rugged and mountainous country. The altitude varies rather abruptly from 300m at the base of the foothills to 7817m at the peak of the Nanda Devi. The region preserves well a chronological record of the great Himalayan sedimentation, tectonic and volcanicity that followed it. The four distinct parallel, longitudinal geo-tectonic zones thus formed are coterminous with physiographic zones, which from the south to north are: (a) Outer or the sub-Himalayan zone (Siwaliks), (b) Lesser or the Lower Himalayan zone (Himachal), (c) Great, or the Higher Himalayan zone (Himadri) and (d) Trans Himalayan zone or the Zaskar Range. Contrast exists in elevation of Valley bottoms and mountain peaks in the region. The absolute relief generally goes on increasing towards the Higher Himalaya, and henceforth decreases gradually towards the Trans Himalaya. All the four ranges have an alignment of North-West-South-East directions. Significantly, the general slopes of the ranges are symmetrical, steeper towards the southern side and gentle towards the northern side. Obviously, the northern slopes are clothed with dense forest growth surmounted higher-up by perpetual snows, while southern slopes are precipitous and bare, either to accommodate snows or support any vegetation, except in valley slopes. Considering the terrain, geology, hydrology, climate, soil and fauna, each of the four physiographic zones represent a distinct geographical personality of its own.

Siwaliks Ranges: Striking the upper Ganga plain in its south, stretches the Siwaliks Himalayan Zone (16 to 24 km wide) of lowly hills, with an average height of 400 m to 1200 m. It is largely composed of the upper tertiary fresh water deposits, and is rich in fossil contents. Further southwards are the undulating thickly forested fertile land of *Bhabar* and *Terai*. Ramganga is only the large river, which drains the Siwalik zone with Mandal as its chief tributary.

Lesser Himalaya (The Himachal) : The Lesser Himalayan zone is characterised by all intermediate aspect of the Himalaya. About 75 km in width, this zone has series of ridges and spurs, divided by deep valleys. The average relief of the ridges ranges between 1500 m to 2700 m, and the valleys between 500 m to 1200 m. The rocks vary in their age, texture and mineral composition. The lesser Himalaya, on its north is bounded by the 'Central Himalayan Thrust', beyond which lies the Great Himalaya. The principal ranges of this zone are: Dhanpur range, Uttain-Kathliand Dudhatoli range. Among the big rivers draining the Lesser Garhwal Himalaya are Alaknanda, Tons, Yamuna and Bhagirathi.

The Great Himalaya: This zone, on an average, is 50 km wide, with a mean relief average between 4800 m to 6000 m. The topography is highly rugged, predominantly consisting of Himalayan meadows, huge 'U'-shaped valleys, horned peaks, serrated crests of high ridges, cirqes and glaciers, deep canyons, torrential rapids, and glacial lakes. There is a marked cluster of the high peaks, which can be broadly grouped into four series; (a) Bandurpunch (6315m), (b) Gangotri (6614m), Kedarnath (6940m), Chaukhamba (7817m), (c) Kamet (7756m) and (d) Nanda Devi (7817m), Dunagiri (7066m), Trisul (7120m). These four groups of peaks are separated by transverse gorges of Bhagirathi, Alaknanda, and Dhauli Ganga rivers, respectively.

The **Zaskar, or trans Himalayas**, the smallest of the four physiographic zones, is separated from the greater himalaya by 'Malari thrust' passing through the Niti region and Malari (Singh 1963 b). It is marked by intense folding, recumbent overturned folds, and small scale thrust (Jhingaran 1981). A rain deficient zone, it contains several glaciers. The average altitude is above 3000m, and most of its remains perpetually snow-covered.

1.5.4 Drainage Pattern

The enormous glacier system of great Himalaya enriches the region with a vast drainage network, which ultimately merges either with Ganga system or with Yamuna system. Both these rivers are of immense religio-cultural value for the major part of the North India.

Bhagirathi- Alaknanda Basin: -Major part of the region, covering the whole of Garhwal (except western part of Uttarkashi district) is drained by Bhagirathi-Alaknanda basin or the Ganga system. The Bhagirathi and the Alaknanda originate from the opposite sides of the Chaukhambha peak (7138m). Below Deoprayag, where these two rivers meet each other, the river acquires the name of Ganga. The Alaknanda rises from Alkapuri Glacier and is longer than the Bhagirathi. The Saraswati River originates from Deotal, meets the Alaknanda near the Manna village, about 3 Km from the Badrinath Temple. The Dhauli Ganga, another important up stream tributary, takes its origin from Kunlung in Niti, and joins the Alaknanda at Vishnuprayag. The Alaknanda flows in a narrow gorge form vishnuprayag to Pakhi. The Birahi ganga, a small tributary but notorious one, bubbles out from the western slopes of the Ghunti and after flowing westward it joins the Alaknanda at Birahi where there was a huge lake (1.6Km x 0.8Km) but completely destroyed in 1970. The Nandakini is another tributary, which takes its origin from Trisul, and after draining in east-west direction, joins the Alaknanda at Nandprayag.The Mandakini originates from Gandhi Sagar, 3 km. above of Kedarnath temple and meets the Alaknanda at Rudraprayag. The Madhu Ganga, originates from the Madhmaheshwar, joins Mandakini at Kalimath, below the Guptkashi. The Pinder originates from the Pindari Glacier (3644m) and after draining in southeast direction, joins Alaknanda at Karnprayag. The river valley is comparatively wide. Atagad River originates from the Western slopes of the Dudhatoli Mountains and joins Pindar at Simli. The Bhagirathi takes its origin from the Gomukh and flows in south-westernly direction up to about 10 Km. down stream of Uttarkashi. It then again turns in south-westernly direction, meeting the Alaknanda at Deoprayag. Bhilangana River with its tributary, Bal Ganga and others, is the important tributary of the Bhagirathi which, after originating from a little southwest of the Gangotri glacier, joins it at Tehri. Other important tributaries of the Bhagirathi are Jad Ganga (Jhanvi) and Kaldi ganga rivers. Nayar is the important tributary of the Ganga, meeting the later at the Vyasghat (420m) near Rishikesh. It drains more than a half area of the Pauri Garhwal district. It has two main tributaries, eastern Nayar and Western Nayar, which meet at the Satpuli. Eastern Nayar originates from the southern slope of the Dudhatoli (2835m) and, after flowing in almost North-South direction; it turns towards west near Chadoli, below Baijro. Western Nayar takes its origin from the northwestern slope of the Dudhatoli. The river has two important headwaters, Syoli Gad and Daijyoli Gad, meeting each other at the Paitani and hereafter; the river is named as Western Nayar. From Painthani to a little above Jwalpa, the river flows in North-South direction and then again turns towards southwest direction meeting eastern Nayar at Satpuli. The river forms many terraces of various sizes throughout of its course.

Yamuna Tons Basin:- The Yamuna has its source in the Yamnotri Glacier lying on the southwestern slope of the Bandarpunch peak. Yamnotri temple is located near the hot spring and it is believed to be the source of Yamuna. Through out of its course, it flows through vast deposit of moraines.Huge deposits of Glacial debris may be seen around Janki chatti. At Dhalipur (402m), river Giri joins the Yamuna on the Right Bank. Tons originating from the northern slope of the Bandarpunchh peak (6102m), is the biggest tributary of the Yamuna and with its total length of 160 Km., drains the North Western part of the region. The Supin, Rupin and the Pabar are the important tributaries of Tons. It joins the Yamuna at Kalsi (514m), about 48 km. west of Dehradun. Tons drains 2.7 times greater volume of water of the Yamuna.

Fig no 1.3

Drainage Map of Garhwal

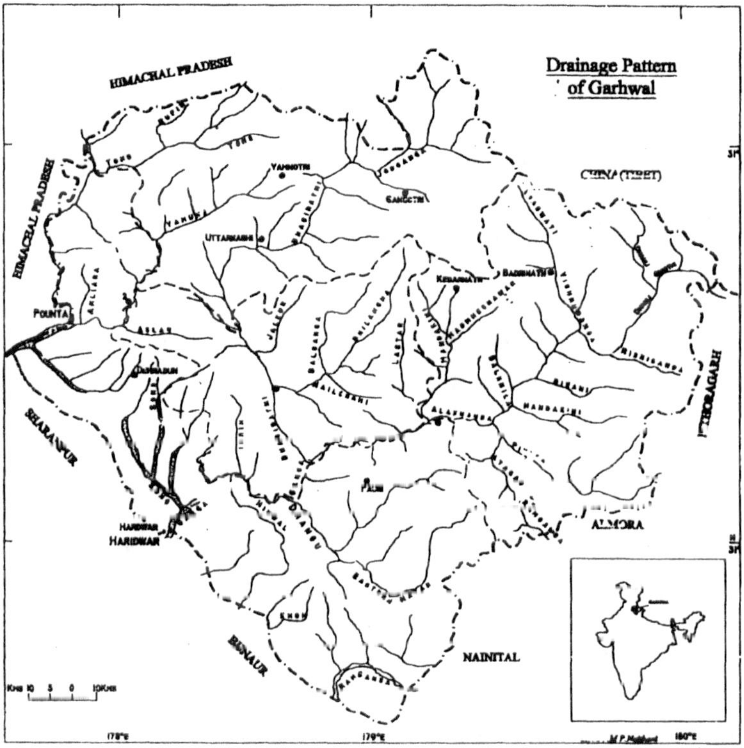

After flowing about 175 km. from its source, the river Yamuna enters the Dun valley. Here, some of the Doon rivers join the Yamuna. Asan after following North-Westernly course of about 40 km. from its source near Ogalwala, joins the Yamuna near Rampur mandi. The Tons nala with its tributary and Nalota Nala, are another important tributaries meeting Yamuna in the Doon valley. The Yamuna leaves this region by passing through a tear fault in the Siwaliks debauching upon the upper Gangetic plain near Badhahi Mahal in Saharanpur district (now in Hardwar district).

1.5.5 Climate

Corresponding to the latitudinal gradients, the region experiences a wide range of climatic conditions. The increase in temperature begins March onwards and reaches its optimum during May-June. During these months the foothills and low-lying valley up to about 1200m experience a very hot and humid climate. Even the river valley penetrating the Lower Himalaya for a considerable distance marks a surprisingly high temperature. However, stations located between 1500-3000m normally enjoy a bracing climate, ideal for health. Beyond 3000m, the rise in temperature is generally experienced during June-August.

Climatic Zones

Kaushic (1959) divides Garhwal into seven broad climatic zones primarily based on altitudes.

Table - 1.2

Broad climatic zones of Garhwal Himalaya

Climatic zone	Altitude	Temperature (oC)		
	(m)	Mean annual	Mean June	Mean Jan
Sub-Tropical zone	300-900	18.9-21.1	27.2-29.4	11.1-13.3
Warm Temp zone	900-1800	13.9-18.9	21.1-27.2	6.1-11.1
Cool Temperate zone	1800-2400	10.3-13.9	17.2-21.1	2.8-6.1

1	2	3	4	5
Cold zone	2400-3000	4.5-10.3	13.3-17.2	1.7-2.8
Alpine zone	3000-4000	3.0-4.5	5.6-13.3	Below zero for six months.
Glacial zone	4000-4800	Ten months below zero, two months between 2.2 and 3.9°c		
Perpetually frozen zone	Above 4800	Cold desert, no vegetation.		

Source :-Kharakwal S.C. (1993), *Physico-Cultural Environment and Development in U.P. Himalaya*, Nutan Publications, Kotdwar Garhwal.

Rainfall

In the region rainfall varies considerably with the height and quality is to a great extend dependent on the situation of the place to windward or leeward of high ridges and peaks.

Table - 1.3

The average monthly rainfall in millimeters and temperature in centigrade is as follows:

	Jan	Feb	Mar	Apr	May	Jun	July	Aug	Sep	Oct	Nov	Dec
Temp	5.5	5.5	10	15	18	20	18	18	16	15	11	9
Rainfall	9.0	9.2	8.2	6.7	9.7	22	52	51	19	01	1.2	3.2

Source : Bagri, S.C., 1994 Report on *Trekking Tourism in Garhwal Himalaya* submitted to Department of Tourism, Government of India.

The monsoon commences towards the mid June and normally ceases towards mid September. Generally, the zone of maximum precipitation lies between 1200-2100 m. The zone above 2400m. experiences smaller amounts of rain, while above 3500 m. there is virtually no rainfall except for mists. The monsoon showers indeed improve thc temperature discomforts and add to the luxuriance and greenery, though, because of landslides and rock falls, it often becomes hazardous to people's mobility, particularly in foothills and *Terai* area. Mid September to mid November is usually the fairest weather with occasional rain. However, in the higher zones, a considerable decrease in temperature is experienced after mid October. December and January are the coldest months. Even in the foothills and the low-lying valleys, several degrees of frost is recorded at nights. Maximum snowfall occurs during mid-January to mid-February. Sometimes the snowfall may be recorded at as low as 1000 m, but it rapidly melts below 2500m.

1.5.6 Flora and Fauna

The flora and fauna show a subsequent variability. The flora is broadly divisible into sub-tropical, temperate and alpine type, which roughly correspond to the Siwalik, Himachal and Higher Himalaya zones. The *Terai* and foot-hills zone is largely dominated by Sal (*Shorea robusta*) and its allies, extending up to 1000 m. The Himachal Zone is predominantly forested with Chir (*Pinus roxburghii*). The other major forest types are those of Ban Oak (*Quercus incana*), Kharsu Oak (*Q. dilatata*), Moru Oak (*Q. semicarpifolia*), Blue Pine (*Pinus excelsa*), Himalayan Fir (*Abies pindrow*), Silver Birch (*Betula utilis*) and the like. Between the timberline and permanent snow line lies the vast stretch of Himalayan meadow lands, witnessing rich and fascinating varieties of flowering herbs, viz., species of *Potentilla, Primula, Gentiana, Geranium, Saussuria*, and the like.

The fauna is as varied as the flora. The *terai* or *bhabar* are significant for the presence of tiger (*Panthera tigris*), Sloth bear (*Melursus ursinus*), Indian elephant (*Elphas maximums*), Spotted deer (*Axis axis*) and Hog deer (*Axis porcinus*). Leopard (*Panthera pardus*), Sambar (*Cervus unicolor*), Barking deer (*Muntiacus muntjak*), Goral (*Nemoerhaedus goral*) and Himalayan black beer (*Selenaretos this betanus*) on the other hand, enjoy a wide range of distribution up to 2700 m and sometimes even higher zone. The Higher Himalayan area represents some of the unique and rare high Himalayan brown beer (*Ursus arctos*), Musk deer (*Moschus moschiferus*), Bharal (*Psedudios nayaur*), birds and the fish fauna.

1.5.7 Land use

As regards the land use, the statistical handbook (1993) reveals 69.8% of the total land is under forests, 8.7% under agriculture, 5.2% under cultivated waste land, 2.5% under pastures, 3.3% under horticulture, 2.2% under miscellaneous uses, 1.2% fallow land and 7.1% barren land. The forest area reported in the official records also includes the snow bound area and the Himalayan meadowland. The imagery interpretation of Gupta (1979) in different watersheds of Garhwal reveals 36.66% land under forests, 8.27% under alpine meadow and 21.44% under perpetual snows. The total forest area in Garhwal region is 23094.72 sq.km. Uttarkashi District accounts for 30.75% of total forest area of Garhwal. Its 88% area is reported under forest. The share of forest area in other districts is Chamoli and Rudraprayag (22.8%), Pauri Garhwal (19.7%), Tehri (17.2%) and Dehradun (9.6%). The areas under major crops in Garhwal are: 33.5% under wheat, 1.5% under sugarcane, 19.7% under rice, 4.7% under maize, 3% under pulses, 37.6% under other major crops.

1.5.8 Demography

Population and Settlement

According to the population census 1991, out of the total population of the region (2982947), about 77% live in rural area (2295589). Urban population is represented by Dehradun district (50.3%), Pauri (11.8%), Chamoli (8.9%), Uttarkashi (7.2%) and Tehri (5.7%). Female population of the region (1461101) is 960 in every 1000 male population (1521846). But female population is more in Pauri (1060), Tehri (1058), and Chamoli (1103) per thousand of male due to male migration as compare to Uttarkashi (918) and

Dehradun (843). The overall growth of population in this region is 21.6% over the previous decade (1981). The population density of the region is about 99 person/sq. .Km, which is maximum in Dehradun District (332 persons/sq. km) and minimum in Uttarkashi (30 persons/ sq.km). This population density is worked out by taking the total area of Garhwal, which does not reflect truly the pressure of population on land as about 70% of the total land is forest. The population density of the Garhwal region is 428 persons/sq.km of the revenue land or measured land. Religion wise the population of Garhwal Comprises of Hindu (94.8%), Muslim (3.3%) Christian (0.4%), Sikh (1.1%), Buddhist (0.2%), Jain (0.2%) and others (0.1%).

Scheduled Caste and Scheduled Tribe Population

The percentage of the S.C. and S.T. population to the total population is 18.25%. The scheduled caste population of region consists of variety of castes such as *Chamar, Koli, Teli, Lohar, Badi, Auji, Tamta* etc. where as scheduled tribe population mainly consists of *Bhotias, Marchas Gaddis, Jads, Boxas, Tharus* etc. All the sub-castes of scheduled caste population are found in almost all parts of the region, while among the scheduled tribes *Bhotias, Marchas, Gaddis* and *Jads* are the tribes of higher Himalayan Valleys and *Boxas* is important tribes in the *Bhabar* and *Tarai* tract of the region. In the region, highest share of SC/ST population to total population of district varies from 32% (Dehradun) to 13.1% (Tehri). The tribal population is mainly concentrated in the *tehsils* of Joshimath, Chamoli (Chamoli District), Bhatwari, Dunda, Rajgarhi and Purola (Uttarkashi district).

The heterogeneity of geographical landscape has largely determined the population structure and settlement patterns, besides limiting the choice of occupations. The foot hills, a fertile and thickly forested zone is now characterised by a rapid economic growth due to such geographical advantages as sub-tropical climate conducive to plant growth, and its location to serve as a contact zone between the plains and the hills. Unlike the mountains lying northwards, this part has always been easily accessible to the plains, which accounts for a great in-migrated population, imported agricultural technology, growth of small and big urban centres, and varied economic activities. This is, however, a post-independence development and a result of colonizational scheme initiated by the Government. The Lesser Himalayan Zone, being the principal zone of habitation, is the scene of all economic activities whether it be in shape of terraced slopes for agriculture, a continuous belt under horticulture or in the form of winding hill roads, or again, scattered rural dwellings and smaller urban settlements. The higher Himalayan Zone, characterised by inspiring mountain scenery, controls the precipitation and serves as a huge reservoir of water. However, on account of highly precipitous terrain,. it is hostile to human settlements, though it excels in super Himalayan pilgrim resorts and fascinating mountain scenery. Out of the difficult physical conditions, wide valleys and basins, river terraces, spurs, gentle sloping up lands and the roadsides present the best possible choice for the settlements. The urban centres have been initiated mainly by the religious, administrative and tourist functions. Commerce and industry are almost underdeveloped and even service centres are few and rare. The development of transport gathered momentum with the beginning of sixties, particularly after the Sino-Indian Conflict in 1962.

Education:

As per the population census 2001 the literacy rate of the study area is 73.5 with male literacy 88 and the female literacy 59.60. Dehradun district had the maximum literacy rate of 78.96, followed by Pauri district with 77.99. The region has 5152 junior basic schools, 1105 senior schools, 691 high schools, 18 colleges and one university (1992-93).

Table: 1.4

Population and Demography (According to 1991 Census)

S.No	Item	Pauri	Tehri	Chamoli	Uttar-kashi	Dehra-dun	Total
1	Geographical Area (In sq. kms.)	5397	4421	9168	8016	3088	30090
2	**Population (In Thousands)**						
2.1	Male	331	282	227	125	556	1521
2.2	Female	351	298	228	115	469	1461
2.3	Total	682	580	455	240	1025	2982
2.4	Village	601	347	414	223	510	2295
2.5	Town/ City	81	33	41	17	515	687
2.6	S.C.	92	82	80	55	137	446
2.7	S.T.	01	01	10	02	84	98
3.	**Literacy (In Thousands)**						
3.1	Male	226	163	150	70	367	976
3.2	Female	146	64	75	22	230	537
3.3	Total	372	227	225	92	597	1513

Source :- District Statistical Department (Pauri).

Table: 1.5

Population Distribution in Garhwal (as per 2001 census)

Districts	Total Population	Density (per sq. km.)
Pauri	6,96,851	129
Tehri	6,04,608	148
Chamoli	3,69,198	48
Rudra Prayag	2,27,461	120
Uttarkashi	2,94,179	37
Dehradun	12,79,083	414
All Garhwal	34,71,380	115

Economy: Leaving out some parts of Dehradun district, the entire region is economically backward. A less developed state of non-primary sector has created a high dependency of the people in the uneconomic cultivation of agriculture, which due to unproductive lands and the environmental limits creates not only a condition of food deficit in many parts, but also disguised unemployment. Pasturing cattle is often taken up as a supplementary occupation with agriculture in the high table lands. A sizable population of the interior areas, especially the tribal populations of *Marchas, Tolchas, Jadhs,* and *Jaunsaries* also use the agriculture-based cottage industry, but non-availability of a suitable market prevents them from earning their wages. Their trade across the Tibetan borders has been stopped since 1962. Out of total workforce of the region 56.9% are farmers, 3.8% are farm labourers, 5.9% are doing business, 3.6% are employed in construction works, 0.7% are engaged in house hold Industry, 2.2% are in transport business and 22.5% are in other types of occupations.

References

Akehurst, G. (1992). European Comunity Tourism Policy. In *Perspectives on Tourism Policy*, P. Johnson and B. Thomas, eds., pp. 215-232, London, Mansell.

Ashworth, G.J. (1995). *Tourism Policy and Planning for a Quality Urban Environment: The Case of Heritage Tourism,* Department of Urban and Regional Planning Faculty of special Science, University of Groningen.

Ashworth, G.J., and J.E. Turnbridge (1990). *The Tourist Historic City.* London: Belhaven Press.

Ashworth, G.J., and P.J. Larkham (1994). *Building A New Heritage: Tourism Culture and Identify in the New Europe*. London: Routledge.

Bagri, S.C., (1997). What Is Tourism? Concepts And Definitions. *IITTM Journal Of Travel And Tourism*, Vol.-1, No.1 April 1996 - March 1997. IITTM, Gwalior

Bisht, H.(1994),*Tourism in Garhwal Himalaya*, Indus Publishing Company, New Delhi.

Bond, Ruskin (1988), *Beautiful Garhwal Heaven in Himalayas,* EBD Educational Pvt. Ltd., Dehradun, pp. 1-3.

Booms, B.H., and M.J. Bitner (1981). Marketing Strategies and Organizational Structures for Service Firms. In *Marketing of Services*, J.H. Donnelly and W.R. George, eds., pp. 47-51, Chicago: American Marketing Association.

Bose,S.C. (1968), *Land and People of the Himalaya*, Indian Publications, Calcutta, pp. 58-59.

Bose,S.C. (1972), *Geography of the Himalaya*, National book Trust India, New Delhi, p. 142.

Burkart, A.J. Medlik, S. (1974). *Tourism, Past, Present and Future*, Heinemann, London.

Butler, R.W. (1980). The Concept of a Tourism Area Cycle of Evolution: Implications for Management of Resources, *Canadian Geographer*, 24:5-12.

Census of India, (1991), Uttarpradesh National Information Science Institute, Lucknow.

Chadwick, R.A. (1981). Some notes on the Geography of Tourism; A Comment", *Chanadian Geographer*, 25.

Cheah, P. (1983). World Heritage Sites and Tourism Potntial, *Heritage Australlia*, PP. 60-63.

Clemmer, J. (1991). *Firing on All Cylinders*. Toronto: Macmillan.

Cohen, E. (1974). Who is a tourist? A Conceptual Clarification, *Sociological Review*, 22, 527-555.

Colling, R.E. (1983). Tourism and Heritage Conservation: The Pacific Experience, *Heritage Australia*. 2(2) P.58-59.

Coltman, Michael, M. (1989). *Tourism Marketing*, Van Nostrard Reinhold, New York.

Cooper, C. (1992). The Life Cycle Concept and Tourism. In *Choice and Demand in Tourism*, P. Johnson and B. Thomas, eds., pp. 145-160, London: Mansell.

Csikszentimihalyi, M. (1975). *Beyond Boredom and Anxiety*. San Francisco: Jossey-Bass.

Dann, G. (1976). The Holiday was Simply Fantastic. *Tourist Review*, 31(3):19-23.

David, L. Edgell, Sr., (1990). *International Tourism Policy*, Van Nostranal Reinhold, New York. P. 6-91.

Dogan, H.Z. (1989). Form of Adjustment: Sociocultural Impacts of Tourism. *Annals of Tourism Research* 16:216-236.

Donalde, E. Lundberg, (1990). *The tourist Business* (sixth Edition), Van Nostrand Reinhold, P. 9-13, 233-243.

Draft National Tourism Policy, (1997). State Tourism Ministers' Conference. *Department of Tourism*, Government of India, New Delhi, 26-27, December, 1997. PP. 20-29.

Fitzsimmons, J.A., and R.S. Sullivan (1982). *Service Operations Management*, New York: McGraw-Hill.

Fowler, P. (1989). Heritage: A Post-Modernist perspective. In *Heritage Interpretation: The Natural and Built Environment* (Vol. I), D. Uzzell, ed., pp. 57-64, London: Belhaven.

Franz, A. (1991). *OECD Manual on Tourism Economic Accounts*, Paris: Organization for Economic Co-operation and Development.

Gansser, Auguste, (1964), *Geology of the Himalayas*, Interscience Publishers, John Wiley and Sons, Surich, p. 261.

Gilbert, D.C. (1992). Conceptual Issues in the Meaning of Tourism in Cooper, C.P. (ed), *Progress in Tourism and Hospitality Management*, Vol. 2, University of Surry, U.K.

Gill Brinda (1998). World Heritage Sites in India. *Indrama*, Vol. XXIII, No. 3, SITA World Travel (India) Ltd., New Delhi.

Greenwood, D. (1972). Tourism as an assent of change: A spanish Basque Case, *Ethnology*, No. 11, pp, 80-90.

Gronroos, C. (1983). *Strategic Management and Marketing in the Service Sector*. Cambridge: Marketing Sciences Institute.

Gruenwald, G. (1992). *New Product Development*, 2nd ed. Chicago: NTS Business Books.

Gunn, C. (1972). Vacationscape: Designing Tourist Regions. *Austin: Bureau of Business Research.*

Gunn, C. (1988). *Tourism Planning* (2nd ed.), New York: Taylor and Francis.

Hall, M., and S. McArthur (1993). *Heritage Management in Newzealand and Australia*. Oxford: Oxford University Press.

Hameng Kubowno, X. (1993). Revitalization of culture Heritage within the context of Tourism. In Universal Tourism: Enriching or Degrading Culture. Proceedings of the *International Conference on culture and Tourism*, W. Nuryanti ed., pp. 20-29. Yogyakarta: Gadjah Mada University Press.

Hardy, D. (1988). *Historical Geography and Heritage Studies*, Area 20:333.

Haywood, K.M. (1985). Can the Tourist Area Life Cycle Be Made Operational? *Tourism Management* 6:154-167.

Heather, Zeppel and C. Michael Halls. Arts and Heritage Tourism, *Alternate Tourism*, P. 47-67.

Heeley, J. (1989). Heritage and Tourism. In *Heritage, Tourism and Leisure*, S. Hebenton, ed., pp. 3-20. Glasgow: The planning Exchange.

Herbert, D.T. (1989). Leisure Trends and The Heritage Market/In *Heritage Sites: Strategies for marketing and Development*, D.T. Herbert, R.c,. Prentice and C.J. Thomas, eds. pp. 1-15. Hants: Avebury.

Heritage Site Working Group (HSWG) (1991). *Tourism and Environment: Maintaining the Balance*, Glasgow: Government of Scotland.

Hewison, R. (1987). *The Heritage Industry*. London: Methven.

Hewison, R. (1989). Heritage: an interpretation. In D.L. Uzzell (ed.), *Heritage Interpretation: The Natural and Build Environment* (Vol. I), London: Belhaven pp. 15-24.

Hunziker, W. Krapf, K. (1942). *Grundriss der allgemeinen Fremdenverkehrelehre*, Polygraphischer verlag AG, Zurich.

Jafari, J. (1989). Structure of Tourism in S.F. and Mountinho, L. (Eds), *Tourism Marketing and Managerial Handbook*, PP. 437-442, Prentice Hall, London.

Jafferson, A. Lickorish, L. (1988). *Marketing Tourism, a Practical Guide*, Longman, Halow.

Jefferson, A., and L. Lickorish (1988). *Marketing Tourism*, Harlow: Longman.

Kaiser, C. Jr., and Helber, L.E. (1978). *Tourism: Planning and Development, Mass*, CBI Publishing, Boston.

Kamlesh Kumar and Nityanand (1989), *The Holy Himalaya: A Geographical Interpretation of Garhwal,* Daya Publishing House, Delhi.

Kaur,J. (1985), *Himalayan Pilgrimages and the New Tourism*, Himalayan Book.

Kaushic, S.D. (1959), Climatic Zones and their Related Socio-Economy in the Garhwal Himalaya: *Geog. Rev.*, Vol. 24, No. 3-4, P. 29.

Kermath, B.N., and R.N. Thomsas (1992). Spatial Dynamics of Resorts: Sosua, Dominican Republic. *Annals of Tourism Research*, 19:173-190.

Khanduri, B.M. (1994), *Archaeology of Alaknanda Valley (Central Himalaya)*, Book India Publishing Co., New Delhi.

Kharakwal, S.C. (1993), *Physico-Cultural Environment and Development in U.P. Himalaya*, Nutan Publications, Kotdwara Garhwal, pp. 3-109.

Konard, V.A. (1982). *Historical Artefacts as Recreational Land use: Perspective on its evolution in Canada*, Carleton University Pres, Ottawa.

Kotler, P. (1983). *Principles of Marketing* (2nd ed.), Englewood Clifts: Prentice-Hall.

Kotler, P. (1984). *Marketing Management: Analysis, Planning, and Control* (5th ed.). New York: Prentice-Hall.

Lapierre, J. (1991). A Proposal for a Satellite Account and Information System for Tourism. Paper presented to the *International Conference on Travel and Tourism Statistics*, July, Ottawa, Canada. Madrid: World Tourism Organization.

Leiper, N. (1990). Partial Industrialization of Tourism Systems. *Annals of Tourism Research* 17:600-605.

Leiper, N. (1990). *Tourism Systems*, Department of Management Systems, occasional paper 2, Massey University, Auckland, New Zealand.

Leiper, N. (1993). Industrial Entropy in Tourism Systems: Rejoinder to Smith. *Annals of Tourism Research* 20:221-225.

Levitt, T. (1981). Marketing Intangible Products and Product Intangibles. *Harvard Business Review* (May/June):37-44.

Lewis, C.C., and R.E. Chamber (1989). *Marketing Leadership in Hospitality* New York: Van Nostrand Reinhold.

Lickorish, L.J. (1970). Planning for Tourism in Burton in T.L. (ed.), *Recreation Research and Planning*, Allen and Unwin, London.

Mace, R. (1980). Facilities and Equipment/Program Accessibility. In *Focus on Research: Recreation for Disabled Individuals*, pp. 131-137. Washington DC: Regional Rehabilitation Institute on Attitudinal, Legal, and Leisure Barriers, George Washington University.

Mannell, R.C., and W. Bradley (1986). Does Greater Freedom Always Lead to Greater Leisure? Testing a Person X Environment Model of Freedom and Leisure. *Journal of Leisure Research* 18:215-230.

Mannell, R.C.R. Larson, and J. Zuzanek (1988). Leisure States and "Flow" Experiences: Testing Perceived Freedom and Intrinsic Motivation Hypotheses. *Journal of Leisure Research* 20:289-304.

Medlik, R. (1988). 'What is Tourism? Teaching Tourism into the 1990s, Published in the proceedings of *International Conference for Tourism Educators*, July 1988, University of Surry, Guildford, U.k.

Medlik, S., and V.T.C. Middleton (1973). Product Formulation in Tourism. In *Tourism and Marketing* (Vol. 13), Berne: AIEST.

Meidan, A. (1989). Tourism Marketing Strategies. In *Tourism Marketing and Management Handbook*, S.F. Witt and L. Moutinho, eds., pp. 525-528. Hempel Hempstead: Prentice-Hall.

Middleton, V.T.C. (1988). *Marketing in Travel and Tourism*,Oxford: Heinemann.

Middleton, V.T.C. (1989). Tourist Product. In *Tourism Marketing and Management Handbook*, S.F. Witt and L. Moutinho, eds., pp. 573-576. Hempel Hempstead: Prentice-Hall.

Mill, R.C. Morrison, A. (1985). The *Tourism System; An Introductory Text*, Prentice Hall, London.

Miller, S. (1991). Heritage Management for Heritage Tourism, P.15-21. In S. Medlik ed. *Managing Tourism*, Butterworth-Heinenmann Ltd., Oxford.

Morley, Clive, L. (1980). *Tourism: A Community approach*, Methuen, New Yourk.

Moscardo, Gianna (1996). Mindful visitors: Heritage and Tourism. *Annal of Tourism Research*, Vol. 23, No. 2, pp. 376-397, Elsevier Science Ltd.

Moutinho, L. (1989). New Product Development. In *Tourism Marketing and Management Handbook*, S.F. Witt and L. Moutinho, eds., pp. 291-294. Hempel Hempstead: Prentice-Hall.

Murphy, P.E. (1985). *Tourism: A Community Approach*,New York: Methuen.

Nautiyal, K.P. and Khanduri, B.M. (1977), "Ranikhet and its Environs: Excavation of an early Historical site in Garhwal", *The Himalaya*, Vol. I, pp. 22-38.

Nightingale, M. (1985). The Hospitality Industry: Defining Quality for a Quality Assurance Programme - A Study of Perceptions. *Service Industries Journal* 5(1):9-22.

Normann, R. (1985). Service Management: Strategy and Leadership in *Service Businesses*, New York: Wiley.

Nuryanti, Wiendu (1996). Heritage and Post Modern Tourism. *Annals of Tourism Research*, Vol. 23, No. 2, pp. 249-260, Elsevier Science Ltd., dLondon.

Ogilive, F.W. (1933). *The Tourist Movement*, Staples Press, London.

Pacific Analytics (1991). *The Tourism Satellite Account: Methodology and Results*, Vancouver : British Columbia Ministry of Development, Trade, and Tourism.

Parasuraman, A., V.A. Zeithaml, and L. Berry (1988). SERVQUAL: A Multiple-Item Scale for Measuring Consumer Perceptions of Service Quality. *Journal of Retailing* 64:12-37.

Pauw, E.K., *Tenth Settlement of Garhwal District*, Govt. Press, Allahabad, 1896, p. 16.

Pearce, D. (1989). *Tourist Development* (2nd ed.). London: Longman Scientific and Technical.

Pearce, Douglas, (1991). *Tourism Today - A Geographical Analysis*, Longman Group, Harlow.

Pearce, Philip, L. (1993). Fundamentals of Tourist Motivation in Pearce, Douglas, G. and Butter, Richard, W, (ed), *Tourism Research*, Routledge, London.

Pisarski, A. (1991). Scope of the Industry: Standard International Classification of Tourism Activities. Paper presented to the *International Conference on Travel and Tourism Statistics*, July, Ottawa, Canada. Madrid: World Tourism Organization.

Prasad,C. and Shasndilya, A.K. (1986), Evolution of Drainage in Himalaya, *Proc. of 73rd Session of Indian Sci. Cong. Delhi.*

Prentice, R. (1993). Heritage Consumers in the Leisure Market: An Application of the Manning Haas Demand Hierarchy. *Leisure Sciences* 15:273-290.

Prentice, R.C. (1993). *Tourism and Heritage Places*. London: Routledge.

Rau, M.A., High altitude Flowering Plants of Western Himalaya, *Botanical Survey of India*, Howrah, 1975, p. 5.

Raveendran, G. (1993). *Tourism Planning and Measurement Methods*. Doctoral Thesis submitted to H.N.B. Garhwal University, Srinagar Garhwal. P. 38-45.

Report of the working group on Tourism for ninth five-year plan *(1997-2002), 1996. Department of Tourism, Ministry of Tourism and Civil Aviation, Government of India. P. 1-14, 13-20.*

Robinson, H. (1976). *A Geography of Tourism*, Macdonald and Evans, London.

Saleh, F., and C. Ryan (1991). *Analyzing Service Quality in the Hospitality Industry using the SERVQUAL Model.* Service Industries Journal *11:352-373.*

Schmoll,G A.(1977). *Tourism Promotion*. London: Tourism International Press.

Schulz, C.N. (1980). Genius Loci: Towards A Phenomenology of Architecture. *London: Academy Editions*

Seekings, J. (1989). Components of Tourism, in Witt, S.F. and Mountinho, L. (Eds), *Tourism Marketing and Management Handbook*, Printice Hall, London.

Silpakit, P., and R.P. Fisk (1985). Participatizing the Service Encounter: *A Theoretical Framework. In* Services *Marketing in a Changing*

Environment, T.M. Bloch, G.D. Upah, and V.A. Zeithaml, eds., pp. 117-121. Chicago: American Marketing Association.

Singh, Shalini, (1996). *Development of Cultural Tourism and Heritage Resources: Case of Awadh Region.* A.P.H. Publishing Corporation. New Delhi. P. 149-150.

Smith, R.A. *(1992).* Beach Resort Evolution: Implications for Planning. *Annals of Tourism Research 19:304-22.*

Smith, S.L.J. (1985). Locational Patterns of Urban Restaurants. *Annals of Tourism Research 17:581-602.*

Smith, S.L.J. (1988). Defining Tourism: A supply side view, *Annals of Tourism Research, 15(2): Pergamon, London.*

Smith, S.L.J. (1989*). Tourism Analysis: A Handbook, Wiley, New York.*

Smith, S.L.J. (1991). The Supply-Side Definition of Tourism: Reply to Leiper. *Annals of Tourism Research 18:312-318.*

Smith, S.L.J. (1993). Return to the Supply-Side. *Annals of Tourism Research 20:226-229.*

Smith, V.L., and W.R. Eadington, eds. *(1989). A Marketing and Product Development Manual for the Freshwater Fishing Resorts of British Columbia,* Victoria: BC Ministry of Tourism and Provincial Secretary.

Smith, V.L., and W.R. Eadington, eds. *(1992).* Tourism Alternatives. *Philadelphia: University of Pennsylvania Press. The Tourism Research Group, The DPA Group, and Mike Hurst and Associates.*

Stephen, L.J. Smith., *(1994).* The Tourism Product. *Annals Of Tourism Research, Vol.-21, No.3, P. 582-595.*

The Economics Intelligence Unit Limited (EIU). (1996). International Tourism Reports, No-1, P. 21-33.

The Way Forward (Multilateral Air Transport Liberalisation) A special report from *World Travel and Tourism Council*, October, 1993.

Tourism Trends World Wide and in South Asia. 1950-90, *WTO Publication.*

Toynbee, G.J. *The Greeks and Their Heritage.* Oxford University Press. PP. 1-3

Travel and tourism Economic Perspective, (1995). *A special Report from the World Travel Tourism Council*, Belgium.

Tucker, K., and M. Sundberg (1988). *International Trade in services.* London: Routledge.

Valdiya, K.S. (1980). *Geology of Kumaon*, Lesser Himalaya, Wadia Inst. of Him. Geology.

Vartaman Uttarakhand (In Hindi), June 1995, pp. 40-41.

Wadia, D.N., (1966), *Geology of India*, Macmillan, London.

Wahab, S. (1971). An Introduction to Tourism theory; ***Travel Research Journal***, No. 1, USA.

Wahab, S., (1995). *Tourism Management*, Tourism International Press, London.

Wahab, S.L.J. Crampon, and L.M. Rothfield (1986). ***Tourism Marketing***, London: Tourism International press.

Wall, G., D. Dudycha, and J. Hutchinson (1985). Point Pattern Analyses of Accommodation in Toronto. *Annals of Tourism* ***Research*** 12:603-618.

World Tourism Organisation. *(1983). Development Of* ***Leisure Time and Right*** *To Holidays.*

WTO (1996). International; Tourism Over View, A special report from the World Tourism Organisation.

WTO *(1998). International Tourism Over View, A* ***Special report from the World*** *Tourism Organisation.*

Yale, P. (1992). *From Tourist Attractions to Heritage Tourism.* ***London. ELM*** *Publications.*

Zeppel, H. and M.C. Hall (1992). Arts and Heritage Tourism. ***In special Interest*** *Tourism, B. Weiler, and M.C. Hall, eds., pp. 47-69.* ***London: Belnaven.***

2

Natural Heritage Tourism Products

2.1 MOUNTAIN PEAKS

The actual attractions of higher Garhwal Himalaya are the towering snow covered peaks. The chains of mountain peaks are divided into different mountain groups by mighty rivers of Garhwal (detail list of peaks is listed in Appendix). The high peaks of Banderpunch (6302 Mt.), Kalanag (6387 Mt.), Swaraga rohini (6252 Mt.) and Yamunotri lie between the Tons and Bhagirathi river. Chirbas (6525 Mt.), Matri (6712 Mt.) and Trimukh Parbat (6422 Mt.) lie between Jadh Ganga and the Bhagirathi rivers. Another cluster of peaks lies in between Bhagirathi and Saraswati (tributary of Alaknanda) rivers. Famous among this cluster of peaks is Chaukhamba (I-7140, II-7070, III-6970, IV-6850 Mt.) situated on the West of Badrinath temple. To the east of Chaukhamba are Parvati Parbat (6257 Mt.), Nilkanatha (6600 Mt.) and Narayan parvat. On the West are Mandani parvat (6190 Mt.), Yaunkbar (5953 Mt.) Kharchakund (6630 Mt.) and Sumeru parvat (6350 Mt.). Gangotri glacier, which starts from Chaukhamba and ends at Gaumukh is almost encircled by snow covered peak. The third important group of peaks lies to the north of Nanda Devi Cluster. These peaks are situated between Saraswati and Dhauli Ganga rivers. Kamet (7750 Mt.) is the highest peak in this group. It does not rise from the main Himalayan chain, but is the culminating point of Zanskar Range. Three equally lofty peaks form a group with Kamet-the western Ibi Gamin (7376 Mt.), the Eastern Ibi Gamin (7367 Mt.) and the Mana Peak (7272 Mt.). In the same chain to the south-east of this cluster are Gauri Parbat (6708 Mt.) and Hathi Parbat (6727 Mt.). The great Snow Mountains that form a conspicuous feature of Garhwal are some 50 to 60 kilometres South of Tibetan Watershed. There are several peaks over 7000 Mt. high and all the great peaks occur in clusters. Nowhere do we find so many clusters of peaks of average unparalleled height (with the exception of Nepal) as those that occurring in Garhwal. The most important cluster of peaks is the inner Nanda Devi Sanctuary. The chief of these groups is Nanda Devi Peak (7817 Mt.), Kalanka (6931 Mt.), Rishi Pahar (6942 Mt.), Changbang (6864 Mt.), Nanda Khat (6611 Mt.), Nanda Ghunti (6309 Mt.), Mrigthuni (6565 Mt.), Maiktoli (6303 Mt.), Devisthan (I-6678 Mt., II-6529 Mt.) and at least a dozen more snow capped peaks.

One can enjoy the beauty of upper Garhwal while trekking or climbing the mountains. But for the normal tourists there are some vantage points to enjoy the best view of these peaks. A view of Nanda Devi can be enjoyed from several points in upper Garhwal like Kuari Pass (4268 m.), Chandrashila (3680 m.) and Auli (3049 m.), but there is none so touching as that seen from the outer Nanda Devi National Park. As one crosses the ridge to reach Dibrughetta one gets the first vision of Nanda Devi, towering from the jaws of Rishi valley. A beautiful view of Trisul can be enjoyed from a ridge above Gwaldam (1940 m.). The northern face of the Trisul massif can best be viewed from Lata Kharak, a ridge above village Lata, in Dhauli Valley. The best view of Chaukhamba is that from Deoriatal and Chandrashila. The Madhyamaheshwar valley sand the Pangarbasa dharamshala at Chopta also offer beautiful views of Chaukhamba. The Kedarnath group of peaks is visible from Deoriatal, Chandrashila and from the shrine of Kedarnath itself.

The best panoramic view of Kamet peak is offered from Kuari Pass (4268 Mt.) and Chandrashila (3680 Mt.). For viewing Kirti Stambha, Jogin etc. near Gaumukh,Panwali meadow is the best place.

Glaciers

The great Himalayan range is a gathering ground of snow, nourishing heap of multinational glaciers. Garhwal is one of the most glaciated regions and here the glaciers maze is amazing. There are three main glacial systems in Garhwal Himalaya: Bhagirthi Glacial System, Alaknanda Glacial System and Dhauli Glacial System.

Some Important Glaciers of the Garhwal Himalaya

Gangotri Glacier: It is located on the western slopes of the Chaukhamba peak. It is 30 km long and about 2 km wide, thus it occupies a little over 200 sq.km. The holy river Bhagirathi, the headwater of the Ganga, takes its origin from Gaumukh, about 4 km. down of its snout. The glacier is fed by a system of tributary glaciers, known as *Rakta Varna, Swet Varna, Nilamber, Pilapani* and *Chaturangi*, depending upon the colour of the surrounding rocks. The height of the glacier is 4040 Mt. with a maximum height of 5200 Mt. at its source.

Kedarnath Glacier: The glacier is about 14 km long with an average width of 500 m. The snout of the glacier is related to the Bhagirathi River. Lateral moraines are well developed along both the sides of the glacier. The glaciers of Bhagirathi and Alaknanda systems are separated by Kalindi Khal (5,968 Mt.) water parting.

Bhagirathi-Kharak Glacier: This is a transverse glacier, extending in about 9 km. The glacier is connected with the Satopanth glacier that lies in the south.

Satopanth Glacier: This transverse glacier is located in the southeast of the Bhagirath-Kharak glacier. The Nilkanth peak is located in the south east of this glacier. A beautiful Satopanth Tal is also located here. The snout of the Bhagirath-Kharak and the Satopanth glaciers are connected each other and the river Alaknanda takes its origin from here.

2.2 LAKES AND KUNDS

Upper Garhwal Himalaya contains numerous beautiful lakes that are usually found around 3000 Mt. above sea level. Many of them are insignificant depressions on ridges receiving seasonal rainwater. All the major higher lakes in Garhwal have rich background and are related to a number of events. The lakes are also visited by people for some fair, festivals and ritual performance. Trekking to these lakes has high potential for Tourism promotion.

Deoriatal: The road-head to the lake is Mastura on Gopeswar-Ukhimath road, at a distance of 8-km Northeast from Ukhimath. After a 5.5 kms of trek from Mastura through a tiny village Sari one can reach the beautiful oval shaped lake surrounded by forests of pine, oak and rhododendron on three sides. The lake is situated on a spur at an elevation of 2440 Mt. It is approximately 200 sq.mt. in area and the maximum depth is 19.80 m. It affords a magnificent view of snowy peaks of Chaukhamba, Kedarnath, whose beauty is doubled, when reflected in the clear water of the lake. In winter the surface of the lake is frozen.

Hemkund (Lokpal Ka-kund): Hemkund-Lokpal is situated about 40 km from Joshimath and the road-head is Govindghat. This lake commands two-fold sanctity, because of its association with *Lakshman*, the younger brother of Lord *Rama* and the Sikh *Guru Govind Singh*.

Satopanth: It is a high altitude glacial lake, situated at an altitude of 4402 Mt. above sea level and 25 km to the north west of Badrinath. It is a triangular lake and has a diameter of one and a half kilometre roughly. The lake is considered as one of the most pious lakes of the Hindu. *Brahma, Vishnu* and *Mahesh* the creator, preserver and destroyer of the Universe are believed to have meditated at the three corners of the lake. Hence the three corners are named as *Bharmaghat, Vishnughat* and *Maheswarghat*. The access to the lake is difficult and beyond Vasundhara fall (5 km away from Mana Village) there is no proper pathway. It is 18 km away from Vasundhra fall. Interested visitors have to visit with guide and all trekking equipment. *Marchhyas* of Mana hold it in great reverence and take their dead to this lake.

Kakbhusandital: It is a small high altitude glacial lake situated at an altitude of about 5000 Mt. in the lap of *Hati Parbat* (6730 Mt.). It is associated with the mythological character of *Kakbhusandi* (the crow). The lake can be approached from two sides, one from Bhyunder village near Ghangaria and the other comparatively more difficult path is from Vishnu Prayag, confluence point of Alaknanda and Vishnu Ganga. The trek from Bhyunder passes through thick bear infested forests, and stretches of stinging nettles without any shelters, except shepherd huts. It is of 18-km trek and involves walking on glacial moraines and slippery rocks over long distances. The approach to the lake from Vishnuprayag runs along ridges and involves steep climbing.

Deotal: The lake remains frozen most of the time in the year. It is considered as the holiest of the holy lakes and situated on the glacial moraines in the inner line area of Chamoli district. It is on the ancient Indo-Tibetan trade route, which passes through Mana pass. On the shore of this lake, a fair is held on *Janamashtami*.

Roopkund: This small, but beautiful mysterious lake is situated below the Trisul massif on a mountain close to Chandanikot (5023 Mt.) peak at an altitude of 4778 Mt. above sea level. Steep rock walls about 25 Mt. high surrounds the lake. This high-altitude glacial lake falls on the Nanda Jat route to Homkund. Debal, the road-head for Roopkund trek is 57 km from Karnaprayag. The base of trek for Roopkund is Mundoli, 7 km from Deval. The popular trek route for Roopkund passes through Mundoli (2134 Mt.), Lohajung (2244 Mt.), Bedni (3354 Mt.), Bistola (4667 Mt.).

Bhaikaltal and Brahmatal: One can visit the tranquil lakes Brahmatal and Bhaikaltal, off the route from Mundoli or wan. These two lakes are easily accessible and are set amidst beautiful environment. Bhaikaltal lies on top of a ridge (2,744 Mt.) about 13 km from the village Phaldiya in Chamoli district. It is surrounded on all sides by dense forest containing fir, birch, and rhododendron with *ringal* forming a dense under growth. These forests make an ideal habitat for wild animals like brown bear, wild bore, deer and a variety of waterfowls. About three kilometres ahead is Brahmatal (3507 Mt.) having similar environs. Ideal conditions exist for developing these lakes for winter sports, as both the lakes remain frozen during winter (December-February) and ice is sufficiently thick. Easy access and availability of level stretches of land around lakes are additional favorable factors.

Vasukital: It is a beautiful lake with an area of half sq.km, at an altitude of 4884 Mt. It is 6 km away from kedarnath temple. The approach is very difficult. Initial trek of 4 km is steep, then half a km is gradual, but the last stretch is the most difficult due to scattered boulders. The lake is surrounded by small hillocks of alpine meadows, full of colorful flowers prominent among them being *Brahma-kamal* and *Neel-Kamal*. It is said that mythological *Vasukinag* (snake) used to live here. On the occasion of "*Krishna-Janmastami*" people specially come to visit this lake and take bathe in it.

Chaurabarital or Gandhi Sarobar: This small and beautiful fresh water lake is 4 km ahead of Kedarnath temple on the Right Bank of river Mandakini The approach to this lake is difficult but interesting. It involves the trekking on the moraines of Chaurabari glacier. The snout of the glacier has to be crossed to reach the lake, which is just on the back of a knife like ridge, made by the lateral moraines of the glacier. The lake might be derived its name due to its hidden quality. It has assumed the new name "Gandhi Sarovar" after the immersion of Gandhiji's ashes into the lake.

Dodital: One of the beautiful lakes of Garhwal, Dodital is located at an altitude of 3024 Mt. above sea level with an area of one sq. km. This lake can be approached from Gangori (5 km. from Uttarkashi on way to Gangotri). At Gangori the motor road bifurcates and one road goes up to Sangam Chatti along the river Ganga. The trek begins from Kalyani (7 km from Gangori) up to Agoda Village (5 km from Kalyani). Agoda 16 Kms away from the lake was the centre of the earthquake in 1991. After crossing many streams and watching waterfalls on the way one can reach Dodital. The lake is filled with fishes including the rare Himalayan trout and for anglers it is like heaven. Thick forests of oak, pine and rhododendron surround the spectacular lake of fresh water. An unnamed stream fills water into the lake and there is an outlet from where the lake water goes out and makes the river Asiganga.

Fig 2.2.1
Dodital Trek

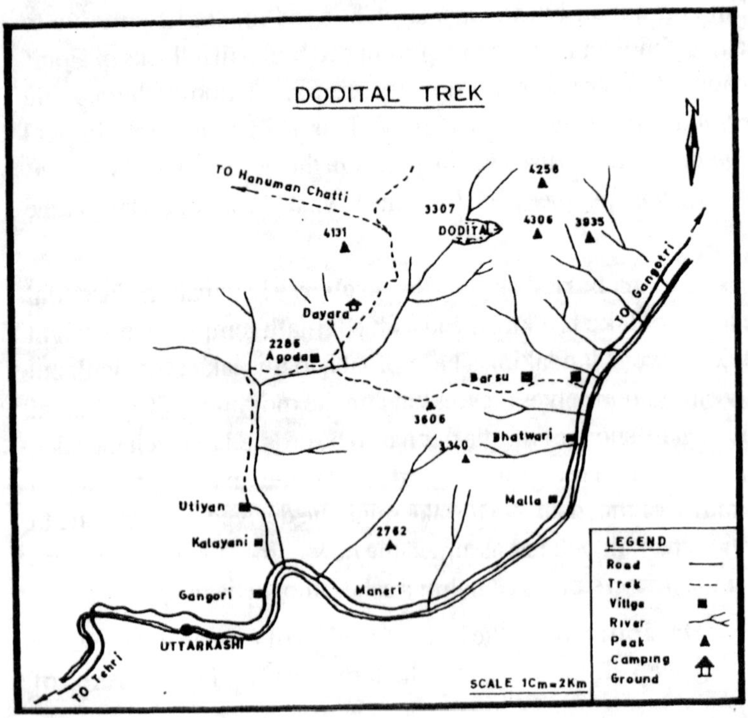

Fig 2.2.2
Sahastra Tal Trek

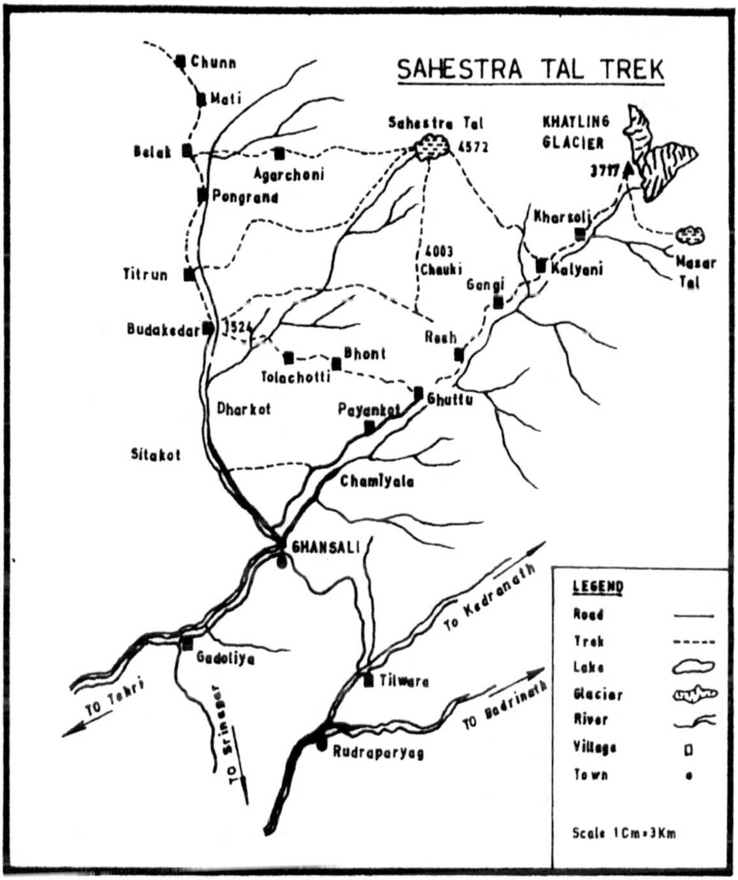

Necessary permission for fishing may be obtained from divisional forest officer at Kotbanglow near Uttarkashi. Near the lake good camping sites are there. Tourist can stay in camps and forest rest house. From Dodital, there is one hard trek route, going towards Hanuman Chatti (last road head of Yamnotri). In this route one has to cross the steep climb of 'Bakriya top' and 'Derva top'. Below the Bakriya top, one can find a series of meadows and it is difficult to find the routes. So one must accompany with a good guide and proper equipment while trekking in this route. From Bakriya top the view of Banderpunch and Gangotri group can be enjoyed.

Nachiketatal: In the east of Uttarkashi, this beautiful small lake is situated at an altitude of 2453 Mt. Chaurangikhal, 23 km. from Uttarkashi is the road head for the lake. From Chaurangikhal one has to trek 3 km. in the thick forest. The lake is easily accessible. One can have enchanting experience of fresh water trout in the lake. There are oak and rhododendron trees in the nearby surrounding of lake. A very small holy temple of *Nag Devta* is located near the lake and every year on *Nagpanchmi* day, people from nearby villages assemble here for celebrating the holy dip and worship. From the west of the lake a vast panorama of Banderpunch region is worth seeing. An adventure-loving tourist can trek from Uttarkashi to Nachiketatal, which is only 16 kms. A few shops and a PWD rest house are there but one can camp near the lake, too.

Kedartal: To reach Kedartal one is required to cover 17-km. trek from Gangotri to Dandi Kshetra. Shepherds mainly use the trek. After a trek of 7.5 kms one arrives at a beautiful campsite Bhojkharak. The Steep climb goes through the pine forest and is hazardous because of rock falls. Drinking water is no problem on the way but firewood is not available. A ridge separates Kedartal from Rudragsira Kharak.

Sahastratal: Sahastratal is one of the upcoming pilgrimage centres in district Tehri situated at an altitude of 4600 m and is worshipped as an abode of Lord Shiva. The pilgrimage to Sahastratal is an annual event for villagers of Uttarkashi and Tehri districts. The trek to this lake begins from Budhakedar, Ghuttu and Malla, which are connected by frequent bus services. The main transit points en route from Ghuttu to the lake are Reeh Village, Gangi Village, Kalyani, Tari Udiyar and Teen Tal, where as from the Budhakedar side the convenient halting stations are Agunda village,

Jhalla Chatti, Pinswar Village, Chatterwana, Khatki pani and Pandav Sera. At Reeh and Gangi Villages, GMVN's Tourist Rest Houses are available. At Kalyani, trek bifurcates for khatling glacier (source of river Bhilangna). The trek is full of natural flowers, green meadows, lakes, fountains, herbs and springs. The fresh water of the lake changes its colour with the glances of sun. The trek to this lake from Malla (25 km from Uttarkashi on way to Gangotri) passes through Shilla, Johra, Karki and Dharamshala. Dharamshala is the base camp not only for reaching to Shastratal, but also for trekking to six other lakes viz., Lingtal, Parital, Darshantal and Daudital etc.

2.3 WILDLIFE PARKS AND SANCTUARIES OF GARHWAL

Garhwal Himalaya represents some of the leading and most fascinating wildlife parks and sanctuaries of the country. Interestingly, country's first ever National Park - the Haily National Park (now Corbett Tiger reserve) is also situated in this part of Himalaya. At present, the region represents as many as five National Parks and two Sanctuaries. Of them, the National Parks are (I) Corbett National Park (Part of Corbett Tiger Reserve) (ii) Nanda Devi National Park (Core zone of Nanda Devi Biosphere Reserve) (iii) Valley of Flowers National Park (iv) Rajaji National Park and (v) Govind National Park (Part of Govind Pasuvihar Sanctuary). The wildlife sanctuaries are Govind Pashuvihar sanctuary and Kedarnath Musk deer sanctuary. Of all the reserves Corbett National park, established in 1935, is the oldest followed by Govind Pasuvihar Sanctuary in 1955 and Kedarnath wildlife sanctuary in 1972. Both Valley of Flowers and Nanda Devi National Park (NDNP) were constituted in 1982. Later Nanda Devi biosphere reserve was made in 1988 and Govind National Park was declared out of the area of Govind Pasuvihar Sanctuary in 1991.

As regards to the area, the Nanda Devi biosphere reserve (with 2236.74 Sq.km area including NDNP with 638.33 Sq.km area) is the biggest followed by Kedarnath Musk Deer Sanctuary (975.25 Sq. km), Govind Pasuvihar Sanctuary (953.12 Sq. km. including

Govind National Park of 472.08 Sq. km), Corbett Tiger Reserve (912.67 Sq. km including Corbett National Park of 329.98 Sq. km in Garhwal region), Rajaji National Park (820.42 Sq. km) and smallest being Valley of Flowers National Park (87.52 Sq. km.). Thus Parks and Sanctuaries cover an area of 4382.30 Sq. km. representing 14.56 per cent of the total geographical area of the Garhwal Himalaya, out of which 7.78 per cent comes under National Park. Among all the reserves Corbett Tiger Reserve and Rajaji National park are situated in the foot hills of the Himalaya and the rest others are exclusively high altitude reserves with rich flora and fauna. The numerous snow peaks, glaciers, glacial torrents, lakes and the beautiful alpine meadows in the high altitude reserves are virtually an asset for naturalists, adventure seekers and bio and geo-scientists. Nanda Devi National Park is the highest reserve in the country and second in the world after the Sagarmatha National Park in Nepal.

In fact, the Parks and Sanctuaries of Garhwal Himalaya are the rich depository of a variety of natural tourist resources viz. wildlife, forests, meadows, water bodies, mountain peaks, glaciers and the like. Some of the reserves are also associated with important historical and religious sites and the tribal settlements. Due to certain outstanding and well defined set of attractive features some of the reserves have become favorite tourist destinations viz. Corbett Tiger Reserve for its rich faunal wealth, Valley of Flowers National Park for the fascinating floral spectrum and Nanda Devi National park for its great many lofty peaks. The National Parks and Sanctuaries are selected for the case studies and the potential of these reserves as important heritage tourism product is evaluated.

2.3.1. Kedar Nath Musk Deer Sanctuary

The sanctuary derives its name from the famous Hindu Shrine of Kedarnath and the Musk deer. The musk pool that the male deer carries is the sole cause behind its persecution. Musk or *Kasturi* used as medicine and perfume making is more valuable than gold. Fortunately, Garhwal Himalaya is still left with some ideal habitats

Table - 2.3.1
Representation of National Parks/Wildlife Sanctuaries in Garhwal Region

		Area (In Sq. Km.)		
Name of NP/WLS	**Year of establishment**	**National Park (NP)**	**Wildlife Sanc-tuaries**	**Tiger Reserve/ Biosphere Reserve**
Rajaji N.P.	1983	820.42		
Corbett Tiger Reserve	1973	502.82		1318.54
Valley of Flowers N.P.	1982	87.52		
Govind N.P. &	1991	472.08	481.04	
Govind Pashu				
Vihar Sanctuary	1955	Total Area	(953.12)	
Nanda Devi				
Biosphere	1988			2236.74
Reserve				(including
Nanda Devi NP	1982	633.33		N.D.N.P.)
Kedarnath				
Musk Deer				
Wild Life				
Sanctuary	1972		975.24	

of musk deer harboring a sizable population of this vanishing deer. In order to provide adequate protection to musk deer in particular and all the high altitude wild life present in the area, Kedarnath Musk Deer Sanctuary was created in Chamoli District (now in Rudra Prayag) in 1972. Sanctuary was notified under Rule 4 of General hunting Rules of U.P., regulating hunting, shooting and fishing in reserved area.

Physical Features and Sanctuary's Attraction

The sanctuary (975-sq. km.) is situated in the northeastern part of Garhwal Himalaya under Kedarnath Forest Division and Ukhimath Tehsil of Chamoli District. The sanctuary lies between 78°54'-79°27E' longitudes and 30°26'N - 30°45'N latitudes. The altitude ranges from 1160 m. (near Phata) to the Peak of Chaukhamba (7068 m). It abounds by numerous named and unnamed lofty mountain peaks like *Kedarnath Parvat* and *Kedar Dome.* The entire sanctuary lies in the northern catchment of Alaknanda River and comprises of a series of mostly north-south oriented river valleys. It is drained predominantly by river Mandakini and its tributaries except for its eastern part. In addition, there are numerous hot and cold springs and waterfalls scattered all along the sanctuary areas.

The sanctuary is snowbound for about three months, following heavy snowfalls in December. 44.4% to 48.8% area of the sanctuary is forested, 7.7% comprises alpine meadows and shrubs, 42.1% is rock or under permanent snow and 1.5% represents formerly forested areas that have been degraded. The tropical zone, which does not occur above 1200 m. is absent. The subtropical zone is represented by chir pine (*Pinus roxburghii*) up to 2000 Mt. Major part of the forests of sanctuary come under temperate zoneand is dominated by banj (*Quercus incana*). The other important trees being *Q. dilatata, Q. semecarpifolia, Rhododendron arboreum, Abies pindrow, Acer ceasium* and the like. The subalpine Zone consists of birch (*Betula utilis)*. Between the timberline and permanent snow line there are beautifully carpeted flower rich *bugyals*, viz., Panar, Chandra Shila, Bisuri, Rudranath, Madhyamaheswar. The herb community of the meadows is dominated by *Danthonia cumminsii*.

The sanctuary is also rich for faunal attractions and is known for Snow leopard, brown bear, bharal, tahr, musk deer in the higher

Fig 2.3.1

Kedarnath Musk Deer Sancturay

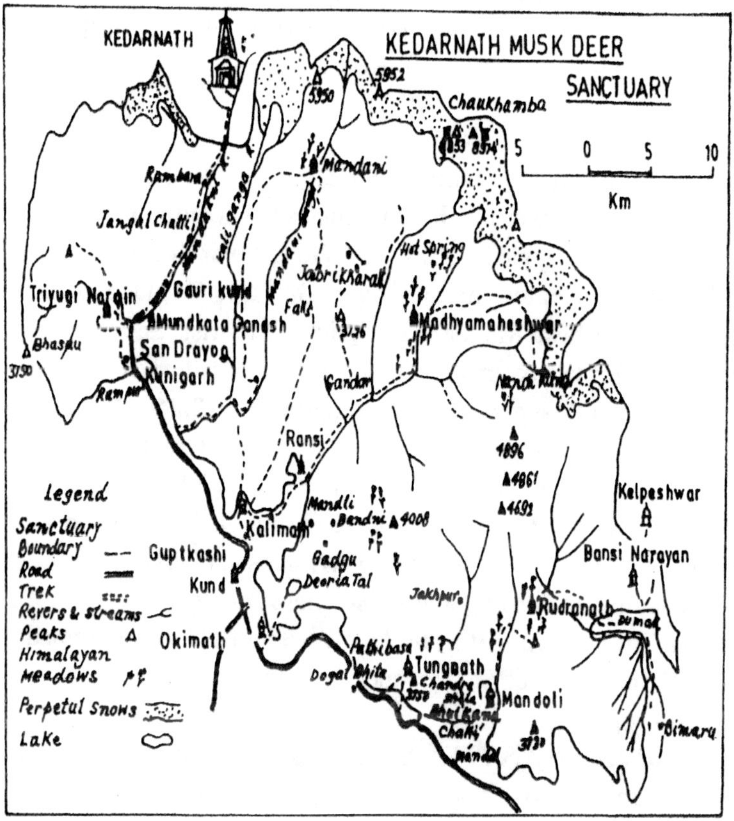

reaches and leopard, Himalayan black bear, Samber, wild boar, serow, barking deer, goral in the lower parts. Himalayan yellow throated Marten, Red Fox, Jackal and Porcupine are interesting mammalian features below the timberline. Some of the important avifauna of the sanctuary is Monal, Koklas, Snow Cock, the Himalayan Cuckoo, Kajeej, Bulbol, Himalayan Tree Creeper and Indian Blue Chat etc. Notable species of reptile include Himalayan

Pit Viper (*Ancistrodon himalayensis*). Some 36 species of fishes have been recorded from the Mandakini River including *Schizothorax* spp. Mahseer (*Tor tor*), *Labeo* spp., *Gara* spp. etc. which is considered to be rare (Singh et.al. 1987). Deoria Tal is a paradise for the anglers, where the snow trout has been introduced.

Management

The office of the wildlife warden Kedar Nath sanctuary is located at Gopeshwar in Chamoli District. The boundary of this sanctuary starts beyond 20 Kms. from Gopeshwar. Tourists visiting Kedarnath can enter the sanctuary through Guptakashi and Okhimath. Garhwal Mandal Vikas Nigam's tourist rest houses are located at Chopta, Okhimath, Sonprayag, Kedarnath and Gopeswar whereas PWD Rest houses are available at Dugalbitta, Okhimath, Phata and Sonprayag. There are also forest rest houses at Augustmuni, Sonprayag and Rudraprayag in addition to a number of Dharamshalas. Unfortunately, due to the lack of appropriate management plan, the sanctuary still remains in blue print. Since it is not possible to shift villagers elsewhere and devoid them from their traditional rights of using forest products. The only remedy lies in the reconstruction of the sanctuary boundary. Under the recent revised proposal for the notification of the sanctuary under the wildlife protection Act 1972, certain areas have been excluded from the sanctuary so as to exclude the villages and the high biotic pressure areas and the areas with duality of control (*Van-Panchayats*).

Further, ill equipped and untrained wildlife staff, deputed there can not do much for the protection of wildlife. Poaching, particularly of musk deer and pheasants, continues in less accessible areas. Grazing by domestic livestock, burning of pastures and collection of forest products and medicinal herbs are usual practice of local people. Research based development plan has further become a priority as the area has suffered an inroads from the secular tourists and trekkers, who are increasing in number day by day.

2.3.2 Valley of Flowers National Park

Valley of flowers, has been known as one of the world's richest treasures of flowers. According to legends Hindu sages used the valley for meditation on account of its exceptional solitude. To the local people it is a fairy land and in Hindu mythology it is named '*Nandan Kanan*' meaning 'Garden of *Indra* in paradise' (Kaur, 1985). Mythically the valley has been associated with the name of '*Hanuman*' and '*Laxman*', the legendary heroes of the Ramayan. *Hanuman* is believed to have procured '*Sanjivani Booti*' (life saving herb) from here to save the life of '*Laxman*'. *Laxman* himself is said to have meditated on the shores of the famous Hemkund Lake where a tiny temple of Laxman still exists besides the massive Hemkund *Gurudwara* of Sikhs.

Frank S. Smythe, a British Mountaineer during his Kamet expedition in 1931, brought this wondrous kingdom of wild flowers to light. He was so fascinated by the beauty of this valley that in 1937 he returned to the valley for an extensive herbarium collection and named the place 'Valley of Flowers'. Subsequently, he wrote a book 'The Valley of Flowers'. His lucid writing made the valley world famous. His contribution to plant geography was indeed praiseworthy. Smyth's work was assisted by England's eminent botanist R.L. Holdsworth followed by John Marget Legg who lost her life there in 1939. The wildlife was briefly survey in 1980 (Green 1980) and visitor survey had been conducted in 1977 (Singh and Kaur 1980) and O.P. Kandari (1984).

Once explored, the valley of flowers gradually caught the attention of naturalists, researchers, and trekkers from the world over. Prior to 1975 higher Himalayan zone was declared as restricted area. In 1975 this area was opened to visitors. Unfortunately, the unplanned display of this spectacular natural heritage proved disastrous, which affected the plant communities and the sensitive ecosystem adversely. Later so as to restore the natural balance and to protect and conserve this unique natural heritage, The Valley of Flowers with 87.52sq.km area was declared as a National Park on September 6th, 1982.

Park Area: Geographical Location and Physical Features

The high altitude National Park is situated in the northeastern part of the Garhwal Himalaya in the Zaskar Range above Ghangaria in the upper catchment of the Bhyundar Ganga - an eastern tributary of river Alaknanda.The National Park starts from the timberline beyond Ghangaria at an altitude of 3200 m and runs in east west direction along both the banks of river Pushpawati up to snow clad peaks of Rataban (6126 m) and Gauri *Parvat* (6590 m). The range of altitude thus varies from 3200 m to 6590 m providing a great diversity of landscapes and microhabitats. Numerous tiny streams and waterfalls dissect the Park. However, *Pushpawati* is the lone river in the park. After having emerged out of the huge Tipra Glacier, *Pushpawati* flows right across the park. After coming out of the park *Pushpawati* joins *Laxman Ganga* (emerging out from Hemkund Lake) at Ghangaria. Onwards this confluence, the river

Fig 2.3.2 (a)

Valley of Flowers Natonal Park

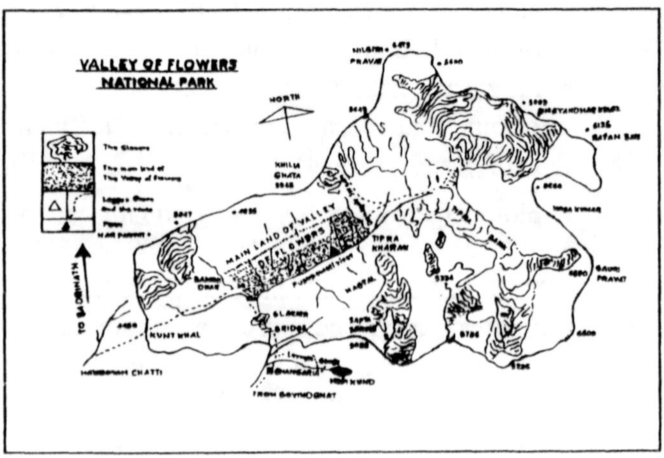

Fig 2.3.2 (b)

Valley of Flowers Trek

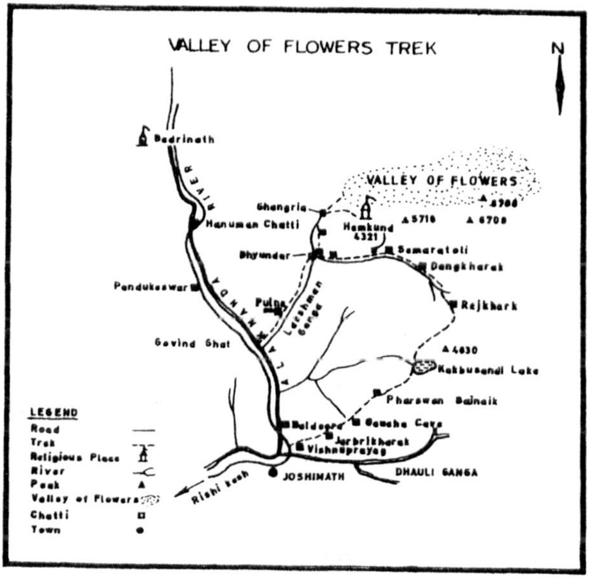

takes its name as *Bhyunder Ganga*, till it merges in the Alaknanda at Govindghat. The major meadows i.e. relatively flat, gently undulating landscapes run in the middle of National Park in the east west direction. The extent of Central Valley is about 10 sq.km. To the north and south of the Central Meadow the slopes rise initially gently but gradually rise in steepness to merge with snow clad mountains and rocky screes of *Nilgiri Parvat* (6479 m) in the north and *Sapta Sringa* (5038 m) in the south. The topography of park consists of highly heterogeneous land formations ranging from low lying flat area, gentle to steep slopes, unstable glacial moraines, stream banks, forest meadow edges and snow bound areas.

Climate

The climate of the area is humid, with short cool summer and long severe winter. The area becomes snow bound up to 7 months (late September to early May). The snowfall begins in

October and continues until the first week of April and the valley remains inaccessible until the first week of May as snow melt begin around mid April. The average temperature for May is 9°C. The daily rainfall fluctuates greatly as it goes up to 47.10 mm in mid August and also register no rainfall during the same month. The maximum rainfall occurs in August (405 mm).

Approach

By 15 km. trek from Govindghat via Phulna and Bhyunder villages one can reach to Ghangaria, the base camp for trekking to the Valley of Flowers or to Hemkund Sahib. A further 4.5-km trek from Ghangaria leads to the Valley of Flowers. Horses, *Dandies*, Ponies and *coolies* are available at Govindghat to carry luggage and tourists to Ghangaria and Hemkund. But from Ghangaria to Valley of Flowers only *coolie* and *Dandi* can be hired. Rates are being fixed by *Zila Panchayat*, Chamoli. The best time to visit the park is in rainy season when Valley is in full bloom. Considering the flowering season, the best time to visit the park is early July to end of August. The weather, particularly, in the Valley is very uncertain.

The Floral Heritage

The floral heritage diversity of Valley of Flowers is due to its landscape diversity and diverse environmental factors like altitude, slopes, flatness of surface, proportions of rocks and boulders, presence or absence of river streams course etc. There are two major aspects in the Park i.e. north facing and south facing as river *Pushpawati* runs in east-west direction. The northern slopes are thickly forested with birch (*Betula Utilis*) and rhododendron (*Rhododendron campanulatum*) up to an elevation of 3800 m. The southern slopes at the base of rock wall consist largely of meadows, where occurs a great variety of alpine flowers for which the Valley is famous. Smythe (1938) has reported as many as 250 genera of flowering plants. To mention a few common, yet fascinating plant genera from the valley are: *Acontium, Anemone (Creamy Colour), Anaphalis, Aster, Ranunculus, Meconopsis (blue), Corydalis, Geranium (Pink), Galium, Gentiana, Fritillaria, Lysimachia, Pontentilla (red), Primula (Blue flower), Polygonum, Pleurospermum, Pedicularis, Nomocharis, Stellaria, Sedum, Viola, Cyananthus, Cynoglossum and Iris.*

Practically, most of the plants in the valley are annual, having medicinal and other commercial values. These are, *Aconitum balfourii (Mitha-bish), Aheterophyllum (Atis), Viola can escens (Dudhi birali), Geranium wallichianum (Ratanjot), Potentilla fulgens (Bajradanti), Bergenia Stracheyi (Pakhen bedh), Tanacetum longifolium (Guggal), Plantago brachyphylla (Isabgul) and Allium stracheyi (Pharan). Saussurea obvallate (Brahm Kamal)* an aromatic herb largely used in religious ceremonies normally grows well above 4000 m.

The valley begins to witness early flowering as soon as snow start melting, generally after mid May. The dwarf Rhododendron is among the first to flower, simultaneously, *Primula denticulata, Oxygraphis polypetala and Gentiana spp.* start flowering. Between mid July and mid August the valley is densely carpeted with flowers of different colours. With the advent of September all colours begin to fade away.

The Faunal Heritage

Unfortunately, the mammalian fauna enjoys comparatively poor distribution in the park. Of the felines, the Leopard *(Panthera pardus)*, snow Leopard (*Panthera unica),* Jungle cat *(Felis chaus)* and Leopard cat *(Felis bengalensis)* are reported from the park. Family Ursidae is represented by Himalayan Black Bear *(Selenarctos thibetanus)* and Brown Bear *(Ursus arctos)*. Family canidae is represented by Jackal *(Canis aureus)* and Red Fox *(Vulpes vulpes)* Order Artidactyla is represented by bovines like serow *(Capricornis sumatraensis)*, Goral *(Nemorhaedus goral)*, Tahr *(Hamitragus jemlahicus)* and Bharal *(Pseudois nayaur)*, while from among the Cervines, Sambar *(Cervus unicolor)*, and Musk deer (*Moshus moschiferus)* have been reported from the park. Game birds like partridges, pheasants are rare in park area. However variety of pigeons, doves, cuckoos, kingfishers, wood packers, bulbuls, finches and like colourful birds enjoy a rich distribution in the park vicinity. But the park harbors spectacular varieties of butterflies.

Product Management

During the last few years some accommodation facilities have come up, with 250 beds capacity at Govindghat and 320 beds at Ghangaria. The Gurudwara management has done laudable work in providing comfortable accommodation with bedding and food to a large number of visitors. The Gurudwara maintains the excellent tradition of entertaining all visitors irrespective of caste, creed or religion. With the start of tourist season tea-stalls and eateries start operating. The Gurudwara and the rest houses have regular catering services. Camping within the Valley is not permitted.

Smythe's account (1932, 1938) gave a wide publicity to the Valley of Flowers. But the real growth of tourism occurred after 1975. Until 1975 higher Himalayan zone was declared as restricted area. After the area opened to visitors in 1975, Garhwal Mandal Vikas Nigam (GMVN) and other travel agents and tour operators came out with attractive packages to this area. The construction of Joshimath-Badrinath Road (1968) has exploded the pilgrim traffic every summer. Pilgrim traffic attains peak in June-September. Interestingly, the flowering cycles and rhythms in valley are also closely associated with these months. This results in the inflow of sizable number of domestic tourists, predominately *Bengalis, Gujratis* and *Maharastrians* in the valley. Sikh hospitality indeed has been the major factor in motivating visitors to the Valley of Flowers. Not many Sikhs care for the valley after their strenuous trek to Hemkund. A major part of the valley visitors consists of researchers and large group of students who visit the valley for their botanical collections or to enjoy their summer vacations. The detail of tourist arrivals, to Valley of Flowers and Hemkund is given in the table.

Table - 2.3.2
Tourist Arrivals in Hemkund and Valley of Flowers

Year	No. of Tourists
1980	25438
1985	24545
1990	57295
1991	60098
1992	50246
1993	22625
1994	15222
1995	15365
1996	16320
1997	72191
1998	101476
1999	109298

Source: Uttaranchal Tourism

Table - 2.3.3
Tourist Arrivals in Valley of Flowers

Year	Indian Tourists	Foreigners
1991	2872	98
1992	3100	246
1993	2033	171
1994	1345	150
1995	1052	38
1996	1156	42
1997	1264	49
1998	453	33
1999	770	07

Source: Uttaranchal Tourism

Until the declaration of National Park (1982) and potential Biosphere reserve (1988), it was exposed to visitors and became the target of unplanned and unguarded tourism. Visitors caused serious damage to the Valley of Flowers. A large number of poachers and herb gatherers also became active in the area. However, with the creation of National Park, opening the check post, appointments of wardens and skilled guards, the degeneration of valley is checked to some extent. Poaching, grazing and herb gathering have been controlled. But ruthless trampling, plucking of flowers by the tourists, especially by the students and researchers, is still a common phenomenon in the valley. Another problem is the littering of debris (Singh & Kaur 1989). During tourist season a few teashops come up on the way. These are constructed with forest timber. Government opened the area for tourists and pilgrims without giving a thought to the basic amenities essential for human beings. Pilgrims, and animals walk on the same trek resulting in dung, mud filth and rubbish on the footpath. All the rubbish and wastewater of shops come on to the trek. But the worst thing is the haphazardly coming up settlement of Ghangaria. For five months at least 300 to 500 people (owner of teashops and their servants) stay there to entertain tourists. A population of 500 mule drivers and porters remain there everyday. Sewage disposal is going to create serious problems in near future. Local shops and Gurudwara require minimum 400 kg. Fire wood per day, which is creating the problem of deforestation. Inside the park under the very eyes of the park authorities the wild weed *polygonum* is spreading menacingly and the heritage of flowers shrinking steadily. Regrettably, even after the imposition of ban on the various unwanted activities, two improvised helipads were seen in the Core area. It may not continue to exist but such tradition is not in agreement with National Parks or protected area.

Need for a Policy for Sustainable Tourism Development

Declaration of the Valley of Flowers as a National park in 1982 has been of course, the most appreciable step taken to ensure the protection and conservation of flora and fauna of the valley and its environs. But due to undefined or hazy policy, the park suffers from the conflicting land use. The problem of deforestation, garbage filth and other untreated waste all around is due to the haphazard planning and programmes. There seems no synergy among land organisers and managers. Hardly any dependable data have been collected on the various aspects of the valley. Valley has not been properly interpreted by the 'guides' who have scant knowledge about the Valley environment and plant families. Practically, no conducted tour seems to have espoused the cause of putting trained guides or authoritative literature with their 'Packages'. It would be better if the whole region with all its floral excellence is identified and sold to tourists in Scientific Manner. (Kandari (1984).

Yet another problem, but of greater magnitude, is the extensive weed growth, which is gradually dominating the flower carpet of the valley. When snow melts in April polygonum and other weeds are the first to sprout. Their growth is so fast that flower plants are left way behind. Grazing at this early stage may result in these wild plants being picked up by the animals, making room for more flowering plants. Prior to ban on grazing, wild foliage had never made its draconian appearance in such magnitude. The park authorities can consider destroying these plants during their early stage of growth in order to rehabilitate the flowers and preserve their beautiful heritage for posterity.

The valley is a vast area and there are pockets of beautiful flowers away from the only trek made for visitors so far. There ought to be some side treks with proper sign indicators towards floral colonies. This will not only afford visitors the opportunity to see the best, but will save the flowers being trampled over. Side tracks and rain shelters are important measures to elicit more disciplined behavior from visitors. Often a large segment of tourists visiting the parks are not aware of conservation values and are not aware of the behavior expected inside the protected areas. A sense of strict discipline can be effectively inculcated with the distribution of brochures indicating do's and don't at the entry point.

To meet the conservation and recreational activities at a time is a challenging job in the present situation, when the planning, policies and, the organisational set up are isolated. Co-ordination among various agencies such as forest, PWD, Tourism, Hydel and regional administration is essential to formulate a perfect planning system. Participation of local people in tourism development should be encouraged. The policy framed should be the result of in-depth findings of the bio and geo scientists and tourism, conservation and planning experts. Thus only scientific and ecofriendly tourism should be undertaken for the sustainable development of the region.

2.3.3 Corbett Tiger Reserve

Corbett National Park, which happens to be the first National Park of India and of the Indian sub-continent, came into existence on 8th August 1936. The Park has a long history of conservation. It celebrated its golden jubilee in 1986. With an area of 323.75 Sq. km. this Park was initially named as Hailey National Park after Sir Malcolm Hailey, the then Governor of United Province. Major Jim Corbett was closely associated with the delineation of the Park boundaries. The name of the Park was changed after India attained independence to Ramganga National Park in 1954. Finally, in 1956-57 the Park was given its present name as homage to Jim Corbett. Corbett died in 1955 in Kenya and after his demise, naming this prestigious Park after him was a befitting tribute, considering his deep involvement in the creation of this Park and his monumental role in creating awareness about the region's rich wildlife through his prolific writings.

The Ramganga River flows through the National Park and imparts to it, much of its renowned charm and landscape beauty. Remarkable ecological change was set in motion when a decision was taken in the sixties to construct a dam on this river at Kalagarh and water started accumulating in the reservoir from 1974 onwards.

Almost 40 sq.km., prime grassland area of the Park, was ultimately submerged in the Ramganga reservoir. With a view to make up for the submerged area and also to make the Park a viable unit an additional area of 197.07 sq. km. was added during 1966 bringing the National Park to its present area of 520.82 sq.km.

Project Tiger Programme

Project Tiger, one of the most ambitious conservation projects ever undertaken, was launched from Corbett itself in April 1973. But the Project actually started functioning here from 1st February 1974. Till then, the Park was being managed by dual authority with forestry operations being under the charge of territorial divisions and wildlife protection and tourism under the wildlife organisation. It was only as late as October 1975 that the National Park could be constituted into one unit.

In spite of being surrounded by a rich buffer of reserved forest that afforded natural security to the Tiger Reserve, the situation continued to be unsatisfactory as the spill over population of wild animals in the buffer area was not getting the attention it deserved, while the animals of the Park continued to freely migrate to and return from these areas.

An attempt was made during 1975-76 to get 1100 sq.km. of adjacent area included under Project Tiger. But the effort proved unsuccessful. Meanwhile an area of 301.176 sq.km. with Kalagarh Forest Division was declared as the Sonanadi Wildlife Sanctuary on 9th January 1987. The basic objective of the creation of this Sanctuary was to afford adequate protection to the rainy season habitat of the wild elephants of Corbett. When the Ramganga reservoir reaches its brim and the valley is inundated, the elephants display local migration and move to upper reaches of the Kalagarh Forest Division of which Sonandi Wildlife Sanctuary forms the major part. The proposal of inclusion of the adjoining reserved forests as buffer of Tiger Reserve remained in abeyance for a period of more than 15 years.

A fresh proposal was sent to the Government of U.P. for the inclusion of entire Kalagarh Forest Division having an area of 611 sq.km. as the buffer area of Corbett Tiger Reserve, and an additional area of 96.69 sq.km. and 89 sq.km. of Ramnagar and *Terai* West Forest Divisions respectively. Fortunately, the proposal was accepted by the Government and a total area of 796.686 sq.km. was handed over to Corbett Tiger Reserve as its buffer on 11th June, 1991.

Reorganised Corbett Tiger Reserve including Kalagarh Forest Division, renamed as Kalagarh Tiger Reserve Division and Corbett Tiger Reserve Division came into operation by May 1994. As a result of this reorganisation there has been decentralisation and delegation of authority leading to increased efficiency and protection. It has also permitted specialization and intensive management.

Area

Corbett Tiger Reserve (CTR) now includes two protected areas namely Corbett National Park and Sonandi Wildlife Sanctuary and legally consists of three different kinds of areas, the National Park, Wildlife Sanctuary and the Reserved Forest. Out of the total 1318.54 sq.km. area of Corbett Tiger Reserve, Corbett National Park spreads out in an area of 520.82 sq.km., Sonanadi Wildlife Sanctuary has an area of 301.18 sq.km. and rest of the area 496.54 sq.km. comes under Reserved Forest. Almost two thirds (329.98 sq. km) of National Park area (520.82 sq.km.) is in Pauri Garhwal, the rest (190.84 sq. km) being in the Nainital district of Kumaon Division. About 8 per cent of the Park area is now submerged land, under Ramganga multipurpose hydel project reservoir. Sonanadi sanctuary lies in the Kotdwar Tehsil of Pauri Garhwal. About one half of Ramganga reservoir falls in Sonanadi sanctuary and is spread over 43 sq.km.

Climate

Climatically, the Park has three seasons, winter, summer and rainy, occurring in November to February, March to mid June, and mid June to October, respectively. December and January are the coldest months, when the minimum temperature is recorded at 3°C, while the maximum temperature rarely exceeds 27°C. During these months; nights are very cold with heavy frost and dew. Dense fog lingers in the low-lying areas like Patlidun, which may persist even after 10 a.m. During the rainy months maximum rainfall occurs in July-September. The Park remains comparatively humid throughout the year but maximum relative humidity of 98 per cent is recorded during monsoon months.

Fig No.2.3.3
Corbett Tiger Reserve

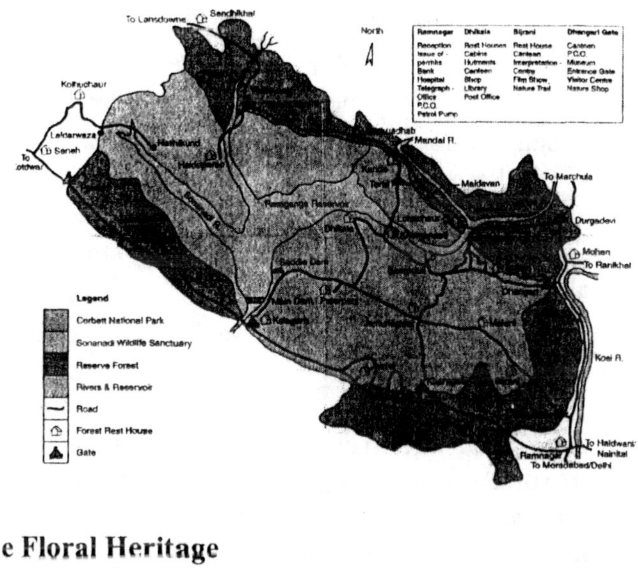

The Floral Heritage

So far, as many as a hundred and ten species of trees, fifty one species of shrubs, thirty three species of bamboo and grasses and, twenty seven species of climbers have been identified from the Park (Kandari and Singh 1982). The vegetation is rather a mixed type, comprising deciduous tropical and sub-tropical species of the plants.

Among the trees, Sal *(Shorea robusta)* dominates, forming almost pure stands, or frequently associated with Haldu *(Adina cordifolia)*. Bakli or Dhak *(Anogeissus latifolia)* is found on the higher ridges. The other popular and more or less common trees within the Park are: Khetwa *(Piliostioma malabaricum)*, Pula *(Kydia calycina)*, Amaltas *(Cassia fistula)*, Amla (*Emblica officinalis)*, Gurial *(Bauhinia variegata*), Dhauri *(Lagerstoemia parviflora*), Ber *(Ziziphus mauritiana)*, Semal *(Ceiba pentandra)*, Nim (*Azadirachta indica*), Tun *(Cedrela toona*), Dhak *(Butea monosperma*), Imli *(Tamarindus indica*), Bahera *(Terminalia belerica*), Kumbhi *(Careva arbora*), Dalchini *(Cinnamomum tamala*), Mahwa *(Bassia latifolia*), Kharik *(Celtis austre'is*), Kanju *(Holoptelea integrifolia*), Khajur *(Phoenix sylvestris*), Bhilawa *(Semicarpus anacardium*), Khaina *(Ficus cunis*), Pipal *(F. religiosa*), Tinla *(F. roxburghii*), and the like.

Sheesham *(Dalbergia sissoo)* - Khair *(Acasia catechu)* association in the Ramganga river, bordering Savannah at Dhikala, is an interesting feature. Trichonia *(Wendlandia heynei)*, Rohni *(Mallotus philippensis)* and Jamun *(Syzygium cumini)* occur on exposed habitats along the dry *(Mullahs)*.

Chir *(Pinus roxburghii)* is the lone indigenous conifer in the Park vicinity, while among the palms, in addition to Khajur (*Phonix acualis)*, *Wallichia densiflora*, a rare tree is also noticeable. Bamboo occurs frequently in several blocks. Among shrubs in the Park, Marorphal or Kapasi *(Helticteres isora*), Dhaula *(Woodfordia fructicosa*), Bashinga *(Adhatoda zeylanica*), Binda *(Colebrookia oppositifolia*), Karaunda *(Carissa spinarum*), Bhanua *(Clerodendron viscosum*), Aak *(Calotropis procera*), Daia *(Callicarpa macrophylla*) and Bhang *(Cannabis sativa)* are a few to mention.

The Faunal Heritage

Of particular significance is the presence of some of the depleted mammals of the Region, i.e., *Panthera tigris* (Tiger), *Felis bengalensis* (Leopard cat), *Cuon alpinus* (Wild dog), *Axis porcinus* (Hog Deer), and, *Manis crassicaudata* (Indian pangolin). *Cervus duvauceli* (Swamp deer), once a common Park in mate has altogether disappeared from the vicinity. *Selenarctos thibatanus* (Himalayan Black Bear) is also a casual visitor to the park, appearing in winters only, descending from its habitat of higher mountains. *Nemorhaedus goral* (Goral), the only goat antelope in the Park, restricts its activities in the northern ridges of the river Ramganga. Common among larger mammals of the Park are, *Elphas maximus* (Indian Elephant), *Macaca mulatta* (Rhesus Monkey), *Presbytis entallus* (Langur), *Canis aurius* (Jackal), *Vulpes vulpes* (Red Fox), *Meluresus ursinus* (Sloth Bear), *Panthera pardus* (Leopard), *Felis chaus* (Jungle cat), and of course, the favorite game animals like, *Axis axis* (Spotted Deer), *Cervus unicolour* (Sambar), *Muntiacus muntiak* (Barking Deer), *Boselaphus tragocamelus* (Blue bull), *Sus scrofa* (Wild Boar), and *Hystrix indica* (Indian porcupine). Among the smaller mammals, hares, otters, mongoose, civets, shrews, hedgehogs, and species of rats, mouse and squirrels are all more or less common.

Both resident and migratory birds, including summer and winter migrants represent avi-fauna. For the winter migrants, river Ramganga is the main attractions. Birds indulge in autumn/winter migration add attraction to the Park. Of the resident birds, almost one fifth indulge in local/seasonal/altitudinal migration (Lamba 1980). The most interesting feature of the Park is its being the meeting place of a number of high altitude and plains and eastern and western races of the birds. To mention a few of the indicator birds species of the Park are: *Elanus caerelescens voceferus* (Black winged kite), *Torgus calvus* (Black vulture), *Francolinus francolinus asiae* (Indian Black Partridge), *Gallus gallus murghi* (Indian Red Jungle fowl), *Pavo cristatus* (Indian peafowl), *Vanellus indicus indicus* (Red wattle lapwing), *Streptopelia chinensis* suratensis (Indian spotted Dove), *Psittacula krameri borealis* (Northern Rose

Winged Parakeet), *Cerryle rudis leucomalanura* (Lesser Pied Kingfisher), *Halcyon smyrnensis fusca* (Indian small Green Bee-eater), *Upupa epos ceylonensis* (Ceylong Hoopoe), *Megalaima zeylanica caniceps* (Northern Green Barbet), *Piscus mymecophoneus* (Little Scaly bellied Green Woodpecker), *Lanius schach erythronotus* (Rufous backed shrike), *Oriolus xanthornus xanthornus* (North Indian Black headed Oriole), *Acridotheres tristis tristis* (Indian Myna), *Pycnonotus cafer intermedius* (Punjab Red-Vented Laughing Thrush), *Gerrulax leucolephus leucolephus* (Himalayan Whitecrested Laughing Thrush), *Copsychus saularis saularis* (Indian Magpie Robin), and *Saxucola caprata bicolor* (Northern Pied Bush-chat). In fine, the park harbors a good deal of avi-fauna, notably Storks, Ducks, Eagles, Vultures, Falcons, Pheasants, Pigeons, Parakeets, Owls, Kingfishers, Horn bills, Barbets, Woodpeckers, Larks, Oriole, Drongo, Myna, Magpie, Bulbul, Flycatchers, Red starts, Thrushes, Tits, Nuthatch, Wagtails, Sun birds, and Bunting.

The presence of four larger threatened reptiles is still another interesting feature of the Park fauna. They are *Crocodilus palustris* (Crocodile), *Gavialis gangeticus* (Gharial), *Python mororus* (Indian Python) and *Naja hannah* (King Cobra). Non-poisonous snakes such as the ornamental, grass and water snakes and also the poisonous kraits and vipers constitute the major part of the reptilian fauna.

The Ramganga harbors a good deal of hill stream fishes, *Barbus tor* (Indian Mahseer) and *Rainmus bola* (Indian Trout) offer a promise for game fishing. *Labeo rohita* (Rohu), has already been introduced in the reservoir of the Ramganga Hydel Project. The insect fauna including the beautiful butterflies, bugs, beetles, bees, moths, termites and dragonflies, is colourful and varied. A census of the Park animals carried out in 1993, revealed the following figures about the population of different animals.

Table - 2.3.4

Corbett Tiger Reserve Wildlife Census Figures

Tiger	**85-95 (Corbett National Park) 30-40 (Buffer areas including Sonanadi Sanctuary)**
Leopard	100-200*
Elephant	400-425
Cheetal	25000-30000
Sambhar	5000- 6000
Barking Deer	2000 2500
Hog Deer	200-300
Bear	40-50*
Wild Boar	7000-8000
Goral	400-500
Monkey	10000-12000
Langur	12000-13000
Muggar	100-150*
Gharial 200-250*	

Note: Figures for all animals except tiger are for the entire Tiger Reserve. *Indicates rough estimate

Source: Newsletter Corbett, Volume 1, Number 1, 1994.

The prime mission of CTR is to maintain nature in all its diversity with minimal disturbance by human activities; to safe guard the endangered species specially the tiger; to mobilise support for biodiversity conservation and; to reconcile conflict between wild animals and human population. Regulated tourism is permitted in designated Corbett Tiger Reserve to provide opportunity to the visitors to view wild animals in their natural environment. It is recognised that unless people from different walks of life see and experience the serenity and beauty of the nature, the sheer richness, complexity and delicate balance that exists within the biological world and the grandeur of rare and endangered species such as wild elephant and the tiger, they are unlikely to appreciate the true value of biodiversity conservation.

Protection: Regular patrolling is done to prevent unauthorized entry and to detect cases of illicit felling and hunting. Offenders are booked under Wildlife Protection Act and prosecuted. The number of *Gharials* has reached a precarious level within Corbett Tiger Reserve. *Gharials* bred in captivity have been released in Ramganga to restock natural population and maintain their viability.

Research institutions have been encouraged to carry out surveys and long term studies of threatened species and the Corbett ecosystem. Annual census is carried out in CTR during summers to estimate the number of tigers and other important animals so as to understand population trends and determine the impact of management practices on wildlife. An Eco-development programme has been initiated to involve villagers in biodiversity conservation and reduce man-animal conflict.

Tourists Traffic in Corbett Tiger Reserve

Considering the pace of growth in the tourist traffic in the Tiger Reserve over last three decades, it is to some extent, encouraging. In 1965-66 the park visitation was merely at 3,900 mark, of which 3,343 were Indians and 553 were overseas visitors. The number of visitors increased to 18,092 in the Year 1982-83, out of which 1,057 were foreigners. This figure now raised to 49,942 in the Year 1996-97. However, despite this significant increase there has been a discontinued trend in the growth rate of the tourist traffic.

Table 2.3.5
Tourist Traffic in Corbett Tiger Reserve

Year	Indian Tourists	Foreign Tourists	Total
1990-1991	36161	2917	39,078
1991-1992	30277	2770	33,047
1992-1993	28480	3483	31,963
1993-1994	37265	6199	43,464
1994-1995	37459	4771	42,230
1995-1996	41283	5415	46,698
1996-1997	45019	4923	49,942
1997-1998	52514	2215	54729
1998-1999	66718	2513	69231

Source: Director, Corbett Tiger Reserve, Ramnagar.

Product Development and Management

Corbett Park's natural heritage allures a large number of visitors who get an opportunity to stay inside its several interiorly located Forest Rest Houses (FRHS). Corbett Tiger Reserve has many other Forest Rest Houses located in the remaining area of Corbett Tiger Reserve other than Corbett National Park, or on its periphery administered by adjoining territorial forest divisions.

Annually, over forty thousand visitors seek accommodation in these FRH's. Many return disappointed at not having been able to stay at Dhikala, CNP's main tourist complex. The details of fare and fee structure are given in the table. For a long time Corbett has been portrayed as being synonymous with Dhikala. This is not true. CTR has got a tremendous variety to offer in terms of accommodation. Each of the twenty-four FRHS has got its own individuality and beauty. The occupancy of some of the FRH'S of

CTR is as low as ten nights a year and yet, they have the potential to offer a singular experience to the visitor. Stay in off beat FRHs requires previous arrangements, as the facilities provided are Spartan. Nevertheless, the stay in these various FRHs is worthy. It is strongly recommended, for those who have already visited CTR earlier as it will provide them with an opportunity to explore the entire range of habitats found in this renowned Tiger Reserve. There are a number of other locations where accommodation facilities are available and the important sites are as follows:

Bijrani: It is a large FRH situated in one of the famous shooting blocks of the past. Surroundings of it are altogether different from the Dhikala zone and it represents drier conditions with tremendous vegetation and bird diversity. Due to the proximity to Ramnagar it has an additional advantage for visitors who are likely to arrive late and may not get entry from the Dhangarhi gate. One can walk along the nature trail accompanied by a guard, look at the nature interpretation centre and see wildlife films.

Dhela: Located close to Dhela village and surrounded by plantations, the FRH has a sprawling campus. Water supply is erratic. It is good for large groups and for holding nature camps with some additional arrangements (particularly water) due to its location close to Ramnagar (13 km.).

Dhikala: Renowned for its panoramic landscape of breath taking beauty, this large complex has a huge establishment resembling a village. The accommodation is varied and includes old FRH, New FRH, cabins, hutment, loghut and annex. It has excellent facilities alongwith restrictions including prohibition on self-cooking. Elephant rides, library and audiovisual show are available to the visitors.

Gairal: The old FRH with two rooms and the new FRH with four are situated next to the Ramganga River. Four hutments, two of them with attached toilets have been added in 1996. The FRH enjoys a tranquil environment of great beauty. Excellent for bird watching, relaxation, and group stay. Crocodile pool is situated at a walking distance. Opportunity for bathing in Ramganga held great charm for old visitors but is now discouraged.

Garjia: The FRH is located on the Ramnagar-Ranikhet highway 10 km from Ramnagar and is accessible throughout the year. It was being closed for a long time but has been recently renovated. One can walk up to the Kosi River and visit the Girja Devi temple. The trail across Kosi is one of the best bird watching places around CTR.

Halduparae: It is the only FRH located in Sonanadi Wildlife Sanctuary and is situated at elevation commanding a panoramic view of the Palain River, which can be enjoyed from a watchtower. It is excellent for bird watching, observing wildlife and enjoying natural surroundings. Halduparo is one of the remotest FRH's of CTR. One must be careful about wild elephants.

Jhirna: Situated next to Jhirna village the FRH was relocated in 1994 and the area is undergoing ecological recovery at a fast pace. Loop roads for wildlife viewing were constructed around Jhirna and Kothirau *chaurs* in 1996. The FRH is good for bird watching, guided nature walks, wildlife viewing and enjoying solitude. Leopard and blue bull sighting are far more common than within CNP.

Kalagarh: The FRH has been renovated in 1996. It is located close to the Ramganga River down stream from the main dam site. The place has public gardens, fountains and viewing spots as well. It is good for educational activities, nature camps and large family groups and is accessible throughout the year. Chances of seeing Goral and Sloth bear are higher.

Kanda: The highest FRH of CTR is located at an elevation of 1019 meter, 61 km from Ramnagar. It commands a magnificent view of the Himalayan Mountains, Patlidun valley, Ramganga reservoir and Dhikala *chaur*. Varieties of birds of cooler habitat are abundant here. The place has been particularly famous because of the shooting of the Kanda man-eater by Jim Corbett. Availability of water becomes a limiting factor during summer but the place is relatively cooler. One can walk up to Teria village from the Teria gate to have a view of a typical Himalayan village. Gorals can be sighted along slopes. On the northern side lies the relatively undeveloped Mandal valley. The ascent to Kanda from Dhikala is fairly steep.

Khinnanauli: It was constructed in 1974. The porch in front of the FRH provides a majestic view of Khinnanauli *chaur* where occasionally tigers can be seen while crossing across towards the river. Alarm calls are easily heard as the FRH is situated in the heart of the forest close to the Ramganga River and therefore, tigers are relatively easy to see.

Koluchaur: The adjoining forests have suffered degradation and also depletion of wildlife. Yet, this old FRH located close to the Koh River has a charm of its own. One can approach Hathikund and Sonanadi from this place via Laldarwaja. One can do fishing and take bath in Koh River.

Lohachaur: The FRH is situated above the Mandal River close to its confluence. The avifauna diversity is fairly different from other parts of CTR. It is highly recommended for fishing, bird watching and nature camps.

Mohan: Located at the bifurcation of the road from Ramnagar to Ranikhet and Tehri, the FRH provides easy access to Kosi River and is well-forested area of CTR. It is an another famous FRH because of its association with the Mohan man-eater killed by Jim Corbett.

Morghatti: It is a beautiful FRH situated amidst ancient trees, but in a run down condition. One can walk up till Tunu sot leading into Sonanadi via a shrine located at Kalu siddha.

Pakhro: The FRH is situated near the entry gate of CTR while coming from Kotdwar. Depending on the condition of the road one may be able to drive up to Kamlaban in Sonanadi Wildlife Sanctuary. Wildlife is sparse here.

Ramnagar: It is a well-furnished and maintained FRH and centrally located in the Ramnagar forest colony. The FRH overlooks the barrage on Kosi River and has scenic surroundings. It is a good place to seek accommodation in times of emergency or when arrival to Ramnagar has been delayed.

Rathuadhab: A modest FRH overlooking the Mandal River and the various inhabitations is situated on its banks. A variety of birds including many rare ones can be seen with ease as they fly back and forth from the up hill Kanda forests to the agricultural fields in the valley down below to feed on grain. The place in well connected by bus throughout the year. It is a good base camp for seeing and trekking to adjoining FRH's and other places.

Sarpduli: It is one of the most beautiful FRH's of Corbett, overlooking the Ramganga and steep sloped hill and is excellent for birdwatching, wildlife viewing and relaxing along the riverside. Tiger and elephant movement is fairly high in the surrounding areas and bird life is rich. Crocodile can be seen basking on sandy banks and occasionally Goral can be sighted on slopes.

Saneh: It is a well maintained FRH situated close to Kotdwar and accessible throughout the year. It acts as a good base to visit the interior areas of Sonanadi Wildlife Sanctuary.

Sendhikhal: The FRH is situated outside Corbett Tiger Reserve. Its location on a hilltop provides a panoramic view of the mountains. Lansdowne cantonment can be easily approached via Dugadda or along a direct steep forest road

Sitabani: This old FRH is now completely renovated and in excellent condition. It is situated at a vantagepoint above the Kaligad sot and surrounded by well-protected sacred grove of the Sitabani shrine. Unlike interior areas of CTR, there is no restriction on walking and one can undertake nature walks on various trails having amazingly rich bird life.

Sultan: It is the first FRH to fall on the Dhangari-Dhikala road of CNP. It lacks additional visitor facilities and visitors are required to drive up till Khinanauli and Dhikala for elephant rides. However, the FRH has the advantage of privacy and solitude. It is good for single night stay or when no other accommodation is available within Dhikala zone. It is meant for large student groups and training classes.

Useful Suggestions Regarding Accommodation

- One should avoid arriving on weekends and during Christmas, New Year, Holi, Good Friday and Baisakhi holidays in order to prevent disappointment in getting accommodation. Corbett Tiger Reserve (CTR) receives maximum visitors during these days.
- One must contact Director, CTR and other officials in case of problem in obtaining accommodation or in case of emergencies.
- One should verify status of road, suitability of your vehicle and condition of a FRH before entering the Park. Rains might have caused damage to the roads.
- One should bring additional rugs during peak winter period, as it may be cold.
- One should book seats for elephant rides on arrival to Dhikala and other FRHs where elephant rides are available. There is tremendous pressure for elephant rides from the visitors.
- Morning elephant ride starts early before sunrise so store sufficient water in buckets in the bathrooms at night so that one may be able to get ready on time.
- One must always hire a guide, as he knows the park and can help in case of any emergency.

Timings

The Park remains open from November 15 to June 15. Day visitors are not allowed to visit Dhikala or to enter from Dhangarhi Gate.

For excursions to Bijrani, day visitors are advised to reach the reception at Ramnagar for entry permits. Only 100 visitors are permitted daily on first come first served basis. Reception offices are located at Ramnagar, Amdanda gate and Dhangarhi gate.

Table - 2.3.6
Fare and Fee Structure in Corbett Tiger Reserve

Entry	Indian (in Rs.)	Foreigner (in Rs.)
Per person for first three days	30/-	350/-
For every additional day	20/-	175/-
Heavy vehicles	500/-	500/-
Light vehicles (Car, Jeep)	100/-	100/-
Mini bus	250/-	250/-
Photography		
Camera Fee Movie	2,500/-	5,000/-
Film (Per day) including		
Videography Feature film	20,000/-	20,000/-
Documentary film	2,500/-	5,000/-
Security money per film		
Feature film	25,000/-	40,000/-
Documentary film	15,000/-	40,000/-
Nature Guide		
(a) Per vehicle day/night (at Dhikala)	150/-	200/-
(b) Per trip of four hours (in Bijrani Tourism Zone)	75/-	100/-

1	2	3
Elephant ride		
Per person (for approximately two hours)	100/-	200/-
For students (for one hour)	40/-	200/-
Minimum charges per elephant (if the number of visitors is less than four, then the charges will be shared accordingly)	400/-	800/-
Conducted Tours (per person)		
Bijrani (for 4-5 hrs)	200/-	600/-
Dhikala (for one day)	400/-	1,200/-
The rates will be 50% for children below 12 Yr. for both Indians and foreigners.		
Museum		
Dhangarhi Museum/Visitor Centre	5/-	10/-
Kaladhungi Corbett Museum	5/-	10/-
For students (both the museums)	1/-	10/-
Accommodation (rates per room per night) At Dhikala		
Dhikala FRH (five rooms)	500/-	1,500/-
Cabin No. 1 ABC, 3 AB and 4 ABC (eight rooms)	300/-	900/-
New FRH (four rooms)	300/-	900/-
Annex 1 to 7 (seven rooms)	300/-	900/-
Tourist hutment 1 to 6 (six rooms, three beds in each room)	160/-	500/-
Log hut (24 berths, bedding not provided) per berth	30/-	100/-
For students, per berth	15/-	100/-

1	2	3
At Khinnanauli		
Three rooms	500/-	1,500/-
Other Rest houses		
Sarapduli (two rooms),	300/-	900/-
Gairal (six rooms)	300/-	900/-
Bijrani (six rooms)		
double bed	150/-	500/-
single bed	150/-	450/-
Kanda, Sultan,		
Malani, Halduparao,	100/-	300/-
Kalagarh, Dhela		
(all with two rooms),		
Jhirna Jhirna (four rooms)		
Fishing		
Rate per rod for one week	26/-	26/-

Cabin 3 AB, Annex 1 to 7 are reserved by U.P. Tourism office at New Delhi; Dhikala FRH, New FRH, Cabin 1 ABC and Khinnanauli FRH are reserved by Chief Wildlife Warden, Uttaranchal and rest by Director, Corbett Tiger Reserve.

Source: Director, Corbett Tiger Reserve 2001.

Guidelines for Regulated Tourism Promotion

To promote sustainable and Eco-friendly tourism, the park authority has framed certain guidelines for visitors, entrepreneurs related to their activities and other aspects of visitation. Some of the important guidelines are as follows:

- Carrying of firearms of any kind is not permitted within the Tiger Reserve.
- No pets can be taken inside the National park.
- Walking or trekking within the National park is strictly prohibited.

- Driving inside the Tiger Reserve after sunset is prohibited.
- Cooking is not allowed within the National Park and at Dhikala and Bijrani tourist complex. In other rest houses visitors can cook within the provided space.
- Visitors are required to carry a litter bag while entering the Tiger Reserve and bring back their non-biodegradable litter (tin cans, plastic, glass bottles, metal foils etc.) outside the Reserve. Throwing litter inside the Tiger Reserve other than in garbage bins will invite severe penalties.
- Officially registered guide is compulsory on excursions.
- Smoking outside residential complex/rest house and lighting of any kind of fire is strictly prohibited.
- Fishing without permission is prohibited. Fishing with permits can be done only in areas outside Corbett National Park and Sonanadi Wildlife Sanctuary and only between 1st October and 30th June.
- Playing of transistors and tape recorders within the Tiger Reserve is strictly prohibited.
- Visitors are required to observe timings for excursions and are prohibited from taking vehicles off the designated routes thereby causing damage to plant or animal life or their habitat.
- Blowing of horns and driving above the speed limit is strictly prohibited within the Tiger Reserve.
- Entry into the core zone by the visitors is prohibited.
- Shouting, teasing, chasing animals or attempts to feed them are prohibited and will invite severe penalties.
- Visitors are advised to occupy accommodation as reserved on the first day itself or send prior intimation to hold the accommodation. Otherwise, the reservation will be treated as cancelled.
- Visitors are compulsorily required to obtain a clearance certificate before leaving their place of residence within the Tiger Reserve.

- Visitors are required to wear clothes of colours, which merge with the natural surroundings (Khaki, olive green, other dull colours).
- Visitors are required to switch off lights, fans and water taps when not in use and park their vehicles at appropriate parking place.
- Visitors have to obtain entry permits at the reception. Entry timings are regulated in such a manner that visitors must reach their place of stay before sunset. Entry into the National Park after sunset is strictly prohibited.
- Day visit to Dhikala Tourism Zone is not permitted except in conducted tours organized by Corbett Tiger Reserve.
- Entry of private buses in Bijrani Tourism Zone is prohibited.
- Consumption of alcohol and non-vegetarian food is prohibited inside CTR forest rest houses.
- Permits issued to the visitors are non-transferable.

2.3.4 Rajaji National Park

Once the favourite hunting ground of Mughals, the Rajaji National park covering 820.42 Sq.Kms of area falls in the Shivalik hills of Dehradun, Hardwar, and Pauri Garhwal districts of Uttaranchal. Named after C. Rajgopalachari, the first Governor General of free India (popularly known as Rajaji), the National park includes three erstwhile sanctuaries namely Rajaji, Motichur and Chila along with some adjoining reserved forest areas of Dehradun East and West, Shivalik and Lansdowne Forest Division, as well as a small area of revenue land between Chila and Motichur on the east side of the Ganga. The three wildlife sanctuaries: Rajaji, Motichur and Chilla were originally established on October 8th 1948, 1935 and 25 January 1977, respectively. The intention to declare Rajaji as a national park was notified on 12 August 1983 by the Government of Uttar Pradesh.

The Delhi - Chutmalpur - Dehradun highway (from Biharigarh to Dehradun) and Rawason river forms the western and eastern boundaries respectively. The park is split by river Ganga (flowing through the park for a distance of about 24 km.) into two parts. Eastern half consists of the former Chila sanctuary and western - half comprising of the former Motichur and Rajaji sanctuaries. The Ganga, Song, Suswa and Rawason are the major rivers flowing through the park alongwith several other seasonal rivulets (which remains mostly dry around the year except monsoons). Dehradun, Hardwar, Rishikesh are the three major urban settlements situated in the outskirts of the Park.

Approach

Rajaji National Park is accessible from many directions viz. Dehradun, Rishikesh, Hardwar and Kotdwar. In total there are eight gates to Rajaji National Park. The details of each gate in given below:

Table 2.3.7

Entry Gates of Rajaji National Park

Name of the Entry Gate	Approach town and distance to Gate	Route
Ramgarh Gate No. 1	From Dehradun 14 Kms.	Delhi-Dehradun highway Via Clement town.
Mohand Gate No. 2	From Dehradun 25 Kms.	Delhi-Dehradun highway
Lachhiwala Gate No. 3	From Dehradun 18 Kms.	Dehradun-Hardwar route (turn right before Doiwala)
Ranipur Gate No. 4	From Haridwar 9 Kms.	Hardwar-BHEL-Mohand Road
Motichur Gate No. 5	From Haridwar 9 Kms.	Hardwar-Rishikesh highway or Dehradun-Hardwar highway

1	2	3
Chilla Gate No 6	From Haridwar 9 Kms.	Via private bus route to Rishikesh
Kunnao Gate No. 7	From Rishikesh 6 Kms.	Via private bus route on Rishikesh-Pashulok route Laldhang
Gate No. 8	From Kotdwara 25 Kms.	Via private bus route to Kotdwara-Chilla

Source: Director, Rajaji National Park.

The Park is accessible by rail, road and air Nearest Railway stations are Hardwar and Dehradun. Jollygrant (Dehradun) airport is only a few Kms from the northern boundary. Mohand (entry gate No. 2) is about 231 Kms. from Delhi.

Topography and Geological Setting

The terrain of the Park falls into two sectors, separated by the valley of the Ganga, which flows approximately north to south between Rishikesh and Hardwar. The sector to the west of the Ganga largely consists of the Siwalik range of hills. The Siwaliks, formed by debris from the older Himalayan range, are composed of sedimentary rocks such as sandstone, clays and conglomerates and present a highly fragmented appearance as the result of extensive erosion, particularly that resulting from rapid run-off during heavy rains.

The Chilla sector to the east of the Ganga consists of flat alluvial land in the south, rising in a series of steep dissected hills, continuous with the outer Himalaya in the north, across the river from Rishikesh. There is no perennial river on the southern side of the Siwaliks but the northern and eastern portions of the park are watered by the Ganga and its perennial tributaries, including the Suswa and Song rivers in the Motichur sector and the Rawason River in Chilla.

Fig. No 2.3.4

RAJAJI NATIONAL PARK

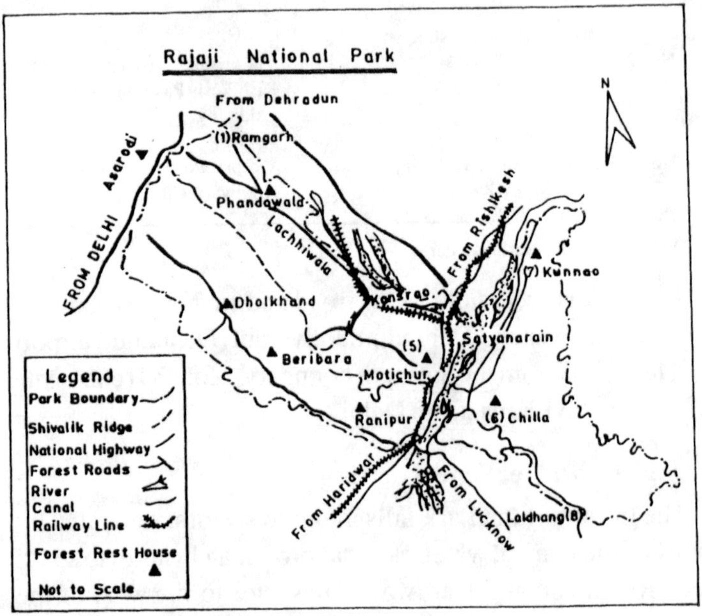

Settlement Patterns

There are over 80 villages, which are on the Park boundary. Further, there are three major urban settlements around the Park. It includes Hardwar Urban Agglomeration with BHEL Ranipur Township, which came up during the seventies and has a current population of over 3,00,000. Dehradun agglomeration has a current population around half a million. Thus the total population around the park including the surrounding villages would be around a million. The settlements around the park comprise of resettlers from various parts of the country who have been settled at different periods.

Settlements inside the Park

There are principally two communities settled inside the park area. The first is a creation of the Forest Department itself. In

1932, in order to increase the labour force for silvicultural operations, the Forest department introduced the *Taungya* system. This system entailed settlement of population with the forest where the settlers were allowed intercropping in exchange of labour for silvicultural operations. The system was most prevalent in the forests of the Upper Gangetic Plains. The *Taungya* system contributed to the forestry operations in a significant manner until recently. Though there are only a few settlements in the park, this has also been one of the issues raised by park authority, as the regulation of a National Park would disallow any human population with it. In 1997 the population was estimated to be around 2500.

The *Gujjar* settlements in the Rajaji Park have been the major reason for the park to be in limelight in the recent past. Originally there were 512 *Gujjar* families along with 4000 licensed buffaloes within the park. Their population and cattle strength have increased enormously and in 1997 the *Gujjar* population and cattle strength in the park were around 25000 and 20000 respectively.

The other inclusion, which has become vital and critical to the movement of animals across the Ganga, is in the Raiwala area itself. Because of the combination of several aspects of development in the region such as BHEL township in the south, the expansion of Hardwar township, construction of a canal for power generation at Bhimgoda the only corridor for movement left is where the oustees from the Tehri Dam site have been resettled.

Vegetation

The vegetation of Rajaji is predominantly Sal forest, of which several sub-types, viz. Moist Siwalik Sal, Moist Bhabar Dun Sal and Dry Siwalik Sal, cover 75% of the Park. In addition to Sal (*Shorea robusta*) common tree species include *Terminalia tomentosa, T. balerica, Anogeissus latifolia, Lannea coromandelica, Cassia fistula, Dalbergia sissoo, Bauhinia racemosa, B. retusa, Acacia catechu, Randia dumetorum,*

Lagerstroemia parviflora, Bombax ceiba, Syzygium cuminii and *Mytragyna parviflora.* Occasional majestic specimens of the Banyan tree (*Ficus bengalensis*) provide favourite resting-places for elephants and other wildlife in the heat of the day. Rohini (*Mallotus philippensis*) is a very common smaller tree of the Rajaji forests and forms a major item of the elephant's diet. *Ziziphus mauritiana (Ber), Phyllanthus emblica, Buchanania lanzan, Semicarpus anacardium, Cordia myxa,* and *Aegle marmelos* (Bel) constitute important food sources for wildlife. Common grasses include *Chrysopogon fulvus, Heteropogon contortus* and *Eulaliopsis binata* or Bhabar grass, a valuable "export" from the area before it was declared a National park.

Park's Faunal Heritage

Among the herbivores, Chital or spotted deer (*Axis axis*) is the most common species, occurring widely throughout the flatter terrain of the Park. A few limited population of the Chital's smaller relative the Hog deer (*Axis porcinus*) occur in several more open areas of Rajaji but they are seldom seen and never in sizeable herds. Barking deer (*Muntiacus muntjak*) is common, especially in forest areas with ample ground cover. Sambar (*Cervus unicolor*) is fairly widespread in Rajaji, especially in the more densely forested areas and on the gentler slopes of the Siwalik Hills. The large Nilgai or Blue Bull *(Boselaphus tragocamelus*) which occurs in the more open forests and woodlands of the drier southern fringes of the park, bordering the Gangetic plain represents antelopes in Rajaji.

The goat-like Goral (*Nemorhaedus goral*) is found in considerable numbers in Rajaji, occupying a specialised niche on the relatively bare rocky slopes at the top of the Siwalik ridges and hills. The animal is seldom seen unless one takes the trouble to climb up the craggy slopes. Wild boar (*Sus scrofa*) is fairly common in the Park. Elephant (*Elephas maximus*) is the most important herbivore in Rajaji National Park and their numbers in the area have shown a steady increase. The construction of a deep concrete power channel to the east of the Ganga, from Rishikesh to Chilla in the mid 1970's put a stop to animal migrations and effectively divided the population into two independent units. The Chilla sector has some 300 elephants whilst there are around 100 in the Rajaji-Motichur sector of the Park west of the Ganga.

Among the carnivores in Rajaji, tiger and leopard (panther) take pride of place. The population of tigers (*Panthera tigris*) is estimated to be 40 to 50 in the entire Park but they are rarely observed. Leopards (*Panthera pardus*) are rather more numbers than tigers. Lesser carnivores are represented by the Jackal (*Canis aureus*), Jungle cat (*Felis chaus*), Leopard cat (*Felis bengalensis*) and Civet (*Viverricula indica*).

Both common Indian primates, the Rhesus macaque (*Macaca mulatta*) and the common langur (*Presbytis entellus*) occur widely in Rajaji. Among the Small mammals the Indian hare (*Lepus nigricollis*) is widely found in the National Park and is especially active at night. Reptiles in Rajaji are represented by a number of snakes including the Python (*Python molurus*), King Cobra (*Ophiophagus hannah*), Common Krait (*Bungarus caeruleus*) and Indian Cobra (*Naja naja*).

Some 240 species of birds have been recorded (Rodgers et.al. 1991). Peafowl (*Pavo cristatus*) is common in open grassy areas. Red Jungle fowl (*Gallus gallus*) is particularly numerous, especially in area with heavy ground cover such as patches of lantana. Kalij pheasant (*Lophura leucomelana*) is not as common but provides a spectacular sight when parties of up to half a dozen birds are seen feeding on the forest edge, especially in the early morning. Other ground birds include the Black partridge (*Francolinus francolinus*) and quail. Raptors in Rajaji include Crested Serpent Eagle (*Spilornis cheela*), Eurasian Kestrel (*Elanus caeruleus*). Among vultures, the Indian griffon (*Gyps *indicus*) is common, as well as the King Vulture (*Torgos calvus*). Great Horned Owl (*Bubo bubo*), Jungle and Spotted Owlets (*Glaucidium radiatum* and *Athene brama*) and Brown Wood Owl (*Strix leptogrammica)* can all be observed. Many varieties of pigeon and dove are present, including the Grey-fronted Green Pigeon (*Treron pompadora*), Emerald Dove (*Chalcophaps indica*) and Blue Rock Pigeon (*Columba livia*). Both Rose-ringed and Blossom-headed Parakeets (*Psittacula krameri* and *P. cyanocephala*) occur, forming noisy flocks as they fly at treetop level in search of fruit. Both the Gray and Pied horn bills (*Tockus birostris* and *Anthracoceros malabaricus*) can also be seen flying in the higher levels of the canopy. Pied Crested Cuckoo (*Clamator jacobilnus*) and other more common cuckoos are present. Woodpeckers are well represented.

Tourism Seasonality

Rajaji Park attracts naturalists and wildlife lovers and the best time to visit the park is from 15th November to 15th June. Climatologically, the park presents comfort regimes during the months of February to April and November-December when weather is pleasant, with more visibility for wildlife sightings. March, April till half of May have clear weather and soothing sunshine. Bird watchers may like winters when avifauna can be seen in abundance. End of June to October is the rainy season when the park becomes inaccessible due to over flow of all the small and big rivulets, which generally remain dry during other season. Tourist inflow into Rajaji has been very limited as compared to other parks of the country. In spite of the fact that Rajaji has a tremendous potential for tourists, the recent statistics indicate a very lean tourist inflow.

Table - 2.3.8

Tourist Inflow in Rajaji Park and Revenue Earned

Year	Domestic	International	Total	Revenue earned (in Rs.)
1989-90	6758	655	7413	1,14,391.00
1990-91	6387	311	6698	1,19,663.00
1991-92	7773	959	8692	1,15,184.50
1992-93	9167	1318	10485	1,26,185.25
1993-94	2678	202	2880	1,04,716.50
1994-95*				
Night Halt	454	10	464	
Day Visitor	4299	235	4534	92,714.50
1995-96*				
Night Halt	342	18	360	
Day Visitor	4574	296	4870	1,84,074.00

Source: Director, Rajaji National Park, Dehradun.

* In 1994. Park authorities started to count Tourist, who visited the park exclusively. Previously, in the early 90s persons happened to pass through the park boundary were included as tourist. But they were not the actual visitors. From 1993-94, only those tourists, who entered the park for wildlife were counted and from 94-95 onwards counting of day visitors and night halters too were done.

Though the park spreads over 820 Sq.kms. of Area, yet only a few places are famous among tourists. Most of the visitors come here for wildlife adventure only. To facilitate wildlife watching, Forest Department has erected a few watchtowers and provides elephant joy ride in some areas. Though whole of the park is evenly distributed with fauna but only a few places are famous among the tourists.

There are several places of tourist interest in and around the park. These can serve as good excursion spots for tourists, while staying in Park. Some of the places are - Dat Ki Devi, Bhadrakali Temple, Laxman Sidh, Neelkanth, Lachiwala, Mansa Devi, Satyanarain, Kanva Ashram, Archaeological sites at Pandu and Laldhang and Small treks/hiking spots.

Management

(a) Watch Towers or Machans

Forest Department has constructed some watchtowers for wildlife viewing near rest houses. A watchtower normally accommodates about ten persons. Some of the watchtowers are easily accessible through jeep while others can be reached after a few hundred metres of walk.

(b) Accommodation

The park can currently accommodate 70 visitors per day in various forest rest houses and a GMVN rest house. There are ten rest houses presently under the control of forest department in park. These rest houses were initially erected by the Britishers and after the independence they came under the Forest Department. Most of the rest houses have two suits except Chilla with five and Satyanarain with four suits. These rest houses have proper electricity fitting, but most of the time either there is no power connection or irregular supply. Similar is the condition with water supply in spite of the well pipefitting and modern toilet amenities. There is a kitchen at every rest house, where except some utensils and crockery no fuel and ration is available. There is no other catering facility available in Park rest houses. One has to carry his own things.

Besides the Forest Rest Houses, Garhwal Mandal Vikas Nigam has also constructed a rest house and few cottages at Chilla. Chilla receives the major share of tourists' inflow of Rajaji as GMVN provides much better accommodation and other facilities.

Table - 2.3.9

Accommodation Available within Park.

Name of Accommodation	No. of suites	Near entry gate nos.	Availability of Electricity
Beribara FRH	2	2,4	Nil
Chilla FRH	5	6,7,8	Yes
Dholkhand FRH	2	2,4	Nil
Ranipur FRH	2	4,2	Yes
Kansrao FRH	2	5,1,3	Nil
Kunnao FRH	2	7,6,8	Yes
Motichur FRH	2	5,1	Yes
Phandowala FRH	2	1,3,5	Yes
Satyanarain FRH	4	Hardwar Dehradun route	Yes
Asarori FRH	2	Dehradun Delhi route	Yes

Source: Director, Rajaji National Park, Dehradun.

(c) Transport System

There are three major roads in the park, two in western part and one in eastern part. Ramgarh-Motichur road via Phandowala and Kansrao and Mohand - Ranipur road via Dholkhand and Beribara are in western part. The Rishikesh-Chilla - Hardwar road is in eastern part. Besides these roads, there are two highways, Delhi-Hardwar - Rishikesh highways running through the park and Delhi-Dehradun highway along the western boundary. Hardwar-Kotdwar road also runs across the park. During the monsoon season (June last - October) these roads become inaccessible for tourists as the rivulets and streams overflow the roads. So this season is stated as non-tourist season.

Currently there is no internal transport available for tourists. One has to take his own vehicle to move around in park. Very limited elephant joy ride is available only at Chilla.

Table - 2.3.10

Accommodation Charges in Rajaji Park

Name of FRH	Charges per suite/per day (in RS.)	
	Indian	Foreigner
Beribara, Ranipur, Kansrao Kunnao, Phandowala, Asarodi & Satyanarain	75	225
Chilla, Motichur	150	450

Source: Director, Rajaji National Park, Dehradun.

Table - 2.3.11

Fees and Fare Structure at Park (in RS.)

Item	Indian	Foreigner
Entrance fee per head for first 3 days.	30	350
For every additional day.	20	175
Students per day	-	-
Road Fee		
Light Vehicle	100	500
Heavy Vehicle	100	500
Camera Fee		
Still	-	50
Movie/Video	100	500
Filming Charges		
Feature film per day	2000	5000
Documentary film per day	1000	2500
Security		
Feature film	15000	25000
Documentary	10000	25000

Source: Director, Rajaji National Park, Dehradun.

Emerging Issues and Development Dilemma

The foremost among the issues in relation to the communities in and around the Rajaji Park is the complete alienation they find with the forest authorities. It is true that the human habitation is significant yet the communities are too diverse to collectively force the Government to change its attitude. However, at the policy level there is a vertical split in the attitude towards protected areas. The Government and several wildlife scientists have been calling for a total isolation of protected areas. The National Wildlife Protection Act categorically states that no human habitations would be allowed inside National Parks. So the major issues in this Park management are :

Resettlement of the Communities Settled inside the Park

(a) *Gujjar* Resettlement

(b) *Taungya* Resettlement

Rights and Concessions of the Peripheral Settlements

The peripheral settlements of Rajaji National park enjoyed traditional rights for grazing of livestock, collection of fuel wood, fodder, household timber (for repair works and social ceremonies), use of paths/routes through park, extraction of minor forest products like bamboo, lac, wax, honey etc. Thus peripheral communities are dependent on the Rajaji forest resources for most of their basic needs. There was no immediate impact observed initially. But later on with the increase of population the requirement of these forest resources also increased. And gradually this dependency of community transformed into pressure on Rajaji.

Forest Corridors

Productive riverine forests tracts connecting Rajaji and Chilla, were the traditional migration routes of Asian Elephants. But this area was given to BHEL, IDPL factories in sixties. It is believed that for a land requirement of 100 ha. BHEL took away more than 1000 ha. The construction of an Army cantonment and rehabilitation of Tehri Dam oustees in Raiwala block, in addition to further settlements in the Ganga Bhogpur area, finally destroyed the corridor between the two sanctuaries. Added to this, the construction of 14-km. long mammoth hydel canal on the eastern bank of Ganga in the seventies, without adequate provision for crossing of wild animals, finally put up an end to annual crossings/migration of elephant population. This resulted in elephants being trapped in western most side, which is degrading rapidly.

Impact of Urbanisation and Industries around Rajaji Park

Large industries of BHEL and IDPL have been set up around the Rajaji Park and whatever may be the laws intended to preserve the park, in the current atmosphere, it is not hard to believe that, laws notwithstanding, the forest would be exploited.

2.3.5 Govind National Park and Govind *Pashu Vihar* Sanctuary

Govind National park and Govind *Pashu Vihar* Sanctuary, with all its bewildering scenic contrasts, rich in colourful flora - fauna and unique cultural heritage is one of the most fascinating wildlife reserves of the country. The British climbers and hunters discovered the Govind Pashu Vihar area for hunting, mountaineering and trekking, in early twentieth century. Prominent among them was J.T.M. Gibson, J.A.K. Martin, and R.L. Holdsworth. Their activities gave a wide publicity to the area. Later, considering the biotic and physical excellence, it was designated as a wild life sanctuary on March Ist 1955. The name of the sanctuary has been coined after Pundit Gobind Ballabh Pant, the first chief Minister of Uttar Pradesh. The Government of Uttar Pradesh notified its intention to constitute part of the sanctuary as a National Park on February 26, 1990.

Location and Approach

One of the largest high altitude reserves of the country after Nanda Devi, it is situated in the northwestern part of the Garhwal Himalaya, between the co-ordinates 30°55' and 31°18'N and 77°49' and 78°55' E. The sanctuary forms the upper catchment of Tons River, which is the most important tributary of river Yamuna in its upper reaches. Thus the area has a significant value as a major watershed for river Yamuna, which is a very important river for the Indo-Gangetic plain. Administratively, it falls under 'Tons Forest Division' in Purola Tehsil of Uttarkashi district of Garhwal region. After Independence in 1949 the vast forests of Tons valley were brought under the Forest Department of U.P. and 'Tons Forest Division' was created with its headquarter at Chakrata. Later the headquarter of division was shifted to Purola. The division had five ranges. But in the year 1988 the administrative control of two ranges of the Tons Forest Division viz. Rupin and Supin, which formed the Govind Pashu Vihar, were shifted from DFO Tons to DFO Nanda Devi National Park (wild life wing).

Naitwar, a typical *Rawain* Settlement, spread on the either side of the river Tons, serves as the entry point of the sanctuary. It can be approached by road from Dehradun, Rishikesh and Chakrata. It is at a distance of 200 km. from Dehradun. Now the motorable road is extended upto Saur, 12 km. ahead of Netwar. The most popular, fascinating and convenient trek into the sanctuary is that of Naitwar to Har-Ki-Dun. Har-Ki-Dun, a beautiful and vast Himalayan meadow, is about 45 km. from Naitwar. The first 24 km. distance, from Naitwar to Taluka, is also jeepable. Onwards, there is a 5 km. descend to Gangarh. The remaining 16 Kms. distance upto Har-Ki-Dun is a gradual ascends. Osla is the last settlement en route, situated at a distance of 7 km. from Gangarh. Har-Ki-Dun is 8 km. away from Osla. Tourist rest houses run by the Garhwal Mandal Vikash Nigam exist at Taluka and Osla. Forest rest houses are available at Naitwar (1402 Mt.), Taluka (1981 Mt.), Osla (2560 Mt.), Har-Ki-Dun (3414 Mt.), Istragad, Satta (1234 Mt.) and Jakhol.

Snow Leopard Project: A venture in Wildlife Conservation

The snow leopard inhabits the inner Himalayas above the altitude of 3,000 m. in an extremely tough, inhospitable and inaccessible terrain in the rugged Himalaya. With the onslaught of its habitat by man its number dwindled considerably making it a highly endangered species. A snow leopard survey was carried out by a team of experts in the mid-eighties to identify possible area for snow leopard conservation. One of the areas identified was the *Govind Pashu Vihar*. The snow leopard project was launched in the Eighth Five-Year Plan for the conservation of snow leopard and part of the *Govind Pashu Vihar* was intentionally notified as Govind National Park and was brought under the project.

Legal Status

The sanctuary was established on March Ist, 1955 through the notification issued by the Government of U.P. spreading over 953.125 sq. km. When the area of sanctuary was brought under the snow leopard project, the Government of U.P. issued the intention notification of the Govind National Park on February 26, 1990, of area 472.08 sq.kms. The final notification for the National Park is yet to be issued, as the settlement of rights yet to be over. There are number of private holdings in the sanctuary as 42 villages exist in it. These vary from agricultural field and small jungles to wastelands and houses.

Area and Boundaries

The original area of the sanctuary was 953.125 Sq. Kms., of which 472.08 Sq. Kms. has been declared as National Park. The external boundaries of Govind Wildlife sanctuary were described in the notification cf 1955.

Physical Features: The entire sanctuary is rather a rugged mountainous terrain, ranging in elevation from 1290 m. to 6325 m. (Banderpunch peak). The higher zones are under perpetual snows or are occupied by glaciers, Black Mountains, moraines and lush

Fig. No 2.3.5

Govind National Park and Govind *Pashu Vihar* Sanctuary

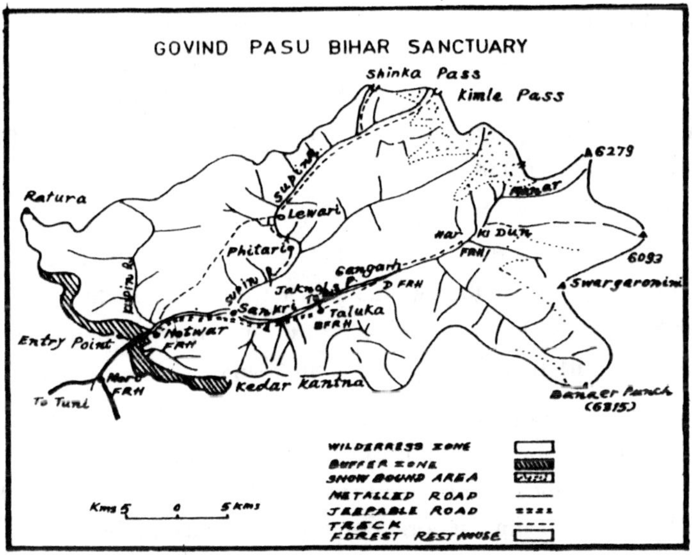

Fig/No. 2.3.6 : Har-ki-Doon Trek

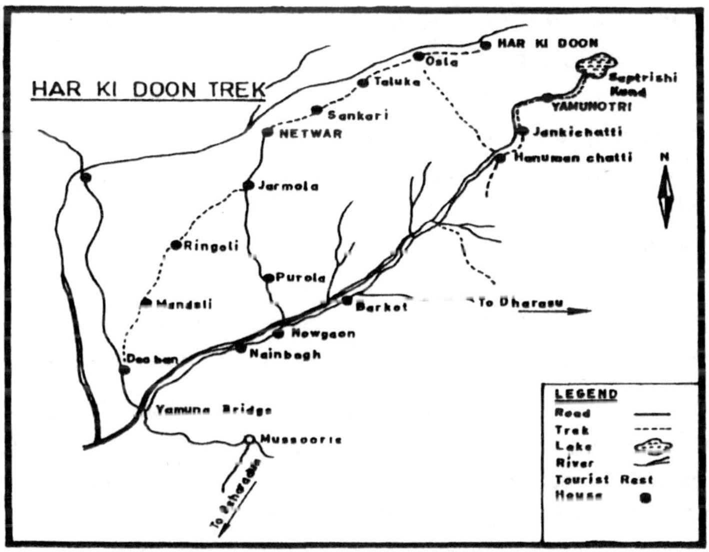

green Himalayan meadows. Lower reaches are dominated by the dense forests.

Geologically, the area is mainly composed of metamorphic rocks, constituted by granites, gneisses and crystalline schist. A series of fragmented rocks such as slates conglomerates and limestones are characteristics of some parts. Granite forms a continuous chain of the rocks in the higher reaches of eastern sides is also present in the bed of Rupin River.

The Tons and its two tributaries, the Rupin and the Supin, are the main rivers in the sanctuary. The Rupin and the Supin meet near Naitwar to form the Tons. Numerous streams, nallahs and waterfalls add to the beauty of the landscape.

Meteorological Aspect: Because of the abrupt altitudinal gradation, the sanctuary witnesses varying climatic conditions from sub-tropical in the lower valleys to arctic in the higher zones. Broadly speaking, the spring phenomenon is experienced in the sanctuary from Mid March to the end of May and is characterised by occasional showers, often accompanied by hail or thunderstorm. Summer is warm and wet in lower heights. Monsoon generally reaches the lower areas towards the mid of June, properly set-in July and generally remains upto second week of August. The annual precipitation varies from 1000 mm to 1500 mm. Autumn (September to the end of October) is generally pleasant with clear sky, though the higher areas begin to record a considerable fall in barometer. Frost starts approaching from first week of October. Winter (mid November to mid February) is severely cold. Snowfall occurs generally above 2000 Mt., which may descend to the lower areas but does not stay longer. Maximum snowfall occurs in January.

Local Human Population: Govind wildlife sanctuary is a fairly well populated area with villages situated as high as 2800 metres above sea level. There are in all 42 villages with a population of 13,000 people (based on 1991 census) and the numbers of live stocks exceed 75,000. The people living in these villages are by and large agriculturist and lead a different life. The main occupation of the people of these villages is rearing livestock and practicing marginal agriculture. The villagers depend on the forest for many of their basic needs. They graze their cattle and other livestock in the forests and also collect firewood. They are provided with timber for the construction of their houses under the free grant.

Tourist Attraction: The area has always been famous for trekking and mountaineering. The Har-Ki-Doon trek is one of the most popular treks in the Himalaya because of its ease, beauty and infrastructural facilities. The sanctuary is specially known for its colourful Himalayan meadows (*bugyals*), dense forests and rich floral and faunal wealth. The flower-spangled meadows, specially the Har-Ki-Doon, present a colourful spectrum when in full bloom during mid July and August. Thus it is a favorite destination of the animal and plant taxonomists, Wild life lovers, naturalists and photographers. During winter these meadows can be suitably developed as skiing grounds.

The visitors are enchanted while passing through the dense and extensive forests of the sanctuary. Many of the forested treks still enjoy a state of primeval glory of nature.

The following treks exist in the area:

- Sankri - Taluka - Osla - Har-Ki-Doon, 38 km.
- Sankri - Taluka - Osla - Ruinsara Tal, 40 km.
- Naitwar - Himri - Droni - Rupin pass - Sangla, 60 km.

This trek lies partly in Himachal Pradesh (Rupin pass - Sangla) and is treated as difficult trek.

- Ruinsara Tal - Yamunotri (High altitude difficult trek), 20 km.

Har-Ki-Doon, Ruinsaratal, Deokyara, Kedarkantha, and Bhratsar are important places of attraction for the tourists. The Black Mountains constitute a special attraction of the sanctuary.

These mountains virtually pose a challenge on rock climbers. There are also some snowpeaks, viz., Kedar Kantha, Swargarohini, and Banderpunch, where mountaineering can be promoted.

Cultural Heritage

The sanctuary area is as rich in cultural attractions as in the bounties of nature. The life style, dress, dialect, folk-traditions, settlement patterns and the religious expressions of the local Rawain population are markedly typical from the rest of Garhwal. Due to the less interference of modern society on the *Rawain* society, their social and religious customs and dresses, buildings and other settlement patterns remain, more or less, in the state of preservation. Both men and women are identically dressed in locally made woolen long coats and trousers. The settlements are suave and small but compact. Buildings, which are mostly double storied, are largely wooden. The settlements are nicely blended with the natural environment. Every settlement has a centrally placed temple, locally called as *Ringh Ghar* (dance house). The temples have beautiful woodcarvings and largely resemble with pagoda. The villagers worship *Kauravas* and *Duryodhan* is the main deity. Most of the temples are related to *Duryodhan* and *Karna*. The important temples of *Karna* are located at *Deora* and *Sarnal* (One and half miles above Netwar). The *Duryodhan* temples at Saur and Jakhol village are particularly beautiful. The society in these pockets is polyandrous and they retain many strange old traditions. However, despite its resource richness, the sanctuary witnesses only a few tourists, mostly the trekkers. These visitors are confined to Har-Ki-Doon only. But since 1991 there is a phenomenon growth in tourists' arrival especially visiting Har-Ki-Doon areas.

Natural Heritage; Flora Distribution

The abrupt change in elevation and subsequent climatic extremes have created a much varied and interesting floristic pattern in the sanctuary; represented by sub-tropical, temperate and alpine to arctic type of vegetation. A vast stretch of land is under perpetual snows. Broadly, the flora of the sanctuary is divisible into the following major types.

- **Sub-tropical Chir-Pine Forest:** Chir pine (*Pinus roxburghii)* is the dominant forest type in the sanctuary, extending upto about 2100 m. However, in the colder aspects of the upper Tons valley, it is seldom found above 1,000 m. Besides forming pure stands, the Chir also grows in association with Ban-oak (*Quercus leucotricophora)*, Rhododendron (*Rhododendron arboreum),* and Kaphal *(Myrica esculanta)*.
- **Sub-tropical Scrub:** This type of vegetation is generally found in the lower Chir-pine forests. It is, however, absent in the northern aspect above 1,500 m.
- **Ban-Oak Forest:** Dense Ban-oak forests are found between 1,500 to 2,100 m, generally substituting the pine forests on their upper limits.
- **Moru-oak Forests:** This type of forests is generally stretched between 2,100 m. to 2,800m. The dominant Moru-oak *(Q. himalayana)* is normally associated with *Q. leucotricophora* in the lower reaches and with *Q. semecarpifolia* in the higher zones. The other common associates are *Betula alnoides*, *Aesculus indica*, *Cornus macrophylla, Acer caesium, A. acuminatum* and *Alnus nepalensis*.
- **Moist Deodar Forests:** Deodar *(Cedrus deodara)* forest is generally present between 2,000 to 2,800 m., and extending upto 3,000m on the dry exposed aspects. Pure stands of Deodar are not common in the sanctuary.
- **Western Mixed Coniferous Forests:** The common trees in these forests are *Picea morinda, Abies pindrow* and *Pinus excelsa*. In moist sites, *Q. leucotricophora, R. arboreum, Pyrus pashia, Aesculus indica, Carpinus uniminae* and *Acer acuminatum* are also present.

- **Moist Temperate Deciduous Forests:** This type of forests is present between 2,100 to 2,750 Mt., in the cold and moist areas. The dominant trees of these forests are *Juglans regia, C. uiminae, Acer pictum, Betula alnoides, Aesculus indica, Cettis australis, Cornus macrophylla, Corylus colurna, Euonymus tingens, E. hamittonianus, Viburnum cotinifolium, Pyrus vestita* and the like.
- **Kharsu-Oak Forests:** Kharsu-oak *(Q. semecarpifolia)* is the dominant tree above the Deodar forest on the southern slopes as also in some exposed sites above fir forests on the cooler aspects. Beginning from about 2,500 m, the Kharsu forests extend upto the timberline. Some other associates of these forests are *Q. himalayana, Sorbus lanata, R. arboreum* and *Euonymus tigens*.
- **Moist Himalayan Oak-Fir Forests:** These forests are generally restricted to the protected sites on the northern aspect, usually replacing the mixed coniferous forests. *Picea morinda, Quercus semecripifolia, Acer pictum* and *Betula utilis* are the common trees in these forests.

Faunal Distribution

Faunastically also, the Govind Pashu Vihar is considerably remarkable. While no attempt so far has been made towards enumerating fauna of the sanctuary, but on the basis of the reports of the Forests and Wildlife departments, the experiences of the local people, particularly, the shepherds and herb gatherers, as also the field observations, it can be established that the sanctuary harbors almost all the major groups of the high altitude mammals and birds known to reside in other parts of the Garhwal.

Among the mammals, the felines are represented by Leopard (*Panthera pardus)*, Snow Leopard (*P. unica)*, Jungle Cat *(Felis chaus affinis)* Leopard Cat *(F. bengalensis)* and the Fishing Cat *(F. viverrina)*. Of course, snow leopard and fishing cat, both are rare. Among bears (Family Ursidae), the area harbors the two high altitude species, viz., Himalayan Black Bear *(Selenarctos thibetanus)* and the Brown Bear *(Ursus arctos isabellinus)*. Family Canidae is represented by Jackal *(Canis aureus)*, Red Fox (*Vulpes Vulpes montanus*) and the Indian Fox (*V. bengalensis*). The presence of Indian Wild Dog (*Coun alpinus*) however is doubtful. Among smaller carnivores presence of common Otter (*Lutra lutra monticola*) Yellow Throated Martin (*Martes flavigula flavigula*), Himalayan Weasal (*Mustela sibrica*), Small Indian Civet (*Viberricula indica wellsi,*) Common Palm Civet (*Paradoxurus hermaphrodistubondar*) and Himalayan Palm Civet (*Puguma larvata grayi*) has been confirmed in the sanctuary.

Order Artiodactyla, a varied assemblage of game animals, is represented by the bovines like, Bharal or the Blue Sheep (*Pseudois nayaur*), Himalayan Tahr (*Hemitragus jemlachicus*), Goral (*Nemorhaedus goral*), Serow (*Capricornis sumatraenis*), and the cervines like, Sambar (*Cervus unicolor niger*), Barking Deer (*Muntiacus muntjak*) and Musk Deer (*Moschus moschus moschiferus*). The Indian Wild Boar (*Sus scrofa cristatus*) is a widely distributed animal in the sanctuary. The most common mammals in the area are, however, the two primates, i.e., the Langur (*Presbytis entellus*) and the Rhesus Macaque (*Macaca mulatta villosa*).

Among the birds found in the sanctuary area, the most interesting birds are, Koklas Pheasant (*Pucrsia macrolopha*), Monal Pheasant (*Lophophorus impejanus*), Kalij Pheasant (*Lophura leucomelana*), Cheer Pheasant (*Catreus wellichii*), Hill Partridge (*Arborophila torqueola*), Chukor Partridge (*Alectoris graeca chukor*), and the Red Jungle Fowl (*Gallus gallus murghi*). The presence of Himalayan Snow Cock (*Tetraogallous himalayensis*), Snow Partridge (*Francolinus francolinus asiae*), Grey Partridge (*F. pondicerianus*), Common Quail (*Perdicula asiatica*) and Jungle Bush Quail (*Coturnix conturnix*) however, could not be confirmed. Some other birds observed in the sanctuary are Wedge Tailed Green Pigeon (*Treron sphenura*), Blue Rock

Pigeon (*C. livia*), Wood Pigeon (*C. palumbus*), Rufous Turtly Dove (*Streptopelia oreintalis meena*), Spotted Dove (*S. chinensis suratensis*), Indian Ring Dove (*S. decaocto decaocto*), Emerald Dove (*Chalcophus indica*), Slaty-headed Parakeet (*Psittacula himalayana*), Pied-crested Cuckoo (*Clamator jacobinus*), Large Hawk Cuckoo (*Cuculus sparverioides*), Indian Cuckoo (*C. micropterus*), Koel Cuckoo (*Eudynamy scolopacea*), Hoopoe (*Upupa epops*), Large Pied Kingfisher (*Ceryle lugubris*), White breasted Kingfisher (*Halcyon smyrenesiss*), Blue-beard Bee-eater (*Nyctyornis athertoni*), Blue-throated Barbet (*Megalaima asiatica*) Large Golden-backed Woodpecker (*Chry socolaptes lucidus*), Large Scaly-bellied Wood pecker (*Picus squamatus*), Alpine Swift (*Apus melba*), Golden oriole (*Oriolus ortolus*), Hair-crested Drongo (*Dicrurus hottentottus*), Black Drongo (*D. adsimilis*) Red-billed Blue Magpie (*Cissa erythrorhyncha*), Yellow-billed Blue Magpie (*C. flavirostris*), Indian Tree Pie (*Dendrocitta vagabunda*), Red-billed Chough (*Pyrrhocorax pyrrhocorax*), Long-tailed Minivet (*Pericrocotus ethologus*), White-cheeked Bulbul (*Pycnonotus leucogenys*), Red-vented Bulbul (*P. cafer*), Streaked Laughing Thrush (*Garrulx lineatus*), Red-billed Leiothrix (*Leiothrix lutea*), Red-billed Leiothrix (*Leiothrix lutea*), White-browed Tit Babbler (*Alcippe vinipectus*) Blue-throated Flycatcher (*Muscicapa rubeculoides*), Paradise Flycatcher (*Terpsiphone paradisi*), Grey-headed Warbler (*Seicercus xanthoschistos*), Little Forktail (*Enicurus scouleri*), Himalayan Ruby-throat (*Erithacus pectoralis*), Spotted Forkatail (*Enicurus maculatus*), Pied Ground Thrush (*Zoothera wardii*), Gray-headed Thrush (*Turdus rubrocanus*), Gray Tit (*Parus major*), Yellow cheeked Tit (*P. xanthogenys*), Red-headed Tit (*Aegithalos concinnus*), White-tailed Nuthatch (*Sitta himalayensis*), Fire-breasted Flower-pecker (*Dicaeum ignipectus*), Red-browed Finch (*Callacanthis burtoni*) White - browed Rose Finch (*Carpodacus thura*) and Striped-throated Yuhina (*Ruhina gularis*). From among the birds of prey, those identified during the field study were, Upland Buteo (***Bueto hemilasius***), Eastern Steppe Eagle (*Aquila nipalensis*), Himalayan Golden Eagle (*A. chrysaetos hodgsonii*), Black Eagle (***Ictinaetus malayensis perniger***), Lammergeier (***Gypateus barbatus aureus***), Henharrier (*Circus cyaneus cyaneus*), Central Asian Hobby (*Falco subbuteo centralasiae*) and Eurasian Kestrel (*F. tinnunculus*).

Heritage Management

State of Natural Environment

While in some parts of the sanctuary, the nature, so far, has been able to retain its primeval grandeur on account of the inaccessibility and remoteness of the habitat, but the natural environment in most of the areas is threatened with undesirable human activities, such as over-grazing, poaching, forest fires, herb gathering, shifting cultivation, green felling and road construction. Because of these activities the fauna of the area is likely to be affected. Some of the animals, like musk deer, snow leopard, serow, bharal, tahr and the fishing cat have already become rare features. Similarly, among the birds, the partridges, Pheasants and quails are also witnessing an alarming decrease in their population. It was observed that most of the villagers inside the sanctuary are in possession of firearms, licensed or mostly illegal. Bulk of the animals are killed in the name of protection of either the crops or the livestock, while others are poached for domestic use and for clandestine trade, which, of late, has proved very lucrative. More game killing happens during winters, when the animals migrate to lower reaches. It has also been learnt that some organised groups of the poachers from the adjoining area of Himachal Pradesh, as also from other parts of Garhwal, are active in the sanctuary.

Collection of Forest Production: Resin tapping which was being done for the department in a small area in Rupin range has been stopped since 1992 with the coming of the Wildlife Protection

Amendment Act of 1991. Medicinal plants, which were been exploited commercially till 1991, are also not been exploited anymore. However the cases of illegal collection of medicine plants do take place occasionally. These are dealt with strong manner by booking an offense. The villagers collect *Guchchi* (Mushroom - *Morsella* sp.) in summers, which they eat and sell.

Live Stock Grazing and Fires

Grazing is probably the biggest problem of sanctuary. According to 1981 census the number of live stock of the 42 villages of the sanctuary was 7348 cows/bulls, Buffaloes, 28278 Sheep and 9771 goats. In addition, buffaloes of *Gujjars* (a nomadic tribe) also graze in the area summers. There is hardly any area that is not prone to grazing. On an average more than 50 live stock animals graze on one Sq. km. which is enough to make any attempt of scientific management in the sanctuary, a failure. The sheep and goats graze in the high altitude pastures thus coming in direct conflict with the wild animals. The cows and buffaloes keep to the lower pastures and forests, playing havoc with the natural regeneration.

Fires are known to occur in the lower parts of the sanctuary mainly in the Chir zone and thus do not pose too much of a problem for the management.

Protection Problems

The high altitudes involved and the very rugged and difficult terrain are the main problems faced by the protection staff. Presence of villages all over the sanctuary ensures presence of villagers all over the sanctuary, which makes the job of protection, staff even more difficult. The staff has to be equipped with the best possible high altitude equipment for them to be able to control the poachers who usually are more used to the difficult climate. A wireless network is in the process of getting established which if maintained properly shall be a great asset for conservation.

Wildlife Conservation strategy and Research

Establishment of a sanctuary was the first step in wildlife conservation. Wildlife guards were posted in the area for better protection. Later wildlife Warden was posted for the sanctuary who was directly under the Chief Wildlife Warden, of the state Government. The territorial control of the forests continued to rest under the Tons forest division. In mid eighties the area was recognised as a potential site for implementing the snow Leopard scheme of Government of India. This led to shifting of territorial control over the area from Divisional Forest Officer Tons to Divisional Forest Officer Nanda Devi National Park under the wildlife wing. This removed the duality of controls and further streamlined the administration. In 1990 an intentional notification for the Govind National Park, in nearly half the area of the sanctuary, has resulted in greater control over the better areas of the sanctuary. Research has been almost non-existent in the area till date. Census of wild animals was carried out in 1989, though the reliability of the same can not be ensured to a great degree. No proper attempts have been made since then for a census. The snow Leopard Project proposal has a provision for a research officer of the rank of an Assistant Conservator of forests and once sanctioned the research officer will be able to justice to the research requirements in the sanctuary. The Zoological survey of India has been entrusted with the responsibility of carrying out a detailed zoological survey of the area, which they would be starting in the current or the next financial year.

Communication in the Sanctuary is only through bridle paths (except for a single motorable road from Naitwar to Taluka). A proper wireless network is proposed to be setup. The feasibility survey for the same had already been completed in the summer of 1992.

Administrative Set-up

The Deputy Conservator of Forests (DFO) Nanda Devi National Park, Joshimath (Chamoli) who looks after the administrative and financial control of the sanctuary, heads the present organisation of the sanctuary. Wildlife staff is as under:

Table - 2.3.12

Administrative Staff at Govind Pashu Vihar

Designation	Sanctioned strength	Presently posted
Wildlife Warden	1	1
Senior Clerk	1	1
Junior Clerk	1	1
Jeep Driver	1	1
Orderly	1	1
Range Officer	1	-
Assistant Wildlife Warden	2	1
Wildlife Guards	26	23

Source: Department of Environment and Forest, Government of U.P., 1996.

Role of Tourism

With its unique natural and cultural assets, the sanctuary provides an ideal recreation environment. Multiple planned tourism activities, *viz.*, mountaineering, rock climbing, trekking, skiing, nature spotting, wildlife watching and nature/culture photography, can promote organic tourism, which ultimately shall benefit the area economically. Economics of Parks and sanctuaries have a vital role to play in people's participation and judicious management of the resources. The number of tourists visiting the sanctuary is gradually growing and almost all of them have Har-Ki-Doon as their destination. Virtually, the area is still looking for an effective tourism development plan, which could take it to international market of tourism. The tourism development Plan should, obviously, be scientifically prepared so as to check the adverse impacts of tourism.

2.3.6 NANDA DEVI BIOSPHERE RESERVE

Nanda Devi has a long history of wildlife conservation. For long the sacred and beautiful Nanda Devi Mountain and its mysterious inner basin remained a cherished dream of naturalists and mountaineers. Even the shepherds of Lata, Reni and other nearby villages, traditionally bringing their flocks to the outer Nanda Devi basin up to Dharasi, could not approach the inner basin. The first known attempt to enter inner basin was made by W.H. Graham in 1882, followed by T.G. Longstaff in 1907 and Hugh Rutledge in 1926, 1927 and 1932, but all proved in vain till 1934, when Eric Shipton and W.H. Tilman ultimately forged their way through the steep and narrow Rishi gorge to reach the inner Nanda Devi basin (Tilman 1935, Shipton 1936). Later in 1936, Tilman and N.E. Odell made the first ascent of Nanda Devi, reputedly the most outstanding mountaineering success of the Pre-Second World War era. Soon after, in 1939, at the instance of Shipton and Tilman the 182.63 sq. km^2 of Nanda Devi basin was declared as Nanda Devi wildlife sanctuary. However, conservation efforts were accelerated in 1982 when the sanctuary was upgraded to National Park to keep a check on excessive trekking and mountaineering ,which had damaged the fragile Himalayan ecosystem. The Park constitutes the core zone of a much larger area (2236.74 Sq. km) which is a biosphere reserve, established in 1988.

Location, Boundaries and Zonation: Nanda Devi Biosphere Reserve (NDBR) is located in the civil district of Chamoli (Garhwal), Pithoragarh and Almora (Kumaon). It is situated between 79°40' E and 80°05' E longitude and 30°17' N and 30°41' N latitude. The entire reserve has been divided into two zones an inner core zone and outer buffer zone.

Core Zone: The area of Nanda Devi National Park minus the small projection leading to Dhauliganga which includes village peng forms the core zone of NDBR. The core zone has a well defined boundary and encircled by some of the important peaks such as Lata Dunagiri (7066 m), Changbang (6864 m), Kalanka

(6931 m), Rishi Pahar (6992m), Mangraon (6765 m), Nanda Devi East (7434 m), Nanda Khat (6611 m), Mrigthuni (6565 m), Trisul (7120 m) and Nanda Ghungti (6368 m). The Nanda Devi peak that lies inside the core is the second highest peak (7816 m) of India. Area of the core zone is 624.62 Sq.Km. Administratively, the area comes under the Badrinath Forest Division of Chamoli district. On its southern and eastern sides, the park meets the boundaries of Almora and Pithoragarh districts of Kumaon Region respectively.

Buffer Zone: The area of the Biosphere Reserve excluding the area of core zone makes the buffer zone. It surrounds the core zone in all sides. The buffer zone also includes the areas of multiple use zones, recreational and special use area. The area of buffer zone is 1612.12 Sq.km. The boundary of Nanda Devi Biosphere Reserve runs along prominent natural features.

Altitude: The entire basin is above 3,500m., apart from the lower Rishi Gorge, which descends to 2100m. Nanda Devi west at 7,817m. is the highest peak.

Approach: Lata, a typical *'Tolcha'* village, situated near the left bank of the Dhauli river, at a distance of 26 km from Joshimath serves as the best entry point for the Park. The 62 km trek beyond this last habitation goes via-Bhelta, Lata Kharak, Dharasi, Dibrugaira (Dibrughetta, 3600m), Deodi (3300m), Ramni (3600m), Bhujgarh and Pathalkhan to ultimately reach the sanctuary camp (Sarson Patal). A further 12-km trek leads to base camp, which is situated at the bottom of Nanda Devi peak on the South Nanda glacier. Besides Lata, Reni and Suraithota villages are situated on the same Joshimath-Malari road at a distance of 24 and 33 km from Joshimath respectively and are other possible entry points. These treks, ultimately meet with the Lata originated trek at Dibrugaira and Lata Kharak respectively. The whole trek is rather a wilderness trail where the shelter is possible under tents or sometimes in natural caves only. The trek from Ramni to Patalkhan is the toughest stretch connecting to the inner core of Nanda Devi.

Fig.No 2.3.7

NANDA DEVI TREK

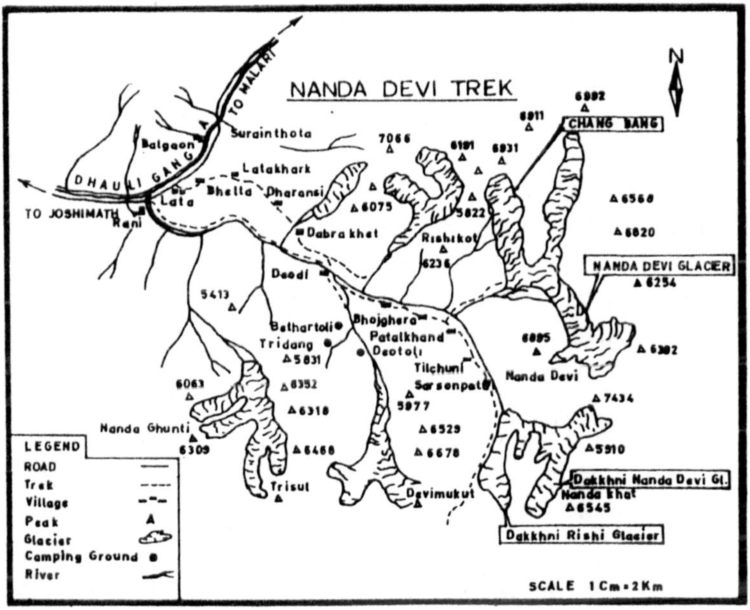

It is a tough steep climb to Bhujgara, and then a long traverse to Patalkhan. Rope is essential between Ramni and Pathalkhan. Sarsopatal (4,000 m) is a vast sprawling alpine meadow for over 10 to 15 kilometer square. It is below the Nanda Devi peak. The Nanda Devi base camp (5,100m) is situated on the southern side of the peak and from this base, mountaineers scale the peak. Again the last 11-km on way to base camp, is an uphill task. The Rishi glacier comes as a blockade and it has to be crossed with courage and skill.

Physiography: Physiographically the whole of the NDBR is a vast glacial basin and consists of many snow laden lofty peaks, large and small glaciers, glacial torrents, waterfalls, alpine meadows, hillocks, colourful boulders, moraines, steep gorges and overhanging cliffs, besides the thick forest down the valley. Access to the national park has become difficult due to closed mountain system. The basin is intersected by a series of ridges with a north-south trend. Most important among these is the Devisthan-Rishikot ridge which divides the Park into two parts i.e., the outer and inner parts, popularly called as the outer and inner sanctuaries respectively. The inner sanctuary is further divided by Nanda Devi Mountain into two parts each supported by a vast glacier system. The northern system is comparatively broader and at a low level and includes three large glaciers i.e., the Nanda Devi North, the Rishi North, and the Changbang. The southern system however, is more active (Khachher 1979) and comprises Nanda Devi North and Rishi North glaciers. Two streams the North Rishi and South Rishi come out of their respective glaciers to meet below Pathalkhan. Beyond this confluence the Rishi River flows through the stupendous upper gorge up to Ramni where it receives the tumultuous Ramni stream. A little further, the Trisul torrent, coming out of the Trisul and Bethertoli glaciers join it. After Ramni the Rishiganga flows between thick forest and after receiving many smaller streams and waterfalls it ultimately comes out of the Park at Reni to join the Dhauli River.

The outer Sanctuary is also divided by the prominent Bethartoli-Malthuni-ridge between Dibrugaira and Dharasi. Both these ridges form magnificent cliffs terminating into the Rishi gorge. Trisul, Ramni and the Bethartoli glaciers are the three prominent glaciers of the outer sanctuary.

Climate: The Rishiganga valley (core zone) and the areas north of its don't get much rainfall due to a high rim of mountains on their south (Nanda Devi, Nanda Khat - Mrigthuni-Trishul). Because of this the Rishi valley, the upper Dhauli valley, the Girthi valley and the upper Goriganga valley are very dry and cold.

The southern, south eastern and south western portion of the NDBR buffer receive full blast of the monsoon, which generally starts by the third week of June. As a result upper valleys of Pinder, Nandakini and Birhi rivers are moist and not as cold. The entire area of the Biosphere Reserve gets snow in the winters in varying quantities. The higher reaches (higher than 4500m) remains snow bound all through the year.

Flora

Most of the areas of NDBR are too high to support any kind of plant growth. The distinctive climate enjoyed by the core zone has of course created a distinctive flora. Forest form very little percentage of the flora of the Park, which is mostly confined to Rishi gorge or some allied valleys. The dominant conifer is the Himalayan fir (*Abies pindrow*). Deodar (*Cedrus deodara*) is present in fine stands near Lata, but is absent inside the sanctuary. Spruce (*Picea morinda*) is significantly absent all along the trail. Himalayan fir has an admixture of Rhododendron (*Rhododendron arboratum*) and both the pink and white varieties of wild roses (*Rosa spp.*). Between Dibrughetta and Reni there is a fine belt of Bhoj forest. A very distinctive feature of this forest is the trailing lichen, festooning the trees, and the understorey of dwarfs Rhododendron (*Rhododendron companulatum*). Broadly the Park can be divided into following ecological regions:

Mixed Temperate and Tropical Forests grows along the Rishi valley from Reni to Dibrughetta. Blue pine, maple, Akhrot, deodar and the like, near the confluence of Rishi and Dhauli, to fine stand of Himalaya fir at Deodi, and thereafter the belt of Bhoj forest up to Ramni.

Temperate Scrub continues above tree line to as high as 14000 ft. The vegetation consists of dwarf Rhododendron, Cottonoeaster, Berberis and Juniper. Strikingly the warm southern aspect has extensive growth of Juniper.

Alpine Grassland: Locally called 'bugyals', it may extend as high as 16000 ft. These grasslands support a wide variety of flowering plants such as *Potentilla, Geranium*, *Primula*, *Pedicularis*, *Cyananthus*, *Gentiana*, *Morina etc.* and medicinal plants such as *Orchis latifolia, Jurinea* sp., *Thalictrum* sp., *Gaultheria* sp. etc.

In NDBR the temperate forests of board leaves and conifers are found mainly in Dhauliganga and Pinder valleys. The forests of Pindari valley are moist and have an admixture of spruce, fir, maples, horse chestnut, walnut, oaks etc. The Dhauliganga valley forests are dry and are dominated by Deodar and blue pine. The area between Suraithota and Malari contains very old over-mature stands of Deodar.

Fauna

The various faunistic surveys in the Biosphere Reserve have resulted in the findings of the presence of 18 mammals and 200 species of birds. Bharal or the blue sheep (*Pseudois nayar*) is the dominant and most conspicuous among the large mammals. The animal seems to be more partial to gentle grassy slopes, however, its trek had also been reported as high as 5300 M, well above the snow line (Khachher 1979). Besides Sarsopatal, Trisul valley, Ramni basin and Dunagiri slopes are other favorite habitat of Bharal. Tahr (*Hemitragus jemlahicus*) is another unsulate to be reported plentiful in the park but is hard to observe, as it frequents the most difficult terrain in the Rishi gorge. Khachher (1978), Dang (1973), Sah (1976) and Lamba (1987) have also confirmed its presence in large numbers. Goral (*Nemorhaedus goral*) is another game animal to be found in the Park in good number. Khachhar (1978) and Dang (1973) and Lamba (1987) have reported this smart creature from sanctuary camp area, and the villagers of Lata and Reni have confirmed its presence in their vicinity. This shows its distribution over a wide range (Kandari, 1984).

Musk deer (*Moshus moschiferus*) is reported to exist in small number in the birch forest of Rishi gorge. Once abundantly found in the Park, this animal has become the victim of ruthless hunting for its prized musk pod.

Among the larger carnivores snow leopard (*Panthera unica*) has been reported from the Park. It is very difficult to observe it due to its difficult habitat and swiftness. While Brown bear (*Ursus arctos*) has not been reported, the black bear (*Selenarctos thibetans*) is quite common in the area, below Dibrughetta.

Park is very rich for the bird fauna specially the high altitude birds. Some of the important high altitude birds found in the Park are Monal pheasant (*Lophophorus impejenus*), Snow cock (*Tetraogallus himalayensis*), Koklas pheasant (*Pucrasia macrolopha*), Chukor pheasant (*Alectoris graeca*), Snow partridge (*Lerva lerva*), Kalij pheasant (*Lophura leucomelana*), Cheer pheasant (*Catreus wallichii*), snow pigeon (*Columba leuconota*) and the Blue rock pigeon (*Columba libia*). Among others the Rufous turtle Dove (*Streptopelia orientalis*), Pied Crested Cuckoo (*Clamatos coromoniuts*), Cuckoo (*Cuculus saturates*), Pied Wood pecker (*Dendrocope himalayensis*), Alpine Swift (*Apus melba*), Nut Cracker (*Mucifraga caryoatactes)*, Red Billed Chough (*Pyrrhocorax graculus*), Stracked Laughing thrush (*Garrulax lineatus*) and White Throated Laughing Thrush (*Garrulex albocularis*) are also common in different parts of the park.

Human Habitation

NDBR ranks among one of the least disturbed protected areas of the country. The human habitation is restricted to the buffer zone of the Biosphere Reserve with 19 villages distributed in three districts. District Chamoli has 12 villages, followed by Pithoragarh and Almora 4 and 3 villages respectively. The population living in the villages belong mainly to two ethnic groups viz. Indo-Mongoloid (also called *Bhotia*) and Indo-Aryan. Most of their winter villages are located outside NDBR. Three villages viz. Samdu, Phurkia, and Dwali are uninhabited. The core zone of the Reserve is free from human population

Mountaineering and trekking activities inside the National Park and surrounding areas have been restricted since 1981. The local population was dependent on these activities for their livelihood as they used to get employment for atleast 5-6 months in a year, besides other indirect incomes in the form of high altitude cloths, ration, utensils etc. Since the ban on mountaineering activities the local is totally dependent on the natural resources of buffer zone for their livelihood.

The people of the area are by and large poor and lead a very simple life. Literacy percentage is very low as the villages are very remote. The villagers practice marginal subsistence agriculture, rear cattle for milk and sheep for wool. They do a lot of weaving of woolens.

Table - 2.3.13
Population of human beings and livestock

District	Name of Villages	Human	Population	Cattle Population
		1981	1991	1981
Chamoli	1. Reni	201	247	860
	2. Peng	123	104	780
	3. Murainda	4	29	-
	4. Lata	325	348	289
	5. Tolma	91	155	368
	6. Suraithota / Sigri	85	-	241
	7. Phagati	65	90	1393
	8. Segadi	85	75	-
	9. Kaga	104	72	463
	10. Garpag	47	49	174
	11. Dronagiri	258	72	270
	12. Malari	759	504	1492
Total		2147	1745	6600
Pithoragarh	1. Kurkuli	-	-	-
	2. Milam	99	-	475
	3. Martoli	31	-	365
	4. Sandu	-	-	-
Total		130	-	840
Almora	1. Phurkia	-	-	-
	2. Dwali	-	-	-
	3. Khatia	197	-	234
Total		197	-	234

Source: The Director, NDBR.

Table - 2.3.14 : General Information of Resident Villages

Parameters	Villages		
	Reni	Suraithota	Peng
Altitute (meters as)	2000	2250	2425
Approximate distance from core zone (km.)	4	8	1
Distance from motorable road (km.)	0	0	4
School	P	P	P
College	A	A	A
Hospital	A	A	A
Veterinary hospital	A	A	A
Post Office	P	P	A
Bank	A	P	A

P - Present A - Absent

Source: G.B. Pant Institute of Himalayan Environment and Development, Garhwal Unit, Srinagar.

Table - 2.3.15
General Information of Migratory Villages

Parameters	Villages								
	1	2	3	4	5	6	7	8	9
Altitude (m as)	2215	2350	2450	2800	3000	3015	3050	3250	3500
Approximate distance from core zone (km)	3	8	1.5	6	7	9	14	11	6
Distance from motorable road (km.)	0	0.5	3	3.5	4	4	0	4	14

	1	2	3	4	5	6	7	8	9
Migratory distance (km)	1	0.5	4	5	3	125 -150	125 -150	125 -150	125 -150
No. of days needed for migration	1	1	1	1	1	7-12	7-12	7-12	7-12
School	P	P	A	P	P	P	P	P	P
College	A	A	A	A	A	A	A	A	A
Post Office	A	A	A	A	A	P	A	A	P
Hospital	A	A	A	A	A	A	A	A	P
Veterinary hospital	A	P	A	A	A	A	A	A	A
Bank	A	A	A	A	A	A	A	A	P

* Villages: 1. Lata 2. Segadi 3. Murainda 4. Tolma 5. Phagati 6. Kaga 7. Garpag 8. Malari 9. Dronagiri P-Present A-Absent.

Source: G.B. Pant Institute of Himalayan Environment and Development, Garhwal Unit, Srinagar.

Heritage Management

Visitors Impacts

Nanda Devi National Park has been attracting a large number of mountaineers from all over the world. These mountaineers and trekkers come to the area to fulfill their urge of adventure since it provides them as many as 90 high peaks to climb and ideal slopes to ski-down from the peaks. It is a paradise for trekkers and nature lovers and its trek route to the base camps is known as one of the most fascinating treks of the world. Since 1934, when the area was first stepped in, up to 1982 when it was closed for 5 years thirty-one expeditions attempted to climb the Nanda Devi East and West peaks alone, from all over the world. The area is very rich in nature resources and still harbors the natural habitat of several endangered species of animals and plants. Thus it attracts a large number of naturalists, wild lifers, ornithologists, botanists, geologists, and researchers etc. of various disciplines.

The educated tourists, who are conscious of the situation take due care of the ecosystem of the area and leave no sign of their visits. On the other hand, the uneducated tourists, with a view to save their time, money and labor and to fulfill their greed, disturb it immensely. During the process, they indulge in whole-scale clearing of the vast areas thus destroying the entire habitat beyond regeneration. Once uprooted, these herbaceous elements are replaced by weeds and shrub vegetation and it creates scarcity of food for the wild animals. Furthermore, a large number of sheep and goats accompany the mountaineering expeditions to carry their loads.

The main threat to the area is from the mountaineering and trekking expeditions, which are accompanied by a large number of porters, goats and sheeps. In the year 1982 alone, in 22 expeditions more than 209 mountaineers with 1,050 porters and 2,500 goats and sheeps visited the area. As these expeditions stay in the area for long periods averaging 20 to 60 days, they carry tons of load in the form of mountaineering equipment, food (mostly tinned), medicines, polythene wares (packing materials) etc. and leave it littered all over.

The porters accompanying these expeditions are not supplied with fuel to cook their food and tents to stay. In order to fulfill their requirements they cut off the trees for firewood. This large-scale felling of trees and shrubs along the trek route and campsites is accelerating the degradation process. Forests are getting thinner, leading to erosion of topsoil and disturbing the ecology of the area. To save their time, labor and money, they dump large amounts of used and unused, unwanted and damaged but undestroyed goods at the campsites. Some such articles for example are: gas cylinders, medicine (especially, capsules, syringes, carbon tetrachloride bottles, first-aid medicine), and polythene as well as tin wares. These articles are found recklessly littered at the campsites and throughout and along the trek route presenting an unsightly view as well as dangerous aspect to the ecosystem. These medicines can get dissolved in water and pollute the river water at its origin. Alternatively, the animals, roaming in search of salt can lick these and thus their physiology and breeding cycles can be disturbed.

Management Activities and Future Plan

Since the establishment of NDBR regular management activities under the heads Eco-restoration and Eco-development, development of data base, protection, education, training and awareness, building construction etc. are being undertaken by the NDBR management. 25 to 50 hec. plantations are being raised and 20 to 30 engineering structures constructed every year. To reduce the pressure on the forests 500 improved stoves have been distributed amongst the villagers. Approximately 30 solar lights are also being distributed every year.

As research and data base development is a major component in the biosphere programme a detailed land use survey was conducted in 1989-90 and 90-91. Funds are being provided to scientific institutions to conduct base line research. A small meteorological station is also being developed.

For better protection arms and ammunition to the wildlife guards and vehicles for patrolling have been purchased and are being used by the staff. Wireless communication network has been installed. Under the education, training and awareness programme frequent film/slide shows are being organised in towns and villages in and around buffer area. Sign boards and other publicity materials have also been installed at conspicuous points. Development of necessary infrastructure in the form of building complex at Gopeshwar is in progress.

In order to achieve the objectives of the Man and Biosphere Programme in a comprehensive and continuous way a detailed management plan for NDBR had been prepared for the period 1993-94 to 1997-98. The main thrust of the plan was in the field of ecorestoration and ecodevelopment. Many new ideas that had been evolved after detailed discussions with the local people were implemented during the plan period. These include development of a cottage level wool industry, cultivation of medicinal plants, poultry, apiculture and promotion of Eco-friendly tourism. Active participation of locals is to be ensured at all levels of implementation as it was done in the planning stage. Research, interpretation and conservation education and infrastructural development is also proposed to receive a boost in the years to come. However local villagers are continuously presserising the central Government to allow them to approach the core zone for their livelihood.

This zone, according to the villagers had sustained their life and formed a part of their culture and customs since time immemorial. Since the Reserve is closed, the local people are unable to protect it and poachers from outside decimate its rich wildlife. As a result, trappers and hunters, mostly from across the Kali River in Nepal, enter its core zone through the Milam glacier in Pithoragarh district. They do not however kill wild boar, bear and other animals, which destroy food crops, and their population has increased alarmingly. The sheep stocks of the villagers have dwindled to one-forth what they were earlier. As the Biosphere, which contained their pastures, is closed, they have been forced to sell their flock.

2.4 ADVENTURE TOURISM

The mighty, magical and the magnificent Garhwal Himalaya is the highest out door laboratory of the world. For the luring, brazen, breed of seekers, who strictly go by the statement "Life is for those who dare", the Garhwal Himalaya offers immense opportunities for adventure tourism viz. trekking, mountaineering, hiking, camping, skiing, aerosports, river rafting and jungle safaris.

Mountaineering: Mountaineering is a preplanned, technical art of climbing the virgin mountain peaks. Before independence mountaineering as a sport was the pleasure and privilege of the Europeans. The Himalayan Club created in 1927-28 had all

European members. The seeds of mountaineering as a sport were planted by two teachers of Doon School, R.L. Holdworth and J.A.K. Martyn, who in the early 1940's took Indian students to the Himalaya for climbing and trekking. The first Indian expedition was in 1951, when another teacher of Doon school, Gurdial Singh, led a team to Trisul and reached its summit. The ascent of Everest in 1953 by an Indian, Tenzing Norgay, along with Sir Edmund Hillary, marked the real beginning of mountaineering in India.The setting up of Himalayan Institute of Mountaineering (HIM) at Darjeeling in 1954 and Nehru Institute of Mountaineering (NIM) at Uttarkashi and more Institutions subsequently, trained thousands of young enthusiasts in the art and techniques of climbing. This resulted in increasing numbers of expeditions as evident from the following figures -

Table 2.4.1
Mountaineering Expeditions In Himalaya

Year	Indian Expedition to Himalayas	Foreign Expedition
1966	15	N.A.
1967	9	———
1968	11	———
1969	11	———
1970	16	———
1971	14	5
1972	14	8
1973	25	13
1974	26	13
1975	26	19
1976	35	36
1977	47	39

1	2	3
1978	59	31
1979	52	50
1980	57	60
1981	74	64
1982	90	72
1983	55	68
1984	91	58
1985	76	62
1986	97	52
1987	103	63
1988	108	61
1989	103	70
1990	88	50
1995	70	48
1996	57	51

Source: Indian Mountaineer, Issue 10, 13, 16, 17, 19, 21, 23, 25, IMF silver jubilee Journal page 61 and NIM Uttarkashi.

In 1988 out of total 61 foreign expeditions to Indian Himalaya, 30 were occurred in Garhwal Himalaya. Similarly in 1988 out of total 108 Indian expeditions to Indian Himalaya, 59 were done in Garhwal Himalaya. In year 1995, 48 Indian expeditions and 24 foreign expeditions occurred in Garhwal Himalaya out of 70 and 48 total expeditions on Indian Himalaya. This shows Garhwal is the most desired destination of mountain climbers and adventure lovers.

Mountaineering Resources in Garhwal Himalayas

There are more than 100 peaks, above 6000 mt. in altitude(list enclosed in appendix). Broadly the mountain peaks of Garhwal Himalayas are divided into three major groups.

1. Kamet Group

2. Gangotri Group

3. Nandadevi Group

1. **Kamet Group**: The eastern and southern limits start from the Kiungla-laa (Niti pass) and continue along the Dhauli Ganga. The western limit is the Mana Pass and Saraswati river which becomes the Alaknanda further south.

2. **Gangotri Group**: It has eastern limit in the *Mana Pass* and *Saraswati* river which becomes *Alaknanda* and the western boundary is Chorgad, the Jadh Ganga and the Bhagirathi river. Because of the size of the group the peaks are grouped into two subgroups.(a) North-Western Gangotri(b) South-Eastern Gangotri

3. **Nanda Devi Group:** The eastern limit starts at the Kangribingri La, goes over the Unta Dhura, through Milam and down the Ghori Ganga. The western limits are from the Kiunglang La (Niti Pass) down the Dhauliganga. It has three subgroups such as: The Eastern Nanda Devi, The Northern Nanda Devi and The Southern Nanda Devi.

Manpower Development:

Indian Mountaineering Federation (IMF) is closely associated with NIM and HIM.Both the Institutes impart training in mountaineering as well as promote Garhwal region. NIM was founded in 1965 and till date has trained thousands of people. The details of foreign trainees trained at NIM up to 15 July 1995 is as follows:

Table: 2.4.2
Foreign Trainees Trained at NIM

Course	Basic Mountaineering course				Advance Mountaineering		Total course		G.T.
	Men	Women	Men	Women	Men	Women	Men	Women	
Australia	1	-	-	-	1	1	2	1	3
Afghanistan	-	-	-		1	1	1	-	3
U.K.	4	-	-	-	2	2	6	2	8
Canada	-	1	-		-	-	-	1	1
Germany	1	-	-	-	3	17	24	17	41
Indonesia	1	-	-	-	-	-	1	-	1
Iran	1	-	-	-	-	-	1	-	1
Netherlands	01	-	-	-	-		1	-	1
Nepal	53	-	16	-	37	2	106	2	108
Pakistan	-	-	-	-	1	-	1	-	1
Singapore	34	10	-	1	-	-	34	11	45
Switzerland	-	-	-	-	4	3	4	3	7
Sweden	1	-	-	-	-	-	1	-	1
Srilanka	1	-	-	-	-	-	1	-	1
Thailand	-	-	-	-	-	1	-	1	1
U.S.A.	8	1	1	-	4	2	13	3	16
Malaysia	1	-	-	-	-	-	1	-	1
Korea	-	1	-	-	-	-	-	1	1
Grand Total	107	13	17	01	73	28	197	42	239

Source: Journal of Nehru Institute of Mountaineering, Volume I, 1995, Page 144-145.

Table: 2.4.3

Details of Training Programmes conducted by NIM

Programme	Duration	Capacity	Remarks
	Basic Mountaineering Courses of 28 days duration		
Basic course	Mar 20 to Apr 16	70	Gents
Basic course	Apr 24 to May 21	50	Gents
Basic course	May 28 to Jun 24	50	Ladies
Basic course	Sep 13 to Oct 10	50	Gents
Basic course	Oct 18 to Nov 14	70	Gents
	Advance Mountaineering Courses of 28 days duration		
Advance Course	Apr 24 to May 21	25	Gents
Advance Course	May 28 to Jun 24	25	Ladies
Advance Course	Sep 13 to Oct 10	25	Gents
	Search & Rescue Course of 20 days duration		
S & R course	Nov 21 to Dec 10	30	Mixed
	Method of Instruction Course of 20 days duration		
M0I Course	Nov 21 to Dec 10	20	Mixed
	Adventure Courses of 20 days duration		
Adventure Course	Jun 08 to Jun 27	35	Girls
Adventure Course	Jun 08 to Jun 27	25	Ladies
Adventure Course	Jun 29 to Jul 18	60	Boys
Adventure Course	Dec24 to Jan12	30	Boys
Adventure Course	Dec27 to Jan15	30	Girls

SNOW SKIING

The snow-clad mountain of Garhwal Himalaya offers immense opportunities for adventure sports. The large slopes in

Garhwal Himalaya when covered with seasonal snow become ideal for skiing in winter months. Skiing is a hot new sport of 90's, because Garhwal Himalaya provides the cheapest ski holidays than anywhere in the world. At present snow skiing is done only at one location in Garhwal, at Auli, 16 km from Joshimath. Auli offers perfect skiing conditions. Seasonal skiers have a clean stretch of 10 to 20 km of absolutely virgin slopes to sport on. These slopes provides excellent opportunities for alpine skiing (racing) and nordic skiing (cross country, relay race, Jumping, acrobatics), slalom and down hill skiing events.The altitude of Auli varies from 2915-3049 mt extend able to Gorson (3400 mt). From Auli up to Gorsontop, a distance of about 6.5 km is the area where beautiful natural slopes, ideal for skiing, exists. The snow capped slopes of Auli are flanked by coniferous and Oak forests which cut wind velocity to the minimum. Auli offers a panoramic scenic view of Himalayan peaks like Nanda Devi (7817 mt.), Kamet (7756 mt.), Mana Parvat (7273 mt.), Dunagiri (7066 mt.), Narparvat (5831 mt.), Gori Parvat (6590 mt.) and Hathi Parvat (6727 mt.) to count a few.

Potential sites for Snow Skiing

The hills of Garhwal provide numerous suitable slopes of varying length where snow skiing is possible besides promotion of different kinds of skiing at Auli. Other areas need to be explored for promotion of different kinds of skiing. Some of these areas provide very extensive slopes where number of cross-country skiing events can be possible. Some of the potential snow skiing sites are given below.

Uttarkashi District

- Kedar Kantha
- Bhim Thanch
- Dayara
- Kush Kalyan

- Lama Tal-Kyarki Bugyal(Bugyal is the local name for mountain meadows)

Tehri District

- Panwali Kantha
- Matya Bugyal
- Kuini Bugyal
- Kadari Bhont Area
- Masor Tal Bugyal

Chamoli And Rudraprayag District

- Bedni Bugyal
- Gorson
- Braham Tal area
- Madhmaheswar valley

Pauri District

- Dudhatoli area.

Training Courses and Facilities

At Auli training courses are conducted in modules of 7-14 days. Training is imparted to the enrolled persons in modern skiing techniques by qualified instructors of Garhwal Mandal Vikas Nigam (GMVN),Indian Institute of Skiing and Mountaineering Gulmarg, Skiing and Adventure Sports Association (SASA), I.T.B.P., NIM (Nehru Institute of Mountaineering) and HAWS (High Altitude War Fare School) etc. The detail programmes are summarised as follows:-.

Table: 2.4.4

Training Programmes for Snow Skiing

Month	**(A) 7 Days non certified course**			**(B)14 Days certificate course**		
	Dates	Course No	Total Seat	Dates	Course No	Total Seat
January	2 to 8	1	30	2 to 15	1	15
	9 to 15	2	30	18 to 31	2	15
	18 to 24	3	30			
	25 to 31	4	30			
February	3 to 9	5	30	3 to 16	3	15
	10 to 16	6	30	19 to 4 Mar	4	15
	19 to 25	7	30			
	26 to 4 Mar	8	30			
March	7 to 13	9	30	7 to 20	5	15
	16 to 22	10	30			
	24 to 30	11	45			

Source: GMVN, Dehradun.

Table: 2.4.5

Fees Structure of Skiing Programme 2001-2002

Courses	Age	Fee
(a) 7 days (non certi-	(a) Students up to 25 Yrs. (Indian)	Rs. 2800/-
ficate course)	(b) General	Rs. 3500/-
	(c) Foreigner (irrespec tive of age)	Rs. 4200/-
(b) 14 days (certific-	(a) Students up to 25 Yrs (Indian)	Rs. 4800/-
ate course)	(b) General	Rs. 6000/-
	(c) Foreigner (irrespective of age)	Rs. 8400/-

Source: GMVN, Dehradun

Other Charges	Charges		
	Clients	Half day	Full day
1.Ski equipment Hiring charges	Adult	Rs. 200/-	Rs. 250/-
	Child	Rs. 150/-	Rs. 200/-
2.Ski lesson	Adult/Child	Rs. 125/-	Rs. 175/-
3.Ski Gloves	Child/Adult Per day	_	Rs. 150/-

Source: GMVN, Dehradun

Infrastructure and Facilities at Auli

GMVN has hotel accommodation at Joshimath and Auli for 350 visitors. Its tariff ranges both from the budget to affluent visitors. Alpine cottages and log huts prove to be a more exciting choice for adventure seekers. Other facilities like catering, heating arrangements, hot water supply are available. A 3.9 km long cable/ car ropeway links Joshimath (1906 mt.) with upper slopes of Auli and terminating at Gorson (3016.6 mt). The cable car rope way is capable of transporting 100 pax down in one hour.A 500mts long ski-lift and 800m long chair-lift link the lower slopes with the upper slopes. Ski equipments are hired on payment basis and assistance of ski instructors and skiers from GMVN and Indo-Tibetan Border Police are available. Medical facilities are available from Army and Civil hospitals. In Auli communication is done by microwave telephones, wireless sets and walkie-talkies. To meet any sort of eventuality emergency rescue facilities by Helicopters is given to visitors. Three official national championships under the aegis of Winter Games Federation of India (WGFI) had been held at Auli since 1986.

Table: 2.4.6
Manpower Development (Skiing)

S.No	Details	95-96	96-97	97-98	98-99
1.	Number of Trainees	1045	510	907	487
2.	Indian	935	459	849	454
3	Foreigners	110	51	58	33

Source: GMVN - Tourism Activities report.

RIVER RAFTING AND OTHER WATER SPORTS

The sport of white water river rafting is practiced mainly in the upper reaches of the Ganga where water is wild and white as it froths and foams, gashing against narrow gorges, rocky out crops and falls at deep gradients. It was all started late in 1930 when the pioneer of float trips on long rafts started the adventure. They were Martyn, Gurdial and Gibson. Since then the river running is an organised event and has been called as white water rafting. The enthusiasm for river rafting increased when in 1987 Sir Edmund Hillary started the G.B. Pant river rafting festival at Devprayag in the month of March. One of the go through was in 1979 by an Indo-New Zealand team which made a successful canoe and run down the Mandakini and Alaknanda 28 km above Devprayag and down further to Rishikesh and Haridwar.The river Ganga offers a number of opportunities of rafting to the professional as well as the amateur. River Alaknanda and Bhagirathi are main tributaries of the Ganga and meet at Deoprayag frothing from their racy decent. The water is of grade IV to V and challenges the experts to survive the thrill. Down river from Deoprayag (70 km from Rishikesh) is perfect for amateur and the novice. From Kaudiyala to Shivpuri and Muni-Ki-Rati (Rishikesh) is the famous sites for white water rafting in Garhwal.

Other Potential sites:

Yamuna River:

- Barkot to Lakhamandal. Both proffesional and tourist stretch.
- Dhamta - Yamuna bridge. Both proffesional and Tourist stretch.

Tons River:

Mori - Tuni.

Alaknanda River:

- Kaliasour to Srinagar - 16 km tourist stretch.
- Srinagar to Bagwan - 20 km, tourist stretch.

Mandakini River:

- Chandrapuri - Rudraprayag - 30 km, professional stretch.

Bhagirathi River:

- Matuli - Dunda - 12 km. Both professional and tourist stretch.
- Dharasu - Chham - 12 km. Both professional tourist stretch.
- Jangla - Jhala - 20 km. Both professional and tourist stretch.

Bhilangana River:

- Ghansali - Godolia - 32 kms professional stretch.

Other water sports are performed at Assan Barrage (40 km from Dehra Dun). Facilities for water skiing, sailing, boating, rowing, kayaking and canoeing are available here.84 tourists and 42 trainees have undertaken water sports activity through GMVN at Assan Barrage in 1996. At present there are around 8-10 Private companies who are organising river rafting in Shivpuri and Bhrampuri area near Rishikesh. GMVN conducts river-rafting courses (both basic and advance) at Kaudiyala.

Table: 2.4.7
Number of Tourists undertaken Rafting (GMVN)

Year	No of rafter
1993-94	267
1994-95	517
1995-96	922
1996-97	819

Source: GMVN, Dehra Dun.

ROCK CLIMBING

It is also a very famous adventure activity of Garhwal region. Nehru Institute of Mountaineering (NIM) is playing vital role in training the youths. Some local agencies based at Pauri Garhwal and Uttarkashi district conduct training programme at local level. GMVN also imparts training to enthusiastic aspirants. The important places that attract youth for rock climbing courses are located at Buranskhantha (Tehri), Songad (Uttarkashi), Tapovan (Uttarkashi), Tharali (Chamoli), Tapovan (Chamoli), Kaudiyala (Tehri) and Pauri. The basic facilities required to complete the rock climbing courses are trained instructors, complete climbing equipments, tents/tourist rest houses, accommodation with catering provisions, transport facilities and first aid.

AERO SPORTS

Since time immemorial man has always dreamt of flying freely like winged species. This has now taken the shape of what we call "Aero Sports" which means the sports, which are performed in air. A few agencies engaged in Aero Sports are Golden Forest Dehradun, Shiba Air Sports Dehradun and Himalayan Para Gliding Institute Pauri. Some of the aero sports activities performed in Garhwal are:

(1) **Para Sailing:** It can be done on a flat of 1000 m x 1000 m average area. It consists of a synthetic fiber canopy, joined with seat harness by lines. It is joined to a vehicle commonly Jeep on the other end. As the jeep starts moving slowly, the same way the sailer starts lifting high in the air. Presently this sport is performed at Jolly grant about 25 Km. from Dehradun.

(2) **Para Gliding:** It is organised by National Adventure foundation (NAF) and a few other private agencies in Dehradun and Pauri. A recently setup private agency Himalayan Para Gliding Institute, Pauri is actively engaged in para gliding activity.

(3) **Hot Air Ballooning:** It is done by army personnel in the Garhwal region.

SOME IMPORTANT TREKS

For those fascinated by the unexplored, Garhwal Himalaya offers breath taking Adventurous trekking routes. Some of the important treks that attracts visitors are:-

(A) National Parks and Sanctuaries;(a)Nanda Devi National Park-Now biosphere reserve(b)Valley Of Flowers National Park(c)Govind Pasu Vihar(d)Kedar Nath Musk Deer Sanctuary.

(B) Panch Kedars Trek.

(C) Glaciers and source of sacred rivers.

(D) Lakes: (a) Roopkund (4778mt); (b) Dodital (3024mt); (c) Sahastratal (4578mt); (d) Hemkund (4578mt).

(E) Meadows cum Valley Of Flowers.

(F) Other treks are (a) Kuari Pass trek (4208mt)(b) Chandra shila trek.

References

Academy for Mountain Environics, Dehra Dun (1996). *Project Report on Mountain Tourism for Local Community Development, Micro-Case Study of Rajaji National Park.*

Agrawala, N.K. (1973). Working plan for the Kedarnath Forest Division 1972-3 to 1981-2. Parts 1 and 2. *Working Plans Circle*, Nainital, Uttar Pradesh, pp. 417.

Aitken, W.M. (1981). The sad saga of Nanda Devi. *Indian Wildlifer,* New Delhi, 1(4):37-41.

Aitken, W.M (1981-2). Nanda Devi Sanctuary revisited, 1982. *The Himalayan Journal*, 39:44-50.

Anon. (1986). Indo-U.S. snow leopard project. Progress report for spring 1986. *Snow Line* 10: 4-5.

Armington, S., (1980). *Trekking in the Himalayas*, Lonely Planet, Victoria Australia.

Bedi, R. (1985). Corbett National Park. *Clarion Books*, Delhi, 388 pp.

Berkmuller, K.L., Mukherjee, S.K. and Mishra, B. (1987). *Environmental Impact of Tourism to Hemkund Lake and Valley of Flowers. Wildlife Institute of India*, Dehradun. Unpublished, pp. 12.

Bhandari, Rajiv, (1994). "Sonanadi opens for visitor" *News Letter Corbett*, Volume 1 No. 1, spring, Page No. 4, published by Director CTR.

Bisht, D.S., (1982). *Guide to Garhwal and Kumoun Hills*, Dehradun, Trishul Publication.

Bisht, Harshvanti, (1994). *Tourism in Garhwal Himalaya: With Special Reference to Mountaineering and Trekking in Uttarkashi and Chamoli Districts*, Indus Publishing Company, New Delhi.

Bond, Ruskin, (1988). *Beautiful Garhwal Heaven in Himalayas*, EBD Educational Pvt. Ltd., Dehradun.

Burton, Lt.-Col. R.W. (1950). Wildlife reserves in India: Uttar Pradesh. *Journal of the Bombay Natural History Society*, 49:749-54.

Clark, A., Sewill, H. and Watts, R. (1986). Pastoralists in an Indian wildlife sanctuary. *Occasional paper*, No. 17, Department of Environmental Studies and Countryside Planning, Wye College, Ashford, pp. 62.

Clarke, M.D. (1979). Ecological impact on the Nanda Devi area. *The American Alpine Journal*, 53:281.

Dabral, S.P., (1965). *Uttarakhand Ka Itihas*, (in Hindi) Veer Gatha Prakashan, Dogadda Garhwal.

Dang, H. (1961). A natural sanctuary in the Himalaya: Nanda Devi and the Rishiganga basin. *Journal of the Bombay Natural History Society*, 58:707-14.

Datar, B.N., (1961). *Himalayan Pilgrimage*, Publication Division, Ministry of Broadcasting, New Delhi.

Director CTR (1996). Brochure on *Corbett National Park Picture Spots and Tips for Good Photos*, Director C.T.R.

Director CTR (1996). Brochure on *Corbett National Park Birds to Watch and Routes and Spots*, Director C.T.R.

Director CTR (1996). Brochure on *Corbett National Park Forest Rest Houses and Facilities*, Director, C.T.R.

Director CTR, (1997). Brochure on *Corbett Tiger Reserve*, Published by Director C.T.R.

Director Rajaji National Park (1996). *Brochure on Rajaji National Park.*

Director, CTR (1994). *News letter Corbett*, Volume 1 No. 3, Monsoon, Published by Director CTR.

Director, Nanda Devi Biosphere Reserve (1995). Booklet on the Nanda Devi Biosphere Reserve.

Fonia, K.S., (1998). *The Traveller's Guide to Uttarakhand,* Garuda Books, Chamoli Garhwal.

Fox, J.L., Sinha, S.P., Chundawat, R.S. and Das, P.K. (1986). *A survey of snow leopard and associated species in the Himalaya of northwestern India. Project completion Report. Wildlife Institute of India/U.S. Fish and Wildlife Service/International Snow Leopard Trust*, Dehra Dun. Pp 51.

GMVN Ltd.,Dehradun,Tourism Activities Report,1996-97.

Green, M. (1995). *Nature Reserves of the Himalaya and the Mountains of Centre Asia* (World Conservation Monitoring Centre in Collaboration with IUCN Commission of National Park and Protected Area), pp. 170-289.

Gupta, R.D. (1986). Elephants in northern India. *WWF Monthly Report*, January 1986: 1-6.

Gupta, S.K., (1998), Tourism In Garhwal Himalaya: Strategy For Sustainable Development, Bhardwaj, D.S., Kandari, O.P., (Eds), *Domestic Tourism in India*, Indus Publishing Company, New Delhi

Hajra, J. (1983b). A new species of Saussurea (Asteraceae) from Nanda Devi National Park, Chamoli District, Uttar Pradesh. *Indian Forester*, 109:77-79.

Hajra, P.K. (1983a). *A contribution to the botany of Nanda Devi National Park in Uttar Pradesh, India.* Botanical Survey of India, Howrah, pp. 38.

Hewett, J. (1938). *Jungle Trails in Northern India.* Methuen and Co., London (Unseen).

Hillary, E., (1979). *From the Ocean to Sky Jet Boating up the Ganges*, Holdder and Stoughton, London.

Hummell, John. (1996). Nature Tourism in Govind Pashu Vihar (U.P.): Case for Ecotourism, in Shalini Singh (Ed) *Profiles of Indian Tourism*, A.P.H. Publishing Corporation, New Delhi.

Indian National MAB Committee (N.D.). The Nanda Devi Biosphere Reserve Project Document 3, Department of Environment, New Delhi, pp. 128.

Jain, S.K. and Sastry, A.R.K. (1983). Botany of Some Tiger Habitats in India. *Botanical Survey of India*. Howrah, pp. 5-8.

Kamlesh Kumar and Nityanand, (1989). *The Holy Himalaya: A geographical Interpretation of Garhwal*, Daya Publishing House, Delhi.

Kandari, O.P. and Singh, T.V. (1982). Corbett National Park, In Singh T.V. (Ed.) *Tourism Wildlife Parks and Conservation*, Metropolitan, New Delhi.

Kandari, O.P. (1982). Nanda Devi India's Highest Himalayan National Park. The Problem of Resource Use and Conservation, Cheetal, *Journal of The Wildlife Preservation Society of India*, Vol. 24, Sept. & Dec. 1982,No.1&2, pp. 28-36

Kandari, O.P. (1984). Wildlife of Garhwal Himalaya: A recreational Resource for Tourism Promotion. *Doctoral Dissertation Submitted to University of Garhwal*, Srinagar Garhwal, (Unpublished), pp. 157-252.

Kandari, O.P. (1985-86). A note on the national Parks and wildlife sanctuaries of Garhwal Himalaya. *Journal of Himalayan Studies and Development* 9 & 10: 31-5.

Kandari, O.P. and Singh, T.V. (1983-84). Govind Pashu Vihar: Exploring Natural Environment. *JOHSARD,* VOL. 7 & 8, 1983-84, PP 117-124.4.

Kaur, J. (1980). On Protecting Nature's Monument, *Tourism Recreation Research*, Lucknow.

Kaur, J., (1985). *Himalayan Pilgrimage and the New Tourism*, Himalayan Books, New Delhi.

Kharakwal, S.C., (1993). *Physico-Cultural Environment and Development in U.P. Himalaya*, Nutan Publications, Kotdwar Garhwal.

Kohli, M.S., (1989). *Mountaineering in India*, Vikas Pub. House, New Delhi.

Kohli, M.S., (1989). *Mountaineering in India*, Vikas Pub. House, New Delhi.

Kumar, N. and Ahluwalia, H.P.S. (Major), (1978). *Trisul Ski Expedition*, Vikas Pub. House, New Delhi.

Lamba, B.S. (n.d.). Impact assessment of bio-ecological changes in the faunal patterns (selected groups) brought about by the partial submersion of Corbett National Park, as a result of Ramganga Multipurpose Hydel Project Dam Ist Stage 1976-1979. *Department of Environment, Govt. of India*, 150 pp.

Mehrotra, B.N. (1979). A survey of medicinal plants around Kedarnath Shrine of Garhwal Himalayas. *Indian Forester*, 105:788-51.

Motwani, M.C. (Ed), *Indian Mountaineer*, Nos. 1 to 25, New Delhi.

Naithani, S.P. (1994). *Uttrakhand Ke Tirth and Mandir* (in Hindi), Pavetri *Prakashan*, Srinagar Garhwal.

Negi, A.S., (1994). Reorganised Corbett Tiger Reserve, *News letter Corbett*, Volume 1 No. 1, spring, Director CTR, pp. 2.

Negi, J.M.S. (1995). *Himalayan Heritage: A Socio-Economic, Cultural and Tourism Analysis*, Gitanjali Publishing House, New Delhi.

Negi, S.S. (1991). *Himalayan Rivers, Lakes and Glaciers*, Indus Publishing Company, New Delhi.

Negi, S.S. (1994). *Garhwal: The Land and People*, Indus Publishing Company, New Delhi.

Negi, S.S. (1995). *Handbook of National Parks, Sanctuaries and Biosphere Reserves in India*, Indus Publishing Company New Delhi.

O'akley, E.S., (1905). *The Holy Himalaya*, London.

Osmaston and Sale, J.B. (1987). *Wildlife of Dehradun and Adjacent Hills*, Natraj Publication, Dehra Dun, pp. 3-104.

Pandey, R.N. and Singh, A. (1986). Management of water resources in Corbett National Park. *Tiger Paper*, 13(3): 12-18.

Pant, P.C. (1976). Plants of Corbett National Park, Uttar Pradesh.*Journal of the Bombay Natural History Society*, 78:287-95.

Pant, P.C., Uniyal, B.P. and Prasad, R. (1981). Additions to the plants of Corbett National Park, Uttar Pradesh. *Journal of the Bombay Natural History Society*, 78:50-3.

Rau, M.A. (1961). Flowering plants and ferns of North Garhwal, Uttar Pradesh, India. *Bulletin of the Botanical Survey of India*, 3:215-51.

Rodgers, W.A. and Panwar, H.S. (1988). *Planning a Wildlife Protected Area Network in India*. 2 Vols. Project FO: IND/82/003. FAO, Dehra Dun.

Rodgers, W.A. and Panwar, H.S. (1988). *Planning a wildlife protected area network in India. 2 vols. Project FO*: IND/82/003. FAO, Dehra Dun.

Sah, Anup (1976). The Nanda Devi Sanctuary, *Cheetal, Wildlife Society of India*, Vol. 18, No. 1 and 2, Sept.-Dec., 1976.

Sathya Kumar, S. (1993). "Nanda Devi: *The Valley of Lost Horizon" Wildlife Institute of India*, Newsletter, January-December, Vol. 68, No. 1-4, 1993.

Sathyakumar, S. (1989). Human-animal conflicts at Kedarnath Wildlife Sanctuary. *Wildlife Institute of India News Letter*, 4(6):25-6.

Sathyakumar, S. (1990). Habitat ecology of major ungulates in Kedarnath Sanctuary, Western Himalaya. Report (March 1989-June 1990). Wildlife Institute of India, Dehra Dun Unpublished, pp. 20.

Semwal, J.K. and Gaur, R.D. (1981). Alpine flora of Tungnath in Garhwal Himalaya. *Journal of the Bombay Natural history Society*, 78:498-412.

Seshadri, B. (1986). *India's wildlife and wildlife reserves*. Sterling Publishers, New Delhi. Pp.92-5.

Singh, A.N. (1982). A survey of the mammalian fauna of the Kedarnath Sanctuary, Uttar Pradesh (India). *Tiger Paper*, 9:8-10.

Singh, H.R., Badola, S.P. and Dobriyal, A.K. (1987). Geographical distributional list of ichthyofauna of the Garhwal Himalaya with some new records. *Journal of the Bombay Natural History Society*, 84:126- 32.

Singh, T.V. and Kaur, J. (1989). The Valley of Flowers in Garhwal Himalaya: An ecological preview. *Studies in Himalayan Ecology (revised edition)* Metropolitan, New Delhi. P. 89-92.

Singh, T.V. (1978). The Valley of Flowers: A case for a Biosphere reserve, *Journal of Himalayan Studies*, vol-3, Srinagar.

Singh, T.V. and Kaur J (Ed), (1985). *Integrated Mountain Development*, The English Book Store, New Delhi.

Singh, T.V. and Kaur, J. (Ed), (1989). *Studies in Himalayan Ecology and Development Strategies*, Himalayan Books, New Delhi.

Smythe, F.S. (1938). *The Valley of Flowers*, Natraj Publishers, Dehradun.

Tilman, H.W., (1937). *The Ascent of Nanda Devi*, Cambridge Press.

U.P.Tourism(Hills)1997,Report On Area Development Plan For The Chardham Circuit in U.P.Hills,Dehradun.

WWF/IUCN. Project no. 1328. *Himalayan musk deer. India: ecological study to identify conservation needs.*

3

Religious and Architectural Heritage

3.1 RELIGIOUS HERITAGE

The origin and evolution of the *Tirtha Yatra* tradition of Hindus seems to be as old as their civilisation or perhaps older than that. With the advent of Hindu civilisation we find some parts of the sub-continent 'Consecrated to the glorious rule'. One such region was the Garhwal Himalaya. Historically the region has a long and prestigious background well documented in the Pauranic literature. Ever since the Pauranic times, it has been a religious sanctuary of the Hindus and thus the most favoured pilgrim zone. The land is closely associated with legendary heroes of the Ramayana and Mahabharat epics who have left their imprint in the names of many places, the devotional lives of the people and even on social customs and cultural activities. Since the dawn of civilization places of pilgrimages like Badrinath, Kedarnath, Gangotri and Yamnotri had been established in this region. Hence since ancient time pilgrims in great number visited this region due to location of the most sacred places like Badrinath, Kedarnath, Gangotri, Yamunotri, Sikh Gurudwara at Hemkund Lokpal, origin of holy rivers like Ganga and Yamuna and holy mountains. The great Adiguru Shankaracharya from Kerala trekked to Garhwal in the 8th century AD and established Badrinath as one of the *Dham* to revive Hinduism. The tradition, which originated in such a remote part, is alive even to this day and there is no dearth of evidence to prove its remarkable continuity. Apart from the various literary evidences, certain inscriptions engraved on the rocks, on or around the temples of Garhwal supply us with valuable information regarding the practice of pilgrimages.

In Garhwal every mountain, peak, river, pool (*kunda*) is held sacred and with this the *tirthas* of Garhwal grew in number. It leads to a longer list of sacred places and satellite *tirthas* besides major pilgrimage places in the region. There are hundreds of temples in the region dedicated to different Hindu deities. Most sacred among them are the '*Panch Badris*', '*Panch Kedars*' and '*Panch Prayags*'. While Badrinath, Kedarnath, Gangotri, Yamunotri and Hemkund Sahib are centres of national significance, others are the centres of regional or of local importance. Besides these main centres, there are a number of pilgrim centres which may more appropriately be called satellites or adjuncts to the major pilgrim centers - such as Guptakashi, Ukhimath, Gaurikund, Ansuya Devi, Gopeswar, Trijuginarayan. Pilgrims use to visit them on their way to major destinations. A study of various pilgrimage places of the region below would reveal the cadre of sacred places.

BADRINATH

Physical Set-Up

Badrinath is a small township with ribbon settlement along the bank of turbulent Alaknanda river that flows South wards, embracing the Rishi Ganga to the south of the township. Located in 30°44'56" North 79°31'20" East, it runs longitudinally into a spacious valley of 4.5 km. long and 1.5 km wide opening up Northwards to the Bhotiya village of Mana, the last human settlement of this region. Badrinath is 3110 Mt. above the sea level and lies in the centre of an open valley between the *Narayana Parbat* on the one hand, and the *Nar Parbat* on the other. River Alaknanda is dividing the valley in two parts. The twin hills form the Badrinath range of peaks. Their tops are permanently covered with snow and appear quite pointed. The *Nar Parbat* is called *Kuber Bhandar* (Treasure of the Lord of Wealth), because it is popularly believed to contain diamonds and emeralds. Beyond the *Narayana Parbat* lies the famous Neelkanth Peak. On the outskirts of the town, there is a confluence of Rishi Ganga and Alaknanda River. The temple standing 15Mt. high faces east and commands a majestic view of the Alaknanda, which flows by gently not far from it. From two well-known railheads Rishikesh and Kotadwar distances are 298 km. and 327 km. respectively. Town with the village Mana is the terminal point of National Highway of Indo-Tibetan Border.

Accessibility

Badrinath is accessible by road transportation. However, the nearest airport is at Jolly Grant (315 km away) and nearest rail heads are at Rishikesh 298 km. away and Kotadwar 327 km. away, which are connected by rail with major cities of Northern India. A new airport at Gauchar is proposed to be constructed and it will make Badrinath easier to approach. Rishikesh is directly connected by rail with Howrah, Mumbai, Delhi, Lucknow, Kanpur, Allahabad, Agra, Amritsar, Ujjain, Varanasi, and Bareilly. There are three major roads to reach Badrinath from Delhi. The first route is via Rishikesh; the second route is via Kotdwar; and the third route is via Ranikhet. The tourists interested to cover both Nainital and Badrinath in one trip opt third option to reach Badrinath.

The main feature of Badrinath terrain is its sloppy land. Landscape is undulating with encircling high bare mountains, superposed by snow-clad ranges and lofty peaks. The mountain Nayarana in the West slopes down abruptly, eastward into the Alaknanda whereas mountain *Nar*, eastwards, leaves adequate space for human settlement. The Neelkanth peak, mysteriously lonely peeps out majestically from the west, where the Rishi Ganga has the source. Drainage system is according to the slopes.

Climate

Due to the elevation of 3110 m. from sea level the climate is cold. Almost for six months the town is snow covered and no human settlement remain there. Yatra starts generally from the first week of May and continues till the mid of November.

Table - 3.1

Climate (Temperature)

Months	Max.	Min.
December-March	Snow bound	Snow bound
April	3°C	0°C
May	5°C	0°C
June	14.2°C	5.9°C
July	18.20C	10°C
August	18°C	10°C
September	16°C	8.5°C
October	12.5°C	5.6°C
November	5°C	0°C

Source: Uttaranchal Tourism, Dehradun.

Mythology

In fact, Badrinath Township should not be studied in isolation. It is a religious belt spreading from *Kanav Ashram* (Kotdwar) to Satopanth - 23 km north of present Badrinath town. This belt is considered highly sacrosanct for religious pursuits where sages and saints, it is believed, devoted major part of their lives. The said belt has often been alluded as *Badrivan or Badrika-Ashram* in Puranic literature. According to Bhardwaj (1973), Hindu missionaries had a purposeful design, in assigning pilgrimage itineraries along the banks of sacred Alakananda in the Badrinath circuit, having the sublimes mountain scenery and the noblest river -aspects, particularly river confluence *(Prayagas*), the five *(Panch) Badris* and the five *Kedars*. A sacred journey to Badrinath is invariably linked up with Kedarnath and it's adjacent. Considering outstanding religious cum scenic resources of this belt, the Hindu expertise seems at its best in *Tirtha* planning and placements of pilgrim centres, in hierarchical order, climaxing in Badrinath. Presently, road system has altered the prescribed pilgrim scheme to Badrinath and has interfered with traditional itinerary.

Badrinath is associated with a number of legendary accounts. According to *Vishnu Purana, Dharama* had two sons, Nar and Narayan, who were inspired by divine to set up *Ashramas* in the *Gandhmadan Parvat* where ultimately they selected, their abode. Since they desired to spread their religious activities on a large scale, they needed spacious Valley in this part of the higher Himalaya. In their search for an ideal place they setup *ashrams* at different places of natural beauty, viz. Vridhbadri, Yogbadri, Dhyanbadri and Bhavisyabadri. Conclusively they found the present Badrinath more suitable for having hot and cold springs besides the Alaknanda waters. In course of time, their followers and devotees gave form to the settlement pattern.

Badrinath it is said, is the other name of Lord *Vishnu*. The mythological story, as to why Lord Vishnu selected this valley as his abode, sounds quite logical and interesting. It is mentioned in *Pauranic* literature that as Lord Vishnu rested on his *seshashayya* on the *kshirsagar* whilst Goddess Laxmi caressed His feet, Narad, the sage, who was a doyen of the highest learning, expressed his displeasure at Lord Vishnu's ways of living in worldly comfort. Lord Vishnu was hurt, and he sent Laxmi away to the *Nagkanyus* and he disappeared into a Himalayan valley. It is said that the valley was covered with *badri*, the wild berries, on which Lord Vishnu fed himself. He assumed a *yogdhyani* posture and meditated there for several years. Laxmi returned from the *Nagkanyas* and on finding the *seshashayya* empty, she went to the Himalaya and found Vishnu in a meditating posture amidst the *badri*. On finding an abundance of *badri*, she addressed the meditating Lord as Badrinath, the Lord of *Badri* and requested him to give up the *yogdhyani* posture and return to his original *sringaric* form. The Lord agreed to do so and called upon the human beings to abide by the following three conditions:-

- that the Valley of Badrivan will remain a valley of meditation and not worldly pleasures;
- that the Lord will be worshipped in both his forms - *Yogdhyani* and *Sringaric*. Gods will worship him in the *Yogdhyani* form and mortals will worship him in the Sringaric form;
- that in the *Yogdhyani* form Goddess Laxmi will sit on the left-hand side and in the *Sringaric* form she will sit on the right-hand side.

Goddess Laxmi is the spouse of Lord Vishnu, and usually the place of a spouse is on the left. As Laxmi is placed on the right-hand side during the *Sringaric* form, it is meaningful. Here the Lord and Goddess are not worshipped as a divine couple, but as an individual deity with no marital relations. It is for this reason that the *Rawal*, the chief Priest of the Lord Badrinath who belongs to Kerala known as *Malawar Desh* in ancient India, must also not be married. The three conditions laid down by the *Yogdhyani Vishnu* were agreed upon and have been strictly adhered to down through the ages. During the summer month, Lord Vishnu is worshipped in his *Sringaric* form by the pilgrims and during the winter, in his *Yogdhyani* form by the gods and sages.

Historical records are not available as to the age of the shrine and the temple. References of Badrinath have been noticed in the *vedas* and perhaps Badrinath was popular Shrine during the Vedic age. But one popular belief is that with the spread of Buddhism, the temple was converted into a Buddhist temple and the idol was thrown into the Narad Kund. In pursuance of divine order as per *Skand Purana*, Adi Guru Shankracharya recovered the idol of Lord Vishnu and re-enshrined it in the eighth Century. The ruler of Garhwal removed it to the present site. The gold canopy of the temple is said to be the gift of Queen Ahilyabai Holkar who has renovated the temple in late medieval period.

Temple Architecture

The temple standing 15 Mt. high from the base, faces east on the Right Bank of the Alaknanda. The temple is built in the form of a cone with a small Cupola,on the top of which is a gilt ball and spire. The main body of the temple is made of flat blocks of stones and plastered with cement that belies its antiquity. Architecturally, the temple has taken after the early Nagar style with a definite hill stamp. It has three parts:

(a) *Garbh Griha* (the sanctum -sanctorum)

(b) *Darshan Mandap* (rectangular shaped where *puja* is performed)

(c) *Shabha Mandap* (outer hall where devotees stand for *darshan*).

Much of its form has suffered a change on renovator's hand as it experienced a number of invasions of avalanches and men. The colourful entrance gate (*Singhdwar*) has put on a Turkish cap, camouflaging the traditional exterior. The shrine, with its attendant services, occupies an area of 0.39 acres which is 1.18 percent of the developed area. The sanctum- sanctorum of the temple contains many idols. The main idol is of *Maha Vishnu* seated in a meditative pose, in *Sidha Ashana* with palms locked and the matted hair flowing over the shoulders. It is made of *Saligram* stone. At its left are the images of Naryana and Nara, the former in *Padmashna* and the latter in *Dhanurasuna*. An idol of Kubera is at his right side. The *Utsava* idol (*Uddhava*) stands in front of

Lord, side by side with a silver image of *Garurda*, and nearby is an image of Narada. The sanctum-sanctorum also contains the "*Sudarshna Yantra* " in silver. Within the courtyard, to the right, stands a small temple of Goddess Laxmi. The idols of Ghantakarna (said to be the guard or *Kshetrapal*) and of Hanuman and Ganesh stand on the wings.

Rituals and Performance

The worship of the deities in the Shrine is done strictly according to the *Agamas* or the science of rituals. At Badrinath, different kinds of *pujas* are performed on behalf of individuals. Every *puja* must be preceded by a holy dip in the *Tapta Kund*. Some of the special morning *pujas* are - *abhishek, mahabhishek, Srimadbhagwat*, and *Geeta path*. Some of the special evening *pujas* are: *Arti* and *Geet Govind*. The morning *pujas* must be booked in the previous day and the evening *pujas* can be booked before noon. The daily ritual is performed with meticulous care. The *Rawal* is assisted in the sanctum sanctorum by a local *Brahmin* priest and outside by learned *Pandits*, who recite the *mantras* and verses.

Darshan

Darshan of Lord *Badrivishal* is available from the *sabha mandap* all the time the temple is open. The temple committee posts volunteers at various points to organise the large crowds. The fragrance of the Himalayan shrubs permeating the air, the chanting of Vedic hymns by the *pujaris* and the *pandits*, together with the chiming of bells, creates a heavenly atmosphere - when emotions run high, with a feeling of complete surrender to the Lord. One leaves the temple blessed, happy and fulfilled because at last a cherished dream has come true. The timings for *darshan* at the temple are 04.30 hrs. to 13.00 hrs. and 16.00 hrs. to 21.00 hrs. The *pujari* of Badrinath is known as the *Rawal* and he is a *Namboodripad Brahmin* of Kerala . *Adiguru* Shankaracharya the reformer of the temple was a *Namboodripad- Brahmin* from

Kerala. For several years, the Shankaracharyas of *Jyotirmath* (Joshimath) were also picked up from *Namboodripad Brahmins*, and they only used to function as the *pujaris* of Lord Badrinath. To become Shankaracharya, it was necessary for one to be a *sanyasi*. For some time no *Namboodripad sanyasi* could be available for the position of Shankaracharya, so the seat at *Jyotirmath* remained vacant. But it was necessary to have a Namboodripad *pujari* at Badrinath, and therefore the *Maharaja* of Tehri Garhwal appointed a non- *sanyasi Namboodripad*, who of course could not qualify to become Shankaracharya, but the *pujari* of Badrinath and the king gave him the title of *Rawal*. From that time, the Shankaracharya, who can be a non Namboodripad also, ceased to be the pujari at Badrinath. The *Rawal* is appointed jointly by the former *Maharaja* of Tehri Garhwal and the Temple Committee, and is assisted by a *naib Rawal* who also must be a Namboodripad Brahmin, as he is the lawful successor to the Rawal. Prior to the Temple Act, the Rawal was considered the supreme administrative and religious head, as well as the controller of temple revenues. He now receives a salary, plus a small percentage of the total puja receipts. He also gets a substantial quota of rations and other items. Altogether, the Rawal is well rewarded for his position and religious status. The *Rawal* must be well versed in Sanskrit and *puja* ceremonials. He is expected to be a celibate and once married ceases to be a *Rawal*.

The *Pandas* (priests)

There are a large number of *pandas* working at Badrinath. The average pandas know Sanskrit, and are well versed in *Karmakand* and often have a good store of mythological knowledge. They are most helpful in performing *pujas* outside the temple. The *pandas* of Kedarnath, Gangotri and Yamunotri come from the nearby villages, but those of Badrinath hail from Deoparayag, 70 km. from Rishikesh. They have always been adventurous and progressive, and so have played an important role in the shaping of *yatra* to Badrinath. The *pandas* of Deoprayag belonged to the

Bhatt communities in South India. They were dedicated to the *Ramanujam* sect and came to Deoprayag in order to propagate the Movement. They settled around the Temple of Raghunathji. Having come all the way from the south they soon became acquainted with the local conditions of *yatra* and helped in organising the difficult *yatra* to Badrinath. During the winter months, they went to the plains and got people interested in the pilgrimage. The *pandas* play an important role in the *karmakand* part of temple affairs and act as friend, philosopher and guide to the *yatris*, for which they are suitably rewarded.

Temple Administration

The administration of the Temples of Kedarnath and Badrinath has come down from the *Maharajas* (king) of Tehri Garhwal to the *Rawals*, and finally to the Badrinath Temple Committee. The committee was formed by the Uttar Pradesh Government through an Act, enacted in 1938, and known as the Badrinath Temple Act. In 1948, the Temples of Kedarnath and others in the area were brought under the administration of the same committee, henceforth known as the Badrinath-Kedarnath Temple Committee. The Chief Executive Officer is the administrative head and is assisted by a separate Executive Officer at Kedarnath. The Chief Executive Officer of the Temple Committee and the former Maharaja of Tehri Garhwal decide the opening day of the temple in consultation with the *Pandits* and the astrologers. The consultation is held with a brief ceremony at Narendra Nagar, on the auspicious day of *Basant Panchmi*. A suitable day is normally found during the last week of April or the first week of May. Special significance is attached to the *Akhand jyoti darshan* on the opening day. The flame in an ancient lamp keeps on burning throughout the year. On the closing day of the temple, *ghee* and oil are put into the lamp to make certain that it will continue to burn, and be available for *darshan* on the opening day. The Chief Executive Officer, the Rawal and the Dharmadhikari decide the closing day of the temple on the day of *Vijaya Dashmi* during the *Dussehra* festival. Normally the day of closing falls during the second week of November. The temple closes with many ceremonies. A woolen *choli*, woven by the *Kanyas* - girls of the *Molapa* families of Mana is offered to the deity. The offering of the *choli* is a part of *Karmakand* in which the faithful participate, thus fostering and fulfilling their religious feelings. After the *choli* is placed on the deity, *bhog* is offered and *mantras* are chanted. It is said that during winter season the Lord takes rest in the *Yogdhyani mudra* and only the Gods and *Yakshas* use to worship Him. The *choli* , which has been on the deity during the winter, is taken off on the opening day and the fibers of it are distributed amongst the *yatris* as *mahaprasadam*. The *Rawal* and other staff members move down to Joshimath for the winter months. The large number of staff members, *pandas*, shopkeepers and others return home for this duration when each will keep the day to day account of the thawing and melting snows, and will eagerly await the auspicious day for the temple gong to ring again.

Heritage Attractions

Essentially a sacred site, Badrinath attracts both religious and secular visitors. The number of secular visitors is steadily increasing. Some of the recreational cum religious resources exists within the township and immediate surroundings. In the vicinity of the temple, hot and cold cisterns (*kund*), *Ghats*, engraved boulders and geologic forms are there.

The Tapta Kund: A *darshan* of Badrinath is always preceded by a "holy dip" in the *Kund*. Many of the hot water baths cause nauseous feeling, but the water of the *Tapta Kund* is pleasantly different. Even though the water may be inviting, it is not wise to stay in too long, as one can suffer from giddiness. Men and women have separate bathing *kunds*. After the holy bath, one's body is reinforced against the cold winds blowing off the icy waters of the Alaknanda River. The hot water springs come out from beneath the *Garur shila* and fall into a tank constructed of stone and cement.

The Narad Kund: The *Narad Kund*, from where the idol of Lord Badrinath was recovered by Adiguru Shankaracharya, is a deep depression in the Alaknanda and just a few yards from the hot water kunds. A dip in the *Narad Kund* is considered very holy, but few choose to do so as the soothing waters of the *Tapta Kund* can be equally or more redeeming in the religious sense. The approach to *Narad Kund*, is very dangerous and pilgrims are advised to avoid any risk nearby.

The Pancha Shilas: Around the *Tapta Kund* there are five blocks of stone, which have acquired mythological importance. They are called the *Narad, Narsingh, Barah, Garur* and *Markandey shilas*.

The *Narad Shila* , Conical in shape - stands between the *Tapta Kund* and the *Narad Kund*. It is said that the sage Narad, meditated on this block for several years.

The *Narsingh Shila* is just below the *Narad Shila* and it stands in the water of the Alaknanda. After killing the demon King Hiranyakashyap,Lord *Narsingh* stayed in the Alaknanda so that the icy water would cool his anger. At the request of the Gods, Lord Narshingh decided to remain in the river forever in the shape of a block of stone. This huge stone looks very much like a lion. Its gaping jaws and hooked claws can clearly be seen from the other side of the river.

The *Barah Shila* has the shape of a boar and it is in the Alaknanda near the *Narad Kund*. Legend has it that the *Barah* incarnation of Lord Vishnu remained in the river in the form of this block of stone.

The *Garur Shila* is near the *Tapta Kund*. Garur, the carrier of Lord Vishnu is said to have fasted and meditated on this stone with the desire of always being in readiness in the service of the Lord.

The *Markandey Shila* is scarcely visible in the flowing waters of the Alaknanda. Acting on the advice of Narad the sage,

Markandey left Mathura and reached *Badrivan* where he meditated on this stone and attained *paramshanti* with the blessings of Badrinath.

***Panch Dharas* - The Five Streams:** The *panch dharas* are famous in Badrinath. They are called the *Prahlad, Kurma, Urvasi, Bhrigu* and the *Indra Dharas*. The water from the *Prahlad Dhara* is lukewarm whilst the water of the *Kurma Dhara* is extremely cold. The *Urvasi Dhara* flows from the Nilkanth ranges and forms the right arm of the Rishi Ganga River. About 1 km. north of Badrinath, *Bhrigu Dhara* flows past a number of caves. The most beautiful is the *Indra Dhara*, about 1.5 km. north of Badrinath, which glides majestically down the rocks of *Narain Parvat*.

Brahma Kapal: It is a flat rock platform on the bank of river Alaknanda. *Hindus* perform propitiating rites for their deceased ancestors here. After the temple, the most hallowed place in Badrinath is a wide rock of stone, jutting into the Alakananda River. It is called the *Brahma Kapal* (or the fifth chopped head of *Brahma*, the Creator). The legend is that *Brahma* was absolved at this place from some sin he had committed. Hence it is believed that *shraddhas* or death anniversaries performed on this rock secure a final salvation for the departed souls and there after their descents are absolved from the periodical or annual duty once for all.

Sesha Netra: On the opposite bank of the Alaknanda, in the lap of *Nar Parvat*, there are two small seasonal lakes filled with lotus. Between these lakes, there is a large block of stone, which carries one eye of the *seshanag*. The formation of the eye is natural, even though it appears to have been carved by man. It is thought that the *seshanag* is patiently watching *Narain* and waiting to accompany Him in his re-incarnation.

Charanpaduka: It is a delightful journey through emerald green meadows, carpeted with wild flowers in the summer, to Charanpaduka. Here is a boulder bearing the footprints of Lord

Vishnu. It is said that when Lord Vishnu descended from *Vaikunth* he stepped on this boulder. The area is full of caves and boulders. Charanpaduka is about 2 km. from Badrinath and the approach to it starts with a climb. Ponies and horses are useful for this trip. But they are not readily available.

Nilkanth Peak - The Shining Pyramid: At the back of the temple, a side valley opens to the majestic, conical-shaped Nilkanth Peak (6596 m), which soars into the Heavens at Badrinath. It is a shining pyramid of white crystals, which are ever ready to change their colour and hue. It reflects the first red glow of dawn into the valley, and at sunset it glitters like a golden temple. Nilkanth embodies all the divinity of this divine land and compels the visitors to wonder and ponder whether it is a mountainous form of *Lord Badrivishal*. The weather is generally uncertain in the afternoon, so the best viewing time is early in the morning. Nilkanth has been scaled by several expeditions, and is a very popular name in the realm of mountaineering.

Urvasi Temple: On the outskirts of the Bamni village, there is a temple dedicated to Urvasi. The celestial nymph is seated on the left thigh of *Narain* who holds a *shankh*, a *chakra*, a *gada*, and a *padma*, in his four hands. A small pond near *Charanpaduka*, where the pride of *Indra* was shattered is named after Urvasi.

Mata Murti: *Dharma Raj* and *Mata Murti* in search of their meditating sons, *Nar and Narain* - decided to stay separately at places given to them. A small temple, in the Alaknanda Valley opposite to the Mana village, is dedicated to *Mata Murti*. Once a year, on the day of *Vamana Dwadashi*, the Narain (*Badrinath*) pays a visit to *Mata Murti*, when the Rawal and the villagers, in a festival of prayer, *havan* and *bhog* worship her. It is believed that Mata Murti has the power of granting *vairagya* to those who are sincere and meditate her. Another belief is that by worshipping Mata *Murti* , preferably on the days of *Shukla Tritiya, Ashtami* and *Chaturdashi* - worried parents will have their wayward children returned to the path of righteousness.

Mana Village: Mana village inhabited by an Indo-Mongolian tribe, is considered as the last Indian village before Tibet. One needs a permit to go beyond it. It is just four Kms away from Badrinath town and is known for the confluence of Alaknanda and the so-called Sarswati River. The confluence is named as *Kesav Prayag*. It is also famous for a rock cave where it is said that Veda Vyas composed the Mahabarata and Puranic commentaries in 2nd century BC. A natural rock bridge of a huge slab of stone over Saraswati river presenting a spectacular view of water thundering down through the narrow passage under the rock, believed to have been placed there by Bhim, the second Pandava.

Vasudhara Fall: Waterfalls have always captivated the human imagination. 5km from Mana village towards the west is the Vashudhara fall with a sheer drop of 145 Mt, set in a background of snowy peaks, glaciers and rocky heights. Violent wind sometimes sprays out the entire volume of the water falling and it appears that the waterfall ceases for a minute or two, giving rise to a lot of superstitious ideas to the locals. Vasudhara is the highest waterfall of Garhwal.

Pilgrim Patterns and Trends

Garhwal is Hindu pilgrim zone with Badrinath as a super shrine resort in the Himalaya where tradition of "*tirth yatra*" seems to be timeless. The "*Badrinath dhama's*" pilgrimage lasts for seven months, mostly in summers and rains (May-November). May - June being the drier months, the majority of visitors take to pilgrimage during this period, to safeguard against inclemency/severe coldness of the weather and road breaches/break. On an average over 2000 pilgrims visit Badrinath every day. However, maximum tourists are recorded in June, when 4000 to 4500 visitors may come in a single day. In August, low profile is noticed due to rain, landslide and slope failure on mountain road. September is the most ideal time with comparatively high profile due to clearer sky and green hills for a memorable journey. In November, traffic flows begin to fade out with the onset of snows. Finally, *Kapat* of Badrinath are closed and the chief priest moves to Joshimath - the winter seat of *Badri Narayan*.

Badrinath Dham attracts visitors from all over the country and from overseas. In 1994, a total number of domestic tourists visited Badrinath were 347,025 besides 390 foreign visitors. In the year 1997, around 5 lakh tourists were recorded. Conducted tours by Garhwal Mandal Vikas Nigam (GMVN), a public sector organisation of Government of Uttaranchal, and other travel agents have encouraged tourist traffic to Badrinath. In the year 1992-93 GMVN conducted 462 tours and carried 6081 tourists to Badrinath and other shrines. In 1994-95 the total number of tours operated by GMVN were 473 and the number of tourists transported to the shrines were 11,104 and in the year 1996-97 it was increased to 820 with 12947 tourists, carried to Badrinath and other shrines. The dominant visitors markets were Maharashtra ,Rajasthan, and M.P. and Bengal. Bengalis prefer September-October months while flow of south Indians continues through out the season. The in depth study of visiting community to Badrinath in 1997 revealed the following figures. In the month of April, out of 1787 visitors maximum 35.60% were from U.P. In May out of 11,731 visitors, U.P. contributed to 33.05% and Maharashtra 25.82% followed by Delhi 18.91%. In June again U.P. was in the top in arrivals with 34.74%, Delhi 28.31%, Punjab 18.22% of the total 7599. In July, out of total 3670 visitors 38.50% from Punjab and 24.35% from U.P. In the month of August Punjab was in the top with 34.71%, Delhi 24.59% out of total 6498 visitors. In September and October U.P. was on the top and in November, Maharastra contributed to 34.57%, Gujrat with 21.36%, West Bangal - 14.26% and Andrapradesh - 7.51% of the total 1423 visitors.

Another notable outcome of the study revealed the change in visitors' attitude. Many of them have wanderlust though Badrinath remains the major pull factor. In another study, conducted by International Centre for Integrated Mountain Development

(ICIMOD) in 1995 revealed that 11.3% of Badrinath's total visitors originated from Garhwal region, 17.5% came from U.P. (excluding Garhwal) and 71.2% originated from other states of India (outside U.P.). Majority of them 74% belonged to 30-60 age group. While the Himalayan pilgrimage have gateways in Kotdwar and Rishikesh, almost 91% visitors prefer entry from Rishikesh, both for transit facilities and enroute attractions, particularly Devprayag, the confluence of the Bhagirathi and Alaknanda. The 300 km long journey is completed with a halt at Joshimath on the onward and Srinagar on the backward journey. Both the stopovers have developed adequate accommodation facilities. Averagely, 2 days stay at Badrinath has been registered.

However, the master plan report of Badrinath revealed that of the total visitors to Badrinath, 18.5% stayed at Badrinath only for one day, 58.5% stayed for 2 days, 19.9% for 3 days and 3.1% stayed for 4 days. It may be observed that the length of stay is directly proportional to recreation resource attractions, facilities, hospitality and travel costs. Badrinath being mainly a religious destination would take some time to cater to the tourist needs, though the trends have set in. Visitor influx to Badrinath shot up after 1973 when metalloid road reached Badrinath for the first time. The highway to Badrinath provided fresh opportunities for opening up of macro tourist destinations viz. - Valley of flowers, Hemkund and various other micro regions are receiving the attention of the developers like the Garhwal Mandal Vikas Nigam (GMVN) and Uttaranchal Tourism.

Badrinath faces many constrain in meeting market demands The major problem is its geography. A town lives only for seven months (May to November) and the rest is sway of the snows. This hard seasonality character is further accentuated by limiting land use adequacy. Manpower resource is another limiting factor for taking up any enterprise, which may benefit locally or regionally. A look into the vital statistics of the hosting town shall reveal the enormity of the situation. Badrinath has semi-resident population that moves to Joshimath and other areas of Garhwal during winter.

Badrinathpuri being the oldest settlement forms the core where the shrine has cluster of *panda* population and services. Here, practically every inch of ground has been used for religious purpose. Mostly all shops of the town are devoted to board and lodging, souvenir and refreshments. A few shops sale cloth, medicine too. In term of civic amenities such as water supply, electricity, hospital and public lavatories the town is poorly served. It receives 100% water supply from the river Rishi Ganga. Struck by avalanches, it has been deprived of electric lights. Use of septic tanks has been introduced and the Jal Sansthan has started laying sewerage lines in the town. The town has allopathic and ayurvedic hospitals, one post office, one telephone exchange, one police station and one information centre. These facilities look pretty impressive for a semi-mobile township that hardly stays for seven months. But considering the vast floating population, pilgrims/ tourists and their heterogeneous needs, these services are all too meager besides very much wanting in grade. The town falls short in accommodation, the foremost distinction facility.

Accommodation Facility

During the season Badrinath can accommodate quite a large number of visitors with around 6355 beds available in its different accommodation units. A large number of these units came up after 1973, when the road to Badrinath was constructed (refer list of accommodation units in Appendix). They are of reasonable standard and quite expensive stay places. On the contrary there are many 'inexpensive' stay places with the *pandas* who look after their clients, on traditional style and charge exorbitantly though at the sweet pleasure of their clients. Since many places are without bath, toilets and other basic facilities, the environment suffers the worst from litter and waste causing health hazard and infection to the visiting community.

The Master Plan

Most agonising feature of the Badrinath pilgrimage is the difficulty in getting a chance to have a look or *darshan* at the deity.

The premise of the temple is too small to accommodate even 200 pilgrims at a time. Pilgrims wait in an endless queue from the early hour of the morning till afternoon. Badrinath is facing serious challenges for the development of an adequate pilgrim cum tourist service system, particularly the constraints of limited land use, close to temple. Across the Alaknanda, beneath the mountain Nar, there is adequate space for further development.

Table - 3.2

Badrinath Master Plan Land Use 1979

Undeveloped Land Use	Area (in Acre)	%	Developed Land Use	Area	%
Agriculture	34.14	36.78	Resident's Housing	9.02	27.28
Open Space	32.40	34.90	Visitor's Housing	6.60	19.96
Low Land	07.18	07.75	Commercial	2.12	06.42
River Sides	19.10	20.57	Govt. Offices D.G.B.R. area	2.52	7.62
			Community Services	0.75	2.27
			Transport Zone	8.56	25.83
			The Temple	0.39	01.18
Total	92.82 (73.72%)	100.00		33.08 (26.28%)	100.00

Source: Badrinath Master Plan, Department of Town Planning, Government of U.P., 1979, p. 25.

Physical land surveys completed by the town planners reveal that the township between Nar and Narain has only 125.90 acres of land available of which about 92.82 acres is 'undeveloped' and only 33.08 is suitable for development. The later should include residents' zone, visitor housing, commercial and official zones, and transport and community services, besides the religious zone of the temple. The above Table provides details of the land use in 1979.

As per projection of the master plan 1979 the number visitor would grow from 1,80,316 in 1979 to 3,53,418 in 1999 and the local population would be 4,000 in 1999. But the actual figures in 1996 was much more than the projected figures and recorded 4.65 lakhs. The west and north part of the town, are the glacial effected zone. Hence the development work can not be taken place on that side. Similarly on the southern side due to more gradients the land can not be used for development work. The only area left for the expansion and development is the eastern side. The new township with pronounced tourist zone is emerging on the eastern side beneath the mountain of Nar. A separate commercial zone has been created here. Proposed area along Nar has been divided into three sectors.

1. Northern sector extends from northern boundary to Hotel Devlok, purporting to be a Regional Commercial Centre.
2. Middle sector to serve as C.B.D., rendering town and regional services. This extends from Hotel Devlok to the Hospital.
3. Southern sector having a regional outlook and it shall have a bus stand, petrol pump station and the like. In the proposal of master plan, the land on the upper side and eastern side of Joshimath-Mana Marg is reserved for local population.

The best land has been reserved to the south of Joshimath - Mana road for tourist accommodation and services. This would also close to the transport zone. Optimal connectivity with tourist service and community service Centre has been planned. Master plan envisages development of all-important activities on a horizontal axis. Keeping off the bus-stand to the southern out skirts to screen off noise and congestion, Joshimath - Mana highway (66' wide) shall pass through the middle of the new town with links to various zones. The only other motor road shall link the P.W.D. rest house to the *Manav Kalyan Ashrama*. There would be recreation parks, socio- cultural Centres and green Belts on the skirts. The proposed land use plan up to 1999 is given below in the table.

Table - 3.3

Proposed Land Use 1999

Land Use	Area in acre	Percentage
Accommodation	67.00	59.04
(a) Visitors Housing	30.50	26.88
(b) Resident's Housing	35.00	30.84
(c) Other populated area	1.5	1.32
Commercial	5.50	4.84
Govt. Offices	5.00	4.41
Community Services	7.75	6.83
Transport Zone	20.75	18.25
The Temple	1.50	1.32
Uncertain Land Use	4.00	3.52
Water bodies land use	2.00	1.76
Total Developed Land Use	113.50	100.00

Source: Badrinath Master Plan, Department of Town Planning, Government of U.P., 1979, Page No. 34.

Much of the town has come up after the plan. The spatio-physical planning should involve the role of different Departments such as Environment, Culture, and Tourism for conserving the sacredness and total ambiance of the super pilgrimage resort, the '*Dhama*'.

KEDARNATH

The shrine of Kedarnath, like Badrinath, is held in equally high esteem. It is one of the twelve *"Jyotirlingas"* of lord Shiva. Kedarnath is located in Rudra Prayag district of Garhwal at 30° 44' 15" latitude and 79° 68' 33" longitude at an altitude of 3583 Mt. on the foothills of *Manapath* mountain of Himalaya. Due to the elevation of 3583 Mt from sea level, the climate is cold. Almost for the six months the town is snow covered and no human settlement remains there. Yatra starts generally from the first week of May and continues to October or mid November.

Accessibility

Kedarnath is approachable on foot 14 km from Gaurikund, which is connected by road with Rishikesh, Kotdwar, Dehradun and other places of Garhwal and Kumaon. However the nearest airport is Jollygrant, Dehradun (239 Km away). Nearest railheads are Rishikesh (223 Km away) and Kotdwar (250 Km away), which are connected by rail with major cities of India. The road route from Rishikesh to Kedarnarth (223 Km) is via Devprayag, Srinagar, Rudraprayag, Tilwara, Agastmuni, Kund, Guptakashi, Sonprayag, Gaurikund and finally 14-Km trek from Gaurikund leads to Kedarnath. Horses, *dandies* and ponies are available at Gaurikund for carrying visitors and luggage to Kedarnath.

Mythology

After the massacre of the *Kauravas* in the war of Kurukshetra, the *Pandavas* set out on a yatra to Varanasi in order to be blessed by Lord Shiva and be absolved from the sin of killing their own kinsmen - the *Kauravas*. Lord Shiva, unwilling to give *darshan* to the *Pandavas*, fled from Kashi to Uttarakhand and lived incognito in Guptakashi. On being detected by the *Pandavas*, *Shiva* went to Kedarnath, but the *Pandavas* followed him. He assumed the form of a bull and started grazing amongst the cattle, but even then could not escape detection by the *Pandavas*. At dusk, when it was time for the cattle to return home, *Bhim* (of gigantic stature, great courage and strength) stretched his legs across the mountains (standing on either side of the Kedarnath Valley) in order to identify *Shiva*. All the cattle passed under his legs, except *Shiva* to whom *Bhim* recognised. As *Bhim* bent down to catch hold of Him, *Shiva* sank into the earth and only his back portion (the hump) remained in *Bhim's* hands. *Shiva* was pleased with the determination of the *Pandavas and* exonerated them from their sin. He gave them *darshan* and advised them to worship his hump. It is from that date , the hump of Shiva is worshipped in the Temple of Kedarnath - in the conical *Shiva Pinda* form. According to the legend, the front portion of the Lord appeared at Pashupati Nath, Kathmandu, and the other four parts - arms, face, navel and hair coils - appeared at Tungnath, Rudranth, Madmaheswar and Kalpeswar in Garhwal.

The Temple

The temple is magnificent in its style and architecture. There is no historical record relating to its origin and construction. It has been constructed on a rectangular platform and built of extremely large and evenly cut, gray slabs of stone. The temple has a *mandap* and a *garbh griha*. In the centre of the *garbh griha* there is a conical rock formation, encircled by a narrow *pradakshina* path, which is worshipped as Lord Shiva. In the *mandap*, right in front of the *Shiva Pinda*, is Nandi, the divine bull and Shiva's mount, whilst in the courtyard facing the *garbha griha* is a very large *Nandi*. There are many idols and small temples on the outer *Pradakshina* path. The *Shiva Pinda* is one of the twelve *jyotirlings* of Lord Shiva. Some of the large gray slabs bear inscriptions, either in pali or Brahmni, but as yet, not being deciphered. They are of great archaeological value and once deciphered, could reveal very important historical information.

Rituals and Performance

The temple of Lord Kedarnath faces east and each day hundreds of devotees throng the *Sabha Mandap* for the cherished *darshan* of Lord Shiva. *Puja* timings are morning and evening. Morning *puja* is called *Nirwan darshan*, when the *Shiva pinda* is worshipped in the natural form *Ghee* and water are the main offerings. Evening *puja* is called *Sringar darshan* when the *Shiva pinda* is adorned with ornaments and flowers. The *pinda* is graced with a golden umbrella suspended from above and the *sabha mandap* bears a glittering scene, charged with emotion. The pandas of Kedarnath reside in the villages around Guptakashi and Ukhimath. Some are scholars of Sanskrit and are also competent astrologers. They are very friendly and helpful. Kedarnath temple opens three to four days before that of Badrinath. The opening date usually falls during the last week of April or the first week of May, and is fixed on the day of *Mahashivratri* by the priests of the temple at Ukhimath. The temple closes on the day after Diwali, with a brief and simple ceremony. *Pujaris* and workers return to their winter resorts and *Bhaironath takes* care of this *Shiva Lok*. The curtain draws on this heavenly theatre of Lord Shiva for the winter months and the next summer, when the land opens fresh and with the melting snows, the pilgrim trail begins again.

Religious cum Recreational Attractions

***Kunds*:** At Kedarnath there are several *kunds,* which are known for their religious significance. Hans Kund, Udak Kund and Ret Kund are the most important.

Bhaironath Temple: This small temple is about 1.5 km. from Kedarnath, and is dedicated to *Bhaironath* who is ceremoniously worshipped at the opening and closing of Kedarnath temple. The belief is held that, when the Temple of Kedarnath closes, Bhaironath protects this land from evil.

Shankracharya's Samadhi: The *Samadhi* of *Adiguru Shankracharya* is located at the back of Kedarnath temple. The Adiguru set up four *maths* and four *dhams* in four corners of India, and revived the Hindu religion which had suffered a setback during the reign of Emperor Ashoka, who had propagated the Buddhist religion. After completing the mission he was born for, the Adiguru's eternal soul passed from his body at Kedarnath at the age of just 32 years.

Gandhi Sarover: Lake Chorabari is about 3.4 km. from Kedarnath. It is usually referred to as Gandhi *sarover*, because Mahatma Gandhi's ashes were submerged in this lake. The floating icebergs and deep blue waters attract trekkers to this spot each year. The access to the lake is through the moraines at the back of the temple of Lord Kedarnath.

Basukital - The Exquisite Lake : Basuki Lake is a pearl set in an unrivalled natural setting. The water is crystal clear and often seen with floating, glistening blocks of ice. During winter, it is completely frozen. From Kedarnath, one can take a track, which winds its way along the right bank of the Mandakini for 5 km to Basukital.

Some of the other popular destinations around Kedarnath are Trijuginarayan, Guptakashi, Ukhimath, Deoria tal, Chopta and other four Kedars of Panch kedar Group viz. Madhmaheshwar, Tungnath, Rudranath, Kalpeshwar.

Facilities and Amenities at Kedarnath

The trek route from Gaurikund to Kedarnath has sufficient facilities for refreshment and meals on route. However the trek route is uneven, *'Kutcha'* road, which is used by pilgrims going on foot, horses, *palkies* etc. The horses, do not have specified lane in the trekking route and there is no regulation of flow of traffic on this route. There is an urgent need for the regulation of the rates and the traffic of horses and *palkies*. There is no proper arrangement for midway shelters where pilgrims can take rest or escape from rainfall or snowfalls. There is a need to improve the trek route and to setup midway facilities such as tin sheds, *sulabh sauchalayas*, fast food centres etc. In order to avoid congestion at the temple, the tourist traffic should be regulated at Gaurikund in the pattern of Vaishno Devi temple of Jammu. The tourist statistics for the Chardhams of Garhwal indicate that tourist traffic is more in easily accessible places. Therefore, if the trek route of Kedarnath can be covered through ropeways, the tourist traffic can be increased. During the season Kedarnath can accommodate quite a large number of visitors with around 1700 beds available in its different accommodation units. The list of accommodation units is mentioned in the annexture. The accommodation units have reasonable standard facilities and are quite expensive. On the contrary there are many inexpensive stay places with the *Pandas* who look after their clients on traditional style.

YAMUNOTRI

Yamunotri, the source of river Yamuna, is the westernmost shrine in Garhwal Himalaya, located on a flank of Banderpunch peak, at the height of 3,323 Mts. The Shrine of Yamunotri is one of the 'four Dhams' of Uttaranchal. The source of river Yamuna lies about 1 km. ahead at an altitude of about 4421 Mts. It is said that sage Asit had his hermitage here. All his life, he took bath both in Ganga and Yamuna everyday. During his old age when he could not go to Gangotri, a soft stream of Ganga appeared in Yamunotri for him. Since then the stream jetting out of rocks is also worshipped here, as Ganga.

The temple of Yamuna is on the foothill of Kalind on the left bank of Yamuna. The temple was constructed by king Pratap Shah of Tehri Garhwal and is not very big. The idol of Yamuna is made of black marble. Both Ganga and Yamuna have been extremely benevolent to mankind and are responsible for nurturing and developing the Indian civilization. Hence both the rivers have been given the place of divine mother. Thus Yamuna, like Ganga, is worshipped both in temple and in her actual form. Close to the temple there are a few hot water springs, where water gushes out from the mountain cavities at boiling point. *Surya Kund* is the most important *Kund*. Near Surya Kund there is a slab of stone known as *Dibya Shila* or the slab of divine light. This slab is worshipped before *puja* is offered to Yamuna. Near the temple another hot water pool known as *Jamuna bai Kund* is located. This Kund is reported to have been constructed by some devout pilgrims during 18th and 19th century. A dip in the Kund is most rejuvenating and refreshing. Taptakund, Suryakund, Gaurikund are the other important kunds near the Yamnotri temple. After Pooja and a heart filling *darshan* of this divine theatre, the pilgrims have to return to Jankibai chatti for the night halt, as there are no adequate accommodation facilities at Yamunotri.

The *pandas* of Yamunotri come from the village of Kharsali, which is on the other bank of the Yamuna near Jankibaichatti. The temple opens each year on the auspicious day of *Akshaya-Tritiya*, which generally falls during the last week of April, or the first week of May. The temple always closes on the sacred day of *Diwali* with a brief ceremony. The temple workers return to their villages and for rest of time the valley is gripped in no-man's silence and covered with white sheet of snow.

Yamunotri is easily accessible from Rishikesh and Dehradun. The Shrine of Yamunotri, source of river Yamuna is situated in the direction opposite to Gangotri and the road bifurcates and goes to Yamunotri from Dharasu, a place between Tehri and Uttarkashi. Yamunotri can also be visited Via Mussoorie-Barkot. Yamunotri is 222 Kms. from Rishikesh via Tehri and Dharasu and 175 kms from Dehradun via Mussoorie-Barkot. Hanuman Chatti is the last road head from where one has to trek 13 km. to reach Yamunotri. On this way one can stay at Janaki Chatti, 7 km. from Hanuman Chatti.

GANGOTRI

In the midst of giant deodars and conifers, nestles the tiny settlement of Gangotri at a height of 3140 m. On the Right Bank of the river is the holy temple of Ganga, whilst on the left bank there are the few *Ashrams* and *Dharamsalas*. According to mythology, Goddess Ganga-the daughter of heaven, manifested herself in the form of a river to absolve the sins of King Bhagirath's predecessors, following his severe penance. The Gorkha Commander Amar Singh Thapa of Nepal originally constructed the temple of Ganga in 1823 and also appointed the *Pandas* of Mukhwa villager near Harshil, as the *pujaries*, and donated the entire forestland between Mukhwa and Gangotri to the temple on *goonth*. The existing temple is said to be the one reconstructed by the Jaipur rulers.

Ganga is worshipped as the sacred river, as well as a Goddess in the temple. Both forms of worship have purposeful significance. The temples and idols arouse faith and devotion, which the Indians have in Ganga and hence the relevance of the Ganga temple in the presence of the real Ganga flowing nearby. All *pujas* are preceded by a holy bath in the river. The *pujaris* are Brahmins from the village of Mukhwa. Every year, ten of them are selected in rotation to take charge of all the functions concerning the

Fig No 3.1

Gaumukh Nandanvan Tapovan Trek

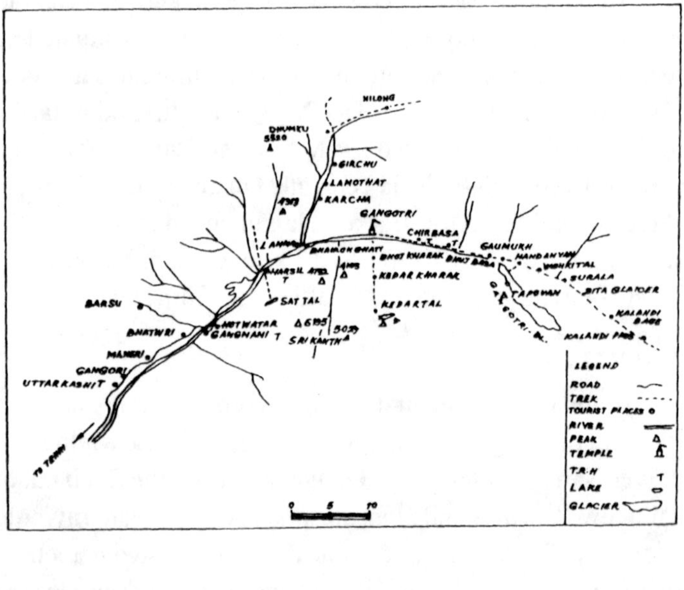

temple. Unlike Badrinath temple, the office of *Rawal* does not exist and the pujaris perform the duties of *Rawal*.

Like Yamunotri, the Shrine of Gangotri opens every year on the auspicious day of *Akshaya-Tritiya*, which normally falls during the last week of April, or the first week of May. The temple opens with a formal *puja* of goddess Ganga both in the temple and on the riverbank. The opening day is duly announced through the press and other media. The temple of Gangotri closes on the day of *Diwali*. The *pujaris*, ir the midst of an array of oil lamps perform the closing ceremony alongwith the usual *puja* rituals. After the closing rituals, the entire temple staff and remaining pilgrims return to their respective places, leaving behind Gangotri to the care of mother Ganga.

Gangotri is accessible from Rishikesh, which is well connected by other places of India. It is 100 km from Uttarkashi and 240 km from Rishikesh. Tourist Rest House, Travelers Lodge, P.W.D. Inspection House, Forest rest house, Temple committee Dharmshala etc. are available. En route accommodations are available at Uttarkashi, Bhatwari, Harsil and Lanka.

Gaumukh

Almost 18-km. northeast of Gangotri at a height of 3980 Mts. Gaumukh is the recognised source of the Ganga. The Ganga is a huge forceful river, which rushes out of the Gaumukh snout. After 8 km. Of trekking from Gangotri towards Gaumukh one can reach Cheedwasa. The place derives its name from the dense forest of Cheed (Pine). It is an enchanting place surrounded by steep mountains. People can take night stay here in *Kali-Kamli Dharamshala*. From Cheedwasa as the pilgrims start further journey towards Gaumukh, there is a dense forest of ***Bhojpatra***, and this place is called Bhojwasa. Beautiful Natural surroundings and pleasant view of Nelang and Bhrigupanth are main attraction of this place. Gaumukh is 6 km. from here.

HEMKUND SHAHIB

Located at an altitude of 4329 Mts. Hemkund is a lake between *Narparvat* and *Rataban* peak. Hemkund or Lokpal Sarovar has been a place of pilgrimage from many centuries, venerated equally by *Hindus* and *Sikhs*. To the Hindus this lake is known as *Lokpal* or *Laxman Kund* and is mentioned in *Narad* and *Vishnu Purans*. Another name for this lake is *Dandapushkarni* lake (lake created by boring), derived from a legend according to which, Lord Krishna created the lake by striking the earth by a rod fashioned from a mountain peak. In 1937 Havaldar Sohan Singh discovered the lake and identified it as that referred to in the Guru Granth Sahib. Bhai Vir Singh, a famous Punjabi Poet and member of Golden Temple Gurudwara committee assisted him.

At this place *Gurudwara Sahib* stands on the shore of Hemkund and it is said that Guru Govind Singh in an earlier incarnation, worshipped fearsome Goddess *Kalika Mata*. Since Guru Govind Singh is honoured and revered by Sikhs, Hindus and pilgrims of other faiths a Gurudwara was built here in 1938. Hemkund Lake was created by marine blockade and is encircled by famous peaks of the Nanda Devi, Nanda Ghunti, Trishul, and others. It is fed by glaciers descending from Hathi Parvat and Sapta Shringa Peaks. On the banks of this lake also stands an ancient Laxman temple, where Laxman is believed to have been brought after he was mortally wounded in battle with Meghnath (Ravana's son). The indigenous *Bhotiyas* traditionally celebrates *Janmashtami* the festival commemorating the birth of Lord Krishna, at Hemkund.

Hemkund can be reached from Rishikesh. Last road head is Govind Ghat, which is 18 kms. from Joshimath on Joshimath-Badrinath road. From Govind Ghat there is 19 kms trek till Ghangharia, from where Hemkund can be reached after a trek of 6 kms. One can also visit the Valley of Flowers, which is 5 kms. from Ghangharia. Various amenities and necessary facilities like Hospital, Bank, Petrol pumps are located at Joshimath. However, post and telegraph facilities are available at Govind Ghat. Horses, *Dandies, Coolies* and Ponies are available at Govindghat and Ghangharia for carrying persons and luggage to Valley of flowers or Hemkund. Accommodations for pilgrims and affluent visitors are available at Ghangariya and Hemkund.

OTHER PILGRIMAGE DESTINATIONS

There are some other places, which are important pilgrimage destination, but at the national level they are somewhat lesser known.

Panch Prayags

Prayag means confluence of two or more rivers. These *Prayags* are termed holy in religious epics like Ramayana and Mahabharata. From Centuries, people take holy bath in these Prayags. It is said that the water of Holy River is supposed to washaway the sins.

Vishnu Prayag: It is located on Joshimath - Badrinath route at an altitude of 1392 Mts. and is the confluecnce of Dhauli Ganga and Alaknanda rivers. From centuries Vishnuprayag is a place of penance and worship of devotees of God Vishnu. According to mythology *Narad* worshipped Lord *Vishnu* here. An ancient Vishnu Temple and *Vishnukund* attract pilgrims here. It is twelve kms. away from Joshimath on Badrinath route. People opting for trek route have an easy three kms descend from Joshimath to Vishnuprayag.

Nanda Prayag: Nand Prayag is 22 kms away from Karnprayag on Badrinath route at an altitude of 914 Mts. Here river Nandakini, originating from Trishul Mountain and Alaknanda meet each other. The place derives its name from Nanda, the Yadava King and foster father of Lord Krishna. It is said that King Nanda organised a grand *Yagnya* here. Besides the confluence, Laxshmi-narayan Temple, famous Gopalji temples, Chandika temple of Goddess Kali and Vishishthaswar Mahadev temples are the main attractions for visitors. In the name of tourist amenities, Tourist Rest House, Banks, Primary Health Centre and Post Office are located here.

Karnaprayag: At an altitude of 795 Mts. Karnprayag is 31 kms. away from Rudraprayag on Badrinath road. The road from here diverts to Adi Badri, Ranikhet, Almora, Kausani and Gwaldam.

It is the confluence place of rivers Pindar and Alaknanda. According to mythology Karna, one of the main character of the *Mahabharata*, worshipped Sun God (Surya) with the help of Goddess Uma at this place. Getting pleased by Karna's devotion Surya blessed him with unpenetrable Guards and Arrows (*Akshaya Kavach* and *Tuneers*). Hence this place is named as Karnaprayag. Besides the confluence, Karn Temple, Uma Devi Temple and Karna Shila where Karna did the penance are the major attractions for the pilgrims here. In the name of amenities accommodation units, Banks, Petrol Pump, Primary Health Centre and Post Office are available here.

Rudraprayag: Rudraprayag is located at an altitude of 610 Mts. on Badrinath highway and 34 kms.away from Srinagar. It is known for the confluence of Mandakini and Alaknanda rivers. This *Prayag* is named after Rudra and there is an interesting legend associated with ancient temple where Shiva is worshipped in the form of Rudra Nath. The sage *Narada* meditated here for several years in order to reach perfection in music. Shiva was pleased and granted the sage's fond wish. Narada became the metaphor for classical music. But this also made him a man of intolerable conceit. Lord Krishna then decided to bring him back to earth by playing a trick on him. He told Narada that Shiva and Parvati had expressly wished to hear him Sing. Krishna then accompanied Narada on his way to Kedarkhand to meet the two. At Rudraprayag, they came across several very attractive women... all with mutilated limbs. In reply to a query they were informed that they were the *Ragas* and *Raginis*. Narada had maimed with distortions in music. This humbled Narada who asked Krishna what he could do to atone for his conceit. Krishna told him to study music under Mahadev. And so Narada learnt under his tutelage, to play the *Veena*.

Best view in Rudraprayag is of *Sangam*, where Alaknanda coming from Badrinath and Mandakini coming from Kedarnath meet each other. The water of Mandakini is slightly blackish because of that it is also called *Kaliganga*. Opposite of this, water of Alaknanda is whitish. This is the reason Alaknanda is also called

Dhauli Ganga. There are down stairs to go to the confluence. Above *Sangam*, the temple of *Rudreshwar Mahadev* is located. According to Kedarkhand *Devarshi Narad* penanced here to get musical powers. 4km. Away from Rudraprayag, temple of Koteshwar Mahadev is located. It is on the Right Bank of river Alaknanda. The deity is inside a cave and the water falls naturally on the deity drop by drop, which attracts tourists.

Rudra Prayag is an important transit point on Badrinath route as the road diverts to Kedarnath from here. Besides various accommodation units, Banks, Primary Health Centre, Petrol Pump, Post Office are available.

Devprayag: Devprayag is 71 kms. from Rishikesh on Delhi-Niti national highway. The river Ganga begins her journey from the confluence of the Alakanada and the Bhagirathi. It is described in *Kedarkhand* that Lord Rama after killing demon king Ravana, came to this place. Later, Dev Sharma, who was a great devotee of Lord Rama, penance here for many years and this place later on named as Devprayag after him.

Architecturally rich, *Nagar style* Raghunath temple is the main attraction for pilgrims. Inside the temple there is a 1.8 Mt. high image of *Raghunath* (Lord Rama) made of black stone. Other images of importance are *Janaki and Lakshmana*. The temple is historical and beautiful. Ancient stone written sculptures are evidence of it. The sculptures on the walls display both Buddhist and South Indian influences. In the compound of temple there is a deity of Garur. It is believed that Lord Shankaracharya built the temple. Deities *of* Badrinath, Kalbhairava, Lord Shiva *and Hanuman* are also there in the compound of the temple. Other places of pilgrim interest around Devprayag are Varahshila, Betalshila, Bharat temple, Suryatirth, Brahmakund and Vasishthakund near Sangam.

Devprayag is en route destination on Rishikesh-Badrinath highway. Tourist rest house and other budget hotels are available here besides Primary Health Centre, Bank, Petrol Pump and Post Office.

Panch Badris

These include Shri Badrinath Dham and four other Badris, which are -

- Adi Badri (Adbadri)
- Yog Badri
- Bhavishya Badri
- Dhyan Badri

Adi Badri: It is 17 kms. from Karanaprayag on Karanprayag-Ranikhet road. It is believed that Badrivishal was worshipped here before the establishment of Badrinath temple. Historians are of the opinion that the temple is of Gupta era. A group of sixteen temples is here, which are quite different from other temples of Garhwal in their style. The most beautiful temple is Narayan temple. Inside the temple there is a three feet tall idol of Lord Vishnu, which is carved, in black stone. PWD Guest House and eateries are available for overnight stay.

Yog Badri: The Yog Badri temple is situated at Pandukeshwar (1920 Mts.), 24 kms. before Badrinath. The image of Lord Vishnu is worshipped here in meditative posture. According to legends the Pandavas retired here after giving over Hastinapur to King Parikshit. Their father, king Pandu, too spent his last days here, doing penance. Some famous copper plates have also been recovered here bearing inscriptions, which provide valuable information about history of this temple.

Bhavishya Badri: Bhavishya Badri (Badri of future) is situated at Subain, beyond Tapovan and 17 kms away from Joshimath on Joshimath-Malari road, at an altitude of 2744 Mts. amidst dense forest. To reach here one has to trek around 3km above the Dhauli Ganga. Legend prophesies that the day will come when the present route to Badrinath will be inaccessible and then Lord Badrinath will be worshipped here. The main attractions for pilgrims in Bhavishya Badri are a deity of Lord Vishnu and two hot water springs in the valley nearby the temple.

Dhyan Badri: The temple of Dhyan Badri is located at Urgam. It is approachable from Helang, which is seven km before Joshimath on the main Rishikesh-Badrinath route. It is believed that Lord Vishnu was worshipped here before the enshrinement of Badrinath by Adi Guru Shankaracharya. Deity of Laxminarayan is main idol, which is worshipped here. Badrinath temple committee looks after the temple. The temple is of local importance. But due to its proximity to the Urgam valley with its enchanting view and the temples of Kalpeshwar, one of the Kedars, Dhyan Badri attracts pilgrims and nature lovers alike. The temple remains open throughout the year. Dharamshala and villagers offer accommodation facilities. However, tourists prefer to return back on the same day of their arrival.

Narsing Badri: There is a great controversy to include it as one of the Badries keeping in view its historic association with Gods and Goddesses. A few historians have identified it one of the Badries. It is located at Joshimath, and serve as the winter seat of the Rawal, the chief Priest of the Badrinath Temple, a *Namboodari* Keralite Brahmin. The image of Lord Vishnu carved from a *Shaligram*, was supposedly crafted in the 8th century. Joshimath was the capital of Katuri dynasty that ruled Garhwal in early medieval period. Later on the capital was shifted to Kumaon. Why Katyuri capital was removed from Joshimath to Baijnath, according to legendary accounts is related to Narshingh. It is said that once on an auspicious day Narasingha visited the palace of king as a Brahmin when the king was away for hunting. The queen entertained him. When the king returned and discovered the Brahmin in his bed he struck and wounded him on the hand. The Brahmin then revealed his real identity and ordered the Raja of Katyuri to move to Baijnath. The wound on the Brahmin's hand is reflected on the idol's hand, which has become weather beaten. People believe that one day the hand will finally fall off and Badrinath Shrine will be shifted to Bhavishya Badri near Tapovan.

Panch Kedars

Kedar is another name of Lord Shiva. Shiva is worshipped at four other Kedars excluding the main temple of Kedarnath. These are -

(a) Madmaheshwar

(b) Tungnath

(c) Rudranath

(d) Kalpeshwar

According to legendary account Rishi Vyas told the Pandavas that they were guilty of '*gotra hatya*' or fratricide and their sins would be expiated only if Shiva pardoned them. So Pandavas began to look for Shiva and Shiva kept avoiding them. The five places, where they spotted him, now hold the five Shiva temples, known as the '*Panch Kedar*s'. Each one is identified with a part of his body. Tungnath, where his shoulders; at Kedarnath, his hump; at Rudranath, his face; at Kalpeshwar, his hair and at Madmaheshwar, his navel were supposedly seen.

Madmaheshwar: Madmaheswar is located at an altitude of 3289 Mts., 24 Kms. away from Kalimath. It has no historical account about the time of its construction. The navel portion of lord Shiva is worshipped here. A *Shivling* of the shape of navel is inside the temple. *Brahmakamal* grows here in abundance. Located against serenity, the temple has no crowd of *Pandas, Pujaris*, shops or the bustle of major pilgrimage centres. The Kedarnath Trust looks after the temple. The sole Pujari is selected by the *Mandir Samiti* and is assisted by four volunteers belonging to panwar family of Gaundar village. The temple is closed for six months during winter, when the silver idols are taken ceremonially to Okhimath for worship. *Saraswati Kund* where '*tarpans*' are offered is close by.

Madmaheswar is 24-km. trek from Kalimath on the main Kedarnath route. The trek from Kalimath is hard and steep. It is a pathway of unparalleled scenic beauty with the magnificent snow capped peaks of Chaukhamba, Kedarnath and Nilkanth. Kalimath, the famous *sidhapith*, is 19 km. away from Ukhimath. Gaundar village, at the confluence of Madmeshwar Ganga and Markanga Ganga, is the last settlement before one reaches Madmaheswar and is 11 km. away. There is a small *Dharamshala* and provisions must be carried from the Village of Gaundar. Tourist Rest Houses are there at Ukhimath, Sonprayag, Gaurikund and Chopta. Banks and Post Offices exist at Guptakashi and Gaurikund and Primary health centres are there at both these places.

Tungnath: Tungnath, the highest Kedar, is located at an altitude of 3680 m. It is 28 km. away from Ukhimath. There are no historical evidences about the time of its construction. But the idol of Shankaracharya inside a temple gives the clue that Adiguru

Fig No.3.2

Panch Kedar Trek

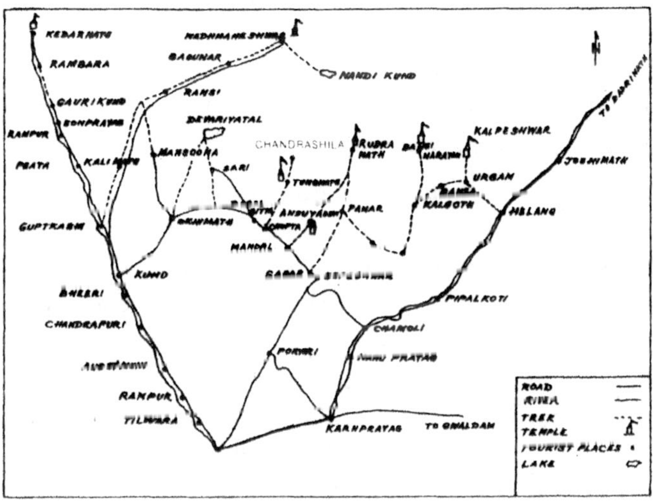

Shankaracharya restored it during 9th and 12th century AD. The main temple is made of stylishly cut stones. The main deity inside the temple is of Lord Shiva. But other smaller deities are also there in the temple. The temple is of Nagar form with Katyuri Shikhara. People worship Shoulder shaped Shivling in the temple. Lord Shiva is worshipped for six summer months in the temple. In the winter the movable deity is taken to Makoomath. Just above the temple, *Ravan Shila* is located and it is believed that Ravana penanced here. Just near Tungnath peak a water source is there which is named as *Papnashini Akashganga* water stream. Tungnath gives amazing view of Great Himalaya. In the East Nandadevi and Dronachal; in North Rudranath, Badrinath, Kedarnath, Gangotri, Yamunotri, in the south Kandolia Mountain of Pauri and in west the shrine of Chandrabadni can be seen. Who have ever spend at least one day in the shore of Deoriatal or wandered through the jungles of Tungnath, they can't forget Garhwal.

From Ukhimath there is 28 Kms. motor route till Chopta, and from Chopta it can be reached after 4 Kms. trek. In route trekkers are rewarded with the sight of varieties of Rhododendron and breathtaking alpine meadows. *Kali Kamli Dharmshala* is located at Tungnath beside a number of accommodations offered by *Pandas*. HNB Garhwal University's High Altitude Plant Physiology Research Centre (H.A.P.P.R.C.) is located here which makes an in depth study of flora of the region.

Rudranath: Rudranath is at an altitude of 2286 Mts., and 23 Kms. from Gopeshwar. To reach there one has to cover 5 km. of the distance by moterable road and rest 18 km. has to be trekked. The trek passes through wild orchards and picturesque *bugyals* and involves trekking over high ridges of 4000 Mt. A cross-country trek from Gopeshwar to Joshimath via Rudranath, Nandikund, and Urgam or Vice-versa is really thrilling. According to *Skandapuran*, Lord Shiva started to live here in Rudranath after killing *Andhkasur*. Since then Rudranath became the worship place of Lord Shiva.

This is the only temple in India, where head/face portion of Lord Shiva is worshipped. Other small temples are also around the main temple. Finely carved statues of *Saraswati* and *Seshasayi* are main features of the temples. In Rudranth lord Shiva is worshipped for six summer months. In winter the worship takes place at Gopeshwar, which is the seat place of Rudranath. The temple is looked after by *Rawal*. Several purified water tanks like *Surajkund, Chandrakund* and *Tarakund* are located near this hallowed site. The legendary river of Hindu faith, the Vaitarni flows near this temple. Anusuya Devi, another famous temple dedicated to Goddess Anusuya Devi, is en route to Rudranath. Accommodation and other amenities are available here as well at Ukhimath, Chopta, Chamoli, and Gopeswar.

Kalpeshwar: It is located in Urgam valley at an altitude of 2,134 Mts. above sea level. One has to trek 11 Kms. from Helang, which is 14 kms away from Joshimath and 17 kms. from Pipalkoti. Most of the trek is gradual climb and 2km before Kalpeswar; one can find the friendly villagers of Urgam.

According to Kedarkhand, *Indra* worshipped Lord Shiva here to get rid of the curse of *Rishi Durwasa*. Being pleased by Indra's devotion, Lord Shiva gave him *Kalptaru*. Hence this place is known as Kalpeshwar. The main temple is a beautiful cave temple renowned for the adornment of Lord Shiva's hair.

Temple of Lord Vishnu is at Urgam 2 km. from Kalpeshwar. It is a favorite destination of pilgrim trekkers. In August this area is ornamented by multicolored flora. River Karmanasha flows here with divine sanctity.

Accommodations and other facilities like Bank, Medical Centres are available at Pipalkoti and Joshimath. The details of Panch Kedars are projected in the table.

Table - 3.4
Treks to Panch Kedars

Kedarnath	3583 Mts. -
Base	-Gaurikund
Trek	-14 kms.
Gaurikund to Kedarnath	
Madmaheshwar	3289 Mts.
Base	-Kalimath and Mansoona
Trek	-24 kms.
Kalimath to Ransi to Gaundar to Madmaheshwar	
Rudranath	2286 Mts.
Base	-Gopeshwar (Sagar)
Trek	- 18 kms.
Tungnath	3680 Mts.
Base	- Chopta
Trek	-4 kms.
Kalpeshwar	2134 Mts
Base	- Helang
Trek	- 11 kms.

Besides these popular pilgrimage places, various other pilgrimage places are there in Garhwal and have their influence due to their sacredness and local importance.

RELIGIOUS DESTINATIONS OF PAURI GARHWAL

Kinkaleshwar Temple: It is an 8th century Shiva temple. The main deities in the temple are *Shiva*, *Ganesh*, *Parvati* and *Kartikey*. Other deities in the temple just behind the main temple are of Lord Ram, Laxman and Sita. One can see magnificent view of Himalaya, Alaknanda Valley and town itself from this place.

Kandolia: A Shiva temple (Kandolia Devta) is located in dense forest on Kandolia hills. Adjacent to this temple is a beautiful park, sports complex. One side of this place gives a beautiful view of Pauri town and other side of it gives view of beautiful *Gagwarsyun* valley. Kandolia is one km. ascend on foot from bus stand or two kms by Motorable road.

Nagdev: It is much-worshipped temple of snake God (*Nag*) and situated in dense forest of pine and rhododendron. On the way to temple a telescope is installed from where one can see the magnificent view of the Himalaya. The temple is located on Pauri - Bubakhal road and 5 km. from bus stop. One can reach there by a trek of 1 km.

Places of Pilgrim Interest around Pauri Town

Jwalpa Devi: It is a famous *Shakti Peeth* of this area dedicated to Goddess Durga. A special worship is offered during *Navratras*. People come from far and near to pray for the fulfillment of their desires. It is 33 km. away from Pauri on Pauri-Kotdwara route. Tourist Rest House and Dharmshala are available here.

Binsar Mahadev: Binsar Mahadev temple is located at an altitude of 2480 Mts. in dense forest of Birch, Rhododendron and Deodar. A grand temple is situated at this place. In the sanctum sanctorum of the temple, deities of *Har-gauri*, ***Ganesh*** and *Mahishamardini* are there. It is believed that Maharaja Prithu built the temple in the memory of his father Bindu. This temple is also known as Bindeshwar.

A big fair takes place here on the occasion of *Vaikunth Chaturdasi* every year. Women taking lamp (*deepak*) on their palms pray for blessing of a baby for nightlong. It is believed that their desires are fulfilled. A 12-km. trek from here leads to Dudhatoli, (3001 Mts.). On the way trekker is rewarded by the sight of beautiful flowers, waterfalls and *Bugyals* (Pasturelands). View of clear blue sky and white spread peaks from here is magnificent. Dudhatoli was the dreamland of great freedom fighter *Veer Chandra Singh Garhwali*. Every year on 12th June a big cultural fair is organised here in his memory. At Brahmadungi 2 km. away from Dudhatoli, a big stone statue of *Veer Chandra Singh Garhwali* is placed.

Binsar is 114 km. from Pauri. Last motorable road is Thalisan 96 km. away from Pauri. Forest Rest House, P.W.D. Rest House and Dharmshala are the accommodation units there.

Srinagar: Srinagar is one of the important towns of Garhwal and was the capital of Garhwal rulers during 18th and 19th Century. Situated on the left bank of river Alaknanda (78°44' 27" E; 30°08" N) at an elevation of 579Mts, it sprawls into a spacious valley (8 km long) with low hills (1500m) in the environs and fertile flood plains, and river terraces. It is an important transit point on the Yatra route leading to Badrinath, Kedarnath, the Valley of Flowers, Hemkund, Nanda Devi, Roopkund, Auli, inviting pilgrims, tourists, naturalists, scientists, and mountaineers from India and overseas. Srinagar is also a centre of learning, housing a University, a polytechnic and Industrial Training centre.

It is believed that during ancient time, a demon named Kolapur lived here. King Satyendra Singh penance here to get *Sriyantra* for killing the demon and was successful in doing so. Since then the place was known as Sripur and later it became Srinagar. Srinagar acquired a legendary character when religious scriptures like the Mahabharat; Purans and the like mention its existence.

Kamleshwar Mahadev, a very ancient Shiva temple, is located here. It is believed that lord Rama worshipped Shiva here and offered lotus flowers to him. Shiva tested Rama's devotion by stealing one of the flowers, and lord Rama was ready to offer his eye to replace the lost flower. On seeing this lord Shiva was pleased and blessed him Sudarshan Chakra. Hence this place is known as Kamleshwar. On the occasion of *Vaikunth Chaturdashi* special worship is performed and a big fair takes place here as organised at Binsar. Women worship lord Shiva for whole night holding lamp (*Deepak)* on their palms. It is believed that by worshipping lord Shiva with such devotion, one's desire for a baby is fulfilled. Kilkileswar and Shankarmath are the other famous temples of Srinagar.

Places of Pilgrim Interest around Srinagar Town

Dhari Devi: Dhari Devi is much worshipped Goddess of the region. It is a Goddess Kali temple. Stone-carved deity of Goddess is in the temple. People are of the opinion that the deity changes face of a girl, woman and of old lady as the day progresses. A myth says that once a severe flood washed away a temple and Dhari Devi's idol was trapped against a rock near the village Dharo. Villagers heard the wail of the idol and a divine voice directed them to install the idol there, where it was found. Another voice from the sky asked them to worship the deity.

Every year on the occasion of *Navratras* special worship is offered to Goddess. People come from far and near to this sacred haunt in large number in these days. An ancient cave is also located near the temple. Village Kaliasaur is on Srinagar-Rudraprayag road. A 2.5 km. cement path takes down to river Alaknanda on whose bank the temple is located.

Raj-Rajeshwari Devalgarh: A 16th Century famous temple of Raj-Rajeshwari (*Durga*) built in a two storied room is at Deval garh. The temple is now partially ruined but is of great importance. Kangda King Dewal established Dewalgarh in 14th century. Deity of Satyanarayan, Bhairav and stone written documents of Pawar rulers Ajaypal and Manshah are also here. A fair is held every year in the month of April in Dewalgarh. It is 17 kms. away on Srinagar-Bughani road. However 9 km. long trek route still exits.

PLACES OF PILGRIMS INTEREST IN TEHRI GARHWAL

Chandrabadni: At an altitude of 2756 Mts., the temple of Chandrabadni is one of the most beautiful temples in the region. Swami Manmathan of Kerala rebuilt this sacred temple in 1990-91. But the sanctum sanctorum is not disturbed. The temple is of hexagonal shape and made up of finely cut red marbles. People come here in large number from far and near to offer *Pooja* especially on the occasion of *Ashtami* of *Chaitra* and *Magh* months. This place has the potential to become a very good hang-gliding place because of high altitude and wide spread valley.

It is 55 kms from Tehri and 36 kms. from Devprayag. Up to Kandikhal en route to Srinagar - Tehri, motor road exists and then temple is an eight kms. walk. One can also approach from Jurana village via Jamnikhal en route Dev Prayag-Tehri. Further, there is a link road up to Nekhari (8 km.) and then a bridle path (2 km.) leading to the temple.

A *Dharamshala* is available in the temple, which is looked after by head Priest of the temple. Boarding facilities are also available in the temple. Bhuvaneshwari Ashram is just below the temple near Anjanisen. Garhwal Mandal Vikas Nigam Tourist Bungalow and other accommodation facilities are available at Devprayag, Tehri and Nekhari (2 km. before temple).

Fig No.3.3: Devi Darshan Circuit

Sem-Mukhem: It is situated in the interior of the district. The people of the area hold the temple of Nagraja at Sem-Mukem in high esteem. Transportation facilities are available up to Khamba khal, a distance of 64 kms, from Tehri. One has to trek about 7 kms. from the road to reach Sem. The temple is situated at the top of a hill about 5 kms. from the village Mukhem, which is 2 kms from Khamba khal. Visitors are requested not to visit this place during rainy season. The 'Pandas' of the village provide accommodation.

Kunjapuri Temple: Kunjapuri temple is situated at about 11 kms from Narendra Nagar and 27 kms from Rishikesh on the way to Gangotri. It is located at an altitude of 1,677 Mts. above sea level commanding a superb view of the Himalayan range on the north and Rishikesh, Haridwar and Doon valley on the south. Kunjapuri hosts a vibrant annual fair on the occasion of *Durga Ashtami* in October. The din of weeklong celebrations and echoes of cultural programmes make Kunjapuri a Sight to behold. The Government is presently considering linking Kunjapuri with Lakhamnjhula by ropeway so that a circuit for heritage sites could be made.

Surkandha Devi: The temple of Surkandha Devi is situated at an altitude of 2,903 Mts. in the dense forest of pine, oak. The temple is of great religious significance and people from far and near visit this temple. A fair is held every year on '*Ganga Dushera*' (May-June) in which thousands of people take part. The place commands a magnificent view of the snow clad Himalayan ranges and also of the neighbouring area. It is located on Mussoorie-Chamba motor road, 38 km from Mussoorie and 22 kms from Chamba. Up to village Kaddukhal, motorable road exists and from there one has to trek 2 km to reach Surkhanda Devi. Every necessary facilities are available at New Tehri, which is newly created District Head Quarter of the District of Tehri Garhwal. It is 12 km. from Chamba. It would become an important centre of attraction on the completion of the dam.

PLACES OF PILGRIM INTEREST IN CHAMOLI AND RUDRA PRAYAG

Joshimath: It is at an altitude of 1875 m. In the eighth century, Adi Guru Shankaracharya attained enlightenment under a mulberry tree inside a cave here and established a *Math* (religious centre) known as '*Jyotir*'. Joshimath is a derivative of the name "Jyotir Math". He wrote the famous Shankar Bhashya in his zest to revive Hinduism. Jyotirmath, the Adiguru's seat is worshipped by hundred's of pilgrims each day and in the evening the Sankaracharya delivers the holy *Pravachan*. Amongst the many temples of Joshimath, the most famous are the Narsingh and the Durga temples. In the eighth century A.D. King Lalithditya Yukta Pida, of Kashmir established the temple of Narsingha. The Statue of Lord Narsingha, an incarnation of Lord Vishnu is carved out of a *Shaligram* and it is an exquisite work of art. It is believed that one arm of the statue is becoming thinner year by year, and ultimately, this will break. When this happens, it will cause a great deluge and catastrophe in the world and the mountains of Jay and Vijaya at Vishnuprayag will collapse, closing the way to Badrinath. Then a new world will emerge and Lord Badrinath will reappear at Bhawishya Badri. Lord Badrinath is worshipped in Narsingh temple during the winter months when Badrinath temple is closed.

Joshimath is the base for visiting many important tourist destinations and for expeditions to important peaks like Trisul, Kamet, Dunagiri, Nanda Devi etc. Hence all the facilities are available to the tourist here.

Anusuya Devi: Anusuya Devi temple is near Mandal in Ansuya village. Goddess Anusuya was the wife of Rishi Atri. She was very much kind and devoted in service of mankind. It is said that once trinity of Hindu religion, *Brahma, Vishnu* and *Mahesh* tried to examine her husband hood but they were unsuccessful in disturbing her sacredness. They were so influenced by her, that they called her Goddess '*Mata*'. Goddess is worshipped as '*Mata Ansuya Devi*'. People from far and near come here to pray for a child. It's believed that their desire is fulfilled. Every year in the month of December on '*Datatray-Jayanti*' a big fair takes place in the temple. Motorable route exists till Mandal, which is 13 km away from Gopeswar. One can reach there by covering 5-km. trek.

Kalimath: This temple is at an altitude of 1403 Mts. near Guptakashi. Main deity in the temple is of *Mahakali*. Other deities are *Saraswati, Mahalakhsmi* and some partially ruined deities of God *Ganesh, Kartikey* and a *Shivling*. Two things in the temple are of great importance. One is stone written sculpture and other is the deity of *Hargauri*. "Deity of Hargauri" is the most beautiful deity of all existing deities of India. Dual dcity is made of a single stone of 40" (inch) in length and 24" (inch) in breath. Adjoining Katyuri style Laxmi temple is of 11-12th century AD. On the outer wall of temple there is a written sculpture, with 20" long and 10" in breadth. Two other temples of Goddess *Rakeswari* and *Kotimaheswari* are located seven and two km from Ranci respectively. It is 6 km. from Guptakashi by motorable road. A small Dharamshala, 7 km. away from the temple is at Ransi.

Trijuginarayan: It is at an altitude of 1982 Mts. on Rudraprayag-Gaurikund-Kedarnath route, near Soneprayag. The village of Trijuginarayan is on the ancient bridle path that goes from Kedarnath to Gangotri. According to legend, wedding of Lord Shiva and Parvati was solemnised here. The nuptial fire has been kept alive down the ages and is ceremoniously sustained even today at the Trijuginarayan temple here. Pilgrims offer wood to the fire that has seen three *yugas*, hence the name Trijuginarayan. The ashes from this fire are supposed to promote conjugal bliss. It is 13 km. by road or 5 km. on foot from Soneprayag.

Ukhimath: Ukhimath is located at an altitude of 1350 Mts. on Kedarnath route. This is the seat place of Lord *Kedarnath*, and during winter when Kedarnath becomes inaccessible due to heavy snowfall, the movable deity of Lord *Kedarnath* is worshipped in

Ukhimath for six months. The Chief Priest of Kedarnath lives here for these six winter months. The temple is made of stone rocks and its Shikhara is of *Katyuri* style, similar to the majorities of temples in Uttarakhand. Near the seat place of God Kedareshwar, a golden deity of *Panchmukhi Mahadev* and *Parvati* are there. In the next room deities of Kunti, and of five Pandavas are there. Ukhimath is 41 kms. from Rudraprayag and 13 kms from Guptakashi.

Guptakashi: At an altitude of 1479 Mts. Guptakashi is a scenic town on the route to Kedarnath and Madhmaheswar. Lord Shiva according to Hindu mythology, is said to have come here elude his pursue, to the Pandavas, who sought absolution for their sins. The temple of Chandra Shekhar Mahadev and *Ardhnarishwar* are located here. In front of the Mahadev temple there is a small pond known as *Manikarnika Kund* which is fed by two springs. It is 39 kms. from Rudraprayag on Kedarnath route.

Gaurikund: It is at an altitude of 1982Mts., 5 km. from Soneprayag and last motorhead for Kedarnath. Two water springs, cold and hot are here. It is believed that Goddess Parwati first took '*Ritu Snan*' (bath) in these kunds. Godess Parvati/Gauri meditated here to win a consort in Lord Shiva. An historic temple dedicated to Goddess Gauri represents the cosmic episode.

PLACES OF PILGRIMAGE IN UTTARKASHI DISTRICT

Places of Pilgrimage in and Around Uttarkashi Town

Uttarkashi was originally a part of Tehri Garhwal. In 1960, it was made a border district with the district headquarter at Uttarkashi. Uttarkashi is a small and beautiful town, en route to Gangotri, situated between two rivers, Varuna and Ashi, whose water flow into Bhagirathi from either side of the town. Elevated, at a height of 1588 Mts., this little town is very similar to Varanashi, in that it has the same kind of temples and ghats and like wise, a north or '*Uttar*' facing river. It is believed that in the second millennium of *Kaliyug*,

Kashi will be submerged and Uttarkashi will replace it as an important religious centre. Of the many temples in Uttarkashi, the major temple is the Vishwanath temple.

Vishwanath Temple is located in the heart of the city. A massive iron trident is erected in the temple, carrying an inscription in Sanskrit. According to it, the temple was built by king Ganeswar, whose son Guh was a great warrior and had the trident forged. The trident is 26ft. high, has a base of 8ft. 9 inch and a top of 1 ft. 1.5 inch in circumference.

TEMPLES IN DEHRADUN

Tapkeshwar Mahadev: This temple is dedicated to Lord Shiva and connected by city bus services up to 'Garhi' five and half kms. from city. A fair is held every year on the occasion of '*Shiva Ratri*' at the temple. The strange thing about the temple is that the water continuously drops on the Shivaling through a small hole in the rock.

Laxman Sidh: It is situated at a distance of 12 km. from Dehradun on Dehradun-Rishikesh road. Vehicles can go right up to the temple. The place is dedicated to a saint known as Lakshmansidh.

3.2 ARCHITECTURAL HERITAGE

On the basis of architectural style the temples of Garhwal can be classified into three-the flat topped temples of early Gupta period; temples of early *Nagara* form; and temples of Nagara form with a modified *shikhara* known as *katyuri shikhara*. Most of the ancient temples of Garhwal are of early nagara form and design (7th-9th century AD). Adbadri, Simli and Tapoban groups of temples belong to this category. However, all the prominent temples of Garhwal have katyuris shikhara and belong to a later date (11th-12th century AD). Temples of Deoprayag, Trijuginarayana, Kedarnath, Badrinath, Ranihat and Dewalgarh can be classed in this category. In addition, they show an impact of hill tradition in the two superimposed parasols one over the *gandi* and the other over the *amalaka*-each resting on a framework of wood and covered by thin slabs of slate. The details of architectural heritage is given in table below:

Table -3.5

Architectural/Artistic Resources of Garhwal

Name of the Centre	Temple Architecture	Description of the attraction Carvings and Sculptures	Other Attractions
Adibadri	Groups of 16 temples of Nagara form, seven of them are more ancient.	Figures of Ganga-Yamuna, Ganesh, Gandharva, Kinnaris and door keepers carved on the doors of temples and statue of Har-Gauri.	
Tapoban	Three Shakti Temples of Gupta period (one of them flat roof); one temple with *Katy-uri shikhara*	Figure of Adinath carved on the door; statues of Mahishamardini, Har-Gauri, Ganesh, Naugrah and Ashtamatris.	Remains of the walls of old temples and some fort or Ashra m; carved stone slabs and pillars scattered all around.
Simli	A collection of temples of Gupta period.	Statues of Har-Gauri, Ganesh, Mahishamardini, a rare piece of three faced scul pture with the face... of Vishnu in the centre and of Barah and Narsingh on either sides.	
Joshimath	A collection of temples of Nagara form with Katy-uri shikhara-many of them dilapidated (partially been overt hrown by earthquakes)	A man sized statue of Vasudeva(Vishnu) beautifully carved in black granite, an example of very superior workmanship; statues of Naudurga Har-Gauri and a brass image of Garura.	

1	2	3	4
Kalimath		Statue of Har-Gauri' excellent specimen of sculpture.	Many broken and damaged pieces of sculpture and Lingas scattered around the temple.
Ukhimath		Statues of Surya, Natraj, Navdurga carved in stone; statues of Shiva, Parvati, Mandhata, Anirudh and Usha in metal.	
Gopesh war	A 13th century temple of Nagara.	Figures of gods and goddesses carved on the outer walls and many broken images signifying iconoclastic activities	A trident in the courtyard of the temple with inscriptions in Brahmi script.
Deoprayag	An ancient temple of Nagara form with Katyuri Shikhara.	A man-sized statue of Raghunathji carved in black stone.	Outside the temple inscriptions on a stone slab in Gupta Brahmi script.
Badrinath	Temple of Nagara form with Katyuri shikhara, renovated several time concealing old structure.	A broken image of Badrinath carved in black stone.	
Kedarnath	Nagara form of temple with Katyuri shikhara (11th-12th century AD).	Eight man-sized statues (including those of five Pandavas); broken statues in smaller temples around the main temple.	
Dewalgarh	A collection of temples (most of them dilapidated); chief temple relatively new (15th century AD).	Beautifully carved statues of Har-Gauri, Mahishamardini and Ganesh.	
Rudranath		Finely carved statues of Sarasvati and Shesh-Shayi.	

1	2	3	4
Moradh-waj	Dilapidated stone temples of Kushana period (4th-8th century AD).	Stucco and terracotta images depicting mythological episodes of Krishna and several human and animal terr-acotta figures of 2nd century B.C. to 1st century AD	Ruins of a fort and a Buddhist-Stupa mai-nly of archaeological interest.
Panduwala	Ancient temple		Carved stone slabs, Pillars and door frames (all scattered in forests); and other material of archa-eological interest.

Source: Kaur, J., 1985, Himalayan Pilgrimages and the New Tourism, Himalayan Books, New Delhi.

Garhwal has some important monuments, which have been declared by the Archaeological Survey of India as protected monuments of national importance. A list of such monuments is presented in the following table.

Table - 3.6

List of Centrally Protected Monuments in Garhwal

Location	**Monuments**
Dehradun District	
Hanol	Temple dedicated to Mahasu (Shiva)
Kalsi	Ashoka's pillar
Karampur	Kalinga monuments
Lakhamandal	Temple and images in its vicinity
Chamoli District	
Adibadri	Remains of 16 temples
Chandpur	Fort with walls and ruins of dwelling homes inside it, and the flights of steps
Gopeshwar	Rudranath temple

1	2
Gopeshwar	Trident of iron with a shaft with one ancient and three modern inscriptions
Pandukeshwar	Two temples
Mandal	Rock inscriptions
Uttarkashi District	
Purola	Ancient excavated site-Stupa of the Kushan period (1st century AD)

Source: Archaeological Survey of India, Monuments Department.

Fig No.3.4

Historical and Archaeological Sites in Garhwal

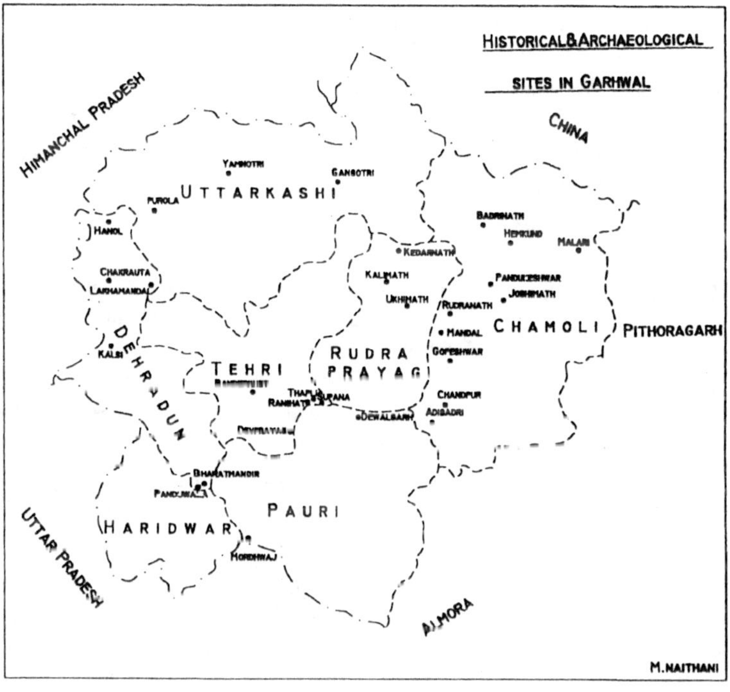

References

Atkinson, E.T. (1973). *The Himalayan Gazetteer*, Vol. III, Cosmo Publication, New Delhi.

Badrinath Master Plan (1979).

Bhardwaj, S.M., (1973). Hindu Places of Pilgrimage in India, Thomson Press Ltd., Delhi.

Bisht, D.S., (1982). Guide to Garhwal and Kumaun Hills, Dehradun, Trishul Publication.

Bisht, Harshvanti, (1994). Tourism in Garhwal Himalaya: With Special Reference to Mountaineering and Trekking in Uttarkashi and Chamoli Districts, Indus Publishing Company, New Delhi.

Dabral, S.P., (1960). Uttarakhand Yatra Darshan, (in Hindi) Veer Gatha Prakashan, Dogadda Garhwal.

Dabral, S.P., (1965). Uttarakhand Ka Itihas, (in Hindi) Veer Gatha Prakashan, Dogadda Garhwal.

Darian, S.G., (1978). The Ganges in Myth and History. The University Press Hawaii, Honolulu.

Datar, B.N., (1961). Himalayan Pilgrimage, Publication Division, Ministry of Broadcasting, New Delhi.

Director, U.P. Tourism (Hills). *Chardham of U.P. Hills*, U.P. Tourism (Hills), Dehradun.

Fonia, K.S. (1987). *Uttarakhand: The Land of Jungles, Temples and Snow*, Lancers Books, New Delhi.

Fonia, K.S., (1998). The Traveller's Guide to Uttarakhand, Garuda Books, Chamoli Garhwal.

ICIMOD (1995). Mountain Tourism for Local Community Development A report on case Studies in Kinnaur District H.P. and the Badrinath Tourist Zone, ICIMOD, Kathmandu, Nepal.

International Centre for Integrated Mountain Development (ICIMOD), (1995). *Mountain Tourism in Himachal Pradesh and the Hill Districts of Uttar Pradesh*, ICIMOD, Kathmandu, Nepal.

Kamlesh Kumar and Nityanand, (1989). The Holy Himalaya: A geogrphical Interpretation of Garhwal, Daya Publishing House, Delhi.

Kaur, J. (1985). *Himalayan Pilgrimage and The New Tourism*, pp.105-125.

Khanduri, B.M. (1994). *Archaeology of Alaknanda Valley (Central Himalaya)*, Book India Publishing Co., New Delhi

Naithani, S.P. (1994). *Uttrakhand Ke Tirth and Mandir (in Hindi)*, Pavetri Prakashan, Srinagar Garhwal.

Negi, J.M.S. (1995). *Himalayan Heritage: A Socio-Economic, Cultural and Tourism Analysis*, Gitanjali Publishing House, New Delhi.

Negi, S.S. (1991). *Himalayan Rivers, Lakes and Glaciers*, Indus Publishing Company, New Delhi.

Negi, S.S. (1994). *Garhwal: The Land and People*, Indus Publishing Company, New Delhi.

O'akley, E.S., (1905). *The Holy Himalaya*, London.

O'akley, E.S., and Gairola, T.D., (1935). *The Himalayan Folklore*, Allahabad.

Patiram, (1917). *Garhwal Ancient and Modern*, Army Press, Shimla.

Raturi, H.K., (1980). *Garhwal Ka Itihas (in Hindi)* Bhagirathi Prakashan, Tehri Garhwal.

Singh, T.V. (1973). *"Badrinath: A Study in Himalayan Pilgrimages", Uttar Bharat Bhugal Patrika*, Gaurakhpur.

U.P. Tourism (Hills) (1997). *Report on Area Development Plan for the Char Dham Circuit in U.P. Hills*, Dehradun.

4

SOCIO-CULTURAL HERITAGE

4.1. FAIRS AND FESTIVALS

The fairs and festivals of Garhwal is important heritage tourism product. They have got religious, cultural, economic and environmental importance. They provide a kaleidoscopic view of the Culture for those both who look from outside and the insiders who are participants and performers themselves. The dazzling variety and numbers of fairs and festivals of Garhwal mirrors an exuberant, throbbing and age old culture which over the years has been trying to assert, define, redefine and reinforce itself. The carnivals of Garhwal can be classified, first, thematically such as religious, seasonal, sportive and agricultural and government sponsored exhibitions. The second classification is regional, varying from valley to valley. Thirdly, it can be divided into *Shabvism*, *Shaktism*, *Vaishnavism*, and local *Shamanism* etc. But the division is useful for the tourists. Whatever be the nature of classification, mapping of the festivals is required to be completed on the basis of cultural units called *Pattis* (*shires*), valleys, Cultural Countries e.g., Rawain and Jaunsar, and finally the districts.

The following are the main cultural Valleys of Garhwal:

1. Tons : (i) Rupin ii) Supin ; 2. Bhagirathi;3. Dhahari (Jalkur); 4. Bal Ganga; 5. Bhilangana; 6. Kamal Nadi; 7. Yamuna; 8. Lastan; 9. Mandakini; 10. Alaknanda; 11. Dhauli Ganga; 12. Nandakini; 13. Pinder; 14. Virahi; 15. Ram Ganga; 16. Atagad; 17. Khankara Gad; 18. Eastern Naiyar; 19. Western Naiyar; 20. Henwal Nadi

If the myths of every village of Garhwal could be collected, one would excitingly find that every stone, well, rivulet, tree, a hillock, cultivation is attributed to the Pandavas, Ram, Laxman, Sita, Gauri (Nanda), Nags, and *Vir Devatas* (the gods of Power). Every river and rivulet sprang up by the grace of gods or goddess sitting at the mountaintop. The remarkable feature of Garhwali ethos is gratefulness to the forces of nature. Accordingly, the patron god of a village or string of villages, called "*Bhumyal*" has to be offered a "*thaul*"* (festival and concomitant rituals) every year as a mark of respect and reverence.The divine powers are worshipped as a deity and invited to earth periodically, their lives are re-enacted through ritual, dance, and drama, and then given a good bye. Thus, the *Jaat*(Processional journey), *Banyaat* (re-enactment) and *Deora* (divine utsitation) are held for several deities of Garhwal. The occasion rituals turns into a massive fair attended by devotees ranging from five to twenty thousands.

To understand exactly what the fairs and festivals of Garhwal are like, profile of a few festivals is given below:-

Processional Performance:

In Garhwal, festivals of large scale are celebrated during processional performances of deities, which go on their human journey through the territory of their devotees, which is deemed to be the territory of the deities themselves. By this, it seeks the participation of entire fraternity and creates an occasion to show

---

* *Thaul* is the term for fairs used in Tehri, Pauri, Uttarkashi districts and Pinder Valley of Chamoli. "*Ausar*" is the term used in a region around Joshimath (chamoli) and "*Mela*" a general term in vogue in all regions of Garhwal.

solidarity among the community members. The heightened and charged atmospherė has its own uniqueness. Although, every festival contains the elements of processional ritual, some of them follow a definite structure sharing commonness with others. These are *Nanda Raj Jaat, Chooti Jaat, Nandikund Jaat, Deoras of shaktis, Tungnath, Madhyamaheswar, Nain, Vasudev, Mahasu, Jaakh, Kans, Dwari, Hariyali, Kartikeya, Trijugi Narayan, Uma Devi, Karn, Someshwar, Ghandiyal, Hooneshwar, Nagarja, Bautya, Kandar, Silgur, Agastyamuni, Kumasen, Saheja Devi and Nagela*. A description of *Jakh* processional ritual around Joshimath will reveal the structure of all such performances.

"*Jakhs*", "*Yakschas*" were the sixty thousand soldiers of *Yakscha Raj* Kuber, the keeper of north direction ("Van Prabha" Mahabharat 139, 5-7). The ballad song in Bembru village narrates him as *Babhru bahan*, the warrior of the Mahabhrat. He lived through the war with his trunk less head. After the war, Bhim took him on a pilgrimage to all sacred places of Kedarkhand (legendary name of Garhwal) as an act of penance for having be-headed him deceitfully by Krishna. The myth is reenacted in *Dummak, Kalangot, Bemru, Baunala, Pokhani, Tangari, Palda, Urgam, Thaing, Rampeer, Raigaun and Lasi* Villages around Joshimath and in Jakhdhar (Near Narayankoti in Mandakini Valley). The event runs over six months in villages around Joshimath while it is concluded in three days at Jakhdhar. On the second of *Baisakh* a thrilling fire walking event is held. It is preceded by a mysterious gothi (sacred pastiament), a procession and mundi (collection and piling of firewood in eleven layers measuring 18 feet). It is burnt and converted into cinders.

1. The ritual recurs after every 24 years.
2. The presiding deity shows inauspicious symptoms to the devout, once the tenure of 24 years is passed. So, the festival is held whenever falling due.
3. On the due date, first a purifactory ritual is held by circling a goat, a pig, and a hen around the village and then they are

sacrificed. The sacrifice is called *Ashtbali* (sacrifice of eight, including animals and fruits).

4. All relatives and *dhiyans* (out married daughter) have been invited with utmost care and attention.

5. With all festive excitements, the *Pooja* (ritual) begins at around 7 P.M.

The image of the deity is given a purifactory ritual (*Shakalikaran*). It is enlivened and then brought out to a thatched tent close by the permanent temple (the space is called *Banatoli*). Now the *maitis* of deity (the villagers of Pokhari in case of the Jakh of Bemru) arrive with *Kandi-Kales* (a big basketful of porridge, deep-fried breads, lentil, cutlet etc.). The main feature of gods and goddesses of Uttarakhand is that every one of them has a *mait* (natal village) *and a sasural* (in-law's village). In Banatoli, Jakh is given a *Kachhana* (make-up, ornamentation, and consecration) by the *maitis*. The deity, *hoisted on the top of a pole*, is animated and endowed with miraculous powers (sixty-four magical properties are consecrated inside the hexagonal ensign of the deity). It then comes to *Kilamuni* (an eminent and fortified space), meant for rest overnight. The history of the deity is sung all-night through. In the next morning, the possessed oracle of Jakh selects three dharis (bearers of the ensigns). The *dharis* have to go on a pilgrimage for six months. In the daytime, the procession of the god reaches a place where he is offered *Chholbhatta* (home-profanation of the sacred with common feast). A goat is sacrificed here. On the fortissimos of *dhol* and *damaun* drums, the shrill sound of *gongs*, the ruffling and gliding blasts of *Bhankoras*, the procession (the sign, *KandiKale*, masks, utensils, the priest, oracles of different attendant deities, and the devotees) moves from door to door. The procession finally terminates at *Panchayati Chowk* (Council Square) where the deity is prayed, in soothing songs, to go to sleep. Around 10 PM, the mask dance-drama begins in the arena. As many as 18 masked characters appear and present some full-length plays, some cameos, and some tableaux. However, the myth of *Narsingh, Baraah, Ram, Laxman* and *Sita* is enacted on the nightlong performances. The dance-dramas with masks are performed every night all through the six-month procession, no matter whether it rains or snows. The dances like *Dhankuri, Chanchari, Jhumalio* are played every night. Staying for three days in the village, the procession then moves towards the other villages on god's territory. First, it goes to Rudranath (one of Panchkedaras), pays its obeisance to lord Shiva and returns. Passing from village to village, the deity, then, goes to Badrinath. Finally it returns to the seat of the God. Wherever it passes through, a *mela* gathers.

Other Processional Performances

The famous *Nanda Raj Jaat, Chhoti Jaat and Nandikund Jaat*, reenact the myth of the post marital journeys of the divine *dhiyan Gaura* or *Nanda*, one of the forms of *Shakti* between her natal place risasan and her husband's place Kailash. The *Raj Jaat* covers the longest traverse of 280 kms from Kansua in Atagad valley to Homkund (Trisul Mountain) and secures participation of near about lakhs of devotees. There are two *Raj Jaat*; one is known as small *Raj Jaat*, which is performed after every second year and ends at Vednikund. *Nanda Raj jaat* or *Bari-Raj-Jaat*, is performed after every twelfth year. The eternal procession of *Chalda Mahasu* on both the flanks of Tons River in Jaunsar tribal area comes next in range and magnitude. The number of devotees present at the time of its movement is calculated to thirty thousand.

The procession of *Nain* (nine serpent sisters) varies in an event called "*Kanspaara*" (tearing out the body of Kansa, the demon maternal uncle of Krishna). But the uniqueness of its is that when the nine km long snake made of grass is pulled towards the river along with the sign of the goddess, representing her violent death in the mythical past, the shaman succeeds in fanning the emotions of the devotees. He sings a wailing song. The male villagers repeat it and some minutes after, a woman or two start sobbing. The sob becomes infectious and more women weep. Then with a lightening speed the snake is pulled to two directions downhill and uphill. The thousand of women present their wail hysterically and rush after the snake, believing that their snake *dhiyan* is going to meet a violent death even as now. In the year 1995 on the final day of Nain of Sankot (Badhan, Pinder Valley) around twenty thousand spectators and devotees were reported present. Besides this the processional performances held on the seasonal migration of the *dolis* (palanquins) and *nishans* (signs) of Badrinath (Joshimath to Badrinath), Rudranath (Gopeswar to Rudranath), Tungnath (Makkoo-Tungnath), Madmaheswar (Okhimath-Madmaheswar), Gangotri (Dharali-Gangotri) and Yamnotri (Khairsali-Yamunotri) also entail sizable melas twice a year.

Fairs at Stations and Altars

The festivals of Heet, Binsar, Narayan, Pandav, Narsing, Chandra Badani, Surkanda, Maniknath, etc. are held at their proper shrines. Several ritual events are held for several deities and massive *melas* occur on the day of special events. Unique fairs are held in Kamleshwar (Srinagar), Anusuya Devi (near Gopeswar), Balkhileswar (Balganga Valley), Mahadev Temple in Kandarsyun (Basar-Tehri), Madhim fair (Dalgaun - Basar, Tehri) and Ghautakaran temple. Punanu (Anjanisain, Tehri) and Kameleshwar (Srinagar) are two famous fairs where young women and their husbands desiring to have an issue perform a nightlong prayer. They keep a standing watch keeping a burning earthen lamp in their palms and in some temples, they also give an abhishek (sacred wash) to the shivling. It is found that most of them are blessed with a child.

Thauls and Ausars

As stated earlier, the term *Thaul*" in Garhwal, refers to fairs held in the name of deities and persons who assumed historical significance in their lifetime. But an individual who wants to perpetuate the memory of his ancestors or any departed member of the family, usually donates a fulsome amount of money or land for holding a fair. Such fairs are baptised as "*Jhankar*".

"*Bissu*" the corruption of the word "Baisakhi" (which fall on April 13 every year) stands alone as a fair and festival. It arouses to gaiety, rhythmic motion, and song in each and every village in Rawain (Uttarkashi), Jaunpur (Tehri), and Jaunsaar-Babar (Dehradun). Participation of each member of the community even if one were in America, is a must. The houses and village streets are decorated with the lines of rhododendron flower; the fields are worshipped, a square representing *Goga* (the god of season) is demolished, and finally the sensational game of bow and arrow, "*Thoda*", is played. After a couple of days *Bissu* is held at a central Place inviting participation of the entire *Patti*. The number of people participated in *Bissus* of Thana Daandaa is approximately twenty thousand.In the game of bow and arrow inflexible rules are followed like hitting the arrow only below the knee, hitting it without disrupting the rhythm of the dance providing the footwork of the sport and in the end begging pardon from the man being hit.

Festivals of annual calendar also throw up small fairs like *Dol Jaatara, Chweela in Chaitra, Maudhavi in Jeshta, Asaris or Jakholis in Aashaar, Saunez in Sharavan, Jagaras in Bhadaun, Haryalakas in Aswin, Burhi Diwali in Margshir, Marojin in Paush-Magh*. Such festivals express gratefulness and obeisance to the power of nature.

Angling the fish and Hitting the Ball (Maun) : *Maun* i.e. *timru* powder or killing the fishes with Timru (*Zanthoxylum alatum*) powder, is the grand sport of Rawain Jaunpur, and Jaunsar - Babar regions. In a subdued manner, it is also held at Satpuli and Massaun (Pauri), Aglad and Bhadrigad (Jaunpur - Tehri), Kamold, Mungaraa and Barahi Gaad (Rawai - Uttarkashi), Daragaad, Kirangaad, Dungiara and Riknaad (Jaunsar - Babar - Dehradun). The claimants to the fish treasure group themselves into two generally consisting of two slopes of the catchment. *Timru* powder is arranged turn by turn every year. The rival groups come to the riverside in a threatening procession, wielding sticks and axes, dancing and singing and typing red and white cloth pieces around their heads as if willing to become martyrs. The parties take position strictly to the places allotted to them at the riverside. The horn plays a signal and the headmen open the powder bags. The powder is poured into the river and the sport begins. Serious clashes also occur, as reported in 1978, over the catch. The catch is taken home and the biggest fish is offered to the village deity.

Gindi Fair : It is commonly known as *Gindi Ka Mela* and is held in Mawakot, Dadamandi, Sangura, Thal Nadi, Kaans Khet, and Ghandiyal (in Pauri District) on Makar Sankranti. A stuffed ball is made out of hard leather with two hooks to hold, measuring one foot in diameter. The parties are divided into two on the basis of slope, catchment, or Patti. The dancing and drumming processions approach with flags and ensigns and stand face to face like two battling armies. The ball is placed in the centre of the field, the trumpets and drums thunder and the game begins. The ball is not kicked like football. It is lifted with hands and is not hitted against the goal post of the adversaries; rather it is to be carried back to one's own boundary. Scores of players stick together to the ball trying to snatch out. The Jostle leads them through bush cobblestones, and sometimes into the riverbed, making all the spaces a playing field. The game continues until a win is registered even if it were midnight.

Other sports Festivals : *Selku* (In Mukhaba, Sauira, Lata, Gorsali, Sainil - Uttarkashi), where the oracle of Someshwar walks on a line of sharp edged axes.

Devlang Festival (Rawain-Gangotri - Uttarkashi): On the occasion of Devlang Parva a tall cedar tree is fixed to which a large number of wooden matches are fixed. After the Pooja, the matches are torched and the devotees are divided into *Sathi* (the 60 *kauravas*) and *pasis* (The five *pandavas*). They try to uproot the cedar tree and tilt it towards each other, as a trial of strength.

Laang Festival (Tehri, Pauri, Uttarkashi): It is performed and held by the *Beda* community. In the *Laang* fair, the performer sets his stomach upon a revolving bearing set upon a 30 feet tall *Laang*. He pirouettes upon it annõuncing loudly the sponsors of each round.

Kathbaddi Festival (Khirsoo-Pauri): It takes place every year at Khirsoo (Pauri). The *Kathbaddi* is treated as a bridegroom visiting Kailash and returning, the third day as "*Ujale Baddi*" (the flaming Baddi)" with burning torches tied to his hands. Seven thousand spectators attended the fair in 1996.

Modern Festivals

Besides the traditional *thauls*, the local administration has been organising sports rallies, autumn festivals, exhibitions and *valmelas*. Fairs like *Gauchar Mela* and Uttarkashi *Magh Mela* draw an incredible crowd and business transactions run into crores. In these festivals attempts are made to bring to the proscenium stage, the folk songs and dances of the people.

Gauchar Mela: Gauchar Mela had been started as a religio-cultural fair, but today it is a trade fair. This starts from 14th November and lasts for a week. Women-folk wear colorful dresses and jewelry. Woolen products (carpets, blankets, shawls, *chugta* and *pankhi*), *ringal* (cane) and wooden artifacts are worth buying at the fair. Today Gauchar and Malari fairs are organised and controlled by government agencies.

4.2 NANDA RAJ JAAT

Nanda Raj Jaat, i.e., going on pilgrimage from Nauti-Ira Vdhani-Nauti-Kansuwa to Shila-samudra is recreated in every twelve years. This is an unique *Yatra* or *Jat* held in every twelve years on *Nandasthami* to escort patron goddess Nanda Devi to her in-laws place near Nanda ghuti Peak.

Myth and Legends

Nanda i.e. incarnation of '*Shakti*' or '*Sati*' or '*Parvati*' was the daughter of Himalaya and Maina Mainduli. Gaura i.e. Nanda, the dearest of them was married to Lord 'Shiva' in the precarious heights of Kailash. The myth of *Nanda jaat* was related to the movement of outmarried daughter (*dhyani*) Nanda to her in-laws house *(sasural)* i.e. Kailash from her mother's home (*maitee*).

At the time of the departure of Gaura, palanquin was prepared for the bride Gaura which was filled with pearls, *rotating chattars* (metallic Umbrella), apexed with golden Umbrella. Thousands of men and women gathered to bid farewell to Gaura. The women burst out and wept before Gaura who also wept ceaselessly. Gaura reached the hermitage of lord Shiva. On the way they halted at Roopkund and Homkund. Thousand of men and women (*maitees*) accompanied Nanda up to Homkund. Lord Shiva requested them to go back and established a *'Sriyantra'* at Homkund. He told that on the "*Astami*" of *Bhadrava*, one could able to see both of them in Sriyantra on worshiping them. Twelve long years after the marriage, Nanda's nostalgia for her *Maika* (Parental home) became intolerable. Mother Mainduli was also longing for meeting her. But it was a difficult task going to invite Nanda who lived in high Himalayas. Then it was *Heet*, one of the four god brothers of Latu, agreed to go to Kailash. Maya Mainduli ordered the *Rudiya* (basket maker) to knit a *Kandi* (basket) and a *Chantoli*(Umbrella) of thin bamboo. She then went to the goldsmith and ordered him to prepare ornaments and the tailor was asked to stitch new cloths. The eatable, ornaments and cloths were packed into the basket. Heet was given the sacred rice and the vocal paper as a protection against the ruinous effect of evil forces.

After twelve years Nanda was able to meet someone from her parental house. She was over whelmed with sentiments and tears. She prepared for the journey to Rishashan. Devi and Heet started for Rishashan. After a few days of stay in her Parental home, the departure of Nanda to the *sasural* (in-laws) took place. With all ritual and musical instruments the farewell was held. All the vintages, eatables, clothes and ornaments were collected and packed. Mother Mainduli's heart became heavier and heavier with the feeling of segregation. With great difficulty weeping Nanda moved out of parental house. Her mother, the menfolk and the womenfolk wept and the atmosphere was sentimental and painful. Nanda went to 'Kailash' through Vyasi, Devprayag, Srinagar, Rudraprayag, Karnaprayag. On the way Nanda and Shiva, passed through Nauti, Kansuwas and a number of other villages of the Himalayas and received healthy welcome and took the promise that she would be invited by them in every twelve years.

Recreation of the Myth: The Jaat

The oldest evidence of *Nanda* cult in Garhwal is found in the three copper plate of Katyuri era found in Yogadhyan temple of Pandukeshwar. The plates bear the royal orders of the three successive Katyuri kings regarding gifting out the piece of land to different temples. In the next plate the kings proudly call themselves the devotees of Nanda. After the kings of Garhwal started accepting Nanda as their patron goddess, the *'Jaat'* was undertaken under their patronage and *"Nanda Jaat"* was named as *"Nanda Raj Jaat"*.

It was difficult to say when *"Nanda Raj Jaat"* was started. But the existence of this *"Raj Jaat"* came to the limelight by historical evidences in the seventh century. In seventh century, Kanakpal, the king of Malwa along with his *purohits* (royal priest) and family members came on pilgrimage to Badrinath. At that time king Bhanupratap, the *chandravanshi* king, was ruling Garhwal. King Bhanupratap had a vision in which Lord Badrinath directed him to marry his only daughter to Kanakpal and to renounce the world and dedicate himself in the service of God. The king went a long way to Rishikesh to receive the prince of Malwa and took him to Chandpurgarhi where the prince and the princes were wedded. King Bhanupratap directed his younger brother Kanasa, kunwar of Kansua to arrange the *Jaat* of patron goddess Nanda on his behalf in future. The *purohits* accompanying the Malwa prince belonged to the family of Bhardwaj rishi (brother of Himalaya) and settled at Nauti. Since Nanda was the daughter of Himalaya, these purohits were considered as the brother of Nanda.

The Adya Gaur Brahmins of Nauti heard the divine beating of *Naubat* (nine drum beats) in the mid of the night and from "*Naubati*" the place derived its name "*Nauti*" and the Adya Gaur Brahmins as "*Nautiyal*". When king Kanakpal heard of the miracle, he asked his royal priests, the *Adya Gaurs of Nauti*, to consecrate Shreeyantra under a square platform there. Through a divine message, the same goddess asked the king to consecrate her shrine at Chandpurgarhi. The remaining attendant *purhoits* of the king settled around his capital and become the twelve *thanis* (Nautiyal, Maithani, Nainwal, Gairola, Chamoli, Semalty, Raturi, Khanduri, Deondi, Semwal, Thapliyal and Nawani) and the *Khshtriyas* become the sixteen *sayanaas* of Badhaan. Whenever Nanda would feel nostalgic to come to Rishashan, she would cause a quadruple horned ram to take birth in Rishashan and the ram would be sent to Kailash as an attending carrier in her return journey.

Rituals of Nanda Raj Jaat

As per the tradition the rishasan folk and the king (now the younger brothers of the king, the kunwars of Kansuwa) decide to invite their *Dhiyan* (married sister) during the plentiful season of *Bhadau* (August-September). A ritual *Manauti* (a ceremonial invitation to Nanda from her husbands home to her parental home) is performed on *Vasant Panchami* and *Heet*, the god brother of *Gaura* is sent to Kailash with a *Ringal Chhantoli* (an umbrella made of hill bamboo). Heet brings the *Chhantoli* from the king's place to Nauti where the detailed programme of *Gaura's* stay and departure is performed. Heet is sent to Kailash symbolically, actually the *Chhantoli* is placed in Shaileswar Math, a Shiva temple near Nauti.Now the dates have been decided and the excitement of seeing Gaura runs high among the folks. On the *pratipada* of *Bhadau* Gaura arrives. Her arrival is celebrated in songs and dances in ritual and in the talks among the folks. From *pratipada* to *shashthi* she stays in her *maika*, dances and plays with her jungle mates, sisters and sister-in laws. She visits the field, the orchards, the herds and the trees. She gourmets to the full of her satisfaction and complains about the hardships of Kailash. On *Saptami*, her emotion laddened, procession for Kailash starts off from Kansuwa, the place of Kunwars (earlier from Chandpurgarhi), the patrons and brothers of Gaura. She walks under the Royal *Chantoli* led by the ram who carries all her luggage.

Gaura's procession, then moves to Nauti, the village of the royal priests and the *Maitees*. From there she goes to meet the descendants of Jaman Singh jadora of Eda Badhani. She is given a red carpet welcome there. She returns to Nauti again and is given the tearful final see off. Gaura bursts out in sobs and tears. Nautiyal Maities *accompany* her who are soon joined by the villagers of Naini who come along with their *Chhantoli*. She then goes to Kansuwa. She passes through Chandpurgarhi where the king of Garhwal gives a grand send off. The *Maities* of Chamola, Gairoli and Chamoli also join her at Ujjwalpur and Sem respectively. She stays at Sem, Koti, Bhagoti, Kulsari and Chepdyun. At Nandkeshari, Gaura joins the great procession of devotees who have also started their procession of sending off the goddess from their own village of Kurur. By this point the devotees of Dasholi, Badhan, Chandpur, and Sirgoor have joined her procession. Next she stops at Faldiyagaon, from there she stops at Mundoli, and then at Wan. At Wan she is accompanied by her god brother Latoo who had once accompanied her from Dhar-Malwa to wan. Latoo leads her way hence forward.

From this place onwards the *Vihar* zone of Gaura begins and she does not allow women, sinners, and omnivorous eaters beyond this point. Also she dislikes noise and dancing in this area. Gaura and her procession halts at Gairoli Paatal, Patar Nachaunyu, Shila Samudra, and on the day of *Durga-Shtami*, Gaura and her animal companion proceed up towards Kailash (Trishul here). Her brother-priests, Nautiyals and Kunwars give her a *pooja* here and with a promise that they will be protected by the goddess, they return along with the other devotees via Chandania ghat, Jaman daali, sutol, and Ghat.. When the *Maities* return back to Nauti, a grand *Yajna* is performed.

Table - 4.1: Nanda Raj Jaat (time table)

Day	Journey	Distance (Kms)
1st	Nauti to Iravdhani(1350mts) via Chaundli	10
2nd	Iravdhani to Nauti(1650mts) via Naini	10
3rd	Nauti to Kansuwa(1500mts)	10
4th	Kansuwa to Sem(1600mts)	10
5th	Sem to Koti(1700mts)	10
6th	Koti to Bhagoti (1650mts)	12
7th	Bhagoti to Kulsari(1000mts) : A special worship at local Kalika temple on New Moon	12
8th	Kulsari to Chepdyun(1350mts)	10
9th	Chepdyun to Faldiagaon(1600mts)	15
10th	Faldiagaon to Mundoli(1850mts)	10
11th	Mundoli to Wan(2400mts) : special worship of Latu Devta	15
12th	Wan to Gairoli Patali(2950mts)	10
13th	Gairoli Patali to Pathar Nachauni(3700mts)	12
14th	Pathar Nachauni to Shail Samudra(4600mts) via Roopkund and Jiura gali dhar	15
15th	Shail Samudra to Chandanighat (Chenshya) in the forest. Special worship at Homkund (4061mts).	16
16th	Chandanighat to Sutol(2200mts)	18
17th	Sutol to Ghat(1500mts)	25
18th	Ghat to Nauti by bus	60
19th	Religious recitation and 'Yagna' started on the first day ends.	

The ritual of the *Jaat* are interesting but not esoteric. The rituals recreate the return of Gaura from her parents home. Thus they are, first recreationary and, then, propitiatory. Gaura becomes a living entity through the rituals. The rituals and the corresponding responses of the vehicle of Nanda are so human that the illusion of performance is cleared out. After Sem, Nanda's vehicle starts weeping because Nauti is no more visible beyond this point. The same happens when Nanda crosses *Kyoor Gadhera* at Narayanbagar and enters the soil of *Sasural* (the area after this rivulet is believed to be her in-law).

Fig No. 4.1

Nanda Raj Jaat Circuit

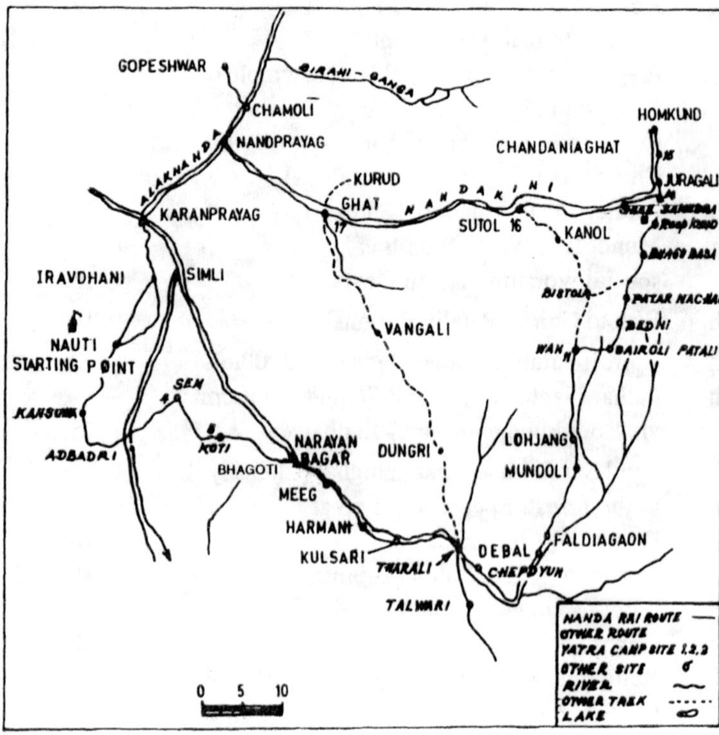

The ritual of *Ashtbali* (eight types of sacrifices) follows on the event of Nanda's life when she had gone under-ground and became *Kali* . *Ashtbali* is given at Chepadiyun, Nandkeshari, Faldiyagaun, Pilkhara, Lohajang, Wan, and Gairoli Paatal. The tradition of *Ashtbali* has been stopped by the anti-bali activists of Garhwal. It has stopped with the *Raj Jaat* since 1968, but continues with the *Chhoti Jaat*. The obsequious rituals are the only extra rituals performed at Baitarani by the royal family and at Shila Samudra by the pilgrims to give oblation to their dead ones. The priests, the members of the royal family, and the devotees walk bare-footed.

Historical Background

When we think of the history of Jaat, a limited evidence is used again and again. The folk history of Nauti and Kansuwa says that the *Jaat* tradition was started by Shalipal, King of Candpurgarhi between 850-858 AD. In the last century , the Nanda Raj Jat was held only five times ;in 1905, 1925, 1951,1968 and 1987. But it has become almost definite that the tradition existed in the 14th century. Swami Pranava Nand has collected a huge number of remains of the dead pilgrims in and around Roopkund most of which prove that the skeletons belong to the *jaat* pilgrims. Broken *Chantolies*, one of the findings, confirm that the dead ones were on *Jaat* pilgrimage. He has corroborated his hypothesis with that episode of *Jaagars* (ballads) sung at Wan and Nauti which sing the sad tale of queen Balampha, her King Jasdhaul and her son Jadela and daughter Jadeeli. According to the *jaagars* the entire army of Balampha perished in the snows for they violated the sanctity of the *jaat* trek. Some of the well known anthropologists have also established the fact through carbon dating process that the skeletons are about 650 years old.

However, there remains a historical puzzle, which of the two *jaats* of Kurur and Nauti-Kansuwa is older. The pre-existence of Nanda cult in Garhwal and the claim by the priests of Kurur that the King of Chandpurgarhi had brought and consecrated the goddess at this capital with the promise that he would bring his *jaat* and merge it with the Kurur *jaat* point to anteriority of Kurur *Jaat*. The ritual of submission of *Raaj Chhautoli* to the *doti* of Kurur also supports the fact. On the other hand the fact of Kanakpal's direct inheritance from the King of Garhwal speaks for facts in favour of Nauti- Kansuwa *Jaat*. The presence of *Shree Yantra* in Nauti and the presence of *Shila Moorti* (stone image) at Kurur again make the rival claims. This puzzle manifested in the sad bifurcation of the two *jaats* at Nandkeshari in 1987 *jaat*. For finding the truth, the researchers will have to take into account the jaat tradition of Urgam, Bemru, Dummak, Kalangot, Lata and Pandukeshwar. The *Jaat* is a grand coming together not only of men but also of the gods and goddess. The deities from all over Chamoli, Pauri, Tehri and Kumaun region meet and embrace one another. The *legion* of the gods starts assembling from Nauti, and it becomes an assembly of about two hundred dancing gods at Van. The *Kotmai Katar* of Nanda meets the procession and returns to Kumaun. Other deities like Dasmdwar Nanda of Kot Kandara; Nanda of Dasoli,;Latoo of Swarkha; Jakh of Lasi; Badrinath of Dimmer; Nanda of Lata, Subhai, and Baloor; Deosing Bhansingh of sutol and numberless others remain with the procession till the end. It becomes a godly pilgrimage and presents a scene of cosmic dancing and cosmic journey.

Touristic Potential

The *Jaat* is a unique heritage tourism product. It gives the opportunity of pilgrimage at different places en route; joy and thrills of adventure through trekking the hills, which provide panoramic view of nature, lakes and high alpine meadows and lively show of colorful dance and dramas along the trek simultaneously. The temples and monuments at each destination of *Jaat* treasure rich historical insights. *Nanda Jaat* has its own mythological and historical background. Nanda was the tutelary goddess of Garhwal and her departure to Kailash became reality,when king recreated the myth by taking the devotees to the high Himalayan region. The religious fervour of the *jaat* continues, but it has now been dominated by the zeal of adventurist and is a real fascinating journey of about 280 km, 4-5 halts of which fall in the uninhabitated Alpine zone. The fascinating beauty of Ali and Bedni pastures; the mysterious water of Roopkund with the ghastly skeletons in it; the deadly slopes of Jyonragali and the Shila Samudra glacier and the forest of Chandnia ghat all fulfill the appetite of adventurers and nature lovers. As a cultural manifestation *jaat* stages a carnival of colour, movements, music, miracles and dances. It documents the socio-ethnic pattern of the folk and the archetypal situation of its emotional growth. Poignant enactment follows one after another along the route of the march. At Madhoghat a place after Kansuwa, the *chhantoli* passes over to the *Deundies*, the *Sasuralies*. The ancient capital with its archaeological importance attract a huge crowd (20,000 during the 1987 *Jaat*). The *Jaat* is greeted with melodious *Jaagars* (ballads) of women and men, the high pitched beats of *dhol-damaun* and the sky-raising symphony of *bhankories*. Every time the procession reaches a new place uncountable numbers of gods and goddesses jump out of the crowds. From Kulsari onward there is a feeling in the air that the tributaries of *Jaat* are flowing parallel. The tributaries, the Ganga of *Raj Jaat* and the Yamuna of Kurur *Jaat* finally make a confluence at Nandkeshari. The myth of king Yasdwal of Kannuj and queen Balpa becomes more mysterious by viewing the "Mystery Lake" of Roopkund. One can see human and equine skeleton remains, sometimes with flesh attached of about 500-600 years ago, well preserved in the alpine condition. Any sensible soul can feel destruction in the snowy winds of the mountains.

It is no small a tribute to the *Jaat* of 1987 that about 3,00,000 (three lakhs) devotees and adventurists participated in it. It became a focus of hot social, cultural and political activities. The lack of infrastructure is creating a lot of problems for the smooth completion of the *Jaat*. The 1951 Jaat had to be abandoned, because of ceaseless hail storm and for want of shelter for the pilgrims. During 1951 and 1968 the basic amenities like medical aid, water and fuel were not available to people participated in pilgrimage procession. The Chamoli district administration helps in providing water, food and medical facilities to the participants in the *Rajjaat* where these are scarse. Otherwise the villagers en route provide all hospitalities to the marching procession. It is no small wonder how a small population dwelling at Nauti and Kulsari ogranise themselves to receive and entertain thousands during Jat celebration. There is a unique custom of keeping everyone's house unlocked in Wan village for use by the *Yatris* on the Jat day, according to the divine instruction of the goddess Nanda Devi. The infrastructure of 1987 Jaat cracked miserably under the pressure of the pilgrims and tourists. At Nauti, from 18th August, 1987 to 20th August, 1987, majority of the visitors found neither proper food to eat nor any place to sleep. There was utter lack of public information system. Mandir Committee made the only sensible but limited arrangement for food. Due to small number of pilgrims the arrangement was all right at Kansuwa, Sem, Koti and Bhagoti. Van faced maximum pressure of pilgrims. The local administration utterly failed in its arrangement of food, fuel and medicine. But the active co-operation of I.T.B. Police *Jawans* came to rescue the pilgrims at various dangerous spots.

Management

An organising committee is functioning for several years named as "Shri Nanda Devi Raj Jat Smiti". It comprises of a President, General Secretary, Joint Secretary and other members. The organising committee constitutes other various committees at various halting points to look after the arrangements. It co-ordinates with the priests of more than 200 Gods and Goddesses of Garhwal-Kumaon and with the Brahmins of 12 *thanis* and 14 *Sayanaas* of *Badhaan*. This organising committee manages all ritual and religious aspects of the Jat. In 1987 Raj jaat, Government spent Rs. 22 lacs and this amount was utilised through different Government channels to build primary infrastructure.

Nanda Raj Jat 2000: The first pilgrimage of the region in the new millennium was held on a grand scale from 21st August, 2000, in a new rhythm but with same faith. Due to media hype and wide publicity even through the Inter net, *Nanda Raj Jat 2000* attracted much more National as well as International interest. District administration had made elaborate arrangement for the Raj Jat 2000 like construction of trek routes, bridges, beautification of sites, provision of accommodation, food, water, electricity, medical and telecommunication facilities. Around Rs. 9.5 lakhs had been sanctioned and spent on development of destination and important spots of Raj Jat circuit like *Raj Rajeshwari Nanda Devi* temple of Karur; the venue of fair at Nauti and Homkund and cleaning of Bedni *bugyal* (meadow) and Bedni Kund. For health and sanitation Rs. 6 Lakhs had been sanctioned. Upgradation of power stations at Karur, Nauti and Faldia gaon took place and lighting facilities was provided at 132 points on the route of the Raj Jat by spending Rs. 7.5 Lakhs . At 19 halting places drinking water facilitiy was made available by spending Rs. 24 Lakhs. For construction and repairing the link roads, trek route and small bridges Rs. 25.55 lakhs was sanctioned and Rs. 13 Lakhs had been specially sanctioned for clearing the land slides. In this Raj Jat reasonably good trek route was constructed up to Roopkund and Jiuragali dhar. A team of Doctors accompanied Raj Jat and telecommunication facility was also provided during the entire route. In spite of all these arrangements, infrastructure was cracked under the pressure of pilgrims and tourists. The en route places especially at high altitudes did not have the infrastructure to meet the needs of great number of tourists. Health and safety problem arose due to bad weather during Raj Jat 2000. From Wan to Bedni around 15,000 to 20,000 tourists / pilgrims were reported. This number reduced to 10,000 at Roopkund and finally 2,000 at Homkund.

4.3. FOLK DANCES AND FOLK SONGS

Four types of important folk dances are prevalent in Garhwal.

1. *Pandav Nritya*

2. *Bagdwal Nritya*
3. *Nag Nritya*
4. *Bhairav Nritya*

Pandav Nritya is performed with bows and arrows displaying fighting posture. Songs are related to the legends of Mahabharat. Dancers disguise themselves as five *Pandavas* and Draupdi. It is prevalent through out the Garhwal.

Bagdwal Nritya is prevalent in the whole of Garhwal except the yamuna valley. It is connected with the legend of Raja Jeet Singh who defeated the Gorkhas and brought back the statue of Someswar. Males and females dance together with *pharsa*(a type of axe) in hand and sing song about the bravery of Jeet Sing. *Bagdwal Nritya* is performed in Niti valley, particularly in Malari village in the months of August and September.

Snake dance (*Nag Nritya*) is performed in a kneeling posture in the courtyard of a house. A saucer of bronze is beaten during the dance.

Bhairav Nritya is just like *Tandav Nritya* of lord Shiva. Furious Postures are exhibited in a great speed and when the dancer is over powered with *Bhairav* he can lick red-hot tongs of iron.

Other popular dances worth mentioning are '*Tharya*' and '*Achhari*'. *Tharya* is a community dance meant purely for fun and enjoyment. In this dance the rhythmical movements of men, women and children, to the accompaniment of *dhol* and *damaun* look extremely graceful.

'*Achharia*' (i.e. literally means "a fairy") is a dance meant only for female dancers. It is performed after the autumn harvest and is the expression of the joy of successful harvesting.

Badi, jagri, das, hurakiya and *miras* sing folk songs. While *badi* sings the songs his wife performs the dance. *Jagri* sings melodious songs related to the legends like Krishna, Pandav, Hanuman, Narsing and other gods and goddess including fairy tales.

During singing one-person drums donr (a medium-sized drum, being beaten by stick on one side by hand on the other) and another beats a bronze plate with a thin stick. These *jagar* songs are sung during night time.

Auji or *Das* sing songs on auspicious occasions like marriage ceremony or *chudakaram* (head-shaving) ceremony at the beat of *dhol*. *Dhol* is a type of drum, which is beaten like dohr, but it is accompanied by *damau* which resemble with tambourine but played with two sticks.

Hurakiya sings *panwada* which is a poetic recitation relating to the history of the terrain and its heroic figures. The people welcome *Panwada* singers who recite the glory of their forefathers and local history. Thus it contains the element of ancestor worship and is sung on the beats of a huraki (a small handy drum with leather mounted on one side and is beaten by one hand). *Mirasi* sings folk songs along with religious songs. They are expert in playing on sarangi.

As the modern civilization is making serious intrusion into the Garhwal culture, the folk dances and music are imperceptibly getting modified and affected. Properly managed heritage tourism can be a savior of such cultural products.

References

Badola, D.N. (1975). *Fairs and Festivals of Pauri District*, Adams Pilgrim Route Report.

Chauhan, S.S. (1977). *Garhwal Himalaya: A Study in Dietic Pattern*, P.R., pp. 25-29.

Devrani, Pitambar (1981). *Garhwal Aur Uska Lok Sahitya* (in Hindi), Garhwal Sahitya Parisad, Allahabad.

Ghosh, A.P. (1990). *Chamoli Charm*, EBD Educational Pvt. Ltd., pp. 34-40.

Hatwal, S.M. (1978). *Fairs and Festivals of Chamoli District*, Adams Pilgrim Route Report, pp. 7.

Kamlesh Kumar and Nityanand (1989), *The Holy Himalaya: A Geographical Interpretation of Garhwal*, Daya Publishing House, Delhi.

Nautiyal Shivanand (1991),*Garhwal Darshan* (in Hindi), Sulabh Prakashan, Lucknow, pp. 72-85.

Negi, R.S. and Singh, J. (1981),Makar Sankranti in Garhwal Himalaya: A Study in Sacred Performances,*Journal of Social Research,* Sept. 1981, pp. 113-123.

Panwar, R.S. (1975). *Fairs and Festivals of Yamuna Valley*, Adams Pilgrim Route Report, pp. 14-19.

Purohit, Beena (1987). *Nanda Raj Jaat: A Case Study of Professional Performances of Garhwal*, PG Diploma in Tourism Dissertation, Department of Tourism, H.N.B. Garhwal University, pp. 40-45.

Purohit, D.R., Personal Manuscript (Unpublished), Department of English, H.N.B. Garhwal University.

Van Prabha, *Mahabharata*, Geeta Press, Gorakhpur.

5

Evaluation of Tourimsm Infrastructure

To attract tourists and to provide them with a satisfying experience, Construction of accommodation, restaurants and passenger transport terminals at tourist places of interest is necessary. These form the superstructure of the region. In addition there must be a sufficiency of roads, railway lines, airport runways, Water, electricity, other utilities to serve not only the local residents but also the tourists influx. These are normally referred to as the infrastructure. If the infrastructure is insufficient to support the total number of people at a destination, both local inhabitants and tourists, then the full potential of a tourist place can't be exploited. In an ideal situation the infrastructure should be created in advance for the overall development of a destination. The infrastructure usually covers a substantial area, takes considerable time to create and involves substantial capital investment. Because of this, it is essential for the central and /or local government to initiate work on the infrastructure. Superstructure elements like hotels and restaurants cover more limited areas and need less capital. They can be developed, owned and run by private sector. In fact, development of infrastructure and superstructure is the prerequisite for the development of tourism. Initially most of the infrastructure had been constructed in Garhwal for the purpose pilgrimage. But recently different kinds of infrastructure are being developed to cater the need of affluent visitors, too.

Existing tourism infrastructure includes the following aspects:-

- Travel links and related transport facilities.
- Accommodation facilities at the places of tourist interest.
- Midway facilities on way to tourist places.
- Tourist offices to disseminate information to visitors.
- Infrastructure for sightseeing.
- Other support and ancillary services

TRAVEL LINKS AND RELATED TRANSPORT FACILITIES

Roads: Till 1925 there were no facilities of transport and communication in Garhwal. Though construction of cart roads started in 1800, only the pilgrims used to traverse this region on foot. The well to do employed coolies to carry their luggage and themselves. However, to complete pilgrimage to Badri-Kedar, Gangotri-Yamunotri was arduous and time consuming. Those days, worst kinds of bridle paths were in existence. The man who took first initiative to construct roads was G.W. Trail, the commissioner (1827-1835) of Kumaon and Garhwal. Prior to him mule and foot tracks were popular here and travel was a tardy and risky job. A 500 Kms length of Pilgrim road between Hardwar-Badrinath, Rudraprayag-Kedarnath, Ukhimath-Chamoli and Karanprayag-Lobha was constructed at his initiative. Road to Rishikesh-Kirtinagar was completed in 1931 and Kritinagar to Karanprayag in 1947, but the network of roads and link roads was formed after independence and particularly after the 1962 Chinese aggression. The Chinese assault stirred us up from slumber and reminded us of our long negligence of roads in Garhwal region. We resorted to quick speedy mechanized construction of roads. The mechanized roads brought landslides, soil erosion and floods. This ultimately forced the planners and policy makers to think in terms of conserving the fragile Eco-system of the region. Though construction of roads made this region accessible, but it destroyed the traditional form of pilgrimage which generated employment for the local people. Even today the condition of roads is not good, most of the roads get obstructed during the rainy season. The details of road is as under and given in table.

Table - 5.1

Major Highways and Connecting Roads in Yatra Route

Constructing Agency	From	To	Via
PWD	Delhi	Yamunotri (SH -57)	Bagpat,Shamli, Saharanpur, Dehradun, Mussoorie, Yamuna Bridge,Barkot, Hanuman chatti.
PWD	Delhi	Rishikesh (SH-45)	Meerut, Roorkee, Haridwar Rishikesh (one road from Roorkee leads to Dehradun also).
DGBR	Rishikesh	Badrinath	Srinagar,Rudraprayag, Chamoli, Joshimath.
PWD	Rudraprayag	Gaurikund (for Kedarnath)	Guptakashi,Sonprayag, August-muni, Kund.
PWD	Kund	Chamoli (From Kedarnath to Badrinath)	Chopta, Gopeswar.
DGBR	Rishikesh	Bhairon Ghati	Narendranagar, Chamba, Tehri, Dharasu, Uttarkashi, Harsil
PWD	Bhairon Ghati	Gangotri (8 Kms.)	

1	2	3	4
PWD	Dharasu	Sayanachatti (for Yamnotri)	Barkot
PWD	Srinagar	Tehri	Gadolia
PWD	Srinagar	Kotdwara	Pauri, Satpuli, Duggadda.
PWD	Karanprayag	Gwaldam	Tharali, Talwari.

Source: Public Work Department (PWD), Government of U.P., Srinagar and Director General Border Roads (DGBR) 1997.

Table - 5.2

Network of Roads in Garhwal Region in 1995

District	Metaled Road (kms.)	Unmetalled Road (kms.)
Uttarkashi	865	694
Chamoli	1324	911
Pauri	3334	1098
Tehri	1525	Not Available
Dehradun	2117	Not Available

Source: PWD, Government of U.P., Srinagar Division, 1996.

Air: Air connection to the region is through Jolly Grant airport at Dehradun (about 16 km. from Rishikesh). However, no airline is flying on this route currently. New airports are coming up at Gaucher (Chamoli) and Chiniyalisaur (Uttarkashi) Which will make this circuit much more approachable if regular flights are operated. A helipad in Badrinath has been built for defense purposes and for high profile visitors.

Rail: Hilly terrain has restricted extension of rail network in the region. For entering Garhwal by railway, the railheads are Dehradun, Rishikesh and Kotdwara. Some important trains connecting Dehradun to other parts of the country make this area accessible to tourists to visit tourist places.

Rail transportation in other areas of Garhwal region is not there as geographic features do not favour further expansion of rail transportation. Though railway out agencies are being run by GMVN (Garhwal Mandal Vikas Nigam) at some places of Garhwal region, but it is not sufficient for greater tourists influx to this area. These railway agencies are connected to Rishikesh or Najeebabad railway station, but it takes a lot of time to make and confirm the reservation to travel out from the area. The only solution to this hurdle is to computerise the booking system and a strong computer network should connect all railways out agencies of Garhwal region to each other.

Road Transport: Most of the routes are well connected by roads. Garhwal was ceremoniously opened for tourism with a network of roads and buses. This was the formal beginning of a new era of tourism in Garhwal, though package tours to *Chardhams* were formally started in 1972 by UttarPradesh Hill Development Corporation. At present there are many transport companies working in the region. The oldest and the largest Transport Company is GMOU (Garhwal Motor Owners Union). G.M.O.U. comprises of motor unions of various districts in the region. During the yatra season all the buses are put in a single pool and buses are taken from this for tourists/pilgrims. In the year 1996 it had 1800 (41 seaters), 60 (27 and 18 seaters) and 36 (13 seaters) buses. In 1976 Garhwal Mandal Vikas Nigam (GMVN) came into existence with a fleet of deluxe coaches given by U.P. Hill Development Corporation. In 1999 it had a fleet strength of 36 buses and 8 cars. Besides it took 80-27 seaters buses on hire. Apart from these, there are buses run by U.P. Roadways, Tehri Garhwal Motor Owners Union Ltd. (TGMOU) and around 1500 taxis operated by Taxi unions and Travel agents.

ACCOMMODATION

Accommodation is one of the most essential tourist facility. Its importance can be measured by the fact that it takes away the largest share of the tourist expenditure pattern. Accommodation includes all available hotels, motels, travelers' lodges, dharmshalas, ashrams, camps and inns. In Garhwal, commercial hospitality system prevails right from the ancient time. It was only pilgrimage , which motivated persons here for solace and salvation. However with the expansion of urbanization more number of visitors started to reach here to see remote places and countryside for rest and recreation.

In Garhwal we see considerably good accommodations for tourists and pilgrims both under public and private sectors, though limited to some key points. GMVN is doing fairly well in this direction whereas private sector entrepreneurs are also coming forward after initial hesitation. Other than GMVN many other government departments have their rest houses and dak bungalow at various tourist centres of Garhwal. Foremost among them are forest rest houses and PWD bungalows. GMVN constructed accommodation at most of the tourist places in Garhwal having 64 accommodation units with 2705 beds, in 1999, but the overall progress is not satisfactory. The available accommodation in Garhwal has been shown in appendix. At points like Rishikesh, Srinagar, Uttarkashi, Joshimath, Badrinath, Gaurikund, Gangotri, Hanuman chatti, and Janki chatti quite a lot has been done for the accommodation. The reason being that a pilgrim or a tourist who comes here has to take his first night halt at Rishikesh before pushing off next day either for Utterkashi or Joshimath (Uttarkshi for Gangotri, Gaumukh and Joshimath for Kedarnath, Badrinath, Valley of flowers and Hemkund-Lokpal). This has resulted in the agglomeration of accommodation at these places.

Apart from Government accommodation ,private owners at various centres run hotels and it includes dharmshalas, chattis, gurudwaras and paying-guest accommodation. But there is a lack of star category hotels in the area. The available total accommodation in Garhwal is not capable of adequately meeting the rush of tourists and may cause many a tourist in busy tourist season to abandon their travel plans to Garhwal. The details of the available accommodation, shortage of accommodation facilities and projection of required accommodation facilities are presented in the tables below. Qualitatively too, the short falls are remarkable. Except for few places like Dehradun, Mussoorie etc. approved star hotels are not available in Garhwal. The GMVN has accommodation at more than 40 places but the facilities offered at these units are of average one star type. Leisure tourists, to whom Garhwal has plenty to offer as well as the myriad young foreign tourists intend to explore the area, face the problem of reasonable quality accommodation.

Table - 5.3

Shortage in Accommodation Facilities (1996)

Particulars	Badrinath	Kedarnath	Yamunotri	Gangotri
Number of visitors	482,900	106,000	99,730	104,335
Number of visitors in Peak Months (25% of annual tourists arrivals)	120,725	26,500	24,933	26,084
Peak number of visitors per day.	4,024	883	831	869
Average stay per tourist	2.5	2.5	3.0	2.0
Peak number of tourist nights (no. of tourists X average stay)	10,060	2,208	2,493	1,739
Number of available beds	5,084	1,673	390	1,469
Add, beds available with pandas& Chatti.	1,271	418	98	367
Total Beds available	6,355	2,091	488	1,836
Shortage of beds	3,705	117	2,006	0
Shortage of rooms (2 beds per room).	1,853	59	1,003	0

Source: U.P. Tourism (Hills), Dehradun.

Table - 5.4

Projection of Required Accommodation Facilities.

	Badrinath	Kadarnath	Yamunotri	Gangotri
	2006	2006	2006	2006
Number of visitors	1,003,678	162,567	171,931	204,709
Number of visitors in Peak Months (25% of annual tourists arrivals)	250,919	42,642	42,983	51,177
Peak number of visitors per day.	8,364	1,355	1,433	1,706
Average stay per tourist	5.0	3.0	3.0	4.0
Peak number of tourist nights (no. of tourists X average stay)	41,820	4,064	4,298	6,824
Number of available beds	5,084	1,673	390	1,469
Add, beds available with pandas& Chatti.	1,271	418	98	367
Total Beds available	6,355	2,091	488	1,836
Shortage of beds	36,736	2,392	3,908	4,987
Shortage of rooms (2 beds per room).	18,368	1,196	1,954	2,494

Source: U.P. Tourism (Hills), Dehradun, 1997

HIGH-WAYS AMENITIES

Highway amenities or roadside amenities play a very important role in tourism promotion. Essential midway amenities include petrol pumps, repair facilities for automobiles, motels, restaurants, cafeterias, road maps and toilets etc. The following table gives the details of petrol pumps and service stations in Garhwal.

Table - 5.5

Petrol Pumps in Garhwal

District	Places where petrol pumps are located
Chamoli and Rudraprayag	Rudraprayag , Karnaprayag, Chamoli, Gopeswar, Pipalkoti, Joshimath, Kund and Simli
Dehradun	Dehradun, Doiwala, Mussoorie, Rishikesh, Vikasngar.
Pauri	Kotdwar, Pauri, Srinagar, Srikot, Satpuli, Lansdowne.
Tehri	Tehri, Muni-ki-Reti, Devprayag, Chamba, New Tehri
Uttarkashi	Uttarkashi, Navgaon, Barkot, Purola.

Source: Uttaranchal Tourism.

Existing wayside amenities are of poor standards. More petrol pumps should be there in the area. The people are sometimes stranded there due to non-availability of petrol, which disturbs travel frequency of visitors. Though most of the places have got service centres but they are not generally located on the way. Vehicle repairs facilities are not adequate and such facilities exist at only limited places after Rishikesh.

Toilets, drinking water, restaurants, eateries, all are in bad shape. Eating places are mostly unhygienic. Toilets made out of hanging gunny bags present ugly sights. Spreading urine and stinking space around the toilets present a deplorable sight. Though opening *Sulabh-Shauchalaya* is a good idea of the state Government, but the scheme is yet to be implemented extensively.

TOURIST INFORMATION CENTRES

Even today all the information regarding treks, trails, climbing equipment, camping kit, porters and other things can not be gathered at one point. Therefore, appropriate and adequate information can not be provided to tourists. The travel agents, accommodation personnel and others who come in contact with the tourists are not properly trained to explain the regions' attractions, routes, country culture, history, geography and archaeology. Such underdeveloped structure of tourism is common in entire Garhwal region. There is a great need of sufficient tourist information centres at different parts of Garhwal, providing sufficient and adequate information to the tourists visiting the area. All the tourist information centres should be linked to each other through a computer network for the sake of rapid communication, providing current information from different areas to the tourists. The tourist information centres provide information to the visitors and are located at Dehradun, Mussoorie, Pauri, Gopeshwar, Narendra Nagar, Uttarkashi, Rishikesh, Srinagar and Joshimath.

BANKING FACILITIES

Banks are also very important for the pilgrims/tourists and the local people. There are sufficient branches of nationalised, non-nationalised, co-operative and scheduled commercial banks in the entire region catering to local people as well as tourists also. But sometimes when a foreign tourist comes in with foreign currency he faces problem of money exchange in Garhwal. So facility of foreign currency exchange are required to be provided at selected destinations like Barkot, Uttarkashi, Srinagar, New Tehri, Rudraprayag, Gopeswar, Joshimath and Badrinath.

TOURISM RELATED INFRASTRUCTURE

Tourism related infrastructural facilities could be mentioned as follows:

- electricity supply.
- clean drinking water.
- disposal of waste and waste water/sewerage system.
- telecommunication.
- medical facilities.

ELECTRICITY SUPPLY

In Garhwal electricity supply is not sufficient and good. Major towns are electrified but the supply is by and large erratic. The percentage of electrified villages in total inhabited villages in entire Garhwal is 60-65 percentage.

The following Tables show working Non-Conventional Energy Development Agency (NEDA) projects in the Char Dham circuit & percentage of electrified villages of Garhwal.

Table - 5.6

Working NEDA Projects in the Char Dam Circuit

Location	Capacity
Ghangaria	50KW
Naini (Chamoli)	50KW
Gangotri*	4 X 5 KW
Pandukeshwar	10 kW
Sahastradhara	10 kW
Deod (Pauri)	50KW
Bilkot (Pauri)	50KW

• Presently only two are in working condition. Source: NEDA

Table - 5.7
Ongoing Power Projects

Location	Capacity
Karanprayag	66 kV substation
Urgam	3 MW Micro Hydel
Kedarnath	100 kW Micro Hydel
Ghangharia	50 kW Micro Hydel
Jankichatti	200 kW
Stargad (Uttarkashi)	200 kW

Table - 5.8

Percentage of Electrified Villages from Total Inhabited Villages

District	Electrified Villages	Percentage of Inhabitants
Pauri	1925	54.59
Chamoli	1087	59.50
Tehri	1312	NA
Dehradun	683	NA
Uttarkashi	491	77.50

Source: NEDA

CLEAN DRINKING WATER

Availability of safe drinking water is a strong hygienic factor for the success of any tourist place. In Garhwal, the responsibility of providing drinking water is of Jal Nigam, which is a state level organisation looking after construction of water supply schemes in the state. These water schemes are operated and maintained by the Garhwal Jal Sansthan in bigger towns and by the Town Area Committee in smaller towns. At present all the major cities/towns in the region have planned water supply schemes, but most of the schemes are very old and need re-organisation. In summer there is scarcity of water supply and the water is not properly treated.

DISPOSAL OF WASTE AND WASTE WATER/ SEWERAGE SYSTEM

To maintain the ecological balance safe disposal of sewage assumes greater significance due to the fact that it would ultimately reach the rivers and pollute the very source of drinking water. Presently, only the following towns have sewerage systems (partial in some towns):

a) Badrinath, b) Chamoli, c) Uttarkashi, d) Rishikesh, e) Dehradun and f) Gopeshwar

There is a definite need to upgrade sewerage systems and set up new sewerage systems in most of the towns in order to provide better facilities to tourists in the yatra circuit.

TELECOMMUNICATION

Good telecommunication services are very essential for tourism development. Speedy means of communication have an added attraction. The facility of telephone and telegraph is not up to the expectation in the region. Radio communication is not yet introduced in a big way. Though GMVN tourist bungalows are having wireless sets for their use, but it is looking after a very small percentage of tourists visiting Garhwal. Lack of radio communication creates great risk to life at the time of accidents on mountains. So poor telecommunication facilities discourage the flow of adventure tourists to snow capped mountain peaks and trekking routes. Other telecom facilities such as STD, ISD services in the area are improving at present at certain important locations like Badrinath, Gaurikund, Kedarnath, Gangotri, Hanumanchatti, yamunotri, Gwaldam, Khirsu and many other interior places of the region. In view of expected increase in tourist inflow in the region it is imperative that the number of lines (for STD/ISD) should be increased at all the location and more public booths should be opened for tourists.

Table - 5.9

Presently Working STD Lines as on December, 2000.

District	Location (Out going + Incoming Lines)
Uttarakshi	Barkot (3+3), Brahmkhal (1+1), Bhatwari (3+3), Chiniyal Saur (2+1), Damta (1BW), Dunda (3+3), Gangotri (4+3),

1	2
	Maidanda (1BW), Maneri (1BW), Naugaon (1BW), Purola (3+3), Ranachatti (3+3), Uttarkashi (15+15) Ranachatti(3+3), Uttarkashi (15+15).
Chamoli	Adibadri (3BW), Auli (4BW), Badrinath (4+3),Bhatoli (15+15), Chamoli(15+15), Chhinka (15+15),Dewal (2BW), Gairsan (4+4), Gauchar (15+15), Ghat (I5+15), Gopeswar (22+22), Gwaldam (4+4),Joshimath(15+15), Karnaprayag (30+30), Kulsari (1BW), Langasu (15+15), Mandal(3BW), Maithan (3BW), Mehalchauri (3BW), Nanda Pandukeswar (3BW), Pipalkoti (15+15),Pokhari (4+3),Simli (4BW), Tapovan (3BW), Tharali (4+3), Talwari (3BW).
Rudra Prayag	Augustmuni (15+15), Basu Kedar (15+15), Bhiri (15+15), ChandraPuri (15+15),Chopta (8+8),Durgadhar(6BW), Gaurikund (15+15), Goltir (15+15), Guptakashi (18+18), Jakholi (3+3) ,Kandai (2+2), Kedar Nath (3+3), Khankra (15+15), Lamgundi (4+3), Okhimath (4+3), Phata (15+15), Rudraprayag (30+30), Saterkhal(15+15), Tilwara (15+15).
Pauri	Agrora (15+15), Bhatoli (15+15), Birokhal (2BW), Bubakhal (15+15), Chilla (15+15),CheluSain (1BW), Dadamandi (2BW) Delchauri (1BW), DobSrikot(15+15), Dhumakhot (4+3) , Dugadda (15+15), Durgapuri (15+15), Ekeswar(15+15), Ghurdari (60+60),Gumkhal(15+15), Kaliasaur (15+15), Kandakhal (1BW), Kanskhet (4+3),Khanda (7+7),Khirsu (15+15), Kisanpuri (15+15), Kot (2BW), Kotdwar-I(Tax), Kotdwar - II (15+15), Lansdowne (15+15), Lawali(1BW), Nanidanda (1BW), Naugonkhal (15+15), Nilkantha (15+15), Pabo(1BW), Patisain (15+15),Pauri(60+60), Pokhra (2BW), Rikhnikhal

1	2
	(4+3), Satpuli(4+4), Srinagar(75+75), Sabdarkhal(15+15), Syunsi (4+3), Thalisain (4+3).
Tehri	Agrakhal (1BW), Anjanisain (6+4), Bagwan (15+15), Bhagira - thipuram (12+8), Bhaldiyana (1BW), Badiyargarh (1+1), Bachhelikhal (15+15), Chamba (5+5), Chamiyala (1BW), Chham (1BW), Devprayag (15+15), Dugadda (1+1), Ghansali (6BW), Gular (1+1), Hindolakhal (1+1), Jakhanidhar (1BW), Jamni Khal (1BW), Kempty (1BW), Kodiyala (15+15), Lambgaon (1BW), Madhi(15+15), Narendra Nagar (6+5), New Tehri (25+35), Nainbag (1BW), Odhadhar (1BW), Paukhal (1BW), Pratap Nagar (5+5), Ranichauri (1BW), Silkakhal (1BW), Satyon (3+3), Shivpuri (15+15), Tehri (15+15), Thatyur (1BW).

Note:- 1. BW (Both way or common for outgoing and incoming lines).

Source:- Divisional Telecom Department, Srinagar.

Similarly good post and telegraph services are very essential for tourism development. The condition of post and telegraph offices is not very good.

MEDICAL FACILITIES

Provision of adequate medical facilities is an important hygiene factor for the development of tourism in a particular area. In a region like Garhwal, medical facilities become all the more important as most of the tourists who come for religious purposes and belong to the lower middle class are always on the move in the hills and the chances of falling ill and having accidents are quite high. The government has made elaborate arrangements for providing medical relief and sanitation services to the tourists.

Table 5.10

Status of Medical Facilities in the Garhwal Himalaya

Medical Facility of Units of the Facility	No. of Places Covered
Medical relief units	15 places
Availability of Oxygen	8 places
Ambulance facility	18 places
Mobile dispensaries	2 places
State Allopathic Dispensaries	32 places
Public Health Centres	21 places
Common Health Centres	4 places
Ayurvedic Medical Centres	17 places
Homeopathic Medical Centres	6 places
Hospitals (including district hospitals)	17 places

Source: Additional Director, Health Department, Pauri.

References

Bhatia, A.K., (1982). *Tourism Developemnt: Principles and Practices*, Sterling Publication Ltd., New Delhi.

Bisht, Harshvanti, (1994). *Tourism in Garhwal Himalaya: With Special Reference to Mountaineering and Trekking in Uttarkashi and Chamoli Districts*, Indus blishing Company, New Delhi, pp., 98-122.

Fonia, K.S., (1998). *The Traveller's Guide to Uttarakhand* Garuda Books, Chamoli Garhwal.

Kaur, J., (1985). *Himalayan Pilgrimage and the New Tourism*, Himalayan Books, New Delhi.

Kohli, M.S., (1989). *Mountaineering in India*, Vikas Pub. House, New Delhi.

Hill Development Department, Government of U.P., 1975-76, Hill Region, Fifth Five Year Plan, Annual Plan (1975-76), p. 61.

Hill Area Development Board, Government of U.P. Hill Area Development Progress, 1994-95.

U.P. Tourism (Hills) (1997), Report on area development plan for the Char dham Circuit in U.P. Hills, Dehradun.

6

Tourist Traffic

In last 10 Years tourist arrivals in erstwhile U.P. hills comprising of Garhwal and Kumaon regions, has been increased. But there is no uniformity in the growth rate of tourist arrivals in erstwhile U.P. hills (now Uttaranchal) in general and Garhwal hills in particular. It can be seen in table below:

Table No: 6.1

Tourist Arrivals in Erstwhile U.P. Hills (now Uttaranchal) and Garhwal Region (in Lakhs)

Sl No.	Year	Tourist Arrivals in Erstwhile UP Hills(now Uttaranchal)			Tourist Arrivals in Garhwal	% share of Uttaranchal
		Indian	Foreigner	Total		
1	1989	106.99	0.40	107.39	78.22	72.84
2	1990	111.99	0.43	112.42	78.41	69.75
3	1991	111.58	0.78	112.36	77.09	68.61
4	1992	91.68	0.56	92.24	60.87	65.99
5	1993	137.93	0.71	138.64	91.45	65.96
6	1994	136.17	0.47	136.64	89.29	65.35
7	1995	139.83	0.41	140.24	97.51	69.53

1	2	3	4	5	6	7
8	1996	160.53	0.47	161.00	109.74	68.16
9	1997	181.40	0.52	181.92	122.91	67.56
10	1998	192.47	0.56	193.03	129.65	67.17
11	1999	193.60	0.64	194.24	121.61	62.61

Source: Statistical Book 2000, Director Tourism (Uttaranchal), Dehradun

Among all the religious shrines in Garhwal, Badrinath is presently the most popular amongst domestic tourists because of it being a key religious destination of national importance, and being a motorable road . The other locations, especially Gangotri and Yamunotri have more regional appeal and are attracting about 100,000 domestic tourists annually. Though

Fig. 6.1

Comparison of Tourist Arrivals in Uttranchal and Garhwal (in Lakhs)

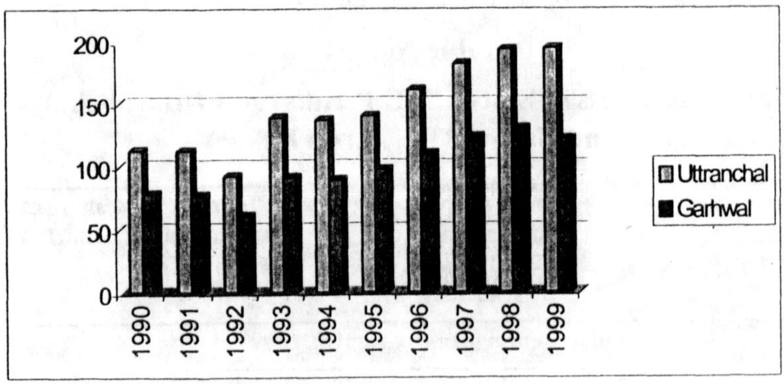

comprehensive data of foreign tourist arrivals was not available, overall the inflow is almost negligible and restricted to 1000-2000 foreign tourists largely for Yamunotri and Gangotri which have a tourism offerings of diverse types (scenic beauty and leisure tourism). The bulk of the foreign tourists come on package tours with adventure sports agencies and their number depends on the number of tours which are conducted. This is the reason, the number of foreign tourists show an erratic growth. The annual tourist traffic from 1975 and the growth rate to 4 major locations have been depicted in tables below. The tourist traffic in the *char dham* circuit does not show any trend. Tourist arrivals at *Char Dham* of Garhwal, starting from 1975 falls and then again rises in 1980 and 1988. It was fairly stable from 1989 to 1993, though with a decreasing trend, and declined in 1994. The growth rate in tourist traffic in these locations had also been very low. The main factors which were responsible for this decline in the number of tourists visiting the *Char Dhams* in 1994,was the environment which was not very conducive for growth of tourism (e.g. demand for separate Uttrakhand State and frequent civic disruption due to this). All these locations are accessible for only 6 months in a year. The gross tourist arrivals in a year thus represent the tourist arrivals for only six months. Because of this curtailed season, this circuit remained relatively underdeveloped than other tourist location in the country and thus tourist traffic has not increased. Out of the four *Dhams* of Garhwal, Yamunotri and Kedarnath are trekking routes, which explains the low tourist traffic in the routes. Since Gangotri and Yamunotri falls in one direction and Kedarnath and Badrinath on the other, therefore the tourist who don't want to cover Yamunotri because of difficult trekking route, also don't go to Gangotri. This explains low tourist traffic in the Gangotri, despite it being a motor able route. The growth of foreign tourists in erstwhile U.P. hills at 12.25% per annum from 1985-1993 is impressive when compared with the growth of the foreign tourists in India, which is only 7.61% per annum for the same period. Also the growing share of foreign tourists visiting Uttaranchal out of the total number of foreign tourists coming to India signifies increasing interest in the region and indicates the vast potential that lies in this area. The domestic tourist figures are based on various sources, which include records kept with various hotels and the number of tourists traveling by road or rail. Hence, these figure are not very reliable and have been used for assessing the direction /trends only.

Tourists going to Yamunoti and Kedarnath need minimum two nights stay at the base camp or other places enroute. For Yamunotri one can stay at Hanuman Chatti, Janki Chatti, Phool Chatti or Yamunotri itself. Tourists going to Kedarnath usually stay at Rampur, Gaurikund, Soneprayag, Rambara or Kedarnath itself. Tourist traffic figures for these locations are presented in table. The number of tourist staying at Gaurikund is the maximum because it is the last stop for vehicular traffic and thereafter one has to travel on foot. Almost 90% of the tourists visiting Gangotri stay at Uttarkashi. Beyond Uttarkashi, accommodation facilities are limited. On the Badrinath route, most of the tourists stay at Joshimath and Pipalkoti.

Table No. 6.2
Average Duration Of Stay Of Tourists

LOCATION	POSSIBLE HALTING PLACES	NO. OF NIGHTS	
		DOMESTIC	FOREIGN
Yamunotri	Chamba, Barkot, Purola, Sayanachatti, Hanumanchatti, Jankichatti, Yamunotri	3	3
Gangotri	Uttarkashi, Harsil, Gangotri, Bhojwasa	2	4
Kedarnath	Srinagar, Rudraprayag, Chandrapuri, Guptkashi, Rampur, Soneprayag, Gaurikund, Rambara, Kedarnath	2.5	3
Badrinath	Chopta, Joshimath, Auli, Badrinath, Pipalkoti, Syalsaur	2.5	5

Source:. Uttaranchal Tourism, Dehradun.

Table No 6.3

Tourist Arrivals in four major destinations of Garhwal Region

Year	Badrinath	Kedarnath	Gangotri	Yamunotri
1975	180000	81549	57000	30000
1976	196000	92218	45000	70000
1977	120000	78362	47000	40000
1978	146568	60839	58382	46621
1979	180442	65480	55210	48621
1980	208041	80690	59421	62492
1981	214080	97202	43097	78307
1982	211982	72349	90615	53697
1983	227395	81819	130261	82000
1984	225200	113323	92000	118000
1985	251867	99803	31000	79000
1986	248565	84164	83000	93000
1987	272858	87629	85980	64543
1988	376819	137094	98520	85227
1989	348592	115856	124127	109455
1990	365000	120000	108175	100672
1991	355774	118750	112860	104640
1992	412597	141784	106538	98200
1993	476560	118659	112132	103710
1994	347415	104638	82690	74110
1995	482900	106000	104335	99730
1996	465928	129230	188827	129552
1997	361313	60500	206536	81662
1998	340510	82000	237689	86307
1999	340100	81090	123124	106252

Source:. Uttaranchal Tourism, Dehradun

Fig. 6.2

Tourist Arrivals in "*Chardhams*" of Garhwal

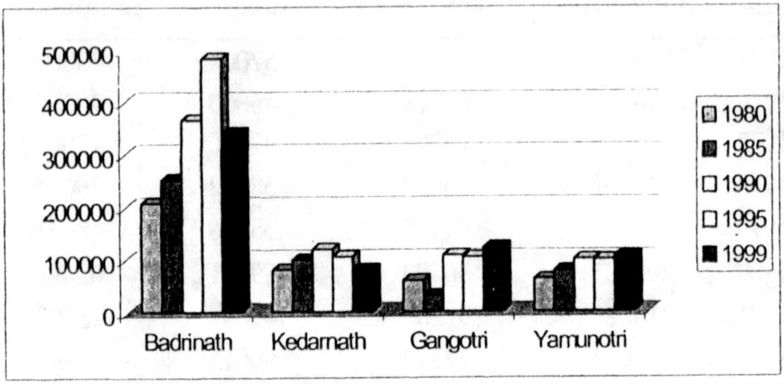

Table No: 6.4

Tourists' Growth Rate in Four Major Destinations of Garhwal

Years	Badrinath	Kedarnath	Gangotri	Yamnotri
1975	0	0	0	0
1976	8.8	13.05	21.05	133.3
1977	-38.7	-15.02	-4.4	-42.85
1978	22.08	-22.35	24.2	16.52
1979	23.28	7.62	-5.42	4.29
1980	15.5	23.07	7.6	28.52
1981	2.8	20.45	-27.46	25.3
1982	-0.98	-25.7	110.25	-31.4
1983	7.3	13.08	43.75	52.7
1984	-0.96	38.5	-29.37	43.9

1	2	3	4	5
1985	11.84	-11.9	42.39	-33.05
1986	-1.31	-15.5	-36.64	17.72
1987	9.7	4.1	3.59	-30.59
1988	38.23	56.46	14.58	30.5
1989	-7	-15.5	26	28.42
1990	4.88	3.45	-12.85	8.02
1991	-2.5	-1.04	4.33	3.94
1992	16.05	19.4	-5.6	-6.15
1993	15.53	-16.3	5.25	5.61
1994	-27.1	-11.8	-26.25	-28.5
1995	38.9	1.3	26.17	34.57
1996	-3.5	21.9	80.98	29.9

Source: U.P. Tourism (Hills)

Table No. 6.5

Tourist Traffic At Major Halting Places

Year	Uttar kashi	Joshi math	Gupt kashi	Pipal koti	Ukhi math	Govind ghat
1985	70,000	35,995	—	17,200	4,500	24,545
1986	70,000	62,324	—	60,614	7,000	—
1987	73,000	51,958	—	52,817	3,820	—
1988	83,500	66,800	27,008	25,150	4,000	32,180
1989	86,215	87,655	—	—	1,255	—
1990	82,538	65,835	18,347	31,450	850	
1991	88,760	69,655	20,126	42,532	982	—
1992	86,996	66,217	23,000	45,040	1,500	—
1993	97,585	45,194	24,024	48,800	2,014	49,025
1994	67,240	30,613	12,297	52,000	1,178	48,970
1995	91,480	—	—	—	—	—
1996	1,11,382	52,396	—	—	—	—
1997	1,46,367	99,320	—	—	—	—

Year	Karna-prayag	Gope-shwar	Ram-bara	Gauri-kund	Sone-prayag	Nand-prayag
1985	18,000	7,445	19,920	56,100	22,205	
1986	19,996	8,644	22,515	55,187	16,005	2,706
1987	25,359	10,008	—	135,000	20,000	3,323
1988	70,110	8,961	23,000	67,000	35,069	15,022
1989	10,350	10,313	5,008	150,025	50,016	
1990	11,389	13,050	6,000	105,297	58,312	17,210
1991	13,552	10,271	6,300	115,522	58,532	19,182
1992	15,200	13,092	7,000	110,000	45,000	19,195
1993	17,350	13,535	8,626	115,024	40,020	16,014
1994	16,245	7,777	8,338	80,182	30,832	9,818
1995		9,681	—	—	—	—

Source: U.P. Tourism (Hills) Dehradun & tourist offies at various locations.

Note: Blanks implies that data was not available for those years.

Tourist Traffic at Other Tourist Locations

Besides the 4 main tourist attractions mentioned earlier data was also obtained on tourist traffic in other major tourist spots which are listed below.The tourist traffic of other tourist locations is presented in table below. Unlike the *Char Dhams* and main stoppages on the *yatra route*, the tourist traffic at major secondary tourist locations has grown steadily over the years with major growth taking place from 1988-1990. The locations are essentially non-religious and come under the category of adventure (trekking,skiing,rafting & mountaineering),wildlife or leisure tourism. The growth in the number of tourist arrivals at these places indicates their increasing popularity and also the scope of promoting adventure

/leisure tourism in this region. Tourist Traffic in Auli picked up after 1991 because of the annual skiing competition which was introduced in that year. Also Auli was developed as a ski resort mainly in 1990-92 when the ropeway from Joshimath to Auli was also built. Thus,the sharp increase in tourists arrivals during 1988-1990 shows the extent of development that took place during that time.

Table No. 6.6

Tourist Traffic at Upcoming Tourist Locations of Garhwal

YEAR	Gau mukh	Dodital	Har-Ki-Doon	Auli	Chopta	Deoriatal
1985		100	450		2,500	
1986	3,000	200	590		4,500	200
1987	4,000	1,000	460	142	7,025	1,510
1988	34,570	5,186	1,634	195	8,000	1,500
1989	43,137	9,018	2,535	285	5,815	806
1990	40,066	8,070	3,259	575	7,347	850
1991	44,906	11,502	24,800	970	10,123	982
1992	39,407	9,828	16,952	2,492	17,922	1,200
1993	46,084	18,422	24,215	3,775	15,993	1,514
1994	34,330	13,580	11,640	7,129	14,758	914
1995	43,655	17,030	15,326	-	-	-
1996	75957	36,961	53711	32,600	-	-
1997	1,36,053	90,606	65,246	35,000	-	-

Source: U.P. Tourism (Hills) Dehradun & tourist offices at various locations.

Fig.6.3

Tourist Traffic at Upcoming Tourist Destinations of Garhwal Tourist Arrivals

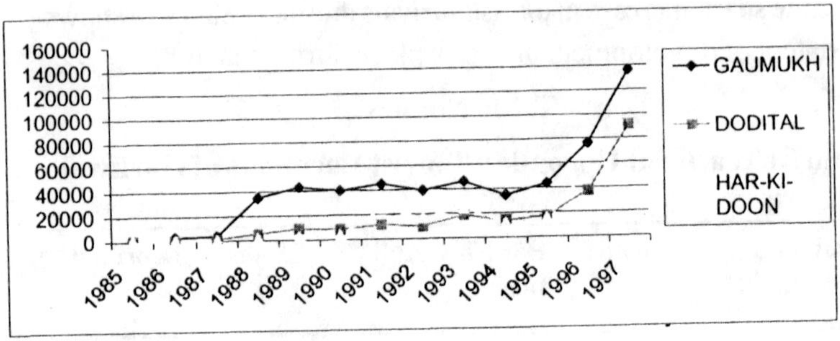

Year

Tourist Arrivals

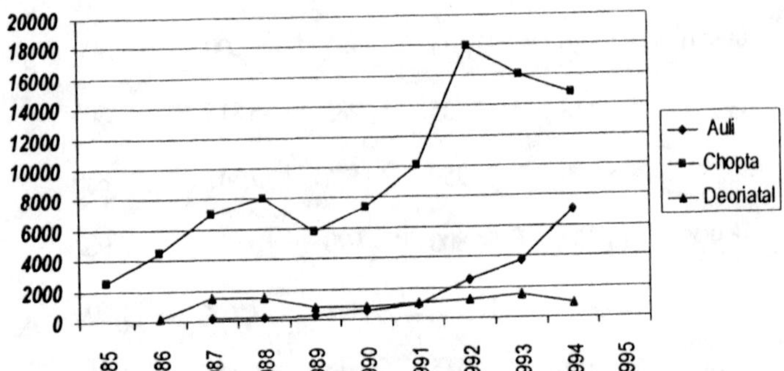

Table No : 6.7: Tourist Arrivals (In lakhs) in some other important places of Garhwal

Tourist Centre Name	1991	1992	1993	1994	1995	1996	1997	1998
Dehradun	12.68	18.28	21.69	11.84	13.31	09.04	12.46	13.45

1	2	3	4	5	6	7	8	9
Mussoorie	15.00	12.57	14.74	12.22	12.82	13.97	15.98	18.42
Dak Pathar	05.82	08.63	07.62	03.06	03.39	01.61		
Rishikesh	47.00	31.20	47.48	58.06	24.54	09.61	13.91	19.01
Kotdwar	0.54	0.54	0.55	0.47	0.65	0.30	0.75	1.87
Pauri	0.30	0.30	0.31	0.23	0.27	0.34	0.49	0.88
Lansdowne	0.59	0.59	0.51	0.52	0.58			
Khirsu	0.03	0.04	0.04	0.03	0.03			
Kanwashram	0.16	0.17	0.17					

Source: U.P. Tourism (Hills) Dehradun & tourist offices at various locations.

Seasonality

The tourist arrivals in the ***Char Dham*** circuit picks up in March and April and is maximum in May and June. The 4 temples at Yamunotri, Gangotri, Kedarnath and Badrinath open every year in the last week of April or the first week of May and are closed in mid November, leaving only a six month season for the pilgrims. A large number of visitors visit these areas during May-November and their percentage of total as are evident from table. This shows the highly seasonal nature of these tourist destinations which also has the implications that any development that is done would cater to tourists for only half the year. However, the maximum number of tourist arrivals is recorded in May and June (more then 50% arrivals are in these two months). Beyond June, monsoons start which hampers travel plan of tourists. The implication of this uneven flow of tourists is that infrastructure for peak level tourist traffic would remain unutilized during off season. However, infrastructure which is unable to cater to peak flows would limit growth of the region and pose security and other problems for the existing tourists and the local people of the area.

Table No. 6.8 : Seasonality in Tourist Arrivals

Month	Uttarkashi		Rishikesh		Joshimath	
	1994	1995	1994	1995	1994	1995
Jan.	2,801	544	3,390	3,653	256	441
Feb.	3,508	406	4,449	3,827	1,319	404
March	1,767	609	3,240	3,793	558	318
April	1,565	1,097	3,758	5,757	213	355
May	9,922	6,390	14,452	12,608	6,070	8,381
June	7,281	7,458	13,875	12,815	11,470	15,629
July	2,914	3,202	9,597	6,560	5,421	5,184
Aug.	1,794	2,542	6,955	4,031	2,933	3,660
Sept.	679	3,345	3,133	2,803	254	4,773
Oct.	679	3,187	3,608	6,746	182	3,586
Nov.	1,418	1,563	3,655	4,391	261	1,597
Dec.	599	742	3,772	4,005	337	774
TOTAL	**34,927**	**31,085**	**73,884**	**70,989**	**29,274**	**45,102**

Source: U.P. Tourism (Hills) Dehradun & tourist offices at various locations.

Fig. 6.4

Seasonality in Tourist Arrivals in Garhwal (Percentage)

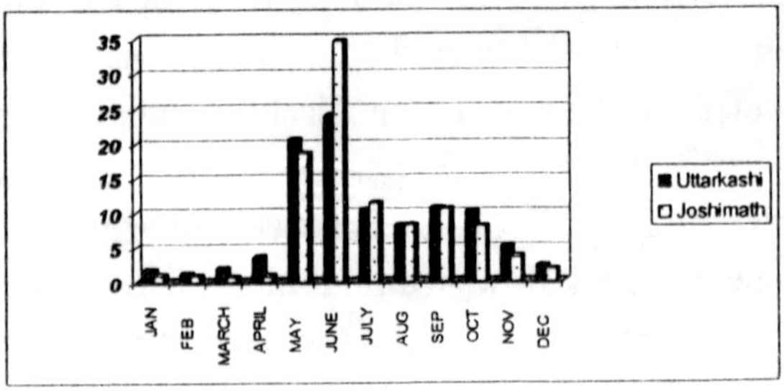

Months *(in year 1995)*

Table No. 6.9

Seasonality In Tourist Arrivals (As Percentage Of Total).

Month	Uttarkashi		Rishikesh		Joshimath	
	1994	1995	1994	1995	1994	1995
Jan.	8.02%	1.75%	4.59%	5.15%	0.87%	0.98%
Feb.	10.04%	1.31%	6.02%	5.39%	4.51%	0.90%
March	5.06%	1.96%	4.39%	5.34%	1.91%	0.71%
April	4.48%	3.53%	5.09%	8.11%	0.73%	0.79%
May	28.41%	20.56%	19.56%	17.76%	20.74%	18.58%
June	20.85%	23.99%	18.78%	18.05%	39.18%	34.65%
July	8.34%	10.30%	12.99%	9.24%	18.52%	11.49%
Aug.	5.14%	8.18%	9.41%	5.68%	10.02%	8.11%
Sept.	1.94%	10.76%	4.24%	3.95%	0.87%	10.58%
Oct.	1.94%	10.25%	4.88%	9.50%	0.62%	7.95%
Nov.	4.06%	5.03%	4.95%	6.19%	0.89%	3.54%
Dec.	1.72%	2.39%	5.11%	5.64%	1.15%	1.72%
TOTAL	**100 %**	**100 %**	**100 %**	**100 %**	**100 %**	**100 %**

Source: U.P. Tourism (Hills) Dehradun & tourist offices at various locations.

Projected Tourist Traffic

Tourism in Garhwal Himalaya is expected to grow in the years to come. However,it depends on economic growth and rising disposable incomes of people, increasing propensity to travel among large segment of population of Delhi and other northern states. Further, focus on promotion of adventure tourism in India on a national level will provide the required impetus to several locations in the circuit which have high worth for adventure tourism. But in the absence of a clear growth trend, historic growth rates for all major locations according to the survey of Uttaranchal Tourism, Dehradun, have been assumed. It is 4-6% per annum for domestic tourists except Kedarnath where the growth has been very slow and its rate was 2% per annum . The share of foreign tourists of the total tourist arrivals is very low mainly because the major tour circuit is more or less of a religious significance for domestic pilgrims where as foreign tourists,mainly come for adventure and leisure tourism. Moreover the foreign tourist season to India falls during the September-March period while the visiting season for the *Char Dhams* is during summers. Hence most of the tourists to India cannot include the *Char Dham* circuit in their tour itinerary during winters.

7

APPROACH TO TOURISM PLANNING

7.1. RESOURCE INVENTORY - APPROACH TO SURVEY AND EVALUATION TECHNIQUE

The attraction features of a country or region provide the basis for developing tourism. They form the most essential element of the tourism product. Without substantial attraction features, pleasure-oriented tourism would not be possible to develop. Although facilities and services are still required for business, government/mission, conference, religious, and other types of obligatory travel. Tourist attractions and activities can encompass a very wide variety, especially because of the great diversity of interests of today's tourist markets. At the same time, some features that local residents believe are of great interest are not so to most visitors. Therefore, imagination, perspective, and objectivity are essential in identifying, evaluating, and developing attractions.

Usually, attractions should be sought that reflect an area's inherent, distinctive, and unique natural and cultural character, and be authentically developed to reinforce that character. Typically, selection and evaluation of tourist attractions and activities should be made relative to the existing and potential tourist markets, that is, the tourist attractions and activities and the tourist markets must be matched together if tourism is to be successful. In some places a product-led approach is applied. This approach implies that the inherent attractions and tourist facilities of the area are developed (or conserved) in the manner that the country believes is the most appropriate for its own environmental and sociocultural benefit, and tourist markets are found that are attracted to that particular product. Often, the approach applied in many places is a combination of market-led and product-led tourism within the framework of balancing economic development and conservation. An important approach is to relate tourist attraction features with tourist activities. One of the trends in tourism is the increasing activity or participatory orientation of tourists who want, for example, to engage in sports and active recreation and learn about the local environment and culture. Therefore, tourist attractions should also be identified and evaluated with respect to the opportunities they offer for development of related tourist activities and involvement.

In order to survey and evaluate tourist attractions, it is important to understand the types of tourist attractions and activities that should be considered in planning tourism and how these can be categorized for analysis purposes. Several elements can contribute to, and enhance, the general attractiveness of a tourist area: a genial climate, a friendly population, good communications, low cost of living, favorable rates of exchange, a politically acceptable government, and so forth. All these elements can be very important but don't determine by themselves the tourist character of an area. The real tourist offer still remains the presence in that area of 'something interesting or unusual to see or to do' which means a set of natural or manmade attraction. Very few tourist areas or countries have organised a complete and systematic inventory of their resource bases. It is not a simple and straightforward subject. Some areas have a well-defined set of attractive features while others have less identifiable resources, which can still be organised into a sufficiently attractive product to suit the interests and preferences of prospective customers. Often there is a complementary rapport among different attractions. One or few outstanding features usually attract the tourist to a certain area, but less important characteristics or local activities can also be mobilised to induce longer visits. Two main issues involves in this are: (a) How to identify the resource base of an area and (b) how to assess the intrinsic value of such resources to their market. It is essential to organise a complete resource inventory and choose an appropriate evaluating methodology. It is necessary to find a suitable method for assessing the value of a disparate mass of tourist resources that differed widely among themselves in nature, function, and usage, so that each of them can become comparable as far as its degree of attractiveness is concerned. From a practical point of view the ultimate test of the appeal of a tourist feature must be the preferences and interests shown by tourists themselves provided, of course, that these preferences do not conflict with local interests and considerations.

Seasonality, Accessibility, Admission, Importance, fragility and *Popularity* are some of the most basic criteria to assess the touristic potential of a destination or area. Accessibility may be described in terms of excellent or adequate or limited or difficult; Admission can be described as no permit or local permit or advance permit required to visit that place; criteria for seasonality include whether the place is visited over six month or over three month or less than three month or less than one month and fragility can be explained by the large development potential or controlled development or no development possibility based on sustainability of the place to withstand tourist pressure without deterioration of its natural characteristics and cultural values. Importance and popularity can be judged by the ranking of the place among the attraction and visitors profile of that place.

Inventory of Heritage Resources

A detailed Survey and Analysis should be made, with inputs from a wide range of disciplines, with a view to establish a comprehensive plan for the protection, enhancement, development and management of it. However, it is suggested to make intensive survey of heritage products of Garhwal that should make in depth analysis of important sites as mentioned below:

1. Its environmental and cultural assets (a Heritage Inventory) such as historic buildings, shrines, rivers, lakes, notable flora and fauna and existing infrastructure including water supplies etc.
2. Its qualitative weaknesses and shortcomings such as polluted air, inadequate sanitation, congestion, outdoor advertising and buildings and other elements that are functionally redundant or have no place esthetically or spiritually in the site.
3. Its potential for tourism development in relation to local community needs: the type of tourism, the carrying capacity, the likely costs of infrastructure development and financial returns, the benefits and disadvantages for the local community including employment, inflationary pressures and the need for education and training.

Based on this information, a comprehensive plan should be created for the region, or district in consultation with historians, the tourism industry, local agencies and institutions and community representatives containing detailed policies for preservation of the main monuments, design and management of zone as a whole, community education and tourism development and management.

The first step in the survey of tourist attractions is document research and interviews of government officials and other local resource persons to determine the general types and locations of attractions available. Then a preliminary list of attraction categories, types of characteristics for which information are to be obtained, and the evaluation criteria are prepared. These may be modified as the survey proceeds. Next, a field survey is undertaken to visit the attraction features. For some types of attractions, the survey may need to be conducted during more than one season to determine seasonal differences of the sites characteristics (for example, of a potential ski resort that also may offer possibilities for summer season tourism, or of a high altitude scenic or historic site to determine whether it can be open to visitors during the winter).

The identification of the attractions should be done systematically, indicating name, type, location, accessibility, special characteristics, type of any existing development and any advantáges or problems of the existing development, including a photograph if relevant, and a written summary description about the feature.
The place-specific attractions should be plotted on a map of the overall planning area so that they can later be analyzed with respect to the transportation system and potential tourism development areas. Other types of attractions such as climate can be described and mapped, and non-place specific cultural attractions such as music, dance, and handicrafts should be described.

The evaluation of attractions should be made relative to their respective importance at the regional, national, and international levels. Evaluation must take into account the potential tourist markets for the attraction features, use of the attractions by residents of the area, national, regional, and local accessibility, relative costs of conservation and development, carrying capacity of the attractions environments, and the environmental and sociocultural implications of development. Accessibility may be a particularly important consideration. The attractions can usually be best evaluated by using a numerical evaluation matrix technique. Criteria of resource attraction assessment of the region are given in the following figure.

Table - 7.1

Criteria for Recreation Resource Assessment

Group	Criterion	Considerations
Natural Factors	• Scenic Beauty	• mountain Scenery: Outstanding mountains, snow peaks, Black Mountains, green slopes, glaciers, snow bridges, vantage points and Panoramic views.
		• Geologic features: special rock structures & formations, figurations.
		• Valley aspects: gorges, glaciated valleys, scenic & wild rivers.
		• Water bodies: Lakes & Kunds, waterfalls, white rivers, riverfronts and confluence's, natural springs (hot water, cold water & mineral).
	• Flora & Fauna	• Forests: local forest types, primitive stands of forest, largest and the oldest trees, unique floral regions.
		• Meadows: The Himalayan meadows-Bugyals and Panyars, flower Valleys.
		• Fauna: The popular fauna type, the rare wildlife and bird life areas, and the insect fauna.
	• Climate	• Temperature, length of sunshine hours, precipitation, atmospheric quality and comfort/ discomfort index.
Social Factors	• Religious Significance	• Pilgrim Centres: of national, regional and local significance.
		• Rituals and religious observances.
	• Fairs and Festivals	• Fairs: religious, religious cum cultural and cultural cum commercial.
		• Festivals.

1	2	3
	• Distinctive local features	• Ethnicity: Tribal groups and settlements, tribal life style, dress and jewelry • Folk traditions, folk lores, folk dances/ music and musical instruments.
	• Artistic and Architectural Features	• Local architecture. • Temples and sculpture. • Paintings.
Historical Factors	• Historical/ Archaeological Sites	• Places of Historical importance. • Ancient ruins. • Sites of archaeological significance.
	• Historical Events	• Legends. • Other historical events
Recreation & Shopping facilities	• Sports facilities	• Sports for adventure seekers : mountaineering, rock climbing. • Sports for adventure cum pleasure seekers: Nature trails, Trekking Mountai-neering, Skiing & Outdoor skating, Canoeing, Rafting. • Other pleasure pursuits: hunting, hiking, camping, angling, nature spotting, sights seeing, outdoor photography, collecting pebbles, drift woods etc
	• Facilities conducive to Health, Rest, Tranquility and Education	• National Parks: Games Sanctuaries; Biosphere Reserves; Zoological Reserves; Botanical Gardens; Picnic grounds and reservoirs
	• Shopping Opportunities and Auto service	• Groceries and necessities • Souvenirs and Gift shops • Handicraft Shops,
Facilities	• Petrol Pumps and auto-service centres.	

1	2	3
Infrastructure and Food and Shelter	• Infrastructure above minimal touristic quality	• Highway and roads, Electricity and gas; Safety services, Communication and Public transport facilities
	• Food and lodging facilities above minimal touristic quality.	• Hotels, restaurants, vacation villages, bungalow, motels.

Source: Kaur, J. 1985, Himalayan Pilgrimages and The New Tourism, Himalayan Books, New Delhi, pp. 49-50.

An important result, the evaluation will be deciding which are the primary attractions, that would induce tourists to visit the area, and which are secondary, that are not sufficiently important to induce tourist to visit but that would serve as complementary features to provide more activities and interest features for tourists and increase their length of stay. Also, the evaluation will indicate which are the predominant types of attractions, such as nature or culturally oriented an important consideration in the market analysis. It is often a combination of attractions that provides the best basis for tourism development.

If, after the evaluation, it is determined that the natural and cultural attractions are not sufficiently important to successfully market tourism, or if additional attractions are needed to meet the development objectives, then consideration can be given to develop special types of activity oriented attractions or specialized recreation and sports facilities, or it may be decided that the limitation of attractions or their high cost of development may preclude the feasibility of developing tourism and expansion of other economic sectors should be examined instead.

7.2. PLANNING ANALYSIS AND SYNTHESIS

There are three main aspects of the planning analysis:

- Market analysis and projections of accommodation and other tourist facility needs and determination of the transportation and other infrastructure requirements.
- Integrated analysis and synthesis of physical (natural and built environment), social and economic factors, including tourist attractions and activities, present policies and plans, and establishment of general tourist carrying capacities at the national and regional levels.
- Analysis of the institutional elements.

7.2.1. MARKET ANALYSIS

From the standpoint of planning tourism development, the market analysis results in tourist arrival projections or establishment of market targets in terms of the number, type, length of stay, and other characteristics of tourists by time periods. This is essential input to planning the tourist attractions and activities, facilities, services, transportation, and other infrastructure required. The market analysis also provides the basis for formulating the marketing strategy and promotion program. At present a number of tourist projection techniques are used for market analysis and a few of them which are relevant for tourism management in Garhwal are mentioned below:

- Time series or straight-line projection of past growth trends especially of pilgrimage tourism profile and visitation to scenic places like Chopta and Dogalbitta etc;
- The experience of tourism growth elsewhere like Himachal Pradesh, Nepal which are of similar tourism situations;
- Market segmentation and catchment analysis;
- Global and Regional trends; and

- Tourist destination capacity or receptivity analysis.

As far as the first two points are concerned we may study official publications and official reports of Centre and State Governments. But the tourism markets especially the visitors reaching Garhwal for different motivations are diversely located. Therefore, market segmentation analysis is typically based on the following factors:

- Socioeconomic or demographic segmentation, which categorizes tourist based on their socioeconomic characteristics such as age, education, and income levels.
- Product-led segmentation, which relates the types of tourists to the particular tourism products such as attractions like temples, shrines, mountain meadows, peaks, celestial abodes, social tourism and facilities that Garhwal Himalaya offers.
- Psycho graphic segmentation, which involves grouping tourists by their attitudes, interests, life-styles, and travel motivations.
- Geographic segmentation, which groups tourists by location of origin as related to the time-distance and cost of traveling to the tourist destinations, and also considers the environmental and cultural contrasts and similarities between the origin and destination.

Integrated Analysis of Tourism Attraction

The physical elements to be analyzed include the following:

- Characteristics of the natural environment such as climate, topography, hydrography, vegetation and wildlife, and important ecological systems;
- Significant resource areas such as lands of high agricultural capability and economically viable mineral deposits;

- Land use and settlement patterns;
- Existing and already planned accommodation, tourist facilities and services; and
- Existing and already planned transportation facilities and services, and other major infrastructure.

The integrated analysis will indicate, for example, the climatically desirable areas for tourism development and places that are environmentally developable as related to location of major tourist attraction features and transportation network. Analysis of land tenure patterns will identify any particular problems of tenure that may arise in making sites available for tourism development, and will provide the basis for determining the best approach to securing the availability of development sites or conserving certain types of attractions.

The analysis of economic patterns will indicate the type and distribution of economic activities and the types, levels, and location of employment and unemployment. It will also identify areas that are economically depressed and therefore need new development such as tourism. Social patterns are analyzed with respect to population distribution, age-sex profiles, education levels, and population projections in total and by area that, along with the economic pattern analysis, will indicate the type and location where future labor supply will likely be available or deficient.

The socio cultural analysis will also identify particular patterns or attitudes that may influence the type and location of tourism development. There may also be the danger of tourism disturbing social systems in some traditional cultural areas like Niti and Mana valley near Joshimath or Rupin and Supin valley in Jaunsar -Babar area of Tehri and Rawain region of Uttarkashi district. In such locations, consideration should be given to not developing mass tourism in those places or developing only eco-tourism, even on very limited scale.

The existing physical, social, and economic policies and plans need to be reviewed in every 2-3 years for introducing new policies that may influence further tourism planning, and for proposed development projects such as new roads, environment friendly accommodation and other infrastructure needs. Both compatible and possible conflicting aspects of the policies and plans should be identified.

Identification of tourism development opportunities and expected constraints should be given utmost consideration to achieve balanced development, meeting environmental, social as well as economic objectives.

Major **opportunities** may, for example, include:

- An outstanding or unique type of tourist attraction like Lakhamandal should be given priority in development and marketing;
- Some highly successful existing tourism development of Gangotri region should be retained and reinforced;
- A particular market segment with much potential i.e. especially visitors coming for pilgrimage and trekking should be promoted as a marketing advantage;
- A well-developed infrastructure component that can be utilized for tourism; or
- A highly motivated service-oriented labor supply who have acquired proficiency in Tourism and Pilgrimage management can be tapped for tourism.

Major **constraints** to be overcome may, for example, include:

- Difficult access to the remote areas like Kedarnath, Rudranath, Goumukh, Yamnotri, Tapovan, Urgam, Kalpeswar etc. requiring wide roads, transport carriers and bus terminals improvements;

- Possible negative environmental or social impacts resulting from certain types of tourism development, necessitating careful environmental planning and controls;
- A poor market image of the area, requiring a special marketing campaign;
- A limited number of existing tourist attractions that need to be augmented by special types of attractions; or
- Poor quality of existing accommodation units that require up gradation.

7.2.2 POLICY AND PLAN FORMULATION

In order to receive maximum benefits and least burdens, tourism development planning in Garhwal is essential. Tourism undoubtedly provides economic, social, and cultural benefits to the residents of a number of holy places and transit destinations on Badri-Kedar and Gangotri-Yamnotri routes, but at the same time it generates various problems such as the loss of potential economic benefits and local economic distortions, environmental degradation, the loss of cultural identity and integrity and above all gross cultural misunderstanding and reinforcing existing prejudices. In brief, planning is important due to following reasons:

- Tourism is a complicated, multisectoral and fragmented activity and closely inter-related with other sectors such as local community, accommodation, eateries and transportation. Planning, Project development and co-ordination are particularly necessary to ensure that tourism should be developed in an integrated manner.
- Tourism brings various direct and indirect economic benefits to local people that can best be optimised through careful and integrated planning. It can not be organised in isolation as it requires particular manpower skills; known to the area very deeply. Satisfying these manpower needs; careful planning for human resource development is required.

- Further balanced tourism development requires marketing strategies, promotional programs, effective legislation and regulation. Without comprehensive planning, these factors can not be implemented.

Efficient organisation and provision of services can be the key to the success of adventure tourism the region is known for. Availability of supplies is necessary and any specialised equipment required must either be brought by the trekkers or locally available. Observance of safety measures can be an important consideration, with medical services and emergency evacuation in trekking areas. Helicopter services must be available for evacuation of ill or injured trekkers and their support staff. Establishing carrying capacities of all major and minor destinations is essential as these type of resources can not withstand excessive use.

Planning Process

- To promulgate tourism policy.
- To understand and analyse the tourists profile.
- To determine facility and infrastructural needs.
- To analyse the positive and negative impacts of tourism development on environment.
- To implement packages of impact control measures
- To arrange tourism training programmes for the human resource development.
- To generate variety of incentives and concessions to local entrepreneurs.
- To implement other inter -related promotional programmes.
- And finally, to adapt the procedure for implementation.

Tourism policy

Adoption of tourism policy for Garhwal region especially for the heritage management indicates that the area has products of natural and cultural interest that have significant importance in all over the country. The important elements of policy is recommended as follows:

- Tourism development should be integrated in to the overall development policy, planning and strategy of the region.
- It should be planned and organised systematically so that it does not result in serious social problems.
- Tourism is to be promoted in a carefully planned, controlled and organised manner so as to conserve endangered flora, fauna and important natural ecological system. Tourism promotion should not result in any type of serious air, water, noise and visual pollution.
- All ancillary services should be designed to reflect and represent Garhwal's distinctive architecture styles and local material.
- It should be put on operation in an efficient and integrated manner to meet the needs of national and international tourists.
- Tourist facilities and services should be designed to meet the range of needs of various youths and pilgrims.
- Emphasis should be placed on employment of local persons and be given maximum opportunity for career development and job satisfaction.
- The local people should be educated so that they could understand the importance of tourism and its role in area's economic development.

At the national level, there must be coordinated planning and a framework must be developed for bringing together all relevant public and private sectors. The community should be involved from the very beginning and be active at all stages, from planning to implementation to revision. The objectives of developing tourism provide the most important basis for establishing policy because policy is the expression of how the objectives can be achieved. For example, if the objective is for minimization of sociocultural impact, then the policy may be for highly controlled, limited tourism development. More generally, tourism policy must reflect the overall development policy and plan of the region. Socioeconomic and environmental factors are very important considerations in policy determination, especially the social and environmental absorptive or carrying capacity of cultural and religious shrines of Chamoli and Uttarakashi districts.Uttaranchal Tourism should assume the lead role in determining tourism policy because policy affects the entire region and its communities and must balance economic, environmental, and social concerns.

Policy and Action Plan of U.P. Tourism (Hill),1998.

The Hills of erstwhile U.P. (now part of newly created Uttaranchal State)have vast tourism potential along with its vivid cultural and traditional customs. It has been the endeavor of the State Tourism Department to promote tourism in these areas without adversely affecting rich cultural heritage, unmindful interference with local values and customs as also keeping in view the fact that ecological balance is maintained. Tourism in Garhwal hills has hitherto been mainly a seasonal activity dominated by pilgrimage. But the Holy Shrines of Badrinath, Kedarnath, Gangotri, Yamunotri, Hemkund Saheb remain closed during whole of the winter season. During this lean patch it has become a challenge to Department of Tourism to promote and harness the large tourism potential available in the winter season.Keeping in view the ultimate goal of sustainable tourism development in the state of U.P. and U.P. Hills in particular, the State Government had declared New Tourism Policy in 1998 with an objective to attract more investment through private sector to create more and better tourism facilities in the hills of U.P. Some of the salient features of this Tourism Policy are as follows:

- Tourism be given the status of an industry;

- Single window system for speedy clearance of proposals;
- Availability of State Government land with the approval of Empowered Committee for the construction of star category hotels @ 20% of the market price. Besides, necessary help is available from District Magistrates of the concerned districts in purchasing land, the ownership of which is in private hands;
- Facilities for composite bars and beer bars in hotels;
- Provision of necessary infrastructure such as metalloid roads, electricity, potable water, etc. by the State Government.
- The land procured from the development authorities in urban areas shall carry no levy or premium on the price and development charges;
- Provision of free land, if available for the development of green belt near the star category hotels.
- Deferment of entertainment tax for a period of five years and concession for new amusement parks as decided by the Empowered Committee;
- Nominal single slab luxury tax @ 5% on hotel rentals exceeding Rs. 250 per day;
- Luxury tax on new starred hotels in thrust areas deferred for five years;
- State financial institutions to provide loans on priority basis.

This way it is clear that efforts have been made to attract larger private investment in tourism sector and with this objective efforts have been made for identification of suitable lands in the whole state. A land directory has been prepared of these available tourism land sites with requisite details, thereof. Provision has been made to provide Government land at concessional rate where it is so identified and available. Steps have been taken to rationalise and simplify the existing tourism related taxation structure which include minimising inspections of tourism sites e.g. hotels/motels/ resorts etc. to remove Inspector Raj System. In the hills of Garhwal for larger private investment opportunities and to ensure local peoples' participation in tourism development process, State Government is providing subsidy of maximum 20% on projects up to Rs. 2.5 lacs under Loan Subsidy Scheme. 887 entrepreneurs have been benefited under this scheme so far by 1997. Another scheme for setting up of tourism facilities like hotels, restaurants, plying of taxies, buses, procuring adventure tourism equipments, etc. up to an investment of Rs. 10.00 lacs has already accepted by State Government in its recently declared policy 1998.This would also open new opportunities for self employment of unemployed youths of Garhwal. Similarly, to attract more private investment the Department of Tourism has introduced a Paying Guest Scheme and a directory for it has also been prepared in order to provide accommodation facilities in tune with local culture and life style. It is hoped that all these efforts would attract private entrepreneurs for investment in tourism sector in Hills of U.P. and thereby attract more tourists in this area. Preparation of Master Plan for the whole U.P. Hills, formulation of Safety and Rescue Regulations for water Sports, Trekking and mountaineering, various steps for sustainable tourism development e.g. promotion of Eco-Tourism keeping in view the fragile ecological system of this area have been taken by Department of Tourism. In the IXth Five Year Plan, submitted to the State Government, it has been proposed to develop potential adventure tourism sports as Mega-projects, integrated tourism development of certain identified tourist places, diversification of pilgrimage routes, identification of new circuits and employment oriented tourism schemes. Outlay has also been earmarked for up gradation of basic amenities like-Water Supply, Electricity, Communication, Roads and Transport etc. Based on the recommendations of the Xth Finance Commission for augmenting the basic infrastructure, work have already been started with an outlay of Rs. 40 Crores. Efforts have been made to promote adventure tourism activities like trekking, rafting, skiing, water-sports, aero-sports activities which have now come up. These are extremely essential in order to make tourism a round the year activity. Two departmental adventure tourism experts have been assigned the job of imparting training to local youths and entrepreneurs. Under the Loan Subsidy Scheme these trained persons are provided opportunities to start adventure tourism activities. Two expedition hostels are being set up at Uttarkashi and Joshimath for better training facilities. Similarly, for Human Resource Development in adventure tourism two adventure Training Institutes are being set up at Joshimath and Didihat. These Institutes are imparting training in various adventure activities. Government of India has principally agreed to establish Aero Sports Institute at Jolly Grant in District Dehradun with initial investment of Rs. 8.00 lacs. State Government has also started a new scheme with financial provision of Rs. 25.00 lacs for providing financial assistance to mountaineering, trekking and other allied adventure activities in Garhwal. This will also help larger NGO's participation in adventure tourism development. Private entrepreneurs willing to set up HRD institutions will also be provided necessary assistance. Two Hotel Management Institutes have been set up for imparting necessary training. Efforts have been made by Garhwal Mandal Vikas Nigam to introduce insurance cover to skiers,trekkers and river rafters but, so far no uniform coverage system could be evolved as Insurance Companies have not taken keen interest for such activities. Efforts are now being made to have a State level Policy in this equally important aspect of adventure tourism. For this purpose necessary provisions have been made in the rules and regulations formulated for adventure tourism. It will be mandatory for the adventure trade agencies to provide necessary insurance cover. Medical facilities available in Garhwal are being depicted in the brochures and publicity material. A State level 'Rescue Coordination Committee' has been set up under the Chairmanship of Chief Secretary, to coordinate various agencies/ departments engaged in safety and rescue of mountaineers and high altitude trekkers. Safety and Rescue training has been included in the training programs being conducted by departmental adventure tourism experts.

Himalayan tourism, which is largely a seasonal activity, should be so planned as to be spaced around the year. Tourists from different parts of the world visit Himalayan area mainly during summer months and in some part of the autumn. Consequently, during rainy and winter seasons, the available tourist facilities remain unutilised. This is one of the major reasons of unwillingness of private entrepreneurs to invest in lesser known-but otherwise, potential areas. To overcome this problem, it is necessary to promote off-season activities so that entrepreneur gets the business for the longer period.

State Government is fully aware of this seasonality problem and it has declared the whole of U.P. Hills as thrust area in its new tourism policy with special emphasis on adventure tourism. Auli has been developed as a ski centre having facilities of 3.9 km. long rope way, 600 meter long chair lift, 400 meter long ski lift with two snow beaters. Government has also provided 58.85 acre land for the Master Plan area for further development. Total 439.75 acres of land is being acquired for making it a Ski centre of international standards. Process of engaging a foreign consultant for preparing its Master Plan is already on.Similarly, to develop Dayara as another Ski resort in district Uttarkashi,prefeasibility report has been already prepared to develop it as winter sports centre.In the IXth Five Year Plan it is also proposed to develop Munsiyari as Ski and other winter sports centre. Rivers of Garhwal Himalaya provide ample opportunities to adventure loving people specially for river rafting. Stretch between Rishikesh and Kaudiyala has become most popular in the river Ganga for rafting companies and presently 13 such companies are doing river rafting.Government is fully aware of the carrying capacity of this area and in consultation with Forest Department this activity is being streamlined to have a single window clearance system in order to have sustainable growth of this sport with ecological balance. 12 new stretches have been identified in other rivers of Garhwal hills to promote river rafting in this area.

Lack of proper and easier accessibility has been one of the major constraint for unwillingness of tourists to visit these virgin Himalayan areas. One air strip at Chiniyalisaur in district Uttarkashi will be operational very soon. Another air strip is to be made available at Gaucher in district Chamoli for which land has already been acquired and construction is under way. All these Air strips will be helpful in making present cumbersome journeys of tourists easier and more tourists would be attracted to visit the area.

Promotion of lesser known but otherwise much more attractive destinations is another step which Government has undertaken as a part of its New Tourism Policy.It has been noticed that there is tremendous pressure on existing popular hill stations like Mussoorie etc. To ease the pressure of these towns,Government has decided to develop satellite towns in near vicinity of these places and develop more places simultaneously. While developing new places, carrying capacity with emphasis on environmental impact is being taken into consideration.It is being seen that an integrated approach is undertaken, so that provisions for basic infrastructural facilities are also made available.

It has been the endeavor of the State Government to attract more tourists in off season and accordingly efforts are on to promote Garhwal as 'winter Destination'. Promotion of local fairs and festivals full of colour and gaiety, which take place mostly in Winters and Autumn are being financed by the Department of tourism. International Yoga Week, Garhwal and Auli festivals are held during the winters and would certainly attract tourists during the off-season.

Hills of Garhwal also have tribal areas like Jonsar Bawar, Ranwai, Necti and Mana areas etc.It has been the tireless efforts of the State tourism Department that promotion of tourism activities do not adversely effect the rich cultural heritage of these areas.Tourism is being promoted in such a way that tribal culture and customs are also promoted and the participation of local tribal people is ensured. Some of these areas are now attracting larger amount for infrastructural investment. These areas are also being promoted as tourist destinations. Care has been taken that tourism in this area is handled carefully. Department of tourism is also providing financial assistance to various fairs and festivals organised in these areas to promote cultural friendly tourism. The festivals like *Darma Devi Mela, Kutti Chhota Kailash Mela, Lakha Mandal Veer Ka Mela, Mahasu mela,Bissu Mela, Ranwai Mela* etc. have already become popular attractions.

Publicity plays an important role in the tourism development. A comprehensive publicity campaign has been launched to lay more emphasis on lesser-known places, adventure tourism, winter packages, circuits and wild life. Do's and Don't have been incorporated in the tourist literature so that ecology of this area is not adversely affected.

It is evident that tourism is the main source of revenue and employment generation in the region. It is hoped that with the active co-operation of various agencies, persons, experts of the tourism trade and other persons associated with the development of this region there would be sustainable growth of the tourism sector and it would ultimately help in socio-economic development of Garhwal.

Tourism Policy, 2001 Department of Tourism, Government of Uttaranchal

Mission: To establish Uttaranchal in the world Tourism map as an international standard tourist destination. To ensure planned and sustainable development of tourism keeping in the view of environment with the active participation of private sector; to make tourism as a mean to provide employment and for the social and economic development of Uttaranchal.

Action Plan: Keeping in view of immense potential of Tourism in Uttaranchal; tourism will be established as an important industry and business activity, so that it can contribute for the economic development of this region and provide opportunity for self-employment. For the quick, planned and sustainable development the following components will be given more emphasis:

- Strengthening of organisation.
- Development of Infrastructure facilities.
- To increase the participation of private sector.
- To increase capital investment from various sources (investment from within the country, from foreign investors and NRIs) for tourism.
- Human resource development.
- Promotion and Marketing.
- To develop Pilgrimage Tourism.
- To develop Cultural Tourism.
- To develop Eco-Tourism.
- Development of Leisure Tourism.
- To develop Corporate/Convention Tourism.
- To develop Adventure Tourism and reconsideration of Inner Line Permit.
- Promotion of Tourism related Souvenir Industry.

Strengthening of Organization

Tourism Development Council

The major reasons of the development of tourism below potential in Uttaranchal are lack of sectoral coordination and proper action plan. In this action plan it is proposed that a high level "**Tourism Development Council**" would be formed by an ordinance of the Government. The main responsiblities of the council would be:

- To Make strategy and policy for the tourism development in Uttaranchal.
- To provide guidelines for the development of infrastructure facilities.
- To make effort for increased private investments.
- To identify the various projects related to tourism and its implementation.

Tourism-Development-Council will be the highest body to advise the Government on the subjects related to tourism. Council will also work as Regulatory and Licensing Authority. The organization structure of the council will be as follow. Minister of Tourism will be the president, State Tourism Development Commissioner will be the Vice-President and Secretary Tourism will be the Chief Executive Officer. The other members of the Council will be the officials of the Departments related to tourism and non-governmental members having expertise and experience in the tourism field. The five main divisions of the counsil will be:

- Infrastructure.
- Capital Investment and Finance.
- Administration.
- Planning and Project Development
- Publicity and Promotion.

The in charge of these divisions will be the officials of the rank of Director and they will be recruited either among the Government officials/sources or on the basis of open advertisement. The existing Directorate of Tourism will be merged in this council. Necessary steps will be taken to improve the organizational structure, work efficiency and coordination of the existing corporations i.e. Grahwal Mandal Vikas Nigam (GMVN), and Kumaon Mandal Vikas Nigam (KMVN).

Development of infrastructure facilities

To develop infrastructure according to the requirement of tourist and as of international standard the State Government will mobilize resources from its own and from the centrally sponsored projects of Government of India and also ensure participation of private sector. Action will be taken to develop, expand and strengthen the following tourism related infrastructure facilities:

- Railway Transport and Aviation services.
- A convenient and high quality road network with way side amenities.
- Creation of accommodation facilities.
- Madern telecom facilities.
- Water and Sewage facilities.
- Regular electricity supplies.
- Availability of land.

Participation of Private Sector and incentives to the private sector

The contribution of private sector in Tourism Industry is essential. To ensure the important role of private sector the following provisions are made in the new policy:

- All recognized new Tourism Units of the state shall be entitled for the facility of exemption/ deferment from the Luxury tax for the period of five years from the date of commencement of operations.
- The norms and procedures for assessment of Luxury tax for hotels will be rationalized.
- New Ropeways established in the state shall be eligible for the facilities of exemptions/deferment of Entertainment tax for the period of five years from the date of commencement of operations.

- Programs shown on television channels in hotels either through dish antenna or cable operator shall be eligible for a compounding scheme to assess the levy of the entertainment tax on the concerned hotel/tourist unit.
- The State Government will exempt the new amusement parks from the Entertainment tax for the period of five years from the date of commencement of operations.
- Facilities for beer bar license would be made available as per rules to recognized hotels units in the private sector, which have restaurant facilities.
- A Tourism self-employment scheme has been prepared for the residents of Uttaranchal with a financial assistance subject to a ceiling of Rs. 10.00 lakhs for starting tourism units such as fast food centres, souvenir sale outlets, buses, operations of taxies, purchase of equipment for adventure sports, small hotel and lodging facilities, information centres, restaurants with PCO facilities, Tent house facilities and projects for establishment of garages.

Capital Investment for Tourism

To develop the infrastructure facilitise and for the various projects in the Tourism sector investors within the country, from outside the country and Non-Resident Indians (NRIs) will be encouraged to invest. Such investments would primarily be helpful in building star category hotels and resorts, to establish golf courses, Eco-parks, amusement parks, Ropeways and winter sports projects. Attempts would be made to get financial assistance from the internatioal financial institutions like World bank and Asian Development Bank, etc.

Human Resource Development

- Higher level training programs like Degrees and Diplomas will be provided from hotel management and food craft institutes and tourism management institutions.

- Various Short term training programs will be arranged in the areas like restaurant operation, catering, food preservation, tourism awareness, guiding skill, culinary art, handling the information centers, etc.
- Special training programs will be organized for adventure sports in Adventure Tourism Training Instituties and more such institutes will be set up in the state.

Advertising and Publicity

- Sign boards related to tourism will be put up on highways, airports and railway stations.
- Tourism information centres will be established at railheads and roadheads of Uttaranchal.
- Posters, pamphlets, guide maps, films and other literatures related to important tourist attractions of Uttaranchal will widely be published and publicized.
- An internet web site will be developed to provide information related to tourism and tourist attractions of Uttaranchal and publicity campaign will be launched through print and electronic media. Reservation facility will be made available through Internet.
- Wide publicity will be ensured for Uttaranchal Tourism by making presentation and participating in seminars and travel trade markest in India and abroad and also organizing those.
- Familiarization Trip (FAM Trip) for various tourist places of Uttaranchal will be organized from time to time involving private entrepreneurs of tourism industry like travel agents, tour operators and hoteliers, media persons, travel writers, departmental officials and employees.
- To give wider publicity to the tourist places of Uttaranchal, attempt will be made to establish Film City in this region and necessary facilities will be developed for shooting films in this region.

Development of Pilgrimage Tourism

- To make the *char dham yatra* comfortable for the tourists and improve the management of the *char dhams*.
- To develop other less developed and lesser-known pilgrimage places like *Panch Prayags, Panch Badris*, etc.
- To keep the religiosity of the *dhams* intact.

Development of Cultural Tourism

Wide publicity of fairs and festivals, traditional lifestyles, dresses and foods of Uttaranchal will be done. Besides certain fairs and festivals will be organized in such a way that they themselves will be developed as complete tourism product. '*Nanda Devi Raj Jaat*' and '*Magh Mela of Uttarkashi*' will be organized like the '*Dussehra*' of Kullu (Himachal Pradesh) to attract the tourists. With the co-ordination of Archaeological Department preservation of important archaeological sites and cultural heritage will be done.

Development of Eco Tourism

With the objective of developing Eco-friendly tourism like Jungle Safari, Nature-walk, camping and displaying the bio-diversity, Botanical Garden-cum-Heritage Centers and Theme Parks will be established. For the conservation of environment, intensive plantation of trees will be encouraged in the campus and surroundings of the accommodations units. Intensive campaign will be launched with the help of private sector to control the plastic waste. Incinerators will be installed to incinerate waste disposal and plastics. Tourism Development Plans of various destinations will be prepared keeping in view of the carrying capacity of those places.

Development of Leisure Tourism

In Uttaranchal a lot of destinations with natural beauty are there to develop them for leisure tourism. In those destinations attempts will be made to establish Yoga, Ayurveda and Naturopathy centers.

Development of Adventure Tourism and Reconsideration of Inner Line Permit

To give new dimension to tourism development in the region, adventure tourism activities will be promoted and for this registered societies of various adventure sports institutes will be formed. For trekking, master plan of various trek routes will be prepared. These trek routes will be properly developed and provision of basic facilities and amenities like drinking water, toilets and shelters will be done. Proper availability of tents, equipment, trained guides and porters will be ensured. Guidelines will be made to protect the environment from these activities. For water sports like white water rafting, besides the present popular stretch from Kaudiyala to Rishikesh, other stretches will be identified and promoted with the active participation of private sector. Other water sports activities will be developed in various places of Uttaranchal like Dodital, Asan-barrage, Tehri dam and Maneri bhali etc. For winter sports Auli will be promoted as an international standard ski resort. Besides Dayara *bugyal* of Uttarkashi and Munsyari will also be developed for winter sports. Since Uttaranchal has high potential for aero sports activities like Hang gliding, Paragliding and Ballooning etc, attempt will be made to promote these activities with co-ordination of private sector. For the promotion of adventure tourism government will give incentives and grants to various institutions related to these sports.

Promotion of Tourism Related Souvenir Industry

Traditional handicrafts of rural areas will be promoted by giving training to the craftsmen and establishing craft villages and craft markets. Space will be provided for souvenir shops in the accommodation units of Department of Tourism.

7.2.3. PLANNING AND MANAGING HERITAGE RESOURCES

The planning and management of heritage resources should be based on national or state tourism policy. In the absence of such policy, the planning team must assume what would be a suitable policy for the area. If there is no adopted policy, it may be appropriate for the project team to recommend in the tourism plan an appropriate policy.

The process of planning heritage attractions should include:

- Determination of the development and conservation objectives;
- Environmental/ecological analysis, including any special surveys required such as of the wildlife, flora, and ecological systems, with identification of special environmental and cultural areas to be preserved;
- Fstablishment of visitor carrying capacities especially for those places attracting thousands of tourist. It may be based on various assumptions and types of visitor use;
- Projection of visitor demand by type of use, such as day tours, hiking, and camping and, if necessary reconciliation be made with the carrying capacity analysis to arrive at optimum visitor use levels;
- Determination of the type of visitor facilities needed and facility space requirements;
- Formulation of the plan, including preparation and evaluation of outline plans based on the plan's objectives and environmental impacts, and finalization of the selected plan with any staging of development indicated;
- Preparation of a visitor use organization and flow patterns plan where appropriate;
- Final environmental impact analysis; and
- Implementation of the plan and continuous management of the resource and its visitor use.

An important prerequisite for the management of cultural resources is to find out their historical development, product characteristics, cultural and religious significance, and other authentic information.

How to Plan Archaeological and Historic Sites?

In planning an archaeological and historical site like Lakhamandal (Dehradun district), Vishwanath temple of Uttarakashi, Guptakashi, Vishnu temple of Pandukashar (Chamoli) and their environs, the major consideration is conservation of archaeological or historic features. We may propose visitor facilities and services which can be determined on the basis of projected visitor use. A visitor use plan should be prepared that indicates the easy access and exit points and flow of visitors through the site. However it is necessary to prohibit direct access to very fragile features but only allow views of them, and to control the total number of visitors at the site at any one time if there is danger of excessive congestion or site deterioration especially on the occasion of annual fairs and festivals. People from different walk of life assemble at Uttarakashi during *Magh Mela* and similar events take place in other areas. Signs can be utilized to explain the background and major characteristics of the site. Brochures printed in local language can also be available on free of cost to explain the significance of the site in more detail. At many sites, well-trained and sometimes multi-lingual guides should be available. Tourists should be informed of any control measures that they should observe, such as not littering or smoking. Continuous monitoring must be maintained of the visitor satisfaction levels and sociocultural and environmental impacts of the facility development and visitor use.

Management of Arts and Handicrafts

Arts (painting and sculpture) and handicrafts are important attractions for tourists in all over the world. Their sales can be a significant source of income for residents, and they represent an important aspect of the cultural heritage of an area. A basic concept in the management of arts and handicrafts is that they must be authentic, at least in terms of utilizing local traditional skills, techniques, motifs, and materials. An approach usually applied is that designs can be modified to suit tourist market demand if the authenticity of skills, techniques, motifs, and materials is maintained. There may be various problems associated with maintaining acceptable quality standards and fair pricing for arts and handicrafts and ensuring that the handicraft producers receive their equitable share of the purchase price of the items. The government should establish its own handicraft centers, which maintain minimum quality standards, pay the producers an equitable price, and set fair sales pricing structure. In Garhwal a special corporation has already been set up that encourages local people to produce attractive pieces of arts and crafts. We come across with a fairly large number of such emporiums, mainly located in the GMVN complexes. What we intend to say that tourists should be informed about these centers, which are an attraction in themselves to visit, where they can observe the quality and pricing, learn about the crafts, and purchase some if they want. Private handicraft shops must usually meet the standards established by the government centers in order to remain competitive, but the quality of products they sell is doubtful. Arts and handicraft-making demonstrations by the artists and craft persons can be an interesting and educational experience for tourists and may induce them to make purchases that they would not have otherwise made. Demonstrations can be done in government centers or private factories and shops or both.

Performing Arts

The management of cultural resources such as dance, music, and drama must be tailored to each specific situation. For traditional dance, music, and drama unique to distinct cultural groups and often an important type of attraction in cultural tourism, a decision must often be made as to whether the performances are effectively presented to visitors in their original setting at the places of tourist interest. Garhwal is known for rich folk and it has heroic past which can be shown in organising *Pandava* dance. A number of books have been published on music and dance. But surprisingly least consideration has been given to organise events and performances for visitors. The time has come when local artists should be encouraged to involve themselves in such performances, which are meaningful not only for restoration of art and culture but also for the employment generation to the community as a whole.

Special Cultural Events

Special cultural events such as religious carnivals, art fairs, dance, music and drama, or general cultural festivals can be significant attractions for residents and tourists. If special cultural events like *Nanda Raj Jaat* already exist, then tourism needs to be organised to take advantage of these by involving more number of participants without generating any serious problems such as congestion or violation of religious codes. In some regions there may not be such special cultural events then it may be possible to organise some unique aspects of the culture, such an annual arts, music, or cultural festival at appropriate place preferably linked with history and religion on periodical basis.

Traditional Cultural Patterns

Traditional cultural patterns of life-styles, belief systems, customs, ceremonies, dress, and economic activities of tribal areas of Uttarakashi and Chamoli is also an important attraction. It can also educate tourists and bring economic benefits to an area, but they are the most difficult to portray to tourists in an authentic manner without the danger of some disruption to the local communities. Exposure to traditional life-styles and activities is most effective if it takes place in the original, authentic settings such as traditional villages, although this is not always possible. If cultural tours are organized to the villages not far away from tourist places it must be carefully organized with knowledgeable guides as well as explanation to tourists of local customs, protocol and control of where the tourists can go and what can be photographed. It is also important to arrange visits only during certain time periods. If it is decided that no tourists should visit authentic traditional villages or rural areas or if it is not feasible for them to make these visits, a common approach is to develop model villages, farms, or other types of replicas as authentic reconstruction as have been developed by Garhwal Mandal Vikas Nigam at Chandrapuri near Rudraprayag. This village also displays, of course, artificial environments, but it can still educate tourists about the traditional life of Garhwal in an interesting manner.

7.2.4. INSTITUTIONAL ELEMENTS AND HERITAGE TOURISM

Tourism Manpower Planning

Manpower planning is a systematic approach to ensure that the right people are in the right job at the right time. This is especially important in tourism, which is a type of service activity, depending in large part for its success on human resources and the quality of personnel working in tourism. Manpower planning in tourism should be approached systematically for all types and levels of tourism-related personnel, including national, regional, and community government tourism administrations, accommodation and catering management and operations, tour and travel management and operations, and related tourist facility and service operations, such as for public and private tourist attractions and road, air, and water transportation operations if their manpower planning is not already being handled by other organizations. This planning takes into account both the types of jobs to be filled and the numbers of people and their requisite training to fill these jobs.

Manpower planning involves the four steps of:

- Evaluating the present utilization of manpower in tourism and identifying any existing problems and needs;
- Projecting the future manpower needed by the number of personnel required in each category of employment and determining the qualifications for each category of job;
- Evaluating the human resources available in the future; and

- Formulating the education and training program required to provide the requisite qualified manpower.

Various types of education and training should be considered in a comprehensive education and training plan. Often combined into a single plan or program to satisfy the various needs, these types of education and training include the following:

- On-the-job training provided in the places of employment, such as hotels and restaurants. For low skill level employees, on-the-job training may be sufficient, without the need for formal training.
- Short courses on various aspects of tourism, designed either on new subjects or for up grading existing skills. Short courses may be given in the place of employment or in a local training institution like in the Department of Tourism, HNB Garhwal University, Srinagar Garhwal, which have planned to conduct short term programmes on a number of themes including ecotourism, marketing and Himalayan Heritage Tourism.
- Formal, regular vocational programs of one-half, one, two, or three years, usually in a hotel and tourism training institution or department of a multi program vocational school. Such courses have been introduced at Institute of Hotel Management, Dehradun.
- Regular university type Diploma, Bachelor's and Master's degree programs (usually one to three years in duration) in hotel, tourism, or transportation management. Department of Tourism, HNB Garhwal University, runs two year Master Degree Programme in Tourism Administration, divided into 4 semesters with 28 modules and one year Post Graduate Diplomas in Tourism and Hoteliering, Front office & House keeping and Restaurant & catering operation.
- Study tours, which include visiting places that offer examples of tourism development and operations, such as

resorts, hotels, and tourist attractions, and meeting with tourism officials and administrators from different places.

- Correspondence courses, which are available on all aspects of hotel, catering, tour operations, and tourism management.

Practical training in tourism may also be given to local people for employment purpose in the following areas:

- Geography: Physical land and landscape
- Flora and Fauna
- Map reading
- Proficiency in conversational English and other foreign languages
- Catering and food nutrition
- Housekeeping and on self attitude
- Art, Architecture, and culture
- Socio-economic traditions.

Education and Interpretation of Heritage Sites

Although heritage education can be mandated on the national level, it must begin with local citizens. It is their site, their culture, they are the ones whom visitors come in contact, and they are key to protecting, interpreting and communicating the essence of their heritage. Local education planning should also include civic groups, local leaders, voluntary organisations and media whose understanding and support is needed.

A high priority should be placed on travel industry education. Tour operators must be given the knowledge to operate in a responsible manner so as not to damage the community or create negative feelings. Visitors should be educated at different stages like pre arrival on site and post visit.

Types of Incentives to Heritage Product Promoters

- Provision of suitable land either on lease or on moderate rates.
- Creation of off-site infrastructure.
- Complete or partial exemption from Customs duties on imported equipment and other necessary items of trekking use.
- Complete or partial exemption from Income taxes, sales taxes and other luxury taxes for specified number of years.
- Provision of grants for development of facilities up to a certain percentage of investment costs.
- Facility of loans up to a certain percentage of investment cost at low interest rates.
- Provision of subsidies both on interest payments of loans and on actual amount of loans.
- Allowance of foreign exchange credits from foreign sources for allocation to investment in facilities.
- Provision of aid for the orientation programme of engaged manpower.

7.2.5. EFFECTIVE MARKETING PLANNING

Marketing

Although some major heritage sites of the region are overwhelmed by crowds, in most places, the heritage product is being undersold. Marketing can only help situation, if marketing is an integral part of tourism management. The Garhwal Himalaya is full of attractions that hardly possible to experience anywhere. Therefore, we have not only to identify the target markets, and consumer reaction to the product cost but also to design advertising and promotional aids. Marketers need to understand how buyers make their purchasing decisions for different kinds of products and service.

Objectives

- Achieving a certain level of sales growth within a given period of time.
- Increasing the profitability of both public and private sectors by a given percentage within an agreed time scale.
- Obtaining a given percentage share of the market within a given period of time.
- Reducing the development risk by including other attractions on routes to major places.
- Obtaining a measured increase in the return on capital employed by public and private sectors within a time period.

Strategic Marketing Planning

Product Differentiation: The operational agencies may choose certain kinds of packages, which are not provided in any part of the Himalayas. The operational tour agencies may include 22 valleys of flowers, adjoining meadows, lakes, and tribal villages.

Market Focus: The planners have to make the attractions and other ancillary goods and services to the precise needs of markets. The marketing manager must always ask himself, why should my customer buy my products rather than those of my competitors. Unless he can provide a sound answer to that question, the success of the product will remain in doubt.

Forecasting: The forecast is to be prepared to reflect the anticipated results with projected sales profitability and cash flow. The forecasts may be made both on short-term (for one season) and for long-term (ranging for 5 to 10 years).

Branding: Giving the heritage tourism product a brand name is not only a useful way of differentiating it from natural and adventure products but also a means of adding perceived value. A brand may be defined as a name, sign, symbol or design or combination of these, intended to identify the products of an organisation and distinguish them from those of competitors.

Branding is necessary due to following reasons:

- It identifies a particular product and distinguishes it from competitors.
- It is helpful for publicity and promotion provided it maintains level of quality.
- As trekking and other tourism services are intangible product, it helps consumers to avoid risks.
- Branding provides the opportunity for service agencies in building their corporate image.
- Detailed research work suggested that without branding the image of a region is confusing to the public.

In Garhwal Himalaya a number of tour and travel companies are involved with adventure tourism. Each company may choose to develop and use a brand exclusively for itself. Other alternative is to franchise brand. In this situation, the company owning the brand allows others to sell the product with certain precondition such as to pay a proportion of the earnings to the franchiser (royalty payments). The GMVN Ltd. can become the leading franchiser as it enjoys:

- Government recognition.
- Facilities and amenities.
- Market credibility.
- Trained and skilled personnel.

The GMVN can establish and popularised the brand in the market before it is launched as a product. The name and symbol of the brand has to be framed according to nature of tourism. However, it should be different from the existing one of GMVN. Names must be easy to pronounce and remember, as well as helping to convey the product benefits. Symbols should be distinctive, in terms of design and colour supporting the product concept.

Fixation of Price

Premium Pricing: In this category, prices are fixed above market price. The higher Himalayan religious shrines reflect the unique status and some of them may have such attractions that are not traceable in any mountain region in the world. Visitors have therefore no hesitation to pay premium pricing especially for the packages covering special cultural heritage areas. For such pricing the trek routes leading to Nandanvan, Nanda Devi, Roopkund and Sahestratal are worth to mention.

Value for Money Pricing: Here the tolerable prices are charged for products and services. Some of the places which are dominated by pilgrimage, and budget tourists, enable the suppliers and tour companies to achieve a good levels for money pricing. Such places mainly include kedarnath, Gaumukh, Yamnotri, Hemkund and Valley of Flowers. In this category low prices are announced so as to attract mass tourists. There are certain trek areas similar to our competitors. Heavy discount is the only way to motivate consumers. The trek routes that may be offered under this category include Dodital, Nagtibba, Kalpeshwar and Tungnath.

Factors Influencing Price Fixation

- The economic condition of Garhwal and the adjoining region.
- Occurrence of natural calamities and avalanches.
- Emergence of virtual reality and pattern of demand for tourism products.
- Levels of competition faced by individual companies.
- The nature of tourists market which will determine what kind of holidays or other travel products they will buy and at what price.

- Problem of Seasonality.

Discounts

Today, with the changing services of travel and tourism industry, the idea of set price for travel services is fast disappearing. In Garhwal region-alluring consumers by giving various discounts has rarely been noticed in travel trade. Marketing theory recognises at least six forms of discounting, although not all these are to be found in the travel and tourism industry. Discounts on cash, Group tours, and length of travel to be given. The product and service suppliers may give the following discounts.

- Discounts for cash payments.
- Price reductions for quantity purchase.
- Trade discounts- Discounts offered to people employed in the trade.
- Trade in allowance- Special allowance on sale of product is given to the employer.
- Seasonal discounts, to charge lower prices during off-season.
- Advance discounts- to give those who makes early bookings.

Marketing Communication

It is to be determined that what message is to deliver to markets. The major elements of message are as follows.

- Kind of message- the nature of subject matter we want to deliver.
- Encode the message- putting the message into a form in which it will be clearly understood.
- Channel choice- nature of media.

Ways to communicate the Message

- By advertising
- Using resource persons in personal selling
- Conducting sales promotion activities.
- Publicity through public relation section and inviting travel writers and media reporters.

Advertising: For right promotion of heritage tourism, the advertisement essentially follows the AIDA principle of:

- Attract attention
- Create Interest
- Foster Desire
- Inspire Action

We may include the following points for result oriented advertisement.

- The material, media and method.
- The number of people to whom it is to be advertised and frequency of advertisement repetition.
- Advertising campaigning in comparison of competitors.
- Timing of the campaigning related to buying pattern.

Advertisement through Publication: If the advertisement is made through Newspapers/ Journals/ Magazines or any other literature in the areas of tourists origin/ market the following are the points to be taken into consideration prior placing an advertisement.

- Whether it is daily, weekly, fort nightly, monthly, quarterly, semi annual or yearly publication?
- What is time duration between literature distribution and tourist season?
- How popular is it in youths, potential for tourism?

- Whether the selling price of publication is within the reach of a common man?
- Of these, how many are distributed in audience and target market? Is there any evidence of their being read by more than one person?
- Are the distribution literature is wanted and unwanted, i.e. paid for or free sheets?
- How frequently are they published and how long is it effective?
- Is colour or spot colour available?
- What is the reproduction method and quality like?

Publishing an Attractive Brochure: The travel brochures are the most authentic and cost effective media of information dissemination. Tourism is a newly setup industry in Garhwal and publicising brochures on cultural places has recently been taken up. Therefore, before publication of a brochure the following points may be considered:

- The printing and paper should be of high quality.
- The matter and design style is to be relevant to the contents.
- Location scaled map, indicating all available services en route destination, is an essential feature of brochure.
- The brochure cover should contain a spectacularly attractive photograph of unique heritage destination of Garhwal.
- The content pages should always be arranged in sections.
- The brochure must posses high quality colour reproduction, descriptive titles for each package tour, route maps, day to day itinerary, and at least three photographs respectively featuring a trail route, a tourist attraction like famous religious shrine or lake or glacier where visitors generally come for solace and salvation.

- The paper thickness and type is an important aspect in brochure publication. If there are many pages we may use thinner paper.
- Photographs should be high in contrasts. Colour pictures should be on transparency film on a large film format as possible.
- Television, Radio, and Travel and Trade exhibitions are also the important tools of promotion.

Besides this on site promotion like special events such as Badri-Kedar Mahotsava, Garhwal Mahotsava can bring much publicity. Special events such as *Nanda Raj Jaat,* Himalayan Car Rally, National Snow Skiing Competition, Meet of River Runner Association can put the area on tourist map.

Sales Promotion Techniques: In addition to advertisement, sales promotion techniques are generally treated as a form of "Below the line promotion". Inbound tour operators for sales promotion can adopt the following techniques.

- Incentives to workers and visitors.
- Bonus to staff members.
- Contests and competitions for visitors.
- Give aways(pens, ashtrays, calendars diaries etc., usually bearing the company name).
- Trade exhibition on the occasion of travel mart.

Direct mail (letters and circulars etc.) to visitors availed holidays with company concerned.

Promotion Programmes

- Publication of literature such as scaled guide maps, route maps, posters, postcards, maps, travel agents manuals and information leaflets and distribution channels must be decided upon.

- Preparation and presentation of audio-visual material such as slide, film and video shows in the places of tourists origin.
- Advertisement in youth related magazines and periodicals having widest circulation.
- Selected heritage tourism trial talk/episode on radio and television under national programme.
- Organising seminars/workshops on heritage tourism in the places of visitors origin.
- Inviting travels writers, photographers and other reference group of well-known newspapers and magazines for the possible coverage of heritage of Garhwal.
- Publication of up dated guide books on all major trek routes of the region and include all information not traceable any where.

How to Select Distribution System?

The new entrepreneurs, have less resources for marketing and sales promotion. In Rishikesh and Hardwar, most of the tour operators are single handed and run business in small size. In such circumstances, they may sell their respective packages through consortia. It is regarded cost effective and viable for seasonal tourism destination. The following are the important points:

- Consortia is a joint travel and tourism marketing programme of various companies while retaining their financial independence.
- Publication of joint brochure for all agencies.
- Each operational company finds place, facilities and packages in brochure at proportionate rate.
- Negotiation of higher rates of commission for group members.
- It provides the means to recruit management expertise on a scale unthinkable for the small company alone.

Franchises

It is another way of marketing. Its benefits are as follows:

- Rights to sell an established brand name product, and the centralised marketing support provided by the franchiser.
- Accumulation of funds with the franchiser helps national and international advertisement campaign. It creates brand awareness and ready demand for the product.
- The Franchisees are their own bosses. They can also be relied upon to work harder to ensure the success of the organisation.

7.2.6 ACTION STRATEGY FOR SUSTAINABLE HERITAGE TOURISM DEVELOPMENT PLAN

According to the World Tourism Organisation (1993) "Sustainability" is a more powerful concept of defining an appropriate approach to tourism developments. Because of the expected continuing growth of tourism, sustainable tourism development is the approach that would be most successful. Because of the pressure on the world's resources, it is the only sensible approach. The most successful tourism development of the future will be sustainable which will not over consume the resources used to attract tourists. How is the concept of sustainability actually implemented for tourism developments? The principles are not difficult, but they do require changes in the way most tourism projects are currently conceived and developed. WTO has suggested (1993) the following principles for sustainable tourism planning.

- Most comprehensive planning.
- More consultative and democratic planning processes.
- New Institutional relationship must be formed.
- Sustainable tourism measures the environment impacts of the development in physical, social and cultural terms.
- Sustainable tourism calculates the carrying capacity at destinations.

The goals of sustainable tourism are:

- To develop greater awareness and understanding of the significant contributions that tourism can make to the environment and the economy;
- To promote equity in development;
- To improve the quality of life of the host community;
- To provide a high quality of experience for the visitor; and
- To maintain the quality of the environment on which the foregoing objectives depend.

The responsibility for the implementation of sustainable development planning may be carried out jointly by the Governments, Non-Governments organisations, Tourism Industry, Individual Tourists and International Organisations. What should be the role of the foregoing agencies in the sustainable tourism development has rightly been discussed in the tourism action strategy committee of the Globe'90 conference on sustained development held in Vancouver, Canada, in March 1990. It defined Sustainable Tourism, as- "the management of tourism resources in such a way that fulfills economic, social and aesthetic needs while maintaining cultural integrity, essential ecological processes, biological diversity and life support system. As tourism development usually involves the financial, socio-cultural and natural resources of an area, it must be designed and managed in a sustainable way in order to achieve economic, ecological, social and cultural sustainability Sustainable implies permanence. This conveys an integrated act in the environment, the "optimum" use of the resources, the involvement of the local population, the preservation and improvement of the surroundings, all of which allow a sustainable and therefore, lasting process as against the popular concept of the maximum use of space and time. But some tourist activities are not sustainable, and, therefore, scientific approach for sustainable development of tourism should be evolved which conserve and not consume the environment, by establishing tourism environment capability. Such a development has to explore the relationship between the natural resources and the visitor community, with special regard to its conservation through sensitive planning and management.

The first step towards sustainable planning and development is to protect the environment and initiate efforts for environment friendly tourism. Governments, in consultation with the Private Sector, can establish and enforce environmental standards for the travel and tourism. To facilitate and recognise this responsibility, the World Tourism Organisation (WTO) has been developing key indicators for the tourism sector to improve decision-making with regard to sustainable tourism development. Like a canary in a coal mine, indicators are used to warn the areas of concern so that action can be taken in time. Tourism currently lacks such a canary as the industry is multi-sectoral. It involves mass movement of people. The actions and activities of many other sectors affect the tourism product. A set of international environmental indicators similar to the well-accepted economic indicators has yet to be developed. The WTO has been sponsoring groundbreaking research in this field and has come up with a set of "environmental indicators" as indicated in figure, to measure the healthiness of tourism destinations. The idea is to devise simple measurements of environmental sensibility, stress on the environment, results of tourist use and the human and biological consequences of tourist use.

Table - 7.2

Core Indicators of Sustainable Tourism

Indicators	**Specific Measures**
Site Protection	Category of site protection according to IUCN index.
Stress	Tourist number visiting site (per annum/peak month)
Use Intensity	Intensity of use-peak period (persons/ hectares).

1	2
Social impact	Ratio of tourists to locals (peak period).
Developing Control	Existence of environmental review procedure of formal controls over development of site and use densities.
Waste Management	Percentage of sewage from site, receiving treatment (Additional indicators may include structural limits of other infrastructural capacity on site - e.g. water supply, garbage).
Planning process	Existence of organised regional plan for tourist destination region (including tourism component).
Critical Ecosystems	Number of rare/endangered species.
Consumer Satisfaction	Level of satisfaction by visitors (questionnaire based)
Local Satisfaction	Level of satisfaction by locals (questionnaire based)

International Union for the Conservation of Nature and Natural Resources.
Source: WTO (1995), Madrid.

Role of Planners

Determining Carrying Capacities:

Carrying capacity analysis is believed to be the most reliable and effective method for Sustainable Tourism Development. The Importance of incorporating carrying capacity analysis into the tourism planning process has been emphasised, for example, by McCool (1978), Getz (1983), O'Reilly (1986) and Romeril (1989) despite some difficulties in establishing precise means of measurement and standards. According to Inskeep (1991) carrying capacities need to be established generally for the planning area (usually based on analysis of the specific major attraction features, development sites, and sometimes tourist-transit points) and calculated more precisely for each development site at the community planning level. Inskeep (1991) emphasised the need to determine the carrying capacity of a destination so that tourism development:

- does not result in serious environmental problems such as congestion, air, water, noise or visual pollution, degradation of ecosystems, or overload of the infrastructure.
- does not result in a loss of cultural identity of the host society or social problems, such as crimes.
- does not create serious economic distortions, while still bringing economic benefits, maintains tourist satisfaction levels so that the desired tourist market continue visiting the area.

According to WTO (1983) to determine the carrying capacity, the two aspects to be considered are:

- **The Indigenous Physical and Socio Economic Environment**:- This refers to the capacity that can be achieved without resulting in damage to the physical (natural and man-made) environment and generating sociocultural and economic problems to the local community, and maintaining the proper balance between development and conservation.
- **The Tourism Image and Tourist Product**:- This refers to the capacity or number of visitors that are compatible with the image of the tourist product and the types of environmental and cultural experiences that the visitors are seeking. The criteria for determining optimum capacity levels include the following:

Physical

- Acceptable levels of visual impact and congestion;
- Point at which ecological systems are maintained before damage occurs;

- Conservation of wildlife and natural vegetation of both land and marine environments; and
- Acceptable levels of air, water, and noise pollution.

Economic

- Extent of tourism that provides optimum overall economic benefits; and
- Level of tourism employment suited to the local community.

Socioculture

- Extent of tourism development that can be absorbed without detriment to the socioculture life styles and activities of the community; and
- Level of tourism that will help maintain cultural monuments, arts, crafts, belief system, customs, and traditions without detrimental effects.

Infrastructure

- Adequate availability of transportation facilities and services;
- Adequate availability of utility services of water supply, electric power, sewage and solid waste disposal and telecommunications; and
- Adequate availability of other community facilities and services such as those related to health and public safety.

The criteria that can be applied in determining carrying capacities relative to tourism image or visitor satisfaction levels include the following:

Physical

- Overall cleanliness and lack of pollution of the destination environment;
- Lack of undue congestion of the destination environment, including of tourist attraction features;

- Attractiveness of the landscape or townscape, including quality and character of architectural design; and
- Maintenance of the ecological systems and flora and fauna of natural attraction features.

Economic

- Intrinsic interest of the indigenous community and culture;
- Quality of local arts, handicrafts, cuisine, and cultural performances; and
- Friendliness of residents.

Infrastructure

- Acceptable standards of transportation facilities and services;
- Acceptable standards of utility services; and
- Acceptable standards of other facilities and services.

How to determine the capacity standards for an individual tourist centre is also problematic. Some standards for rural and recreation activities are cited by the WTO (1983) as follows, expressed in visitors per day per hectare except where noted:

- Forest park : up to 15.
- Suburban nature park : 15-70.
- High-density picnicking : 300-600.
- Low-density picnicking : 60-200.
- Sports/team games : 100-200.
- Golf : 10-15.
- For water - based activities:

  1. Fishing/sailing : 5-30.
  2. Speed boating : 5-10; and
  3. Water skiing : 5-15.

- For nature trails in persons per day per kilometer

  1. Hiking : 40; and 2. Horse riding: 25-80
- For ski resorts, a general guide is 100 skiers per hectare of trailways.

Role of Government in Promoting Sustainable Heritage Tourism Development

- Government should undertake area and sector specific research into the environmental, cultural and economic effects of tourism.
- Government should develop standards and regulations for environmental and cultural impacts assessments, monitoring and auditing of existing and proposed tourism developments.
- Government should apply sectoral and/or regional environment accounting systems for the tourism industry.
- Government should design and implement public consultation techniques and processes in order to involve all stockholders in making tourism related decisions.
- Government should design and implement educational and awareness programmes which will sensitise people to the issue of sustainable tourism development.
- Government should develop design and construct standard which will ensure that tourism development projects are sympathetic with local culture and natural environments.
- Government should ensure that carrying capacities of tourism destinations reflect sustainable levels of development and are monitored and adjusted appropriately.
- Government should regulate and control tourism in environmentally and culturally sensitive areas.
- Government should include tourism in land use planning.
- Government should create tourism advisory boards that involve all stake holders (the public, indigenous populations and etc.).

- Government should ensure that all Government Departments involved in tourism are briefed on the concept of sustainable development. The respective ministries (e.g. Environment, Natural Resources, etc.) should collaborate to achieve sustainable tourism development.
- Ensure that national and local tourism development agreements stress a policy of sustainable tourism development.

Role of Non-Government Organisation (NGOs) in Promoting Sustainable Heritage Tourism Development

- NGOs should be part of sustainable tourism advisory boards at all levels of government and or industry and offer input into sustainable tourism planning and development.
- NGOs should promote the use of local residents to assist in sustainable tourism research and data collection.
- NGOs should offer to other agencies information on locally innovated sustainable tourism products and proposals including the use of locally appropriate technologies.
- NGOs should be more involved in public education and awareness programmes.
- NGOs should be encouraged to identify and communicate to the appropriate agencies those issues related to sustainable tourism as well as solutions to these problems.

Role of Tourism Industry in Promoting Sustainable Tourism Development

- Protecting the Biosphere, for example by minimizing and eliminating pollution which causes environment damage and by supporting parks and reserve at key sites.
- Sustaining the use of Resources, for example, by ensuring sustainable use of land, water and forests in tourism activities.

- Reducing and Disposing of Waste, for example, by recycling, reusing, and reducing wherever possible and by having high standards for sewage treatment and waste disposal.
- Adopting energy efficiency practices, for example, by maximizing when possible the use solar power, etc.
- Minimising environmental risks e.g. avoid hazardous locations such as malarial swamps.
- Undertaking Green Marketing, for example, by promoting "soft" tourism that minimises adverse environmental and cultural impacts as well as informing tourists of the impacts of their presence.
- Mitigating damage, for example, by replacing or restoring degraded environments and compensating for local adverse effects.
- Providing complete and credible information to tourists, for example, by disclosing hazardous locations.
- Incorporating environmental Values in Management of operations, for example, by ensuring environment representation at the executive level on board or management groups.
- Conducting regular environmental audits, for example, by conducting independent assessment of environmental performances of the entire business operations (e.g. monitor water quality, carrying capacity, energy consumption, environmental aesthetic and sewage etc.).

Role of Individual Tourist in Promoting Sustainable Heritage Tourism Development

- Choosing an operator which has the reputation of being ethical and environmentally responsible.
- Learning about and respecting the human and natural heritage of the host.

- Traveling in culturally and environmentally sensitive manners.
- Refraining from purchasing or using those products, service and transportation which endanger the local ecology and culture.
- Practicing minimal-impact travel and following environmental regulations in natural and cultural heritage areas.

7.3 HERITAGE TOURISM : IMPACT ASSESSMENT

7.3.1 ENVIRONMENTAL IMPACT

The relationship between tourism and the environment is complex and multifaceted. The range of recreational activities in mountain tourism, such as mountaineering, trekking, hiking, exploration, sightseeing, horse riding, rafting and other adventure activities are closely linked to the environment. Biophysical assets of the natural environment and the cultural heritage of the socioeconomic environment have proved to be the main attractions for mountain tourism (Shrestha; 1995). On the basis of motivational study of trekkers (Bagri, 1994) it is revealed that the study of physical environment comprised of the land, soil, topography, geology, water, flora and fauna and ecological system are the first choice of trekkers followed by socio-cultural milieu. The estimated number of trekkers were 50,000 in 1980 (Negi, 1982). Today over 1,00,000 people migrate to Himalayas for climbing, trekking and other adventure sports (Kohli, 1991). However, the statistics of trekkers to Garhwal, compiled by U.P. tourism, reveals, that in 1990 alone the Kedarnath trek (1,20,000), Yamnotri trek (1,00,672) and Hemkund and valley of flowers trek (59,778), attracted more visitors in comparison to kohli's (1991) estimation. This resulted in haphazard road construction, indiscriminate wood cutting, figure unplanned and unguarded infrastructure development, miserable poor resource Management and finally opening of unscrupulous agencies, which have actually led to help destroy the environment. Using the Alps as an example, it is generally understood that the immediate cause of environmental degradation is population growth and increase of influence of people living outside the mountains. This led especially since 1950 to rapidly increase demands for the developments of mountains especially for recreation with an overwhelming emphasis on water sports (Ives, 1985). Studies in Nepal (Bjonness, 1979) stress the point that trekking, and trekkers related activities are leading to accelerating rate of deforestation in the Sagarmatha area, thereby destroying the habitat for numerous wild animals and the rare high altitude plants. This has led to the need to close down the Nanda Devi National Park for trekkers and shepherds. The Nanda Devi National Park is the worst affected example that experienced environment erosion of its unique and virgin wilds. In the sixties, there used to be 1 to 3 expeditions per year in the area, viz. Nanda Devi, Nanda Devi East and Nanda Kot. In the seventies, this trend changed. In 1980 up to 10 trekking cum climbing expeditions enter the Nanda Devi area. This has led to unprecedented pollution in this area. Rheinberger, leader of the Australian Changbang (6864 M) expedition (1980), expressed his great surprise over the considerable amount of litter found at the camp sites along the Rishi gorge and at base camp within the Nanda Devi Northern Sanctuary. The Gangotri region is also most polluted. Unplanned and unauthorised constructions in Gangotri are in full swing. Deforestation has been increased for the commercial purposes, causing to soil erosion and land sliding and disrupting the normal hydrological cycle. Mountaineers all along the trail leave behind garbage and refuse etc. Foreigners are allowed access to many hitherto prohibited areas and streams of expeditions to a number of popular peaks led to serious depletion of the limited biological wealth during the crucial growth period in the few summer months. The slow growth of plants can be judged from the fact that birch tree in Gangotri region attains a diameter of two centimeter while a juniper bush takes twenty years for the same growth (Jayal, 1990). Local people for meeting the requirements of visitors are cutting such valuable trees on mass scale for domestic and commercial use. Bhojwasa and Chirbasa, once known for the thick vegetation of birch and pine forests are converted into barren land. The Gangotri

Glacier, on the basis of annual observation from 1935-1976, has already been receded 600 metres within 41 years duration (Vohra, 1981). Receding Glaciers leave behind unconsolidated debris, which may become the source material for landslides etc. Gangotri and Khatling area is more or less without vegetation cover. Har-Ki-Doon and Kedarnath Sanctuaries' wildlife like Musk Deer, Snow Leopard, Bharal, Tahr and the fishing cat have become rare features. Similarly, among the birds, the partridges, Pheasants and quills are also witnessing decrease in their population. The Bhuyandar Valley of Flowers attracts more numbers of visitors and offers world's unique rock garden of wondrous plants with amazing life cycle and mosaic of color. These environments of sensitive resources in fact should be made restricted to mass flow of visitors. On the basis of practical study the following positive and negative impacts of tourism on the Garhwal Himalayas have been noticed.

Typology of Impact

Positive Impacts

- Conservation of the endangered flora and fauna.
- Restoration of the archaeological and historical sites and architectural character of pilgrimage shrines.
- Improvement of environment by promoting aforestation programmes.
- Creation of environment oriented infrastructure and wayside amenities on trek routes.
- Increasing environment awareness among hosts and guests.
- The importance of scenic landscape, flora, fauna, barren landmass and other neglected natural resources of the Himalaya are being realised.
- General awareness about the pollution (air, water, noise, garbage and trash).
- Accessibility of mountaineers and trekkers to remote and difficult areas makes the poacher scare from poaching.

Negative Impacts

- Water pollution of sacred lakes, rivers and fountains.
- Noise pollution by mass pilgrims and trekkers.
- Visual pollution by unplanned and unguarded structures.
- Waste disposals generate both litter and environmental health problems on all major trek routes.
- Ecological disruption on account of uncontrolled trekking expeditions.
- Garbage trails and dirty campsites are developing like on Gangotri-Gaumukh trek route and Bhojbasa campsite.
- Destruction of Alpine flora from trampling, haphazard camping and collection of endanger and some rare species.
- Unplanned and unscientific road construction is leading towards landslides and floods.
- The disturbance of topsoil of trek route by the hooves of ponies and mules is causing soil erosion.
- Studies have shown that regular disturbance caused by visitors to nesting birds make the eggs vulnerable to predator attacks.
- Removal of beautiful flowers of particular species by a large number of visitors may reduce the chances of regeneration and long term survival of that species.

Environment Impact Control Measures

- Use of proper solid waste disposable techniques with recycling of waste products to the greatest extent feasible.
- Construction of adequate pedestrian paths in order to prevent traffic congestion.
- Careful management of visitors flows and where necessary, application of visitors use controls at natural and cultural tourist attractions to avoid congestion and environmental deterioration of these places.

- Application of suitable architectural design standards and use of building material for all structures in trekking area so that they are architecturally compatible.
- Requirement for underground of utility lines in trekking areas and careful siting and landscape screening of utility stations.
- Control on littering through trekking tourists and general public education.
- Control or prohibition on use of animals for trekking purpose.
- Prevention of cutting of trees for use as firewood in camping and trekking areas.
- Prohibition on grazing is necessary as it disrupts the natural ecosystem balance.

Table 7.3

Measure and actions as part of a plan to maintain and preserve Heritage Tourism in the mountain environment.

Category of measures		Type of action
1. Preventive measures	a.	Conduct periodic cleaning operations
	b.	Provide alternative fuel to porters, instead of kerosene oil.
	c.	Establish refuse collection areas at base camps which are to be cleaned regularly in May and June under Government supervision.
	d.	Construct micro hydroelectric power units, where feasible.
	e.	Use firewood saving technology.
2. Improvement measures	a.	Organise aforestation best suited to the local ecology.
	b.	Plant vegetation ,which cannot be used as fuel or wood.

1		2
	c.	Institute range management and control against over grazing by animals such as sheep and goats.
	d.	Construct latrines appropriates to the local style and disposal bins that suit local conditions.
3. Information measures	a.	Use electronic media to publicise environmental awareness.
	b.	Train people in local administration and in elected bodies through lectures, slide shows etc.
	c.	Hold international conferences.
	d.	Prepare billboards, T-shirts and similar general information devices.
	e.	Train porters.
4. Enforcement measures	a.	Ban expedition parties who pollute.
	b.	Take action against liaison officers who fail to implement and enforce rules.
	c.	Use existing punitive policies selectively.
5.Incentive measures.	a.	Give cash and/or certificates to individuals, parties and officers of the local administration for effective performance.
	b.	Publicise the positive work of people or parties who are effective in preserving the mountain environment.
	c.	Reward expedition parties who comply fully with rules and regulations about pollution.
6. Management measures.	a.	Periodically close peaks and routes that are most heavily damaged due to over-use.
	b.	Charge variables rates of royalty to expedition parties based on the pollution factors for various peaks.
	c.	Gradually introduce peaks that have not generally been known and used through a variety of incentives.

1	2
	d. Campaign to promote winter tourism in order to reduce congestion during the summer season.
	e. Continue research in order to access relevant agencies.
	f. Promote close coordination among relevant agencies.
	g. Share the distribution of royalty proceeds with local bodies, or allow them to impose a Ceases to cover expenses for cleaning and restoring the environment.

Source: ESCAP, United Nations, New York, 1993.

Policy Options for Conserving the Heritage Products in Mountain Environment

Policy options need to be based on careful study of the actual conditions in the mountainous areas. It is also important to establish priorities, and the finding presented by the Economic and Social Commission for Asia and Pacific (ESCAP), United Nations, (1993) can provide a preliminary guideline. At least nine factors have been identified for policy consideration:

1. Identification and ranking the seriousness of the main types of Environmental degradation is required. This study has identified six main types of pollution, listed below in order of importance: (a) Human and animal waste, (b) Discarded mountaineering gear, (c) Discarded containers, (d) Damage to wildlife, (e) Cutting of forests, and (f) Soil erosion.
2. Examination of the most heavily polluted areas is needed.
3. The rate of pollution needs to be assessed.
4. Careful examination of the time frame is required in order to have effective implementation.

5. Linkages need to be established between the policies and the institutional structures in order to assure proper implementation as well as effective coordination.
6. The role of the public sector and the private sector needs to be examined since both sectors are required if policies and programmes are to be successful.
7. Relationship needs to be developed with regional and international agencies, especially where there is an impact beyond national boundaries.
8. Action plans must be complete and include strategies, responsible institutions, time frame and cost estimates.
9. A monitoring system is needed to evaluate the effect of policies over time in order to consider the need for adjustments.

7.3.2 SOCIO-ECONOMIC IMPACTS

Positive Impacts

Economic Benefits: Garhwal Himalaya is a economically depressed area. The employment and income provided by tourism especially to porters, guides, eatery runners and other sectors, may help to stem out migration from this isolated region.

- Creation of Tourism industry related infrastructure and other essential services assist in general economic development.
- Economic development further accelerates the expansion of other activities such as catering, manufacturing of Souvenirs and creation of handicrafts.
- Tourism activity encourages rural people to adopt regular employment habits and work for the things they want

Conservation: Tourism helps in conservation of historical temples and religious shrines, conservation and revivation of traditional arts, handicrafts, dance, music, drama, customs and manners, dresses and ornaments, faiths and beliefs, and other certain aspects of traditional life style.

Financial incentives and assistance are provided for opening of rural and crafts museums and for organising fairs, festivals and pilgrimage processions and events.

Realisation of Cultural and Social Values: When tourists appreciate visiting area's cultural milieu and social systems, a sense of pride automatically generates inside the local people.

Cross -Cultural Exchange: Domestic trekking tourists coming from all direction to Garhwal for solace and salvation can achieve cross-cultural understanding and build a sense of national unity among diverse casts and creed of people.

Negative Impacts

- Loss of economic benefits to the local area can occur if tourism facilities and services are owned and managed by outsiders or by influential local person.
- Economic distortions can take place geographically if tourism activities are conducted in selected areas.
- Overcrowding of facilities, amenities and ancillary services can cause irritation to the local inhabitants.
- Commercialisation of scenic routes can leave negative impact on the cultural characters of region.
- Problems of social abuse like drugs, alcoholism, crime and prostitution may be exaggerated by tourists.

Impact Control Measures

- To develop tourism in gradual manner so that local residents have sufficient time to understand and to participate in it.
- Local people should be involved in the decision making.
- Integrated tourism development with other sectors of local economy and encourage local entrepreneurs to the greatest extent possible.
- To maintain the authenticity of local heritage.

- Financial assistance for local people participation in business operations.
- Control measure should applied to prevent overcrowding.
- Awareness programme to residents about the benefits and burdens of tourism and brochures of information about local customs and do's and don'ts' for trekkers and tourists should be published.
- Tourist facilities according to local design and architecture should be promoted.
- Incentives should be given to those tourists and adventure tourism agencies that appreciate and respect the local culture and traditions.
- Encourage local residents to opt blue-collar job maximally so as to reduce the number of migrant workers to urban areas.
- Award severe punishment on finding the involvement on drugs, crime and prostitution.

References

Bagri, S.C., (1994). Strategy for Sustainable Tourism Development for Trekking Tourism Promotion and Environment Conservation in Garhwal Himalayas, Vol. 2, *Journal of Tourism*, HNB Garhwal University, Srinagar Garhwal.

Bagri, S.C., (1994). *Trekking Tourism in Garhwal Himalayas* A Report Submitted to Department of Tourism, Government of India, New Delhi.

Bagri, S.C. and Bhatt, A.K. (1997). Sustainable Tourism Planning and Development in *Report of the Conference on Sustainable Tourism Planning and Development*, IITTM, Gwalior.

Bisht, Harshvanti, (1994). *Tourism in Garhwal Himalaya*, Indus Publishing Company, New Delhi.

Bjoness, I., (1979). *Impact on a High-Mountain Ecosystem. Recommendations for Action Sagarmatha (Everest) National Park*, Kathmandu.

Bosselman, Fred P. Ed. (1978). *In the Wake of the Tourist: Managing Special Places in Eight Countries.* Washington, DC: The Conservation Foundation.

Brown, Graham. (1990). "South Asia Tourism Development." *Tourism Management*. 9(3):240-245.

Cohen, Eric. (1978). "Impact of Tourism on the Physical Environment." *Annals of Tourism Research*. 5(2):215-237, London.

Dasman, Raymond F., John P. Milton and Peter H. Freeman. (1973). *Ecological Principles for Economic Development*, New York: John Wiley and Sons.

de Kadt, Emanuel. ed. (1979). *Tourism: Passport to Development?* New York: Oxford University Press.

Dogan, Hasan Zafer. (1989). "Forms of Adjustment: Sociocultural Impacts of Tourism." *Annals of Tourism Research*, 16(2):216-236.

Dowling, Ross, (1993). An Environment-Based Planning Model for Regional Tourism Development, in *Journal of Sustainable Tourism*, Vol. 1:1, (1993), Channel View Books, Multilingual Mattres Ltd., U.K.

Edington, John M. and M. Ann Edington. (1986). *Ecology, Recreation and Tourism*. Cambridge: Cambridge University Press.

Edwards, Jonathan R. (1987). "The U.K. Heritage Coast: An Assessment of the Ecological Impacts of Tourism." *Annals of Tourism Research*. 14(1):71-87.

Ferrario, F. Franco, (1982). Method Approach for Evaluating Tourist Resources: Case of South Africa in T.V.Singh (Ed.) *Studies in Tourism Wildlife Parks and Conservation*, New Delhi, Metropolitan.

Fitch, James Marston. (1982). *Historic Conservation: Curatorial Management of the Built World*. New York: McGraw-Hill.

Fletcher, John E. (1989). "Input-Output Analysis and Tourism Impact Studies." *Annals of Tourism Research*. 16(4):514-529.

Fonia, K.S., (1987). *Uttarakhand: The Land of Jungles, Temples and Snow*, Lancer Books, New Delhi.

Gartner, William C. (1987). "Environmental Impacts of Recreational Home Developments." *Annals of Tourism Research*. 14(1):38-57.

Gunn, Clare A. 2nd ed. (1988). *Tourism Planning*, New York: Taylor & Francis.

Hall, Peter. (1987). "Urban Development and the Future of Tourism." *Tourism Management*. 8(2):129-130.

Hodgson, Peter. (1990). "New Tourism Product Development: Market Research's Role" *Tourism Management*. 11(1):2-5.

India Department of Tourism and National institute of Design, *Fatehpur Sikri: Integrated Development Plan*. New Delhi: Government of India.

Inskeep, Edward, (1991). *Tourism Planning: an Integrated and Sustainable Development Approach*, VNR Tourism and Commercial Recreation Series, New York, Van Nostrand Reinhold.

Inskeep, Edward. (1987). "Environmental Planning for Tourism." *Annals of Tourism Research*. 14(1):118-135.

Ives, Jack D., (1985). The Mountain Malaise: Quest for an Integrated development, Introductory notes in the T.V. Singh (Ed.), *Integrated Mountain Development*, New Delhi, Himalayan Books.

Jafari, Jafar, (1991). The Significance of Youth Tourism, Socio-Cultural Dimensions in the *Proceeding of WTO International Conference on Youth Tourism*, New Delhi, India, 18-21 November, 1991.

Jafari, Jafar. (1987). "Tourism Models: The Sociocultural Aspects." *Tourism Management*. 8(2):151-159.

Jayal, N.D., (1990). 'Himalaya - Our Fragile Heritage' in the *Souvenir of Institute of Mountaineering 25 Years*, Uttarkashi.

Jenkins, C.L., and B.M. Henry, (1982). "Government Involvement in Tourism in Developing Countries." *Annals of Tourism Research*. 9(4):499-521.

Kaur, J., (1982). 'Pilgrimage Progress to Himalayan Shrines' in T.V. Singh (ed.), *Studies in Tourism Wildlife Parks and Conservation*, New Delhi, Metropolitan.

Kaur, J., (1985). *Himalayan Pilgrimage and the New Tourism*, New Delhi, Himalayan Books.

Keating, M., (1993). *The Earth Summit's Agenda for Change, Centre for Our Common future*, Geneva.

Krippendort, Jost, (1987). *The Holiday Makers: Understanding the Imact of Leisure and Travel*. Oxford, Heinemann.

Lew, Alan A. (1987). "A Framework ofTourist Attraction Research." *Annals of Tourism Research*. 14(4):553-575.

Long, Veronica, (1993). Communities and Sustainable Tourism Development: Techniques to Mitigate Social Impacts in Round Table on Planning for Sustainable Tourism Developemnt, Bali, Indonesia, W.T.O.

Lundberg, Donald E. (1985). *The Tourist Business*. New York: Van Nostrand Reinhold.

Mahesh, V.S., (1993). Human Resource Planning and Development: Micro and Macro Modules for Effective Growth in Tourism in the *Human Resource Development*, London.

Mathieson, Alister, and Geoffrey Wall. (1982). *Tourism: Economic, Physical and Social Impacts*. New York: Longman Group Ltd.

McCool, Stephen R. (1978). "Recreation Use Limits: Issues for the Tourism Industry." *Journal of Travel Research*. 17(2):2-7.

Middleton, Michael, (1992). Guideline for Tourism Management at Heritage Sites, *HMG/N-PATA-UNESCO Conference*, Kathmandu, 21-23 September, 1992.

Mill, Robert Christie, and Alastair M. Morrison. (1985). *The Tourism System: An Introductory Text*. Englewood Cliffs, N.J.: Prentice Hall, Inc.

Mings, R.C., (1988). "Assessing the Contribution of Tourism to International Understanding." *Journal of Travel Research*.

Murphy, Peter E. (1985). *Tourism: A Community Approach*. New York: Methuen.

Nash, Dennison and Richard Butler. (1990). "Alternative Forms of Tourism." *Annals of Tourism Research:* 17)2):302-305.

Negi, Sharede Singh, (1982). *Environment Problems in Himalaya*, Dehradun, Bishen Singh, Mahendra Pal Singh.

Nepal Ministry of Tourism. (1988). *Some Regulations Relating to Mountain Tourism in Nepal*. Kathmandu: His Majesty's Government.

O'Reilly, A.M. (1986). "Tourism Carrying Capacity: Concepts and Issues." *Tourism Management*. 7(4):254-258.

Paliwal, G.S. and Badoni, A.K. (1989). Influence of Tourism on Plant Wealth in Garhwal Himalaya: A Look on the Scene in S.C. Singh (ed.), *Impact of Tourism on Mountain Environment*, Pooja Publication, Delhi.

PATA (1992). PATA Code for Environmentally Responsible Tourism, *PATA*, San Francisco.

PATA Foundation (1991). Preparing an Inventory of Heritage Resources, *Pacific Asia Travel Association* San Francisco.

Pearce, Douglas. (1987). *Tourism Today: A Geographical Analysis*. Harlow, England: Longman Group.

Pearce, Douglas. (1987). *Tourism Today: A Geographical Analysis*. Harlow, England: Longman Group.

Pearce, Philip L. (1989). "Towards the Better Management of Tourist Queues." *Tourism Management*. 10(4):279-284.

Pigram, J.J., (1980). Environmental Implications of Tourism Development, In *Annals of Tourism Research*, 7(4):554-583.

Plog, Stanley, C., (1974). Why Destination Areas Rise and Fall in Popularity in *Cornell Quarterly*, 14(4):55-58.

Price, Marti F., (1990). The Sustainable Future of Mountain Communities: Resources and Tourism in the Context of Climate Variability and Change, MAB UMESCO.

Romeril, Michael. (1989). Tourism and the Environment - Accord or Discord? *Tourism Management*. 10(3):204-208.

Salm, R.V. (1985). "Integrating Marine Conservation and Tourism." *International Journal of Environmental Studies*. Vol. 25:229-238.

Sharma and et. al., (1990). Environmental Studies and Management of Lakes in Garhwal Himalaya: Constraints and Prospects in *Journal of Himalayan Studies* and *Regional Development,* Vol. 13-14, 1989-90, p. 63-67, Srinagar Garhwal.

Shrestha, Tirtha B., (1995). Mountain Tourism and Environment in Nepal, *International Centre for Integrated Mountain Development*, Kathmandu.

Singh, Joginder, (1986). The Joys of Trekking Appeared in the *Travel Times, The Times of India,* New Delhi, March 29, 1986.

Smith, Stephen L.J. (1987). "Regional Analysis of Tourism Resources." *Annals of Tourism Research*. 14(2):254-273

Smith, Valene L. ed. 2nd. (1989). *Hosts and Guests: The Anthropology of Tourism*. Philadelphia: University of Pennsylvania Press.

Thorburn, Andrew. (1986) "Marketing Cultural Heritage." *Travel & Tourism Analyst*. December 1986:39-48.

Travis, Anthony S. (1982). Managing the Environmental and Cultural Impacts of Tourism and Leisure Development, *Tourism Management*, 349:265-262, London.

UNEP, (1989). Asia/Pacific Consultative Meeting on Conservation of Critical Ecosystems and Economic Development, Bangkok, UNEP Regional Office for Asia and the Pacific.

UNESCO. (1976). "The Effects of Tourism on Sociocultural Values." *Annals of Tourism Research*. 4:74-105.

Waters, Somerrest, (1967). *Tourism: A New Path to Economic Improvement in Developing Nations*, New York: Child and Waters.

World Tourism Organization. (1977). *Integrated Planning*. Madrid: World Tourism Organization.

World Tourism Organization. (1980). *Manila Declaration*. Madrid: World Tourism Organization.

8

Conclusion and Recommendations

In a bid to promote tourism, India has grown out from the selected growth centres metropolitan tours of historical, cultural centres to religious destinations and wildlife areas. With respect to tourism, the word heritage has been employed in cultural and natural context. In cultural arena, heritage can be used to describe material forms such as monuments, historical or archaeological remains and artifacts on display in museums; immaterial forms such as philosophy, traditions and art in all their manifestations; the celebration of great events or personalities in history; distinctive way of life; and education as expressed for example, through literature and folklore. In the natural arena, heritage has been used to describe gardens, landscapes, National Parks, Wilderness areas of Scenic beauty, mountains, rivers, islands and components there of such as flora and fauna. Heritage is increasingly becoming major catalysts for the whole travel experience. A fairly large number of persons visit heritage sites and many world heritage sites are major tourist destinations. Heritage tourism represents a growing market segment for both domestic and international tourism and can be viewed as being a type of special interest tourism market. Heritage tourism is rapidly becoming integrated in mainstream tourism. Heritage resources are converted into products through an assembly process involving interpretation and packaging. Selection, interpretation and packaging involve a series of choices about which product is being produced and, thus, which resources are to be used and in which ways. It is product defined by, and intended to be consumed by defined market. In case of market defined heritage tourism product, quite different markets can create quite different products from the same environment, which are then sold to different consumers at the same physical locations. The Himalaya with all its nature offerings was considered as the best heritage tourism product for touristic sale. While traditional pilgrimage to Himalayan shrines have had their holy past and a unique tradition of religious tourism, the new tourism paved its way into the Himalaya in the second half of the 19th century giving birth to hill stations, health centres and summer head quarters, which over time flourished into tourist resorts. This study of Garhwal region has been taken to examine the heritage of the region in its historic perspective and to study the product development and management of heritage tourism to safeguard the ecology and economy of the region and attain sustainability, based on scientific research methods.

The region has a remarkable heterogeneity in all its natural and cultural environments. Altitude varies rather abruptly from 300m (Terai) to 7817 m (Nanda Devi). Garhwal Himalaya has a glorious past and enormous natural scenic wealth. The diverse and yet extensive and undisturbed plethora of tourist spots offer immense opportunities for the development of religious tourism, leisure tourism, adventure sports, natural environment and wild life parks. The Garhwal himalaya, with all its nature offerings is considered as the best tourism product for touristic sale. The char dham circuit has high religious significance as some of India's holiest Hindu and Sikh shrines viz. Badrinath, Kedarnath, Gangotri, Yamunotri, and Hemkund saheb are located in this region. Beside offering a number of religious locations, the circuit also offer plenty of opportunities for adventure seekers (water sports, mountaineering, trekking etc.), recreational tourism and wild life lovers. The region as a whole, is a multi attractional all-purpose area, which can attract all kinds of tourists. However, the circuit doesn't have the support structure to be able to attract all kinds of up market tourist who can stay on and enjoy the tourist offerings for a few more days thereby benefiting the locals by way of increased tourist expenditure in the region. In order to fully exploit the potential of the area for product development and management, it is recognised that considerable investment are required for the development, conservation and enhancement of the primary and secondary tourist offerings along with investments in tourism related superstructure and infrastructure.

Development and Improvement of facilities/amenities in the Kedarnath trekking route (14 km, altitude 1982 Mt. to 3583 Mt.) should be on the lines of the Vaisno Devi trekking route. This would include improvement of trekking route, setting up of midway facilities such as tin sheds, *sulabh shauchalayas*, fast food centres etc., setting up of proper office for the regulation of the rates and the traffic of horses and *palkies*. In order to avoid congestion at the Kedarnath temple it is recommended that a slip should be issued at Gaurikund, which allows people to enter the temple. There is a need of setting up tourist information/reception centres at Gaurikund. This would also monitor the cleanliness of the yatra route and conduct checks on sweepers and horse owners. Most of the recommendations and suggestions pertaining to Kedarnath trekking route hold good for Yamunotri also, as condition of the Yamunotri trekking route (14 km) from Hanuman Chatti to Yamunotri is similar to that of Kedarnath. To enhance the present tourism offerings of the region, repairs and beautification of heritage attractions at Kedarnath, Yamunotri and Gangotri are required. Reconstitution of Badri-Kedar temple committee and Yamunotri/Gangotri temple committee should be done for better management of our heritage and culture.

A comprehensive promotion and marketing strategy is to be prepared, as marketing is a critical input for successful tourism.

With improved transport and travel links, the religious attractions of the Garhwal Himalaya could be marketed together with the already popular tourist attractions like Mussoorie, Jim Corbett park etc. The objective of the promotion should be to attract up market tourists who would essentially be leisure or adventure oriented. For this purpose, Uttaranchal Tourism should attempt to tie-up with travel agencies, attend tourism festivals and represent in tourism conferences held from time to time in India and abroad. Special publicity campaigns in the relevant potential market need to be tapped and focused upon. A proper national and international media strategy and planning needs to be evolved to increase media reach and efficiency.

The tourist traffic statistics for the region indicates that tourist traffic is more on easily accessible places. Therefore, it is suggested that, if the tracks can be converted into motor able roads and rope ways are installed at selected places, the tourist traffic can increase tremendously. Moreover these rope way would solve the time and distance problems, blasting of mountains for constructing roads, cutting of trees. Ropeway would be a tourist attraction in itself as it would provide an excellent panoramic view of the snow-capped mighty Himalayas.

Like other parts of Himalayas, Garhwal normally receives maximum number of tourists during summer and autumn months only. Because the main purpose of tourists is to visit the Char Dham circuit. The main business from tourism lasts for only about 6 months. The tourist arrivals in the Char Dham circuit start in April and remain at peak in May and June. The 4 temples at Yamunotri Gangotri, Badrinath and Kedarnath, open every year in the last week of April or the first week of May and are closed in the mid November, leaving only 6 month season for the pilgrims. Bulk of the tourists visit the region during May-November (more than 75%). This shows the highly seasonal nature of these tourist destinations. For breaking this seasonality and for off season, an attempt should be made to increase the number of domestic tourists, foreign tourist by enhancing the tourism offerings, promotion and publicity, by bringing lesser known destination such as Chopta, Khirsu, Kalsi, Dhanolti to lime light. In order to develop our product mix and promote tourism, round the year, various other kinds of tourism like adventure and leisure needs to be developed and promoted to the tourists (both domestic and foreign). These activities are trekking, mountaineering, skiing, white water river rafting and other water sports,rock climbing, fishing and angling, jungle safaris,car rallies etc.

The region abounds with mountains and peaks which offer good trekking routes of varying degree of adventure. The major trekking routes in this region need special attention for development which are as follows:

- Ukhimath to Deoriatal.
- Gaurikund to Kedarnath.
- Govindghat to Ghanharia and to Valley of Flowers.
- Uttarkashi to Dodital.
- Hanuman Chatti to Yamunotri.
- Gangotri to Gaumukh.
- Dodital - Hanuman Chatti to Yamunotri.
- Helang to Kalpashwar Temple.
- Kedarnath to Vasukital.

However, in order to attract tourists, investments would have to be made in marketing and publicising these routes in metros especially in Delhi and Mumbai with proper maps and information. There should be a need to market the schemes to various tour operators and lobby for these trekking routes to be included in the itinerary.

Garhwal Himalaya represents some of the leading and most fascinating wildlife parks and sanctuaries of the country, which are unique heritage tourism resources. Interestingly country's first ever National Park - the Haily National park (now Corbett Tiger Reserve) is also situated in this region. At present the region represents as many as five National parks and two Sanctuaries covering an area of 4382.30 Sqkm. representing 14.56 per cent of the total geographical area. The National Parks are (i) Corbett National Park (Part of Corbett Tiger Reserve) (ii) Nanda Devi National park (Core Zone of Nanda Devi Biosphere Reserve) (iii) Valley of Flower National Park (iv) Rajaji National Park, (v) Govind National park (Part of Govind Pashuvihar Sanctuary) and the sanctuaries are Govind Pashuvihar and Kedar nath Muskdeer Sanctuaries. Apart from the wildlife parks and sanctuaries, there are many other rich pockets in Garhwal, which demand a special care and attention for the recreational use of the wildlife and variety of other natural tourist assets. The environs of Panwali-Khatling (Tehri), Dodital and Gaumukh - Nandanvan - Tapovan (Uttarkashi), Bedni - Roopkund (Chamoli) and Dudhatoli (Pauri) are specially note worthy. The prime requirement for enhancing the potential of the wild life sanctuaries, National parks and Biosphere reserves is to exercise proper control on the ecological balance of the region and to provide information and education to the tourists on the flora and fauna over there so as to enrich their experience. There should be detailed guidelines to minimise ecological damage from over use and also to protect the floral and faunal wealth of the region. Collection of rare plants or removal of plants, disturbance of birds and animals by tourists, deforestation, leaving plastic bags in the national parks, protected areas and sanctuaries must be prohibited. There should be standard code of conduct for all the visitors to the sanctuary. Regular disposal of waste, afforestation programme, investment for breeding and health care of flora and fauna, repairing and creation of tourist trails, construction of *chawkies*, printing publicity brochures and promotion materials should be undertaken.Impact assessment studies must be done at regular intervals.

The Garhwal Himalaya offer more than 100 peaks which are above 6000 metres (20,000 ft.) in height for mountaineering. However, at present number of mountaineering expeditions are very low in this region. There is low level of awareness about the opportunities that exists in this circuit. Besides non-availability of proper training facilities, delays in getting approval for foreign tourists from the Ministry of Defense, inadequate rescue arrangements in case of mishap are the other factors responsible for less expedition. However, there is an active need for promoting the sites available, providing necessary guidance and assistance and by providing training to local youths in the region in mountaineering. Unlike mountaineering, skiing is presently done at only one location in Garhwal, at Auli, 16 km from Joshimath on the Rishikesh-Badrinath route. Auli is the major skiing centre in the region and is quite well developed with respect to equipments and machines. Slopes of Dayara Bugyal, Kedarkhantha and Mundoli can also be developed on the lines of Auli for skiing and development project for these areas should be taken up to promote skiing in the entire region. In addition to skiing, winter sports like ice hockey and skating ring can also be developed in Auli to attract more number of tourists. Technical feasibility study of setting up such sports needs to be done. Winter sports festival at Auli should be promoted on a larger scale to attract more foreign tourists. There is an acute need of encouraging private sector to invest in establishing base camps, skiing training school etc.

The region offers good opportunities for water sports lovers as there are numerous rivers which flow throughout the region. The various sports which can be undertaken are rafting, canoeing, Kayaking, boating, water skiing, sailing and rowing. At present only white water river rafting is being undertaken in the Garhwal region by GMVN's adventure sports division and around 8-10 private companies in Shivpuri and Brahampuri areas near Rishikesh. Other potential location for developing rafting are: (1) Kaliasaur to Srinagar (Alaknanda river), (2) Matuli to Dunda (Bhagirathi river), (3) Barkot to Lakhamandal (Yamuna river), (4) Dharasu to Dham (Bhagirathi river). Similarly there is an opportunity to develop water sports resorts of the nature of the one existing at Assan barrage (50 km from Dehradun, on Dehradun - Chandigarh highway) at Maneri Bhali Dam and Kalagarh Dam.

A large section of tourists particularly the foreign tourists having interest in Yoga come to Muni-Ki-Reti in Rishikesh in search Yoga and meditation facilities. The Government of India has also been organizing 'International Yoga week', with the help of Uttaranchal Tourism. This has also helped in bringing foreign tourists for Yoga purposes to Rishikesh. Considering the potential of Yoga centres, it is recommended that these should be established at the locations viz. Augustmuni, Joshimath, Muni-Ki-Reti, Chandrabadni, Kunjapuri, Khirsu, Srinagar, Bhatwari, Barkot because of their calm and quite peaceful environs.

In Garhwal a number of tourists/pilgrims take holy bath in the river Ganga and hot water *kunds* at various locations. These *ghats* and *kunds* are popular both because of their religious significance, as they provide purity to mind and body. The conditions of these *ghats/kunds* are not proper (because of garbage accumulation and layers of dust and greasy waters) and needs improvement. The ghats of *'Panch - Prayagas'* are very popular and need to be developed in proper way, keeping in mind their religious significance. The potential places for developing *ghats* in the region are - Srinagar, Rishikesh, Devprayag, Rudrapryag, Nandprayag, Vishnupryag, Karnaprayag, Uttarkashi, Gaurikund, Gangnani, Badrinath Kund etc.

The study area has some monuments which have been declared by the Archaeological survey of India as protected monuments of national importance viz. Hanol, Kalsi, Lakhamandal and Karanpur in Dehradun District; Adbadri temples, Chandpur fort, Gopeshwar temple, Gopeshwar trident of iron with shaft and engraved inscriptions, Pandukeshwar temples, Mandal rock inscription in Chamoli District; Purola ancient excavated site in Uttarkashi.

Local people of these areas should participate in tourism activities, which will reduce any socio-cultural problems and provides opportunity for cross cultural exchange between tourists and residents and promote local handicrafts and culture. Based on discussions with the tour operators, GMVN, private bus operators and tourists, the followings are recommended to improve the accessibility and transport services in the region.

- Provision of tourist information booths at the different points.
- Provision of computerised railway reservation system at Rishikesh and Kotdwar and out ticketing agencies for railways at key locations like Srinagar, Rudraprayag and Joshimath.
- GMVN requires more deluxe buses to cater to the peak season demand for its package tours.
- Capacity of bus stands at Rishikesh, Chiniyali Saur, Uttarkashi, Gangani, Hanuman Chatti, Gauchar, Rudraprayag, Joshimath, Govind Ghat needs to be enhanced.
- A helipad at Auli is considered necessary and private opera tors should be encouraged to start helicopter services there.
- Additional petrol pumps need to be set up at Badrinath, Sonprayag, Phata, Rampur, Dharasu, Lanka. Hoarding should be set up at the last petrol pump on particular leg of the circuit, indicating that no petrol would be available after that point.

The accommodation facilities in the Garhwal region comprise mainly of economy hotels, dharamshalas, and paying guest accommodation besides a number of fairly well maintained tourist bunglows run by GMVN. Various other Government department like the PWD, Forest Department, Irrigation Department, Border Roads Organisations also have their guest houses at most of the locations. The dharamshals accounts for 52% of the beds supply in the region. These dharamshals typically offer dormitory type accommodation with common toilet facilities. There are a few star category hotels and GMVN's tourist bunglows are the best available mode of accommodation in Garhwal hills. They are at best categorised as basic and not for up market and international tourists. So there is an urgent need for more up market accommodation facilities in this region. In the peak season of May and June shortage of accommodation is felt. Various project and new hotels are coming up at all the major places in the Char Dham circuit. Apart from these, Uttaranchal Tourism would have to take initiative and construct tourist bunglows and fiber glass huts at various up coming destinations which have potential to attract tourists like Deoriatal, Tapovan, Rudranath. To accommodate the increased tourist traffic at trekking and mountaineering sites, tented accommodation and camping sites can be developed. Apart from accommodation, the mid ways including fast food centres and toilet facilities in the region need to be improved. For up market tourists, who are willing to pay more for better services, it is essential to set up fast food centres on the lines of the one set up in kund at Pakhi and Rajasthan Tourism. The toilet facilities for general public require setting up of *sulabh shauchalayas* at every halting places. This would minimise the serious implications on the hygiene and environmental conditions.

To market the tourist spots in the region and to provide information about city, accommodation and transportation, the major towns in Garhwal have tourist offices viz Dehradun, Uttarkashi, Rishikesh, Srinagar, Joshimath. New tourist offices needs to be opened in Rudraprayag and Barkot. The tourist offices need to be located at convenient locations for tourists and there should be proper board/display signs indicating particular location.

As regards the banking facilities, foreign exchange counters are only available at Rishikesh and Dehradun and not in the other parts of the region. There is an acute need of setting up foreign exchange facilities at various important locations for foreign tourists like Barkot, Uttarkashi, Srinagar, New Tehri, Rudraprayag, Guptakashi, Gopeshwar, Joshimath, Badrinath.

Vehicle repair facilities existed at only 4-5 places in the entire hills of Garhwal after Rishikesh. The tourist are exposed to innumerable hardships because of lack of such facilities. It is therefore suggested that vehicle repair facilities should be set up at the following locations viz. Chopta, Lakhamandal, Dharasu, Bhatwari, Barkot, Chamba, Chiliasaur.

The narrow roads of Garhwal is not suitable to cope up with the tourist traffic during the yatra season. There is a need of resurfacing or black topping, widening and construction of parapets on turnings.

Availability of safe drinking water is a strong hygienic factor for the success of any tourist place. Most of the water supply schemes of the region need reorganisations and augmentations in order to cater to the demand in future with expected increase of population of town and tourist traffic. Also in Uttarkashi some of the schemes need reorganisations because of the earthquake which dislocated the source. There is a need of assessment of sewerage systems, to maintain the ecological balance and to protect the environment. There is a definite need to up grade the sewerage systems and set up new sewerage system in most of the town in order to provide better facilities to the tourist in the yatra circuit. In view of increased tourist inflow in the region, it is imperative that the number of lines for (STD/ISD) Telecommunication should be increased at all the locations especially Gaurikund, Kedarnath, Hanuman Chatti Yamunotri, Gangotri and Badrinath.

Provision of adequate medical facilities is an important hygiene factor for the development of tourism in a particular area. Most of the medical facilities are not up to the mark in Garhwal hills. The state dispensaries of some places do not have even enough medicines and equipments. There is an acute need of setting up new medical relief units, providing proper equipment and adequate medicines for all hospitals.

Due to lack of sustainable tourism development approach, high level of pollution are noticed. On most of the tourist places we find mostly human waste, animal litter and discarded containers. It has been observed that porters and load carrying animals accompanying tourists are a significant source of pollution on all major trek routes. On Gangotri-Gaumukh, Gaurikund-Kedarnath, Govindghat-Hemkund and Hanumanchatti-Yamunotri, the eateries runners tend to cut trees and vegetation indiscriminately and dispose off. Upper regions like Chirbasa, Bhojbasa and Nanda Devi biosphere reserve face utter deforestation, poaching and landslides. Indiscriminate wood cutting for fuel creates landslides and soil erosion. Unauthorised possession of land for construction of huts, ashrams and tea shops is most noticeable. Chirbasa, once famous for its blue pine forests, has been deprived of its glory. Birches of Bhojbasa are still finished and the juniper bushes have disappeared from nearby areas, and now the attack is on far distant Juniper bushes and birch trees. Tourism has also affected demography and human settlement. The new construction on tourist places is in full swing and encroachments on protected land have become common. The fuel and energy crisis of settlement pattern have converted the surroundings into barren mountains. The Bhuyandar Valley of Flowers, once known for kaleidoscopic flowers, has turned into a grass field. The environment degradation of these places which are visited by lakhs of tourists every year from all parts of the country and abroad have forced the planners and decision makers both at the State and the Central levels to wake up and take stock of the decline. The Nanda Devi National Park and Valley of Flowers are the two main examples. Both the places over the years, polluted with garbage and over exceeding carrying capacity. But due to the timely intervention of the Department of Environment and Tourism, the deterioration of the both the places have been checked.

The hills of Garhwal have vast tourism potential alongwith its vivid cultural and traditional customs. It has been the endeavor of the State Tourism Department to promote tourism in this area without adversely affecting rich cultural heritage, unmindful interference with local values and customs as also keeping in view the fact that ecological balance is maintained. Keeping in view the ultimate goal of sustainable tourism development in Garhwal, State Government has declared New Tourism Policy with an objective to attract more investment through private sector so that more and better tourism facilities are created in this region. Preparation of master plan for the whole Garhwal Himalaya, formulation of Safety and Rescue Regulation for adventure activities, development planning for sustainable tourism development e.g. Promotion of Eco tourism, development of lesser known but otherwise much more attractive destinations, publicity of fairs and festivals and tribal areas have been initiated by Department of Tourism on wider scale.

Appendices

APPENDIX-1

1. ACCOMMODATION UNITS IN GARHWAL

A) Accommodation Units in District Uttarkashi

TOWN/PLACE	TYPE/OWNERSHIP	NAME OF THE UNIT	BEDS
Angoda	Forest Department	Forest Rest House	4
Arakot	GMVN	Tourist Rest House	6
Arakot	PWD	Inspection House	4
Arakot	Forest Department	Forest Rest House	4
Barkot	GMVN	Travellers Lodge	44
Barkot	Forest Department	Forest Rest House	4
Barkot	PWD	Inspection House	4
Barkot	Private Hotel	Meghdoot	20
Barkot	Private Hotel	Raturi	30
Beef	GMVN	Travellers Lodge	50
Bhaironghati	GMVN	Travellers Lodge	32
Bhaironghati	Forest Department	Forest Rest House	4
Bhaironghati	PWD	Inspection House	2
Bhatwari	PWD	Tourist Bunglow	4
Bhojwasa	GMVN	Tourist Rest House	50
Chaurangikhal	Forest Department	Forest Rest House	4

1	2	3	4
Chiniyalisaur	GMVN	Travellers Lodge	4
Chiniyalisaur	GMVN	Motel	4
Chiniyalisaur	PWD	Inspection House	4
Deoriatal	Forest Department	Forest Rest House	4
Dodital	Forest Department	Forest Rest House	100
Gagnani	GMVN	Tourist Rest house	20
Gangotri	GMVN	Tourist Rest House	.62
Gangotri	GMVN	Tourist Rest House	20
Gangotri	Forest Department	Forest Rest House	8
Gangotri	PWD	Inspection House	32
Gangotri	Dharamshala	Baba Kali Kamli	4
Gangotri	Dharamshala	Punjab Sindh Shetra	50
Hanumanchatti	GMVN	Tourist Rest House	30
Hanumanchatti	Forest Department	Forest Rest House	4
Harikidoon	GMVN	Tourist Rest House	20
Harikidoon	Forest Department	Forest Rest House	20
Harsil	GMVN	Tourist Rest House	30
Harsil	Forest Department	Forest Rest House	4
Harsil	PWD	Inspection House	40
Jankichatti	GMVN	Passenger Lodge	78
Jankichatti	Forest Department	Forest Rest House	4
Jankichatti	PWD	Inspection House	10
Jarmola	Forest Department	Forest Rest House	4
Lanka	GMVN	Passenger Chadak	100
Lunigad	Forest Department	Forest Rest House	
Mori	Forest Department	Forest Rest House	
Mori	PWD	Inspection House	4
Osla	GMVN	Tourist Bunglow	20
Osla	Forest Department	Forest Rest House	4
Osla	PWD	Inspection House	4
Purola	GMVN	Tourist Bunglow	20
Purola	Forest Department	Forest Rest House	6
Purola	PWD	Inspection House	6
Sayanacnatti	GMVN	Travellers Lodge	18
Sayanachatti	PWD	Inspection House	4

1	2	3	4
Saur/ Sankari	GMVN	Tourist Rest House	20
Seedh	Forest Department	Forest Rest House	4
Taluka	GMVN	Tourist Rest House	20
Uttarkashi	GMVN	Tourist Rest House	120
Uttarkashi	GMVN	Travellers Lodge	16
Uttarkashi	Forest Department	Forest Rest House	4
Uttarkashi	PWD	Inspection House	10
Uttarkashi	Zila Panchayat	District HQ Panchayat Bhavan	26
Uttarkashi	Dharamshala	Birla	200
Uttarkashi	Dharamshala	Punjab Sindh Shetra	10
Uttarkashi	Private Hotel	Bhagirathi	34
Uttarkashi	Private Hotel	Bhandari	76
Uttarkashi	Private Hotel	Gaumukh	64
Uttarkashi	Private Hotel	Hari Om	38
Uttarkashi	Private Hotel	Kashmiri	48
Uttarkashi	Private Hotel	Lakshmi	60
Uttarkashi	Private Hotel	Vijay Lodge	50
Uttarkashi	Private Hotel	Joshi Tourist Lodge	54
Yamunotri	GMVN	F.R.P. Huts	20
Yamunotri	Forest Department	Forest Rest House	4
Yamunotri	Dharamshala	Baba Kali Kamli	8

B) Accommodation Units in District Dehradun

TOWN/PLACE	TYPE/OWNERSHIP	NAME OF THE UNIT	BEDS
Anu	Forest Department	Forest Rest House	4
Atal	PWD	Inspection House	4
Atal	PWD	Inspection House	4
Bhaniyawala	GMVN	Motel	4
Chakrata	Forest Department	Inspection House	4
Chakrata	GMVN	Inspection House	4
Dakpatthar	PWD	Tourist Bunglow	38
Dakpatthar	Irrigation Department	Inspection House	10
Dakpatthar	PWD	Inspection House	4
Daragarh	PWD	Inspection House	4
Dehradun	GMVN	Hotel Drona	202

1	2	3	4
Dehradun (Sahestradhara)	GMVN	Tourist Rest House	4
Dehradun	Irrigation Department	Inspection House	8
Dehradun	PWD	Circuit House	22
Dehradun	PWD	Inspection House	20
Dehradun	Dharamshala		500
Dehradun	Dharamshala	Aggarwal	158
Dehradun	Private Hotel	Ajanta	50
Dehradun	Private Hotel	Akashdeep	50
Dehradun	Private Hotel	Aketa	40
Dehradun	Private Hotel	Aroma	28
Dehradun	Private Hotel	Chandra Lodge	15
Dehradun	Private Hotel	Deep Lodge House	20
Dehradun	Private Hotel	Deepshikha	30
Dehradun	Private Hotel	Doon View	17
Dehradun	Private Hotel	Dunga House	16
Dehradun	Private Hotel	Dynax	36
Dehradun	Private Hotel	Dynax Guest House	12
Dehradun	Private Hotel	Great value	106
Dehradun	Private Hotel	Hilton	48
Dehradun	Private Hotel	Inderlok	105
Dehradun	Private Hotel	Krishna Lodge	12
Dehradun	Private Hotel	Madhuban	76
Dehradun	Private Hotel	Mandakini	NA
Dehradun	Private Hotel	Meedo Grand	52
Dehradun	Private Hotel	Nishima	52
Dehradun	Private Hotel	Nivesh	28
Dehradun	Private Hotel	Orient	50
Dehradun	Private Hotel	Park View	15
Dehradun	Private Hotel	President	36
Dehradun	Private Hotel	Prince	39
Dehradun	Private Hotel	Priya	25
Dehradun	Private Hotel	Quality	35
Dehradun	Private Hotel	Rangmahal	32
Dehradun	Private Hotel	Ranjit	30

1	2	3	4
Dehradun	Private Hotel	Regent	40
Dehradun	Private Hotel	Relax	50
Dehradun	Private Hotel	Shahanshah	50
Dehradun	Private Hotel	Shipra	50
Dehradun	Private Hotel	Tourist	12
Dehradun	Private Hotel	Victoria	60
Dehradun	Private Hotel	Vishal Bharat Lodge	28
Dehradun	Private Hotel	White House	16
Jyadi	PWD	Inspection House	4
Kalsi	Forest Department	Forest Rest House	4
Kalsi	PWD	Inspection House	4
Lakhwad	PWD	Inspection House	4
Mussoorie	GMVN	Tourist Bunglow	78
Mussoorie	Govt. Accommodation	Haryana Tourism Guest House	NA
Mussoorie	Govt. Accommodation	Punjab Tourism Guest House	NA
Mussoorie	PWD	Inspection House	4
Mussoorie	Private Hotel	Abhinandan	88
Mussoorie	Private Hotel	Adapt	48
Mussoorie	Private Hotel	Agar/Samar	64
Mussoorie	Private Hotel	Ajay	36
Mussoorie	Private Hotel	Ambika Palace	46
Mussoorie	Private Hotel	Anupam	55
Mussoorie	Private Hotel	Apsara	64
Mussoorie	Private Hotel	Ashiana Picaddly	135
Mussoorie	Private Hotel	Ashoka Palace	32
Mussoorie	Private Hotel	Avlon resort	74
Mussoorie	Private Hotel	Bookhill Cottage	26
Mussoorie	Private Hotel	Brent Wood	147
Mussoorie	Private Hotel	Broadway	27
Mussoorie	Private Hotel	Carlton Palisance	37
Mussoorie	Private Hotel	Clarks	30
Mussoorie	Private Hotel	Country Inn	21
Mussoorie	Private Hotel	Claridges Nabha Palace	44

1	2	3	4
Mussoorie	Private Hotel	Classic Heights	24
Mussoorie	Private Hotel	Clouds & Resort	70
Mussoorie	Private Hotel	Connaught Castle	56
Mussoorie	Private Hotel	Doon Palace	NA
Mussoorie	Private Hotel	Dwaper	
Mussoorie	Private Hotel	Drapan	60
Mussoorie	Private Hotel	Deckmans Grand	112
Mussoorie	Private Hotel	Deep Mountain View	72
Mussoorie	Private Hotel	Doon View	69
Mussoorie	Private Hotel	Dunservid Court	84
Mussoorie	Private Hotel	Eagle	24
Mussoorie	Private Hotel	Everest	24
Mussoorie	Private Hotel	Evergreen	25
Mussoorie	Private Hotel	Filigree	36
Mussoorie	Private Hotel	Galaxy Garden	NA
Mussoorie	Private Hotel	Goyal Palace	NA
Mussoorie	Private Hotel	Garhwal Terrace	NA
Mussoorie	Private Hotel	Glen Villa	189
Mussoorie	Private Hotel	Greencastle	72
Mussoorie	Private Hotel	Gresmount	93
Mussoorie	Private Hotel	Gulmarg	25
Mussoorie	Private Hotel	Hill Queen	74
Mussoorie	Private Hotel	Hill View	28
Mussoorie	Private Hotel	Himalaya Club	320
Mussoorie	Private Hotel	Holiday Inn	24
Mussoorie	Private Hotel	Honeymoon Inn	98
Mussoorie	Private Hotel	Howard International	127
Mussoorie	Private Hotel	Humming Meadows Jungle Resort	NA
Mussoorie	Private Hotel	Imperial	36
Mussoorie	Private Hotel	India	72
Mussoorie	Private Hotel	JP Resedency Manor (5 star)	180
Mussoorie	Private Hotel	Kahkashan	NA
Mussoorie	Private Hotel	Kanak	NA

1	2	3	4
Mussoorie	Private Hotel	Kamasmadda	38
Mussoorie	Private Hotel	Khayyam	24
Mussoorie	Private Hotel	Lakshmi Palace	20
Mussoorie	Private Hotel	Mainfield	92
Mussoorie	Private Hotel	Mall Palace	63
Mussoorie	Private Hotel	Mansarovar	80
Mussoorie	Private Hotel	Mayur	46
Mussoorie	Private Hotel	Minerva	64
Mussoorie	Private Hotel	Mitson	52
Mussoorie	Private Hotel	Mussoorie Club	62
Mussoorie	Private Hotel	Mussoorie International	55
Mussoorie	Private Hotel	Naaz	20
Mussoorie	Private Hotel	Nandvilla	74
Mussoorie	Private Hotel	Nanda Tales	NA
Mussoorie	Private Hotel	Naveen	60
Mussoorie	Private Hotel	Neelam International	38
Mussoorie	Private Hotel	New Bharat	73
Mussoorie	Private Hotel	Nishima	50
Mussoorie	Private Hotel	Padmini Niwas	60
Mussoorie	Private Hotel	Palki	20
Mussoorie	Private Hotel	Paramount	28
Mussoorie	Private Hotel	Park Lodge	30
Mussoorie	Private Hotel	Peak View	55
Mussoorie	Private Hotel	Picnic	62
Mussoorie	Private Hotel	Pine Retreat	
Mussoorie	Private Hotel	Pilogri	36
Mussoorie	Private Hotel	Pioneer	74
Mussoorie	Private Hotel	Poornima	32
Mussoorie	Private Hotel	Prince	125
Mussoorie	Private Hotel	Priya	76
Mussoorie	Private Hotel	Raghushree	94
Mussoorie	Private Hotel	Raj Deluxe	98
Mussoorie	Private Hotel	Rama	81
Mussoorie	Private Hotel	Ratan	26
Mussoorie	Private Hotel	Regal	39

1	2	3	4
Mussoorie	Private Hotel	Riviera	59
Mussoorie	Private Hotel	Rock Palace	50
Mussoorie	Private Hotel	Rocksee	48
Mussoorie	Private Hotel	Rockwood	94
Mussoorie	Private Hotel	Roop Midtown	124
Mussoorie	Private Hotel	Rosaline	87
Mussoorie	Private Hotel	Royal Classic	22
Mussoorie	Private Hotel	Samrat	42
Mussoorie	Private Hotel	Saraswati	24
Mussoorie	Private Hotel	Savoy	222
Mussoorie	Private Hotel	Shalimar	30
Mussoorie	Private Hotel	Sheela Lodge	20
Mussoorie	Private Hotel	Sherlin	65
Mussoorie	Private Hotel	Shilton	122
Mussoorie	Private Hotel	Shingar	56
Mussoorie	Private Hotel	Shining Star	42
Mussoorie	Private Hotel	Shipra	174
Mussoorie	Private Hotel	Shiva Continental	80
Mussoorie	Private Hotel	Shockair	20
Mussoorie	Private Hotel	Silverton	305
Mussoorie	Private Hotel	Snow View	26
Mussoorie	Private Hotel	Solitaire Plaza	56
Mussoorie	Private Hotel	Sterling Resorts	120
Mussoorie	Private Hotel	Summer Meedo	25
Mussoorie	Private Hotel	Summer Nest	18
Mussoorie	Private Hotel	Sun & Snow	24
Mussoorie	Private Hotel	Sunny Cot	26
Mussoorie	Private Hotel	Sun & Star	NA
Mussoorie	Private Hotel	Super Hotel	NA
Mussoorie	Private Hotel	Sunview	38
Mussoorie	Private Hotel	Surya Kiran	28
Mussoorie	Private Hotel	Tamers International	52
Mussoorie	Private Hotel	Tourist Delight	20
Mussoorie	Private Hotel	Urvashi	38
Mussoorie	Private Hotel	Valentine	79

1	2	3	4
Mussoorie	Private Hotel	Valley View	36
Mussoorie	Private Hotel	Vikas	74
Mussoorie	Private Hotel	View Point	
Mussoorie	Private Hotel	Vikram	71
Mussoorie	Private Hotel	Vishnu Palace	84
Mussoorie	Private Hotel	Walnut Grove	81
Mussoorie	Private Hotel	Westend	20
Mussoorie	Private Hotel	Whispering Windows	52
Mussoorie	Private Hotel	Wild Palawar House	30
Mussoorie	Private Hotel	YWCA	66
Nagdhat	PWD	Inspection House	4
Rishikesh	GMVN	Tourist Rest House	200
Rishikesh	D.O.T.	Rain Basera	30
Rishikesh	Dharamshala	Aggarwal	300
Rishikesh	Dharamshala	Andha Ashram	75
Rishikesh	Dharamshala	Asha Bhai	100
Rishikesh	Dharamshala	Baba Kali Kamli	3200
Rishikesh	Dharamshala	Bhagwan Ashram	400
Rishikesh	Dharamshala	Bahaman	200
Rishikesh	Dharamshala	Bharat Mandir	100
Rishikesh	Dharamshala	Chetanya Bhakti Ashram	7
Rishikesh	Dharamshala	Gopal Kuteer	150
Rishikesh	Dharamshala	Gujarati	150
Rishikesh	Dharamshala	Hemkund Saheb	1050
Rishikesh	Dharamshala	Jabram Ann Shetra	250
Rishikesh	Dharamshala	Jeevni Bhai	300
Rishikesh	Dharamshala	Kanpur Wali	250
Rishikesh	Dharamshala	Manali Shetra	17
Rishikesh	Dharamshala	Mansi	150
Rishikesh	Dharamshala	Punjab Sindh Shetra	2500
Rishikesh	Dharamshala	Rakamgad	360
Rishikesh	Dharamshala	Saharanpur Wali	300
Rishikesh	Dharamshala	Sindhi	200
Rishikesh	Dharamshala	Sujawali	100
Rishikesh	Private Hotel	Ashoka	51

1	2	3	4
Rishikesh	Private Hotel	Akash Ganga	NA
Rishikesh	Private Hotel	Deep Maya	NA
Rishikesh	Private Hotel	Basera	56
Rishikesh	Private Hotel	Ganga Kinare	76
Rishikesh	Private Hotel	Gangotri	50
Rishikesh	Private Hotel	Girwar	40
Rishikesh	Private Hotel	Hari	22
Rishikesh	Private Hotel	Himalayan Tourist	75
Rishikesh	Private Hotel	Inderlok	51
Rishikesh	Private Hotel	Jan Tourist Lodge	20
Rishikesh	Private Hotel	Krishna Tourist Lodge	20
Rishikesh	Private Hotel	Mandakini International	62
Rishikesh	Private Hotel	Menka	22
Rishikesh	Private Hotel	Natraj	98
Rishikesh	Private Hotel	Rajhans	17
Rishikesh	Private Hotel	Saket	NA
Rishikesh	Private Hotel	Shipra	NA
Rishikesh	Private Hotel	Shivlok	NA
Rishikesh	Private Hotel	Suruchi	NA
Rishikesh	Private Hotel	Social Palace	NA
Rishikesh	Private Hotel	Tourist Lodge	12

C) Accommodation Units in District Tehri

TOWN/PLACE	TYPE/OWNERSHIP	NAME OF THE UNIT	BEDS
Agrakhal	GMVN	Tourist Bunglow	4
Chamba	GMVN	Tourist Bunglow	20
Chamba	Forest Dept.	Forest Rest House	4
Chamba	Private Hotel	Alka	20
Chamba	Private Hotel	Ramola Lodge	10
Chamba	Private Hotel	Trishul	50
Chandrabadni	GMVN	Tourist Bunglow	20
Devprayag	GMVN	Tourist Rest House	32
Devprayag	D.O.T.	Rain Basera	30
Devprayag	PWD	Inspection House	4

1	2	3	4
Devalsaree	Forest Department	Forest Rest House	4
Dhanaulti	GMVN	Tourist Bunglow	50
Dhanaulti	Forest Department	Forest Rest House	4
Dhanaulti	Private Hotel	Dhanaulti Retreat	20
Dhanaulti	Private Hotel	Dhanulti Bridge	50
Dharasu	Forest Department	Forest Rest House	4
Dhatyud	PWD	Inspection House	4
Gangi	GMVN	Tourist Bunglow	20
Ghansali	Forest Department	Forest Rest House	4
Ghansali	PWD	Inspection House	4
Ghuttu	GMVN	Tourist Bunglow	20
Ghuttu	Forest Department	Forest Rest House	4
Ghuttu	PWD	Inspection House	4
Jakholi	PWD	Inspection House	4
Kaddukhal	PWD	Inspection House	2
Kanatal	Private Hotel	Filogri	20
Kaudiyala	Forest Department	Log Huts	30
Kempty Falls	GMVN	Forest Rest House	2
Kempty Falls	Private Hotel	Urpuri	5
Lakshman Jhoola	Private Hotel	Tapovan	20
Muni -Ki-Reti	GMVN	Passenger Chadak	148
Muni -Ki-Reti	GMVN	T.R.H.	50
Muni -Ki-Reti	D.O.T.	Rain Basera	30
Muni -Ki-Reti	Dharamshla	Kailash Ashram	
Muni -Ki-Reti	Private Hotel	Shiva	50
Nainbagh	PWD	Inspection House	4
Nainbagh	PWD	Inspection House	4
Narendranagar	PWD	Inspection House	6
Narendranagar	Private Hotel	Kunjapuri	24
Narendranagar	Private Hotel	Ananda Resort	150
Narendranagar	Private Hotel	Sunview	40
Reeh	GMVN	Tourist Bunglow	20
Shivanand Nagar	Private Hotel	Inspection House	40
Surkunda Devi	Dharamsala	Temple Committee	
Tehri	PWD	Inspection House	4

1	2	3	4
Tehri	Private Hotel	Alka	20
Tehri	Private Hotel	Garland	20
Tehri	Private Hotel	Riverview	25
Tehri	Private Hotel	Tourist	20

D) Accommodation Units in District Pauri

TOWN/PLACE	TYPE/OWNERSHIP	NAME OF THE UNIT	BEDS
Binsar	Forest Department	Forest Rest House	NA
Binsar	PWD	PWD Rest House	NA
Chilla	GMVN	Tourest Bunglow	25
Danda Nagraja	D.O.T.	Rain Basera	30
Dugadda	D.O.T.	Rain Basera	30
Dugadda	PWD	Inspection House	4
Jwalpadham	GMVN	Tourist House	4
Kandolia	District Administration	Inspection House	8
Karnavashram	GMVN	Tourist House	10
Khirsu	GMVN	Tourist Rest House	20
Kotdwar	GMVN	Tourist Bunglow	20
Kotdwar	Forest Department	Forest Rest House	4
Kotdwar	Forest Department	Forest Rest House	4
Kotdwar	Irrigation Department	Inspection House	4
Kotdwar	Dharamshala	Hindu Panchayati	100
Kotdwar	Dharamshala	Rajaji	60
Kotdwar	Private Hotel	Bhakti Vishram Grah	20
Kotdwar	Private Hotel	Inspection House	4
Kotdwar	Private Hotel	Bhakti Vishram Grah	29
Kotdwar	Private Hotel	Bharatbhoomi	60
Kotdwar	Private Hotel	Grover	12
Kotdwar	Private Hotel	Paramount	28
Kotdwar	Private Hotel	Pratap	14
Kotdwar	Private Hotel	Sewak	21
Kotdwar	Private Hotel	Uttarakhand	22
Kotdwar	Private Hotel	Vellodore	10
Kotdwar	PWD	Inspection House	6

1	2	3	4
Lansdowne	GMVN	Tourist Bunglow	20
Lansdowne	PWD	Inspection House	6
Lansdowne	Army	Army Rest House	3
Lansdowne	Private Hotel	Garhwal Lodge	6
Lansdowne	Private Hotel	Mayur	6
Lansdowne	Private Hotel	Mishra Bhawan	6
Lansdowne	Private Hotel	Tourist Lodge	8
Neelkanth	Dharamshala	Kali Kamli	200
Paithani	D.O.T.	Rain Basera	30
Pauri	GMVN	Tourist Rest House	38
Pauri	Forest Department	Forest Rest House	3
Pauri	PWD	Inspection House	3
Pauri	Nagarpalika	Nagarpalika Rest House	4
Pauri	Zila Parisad	Zila Parisad Rest House	3
Pauri	District Administration	Circuit House	7
Pauri	Dharamshala	Badri Kedar Temple Committee	14
Pauri	Private Hotel	Frontier	16
Pauri	Private Hotel	Himalaya	22
Pauri	Private Hotel	Mansarovar	19
Pauri	Private Hotel	Hillman	30
Pauri	Private Hotel	Nidhi Tourist Lodge	06
Pauri	Private Hotel	Shivalik	16
Pauri	Private Hotel	Sky Lark	10
Pauri	Private Hotel	Sun & Snow	53
Pauri	Private Hotel	Suman	10
Ritu	GMVN	Tourist Bunglow	20
Satpuli	PWD	Inspection House	4
Satpuli	D.O.T.	Rain Basera	30
Srinagar	GMVN	Tourist Bunglow	204
Srinagar(Srikot)	GMVN	Tourist Bunglow	52
Srinagar	D.O.T.	Rain Basera	30
Srinagar	PWD	Inspection House	4
Srinagar	Dharamshala	Dalmia	20
Srinagar	Dharamshala	Gurudwara	450

1	2	3	4
Srinagar	Dharamshala	Jain	NA
Srinagar	Dharamshala	Kali-Kamli (New)	24
Srinagar	Dharamshala	Kali-Kamli (Old)	300
Srinagar	Dharamshala	Sant Lal	170
Srinagar	Private Hotel	Urvashi	40
Srinagar	Private Hotel	Ahinsa Lodge	25
Srinagar	Private Hotel	Devlok	20
Srinagar	Private Hotel	Jwlapa Lodge	10
Srinagar	Private Hotel	New Menka	50
Srinagar	Private Hotel	Prachi	54
Srinagar	Private Hotel	Pine Inn	14
Srinagar	Private Hotel	Rajhans	30
Srinagar	Private Hotel	Samarat	20
Srinagar(Srikot)	Private Hotel	Crystal Konark	60
Srinagar(Srikot)	Private Hotel	Rama	50
Swargashram (Rishikesh)	D.O.T.	Rain Basera	30
Thalisain	D.O.T.	Rain Basera	30

Accommodation Units in Districts Chamoli & Rudrapryag

TOWN/PLACE	TYPE/OWNERSHIP	NAME OF THE UNIT	BEDS
Auli	GMVN	Tourist Rest House	134
Adibadri	PWD	Inspection House	4
Augastmuni	GMVN	Fibre Glass Huts	30
Augastmuni	PWD	Inspection House	4
Augastmuni	Private Hotel	Vinod Tourist House	19
Badrinath	GMVN	Hotel Devlok	60
Badrinath	GMVN	Inspection House	72
Badrinath	GMVN	Passenger Lodge	30
Badrinath	D.O.T.	Rain Basera	30
Badrinath	PWD	Inspection House	6
Badrinath	Yatri Niwas	Yatri Niwas	500
Badrinath (Bus Stand)	Yatri Niwas	Yatri Niwas	450
Badrinath	BKTC Unit	Chand Cottage	32

1	2	3	4
Badrinath	Badri Kedar Temple Committee	Modi Bhawan-I	16
Badrinath	Badri Kedar Temple Committee	Modi Bhawan-II	16
Badrinath	Badri Kedar Temple Committee	Jhunjhun Wala Cottage	6
Badrinath	Badri Kadar Temple Committee	Narayan Sadan	24
Badrinath	Badri Kedar Temple Committee	Shankaracharya Sadan	112
Badrinath	Badri Kedar Temple Committee	Gujrati Bhawan	4
Badrinath	Badri Kedar Temple Committee	Andra Bhawan	8
Badrinath	Badri Kedar Temple Committee	TTD Dharamshala	100
Badrinath	Badri Kedar Temple Committee	Badri Sadan	60
Badrinath	Private Hotel	Mittal Cottage	6
Badrinath	Private Hotel	Garhwal Hotel	42
Badrinath	Private Hotel	Manisha Lodge	8
Badrinath	Private Hotel	Rupali Lodge	6
Badrinath	Private Hotel	Shri Ram Lodge	10
Badrinath	Private Hotel	Panchali Guest House	12
Badrinath	Private Hotel	Himshikhar Rest House	10
Badrinath	Private Hotel	Nepali & Daramshala	8
Badrinath	Private Hotel	Shir Hans Seva Kutir	58
Badrinath	Private Hotel	Man Singh Dharamshala	26
Badrinath	Private Hotel	Halwasia Dharamshala	12
Badrinath	Private Hotel	Sh. Jeeva Baba Dharamshala	4
Badrinath	Private Hotel	Dhajuria Hharamshala	16
Badrinath	Private Hotel	Dukha & Hair Dharamshala	40
Badrinath	Private Hotel	Manav Kalyan Ashram	120
Badrinath	Private Hotel	Iodi Sewa Sadan	28
Badrinath	Private Hotel	Gujrati Bhawan	16

1	2	3	4
Badrinath	Private Hotel	Geeta Mandir	34
Badrinath	Private Hotel	Anant Math	102
Ba rinath	Private Hotel	Bhola Giri Ashram	62
Badrinath	Private Hotel	Achraya Sadan	20
Badrinath	Private Hotel	Panch Puri Sadan	40
Badrinath	Private Hotel	Uttrakhand Draramshala	42
Badrinath	Private Hotel	Punjab Sindh Kshetra	92
Badrinath	Private Hotel	Njarat Sevasjra, Samgj	143
Badrinath	Private Hotel	Astakshri Dharamshala	240
Badrinath	Private Hotel	Jain Athiti Grih	58
Badrinath	Private Hotel	Balanand Ashram	57
Badrinath	Private Hotel	Maharashtra Dharamshala	180
Badrinath	Private Hotel	Parmarth Lok	286
Badrinath	Private Hotel	Bhajan Ashram	120
Badrinath	Private Hotel	Meerutwali Dharamshala	20
Badrinath	Private Hotel	Patliputra Niwas	12
Badrinath	Private Hotel	Banged Dharamshala	64
Badrinath	Private Hotel	Rajisthan Niketan	36
Badrinath	Private Hotel	Ganesh athiti seva Niketan	12
Badrinath	Private Hotel	Varun Lodge	32
Badrinath	Private Hotel	Jalaram Dharamshala	60
Badrinath	Private Hotel	Taluka Kharamshala	4
Badrinath	Private Hotel	Pitchi Dharamshala	80
Badrinath	Private Hotel	Baba Kali Kamli Dharamshala	150
Badrinath	Private Hotel	Parmarth Loke	200
Badrinath	Private Hotel	Girish	22
Badrinath	Private Hotel	Birla	50
Badrinath	Private Hotel	Anant	38
Badrinath	Private Hotel	Kala Bhadea Brahmachari Ashram	120
Badrinath	Private Hotel	Kedia	20
Badrinath	Private Hotel	Mudarand Dharamshala	84
Badrinath	Private Hotel	Pokhran Dharamshala	8
Badrinath	Private Hotel	Punjabi Dharamshala	300
Badrinath	Private Hotel	Santashram Dharamshala	125

1	2	3	4
Badrinath	Private Hotel	Tanthia Dharamshala	30
Badalpur	Private Hotel	Devlok	36
Birahi	GMVN	Fibre Glass Huts	—
Chamoli	Forest Department	Forest Rest House	4
Chamoli	Irrigation Department	Inspection House	4
Chamoli	PWD	Inspection House	4
Chamoli	GMOULtd	Guest House	48
Chamoli	Dharamshala	Temple Committee	11
Chamoli	Dharamshala	Kali-Kamli	80
Chamoli	Private Hotel	Kandpal	4
Chamoli	Private Hotel	Raj	10
Chamoli	Private Hotel	Darpan	24
Chamoli	Private Hotel	Radhu	24
Chamoli	Private Hotel	Heaven	27
Chandra Nagar	GMVN	Tourist Bunglow	4
Chandra Nagar	GMVN	Nodal Pilgrimage Center	8
Chandra Nagar	GMVN	Tourist Rest House	24
Chandra Puri	GMVN	Tourist Rest House	NA
Chandra Puri	GMVN	Tent Colony	NA
Chandra Puri	Private Hotel	Himlok	8
Chandra Puri	Private Hotel	Paryatan Gram Siyalsaur	38
Chandra Puri	Private Hotel	Gavani Lodge	36
Chopta	GMVN	Fibre Glass Cottage	20
Chopta	GMVN	Tourist Bunglow	8
Chopta	Private Hotel	NEGI Hotel	12
Chopta	Private Hotel	Highhill Panchwati Tourist	18
Chopta	Private Hotel	Bachan Singh Hotel	10
Darani	Private Hotel	Himalaya	4
Dewal	GMVN	Tourist Bunglow	12
Dewal	Forest Department	Forest Rest House	4
Dewal	Private Hotel	Jaishri Lodge	12
Dewal	Private Hotel	Bhootpoorv Sainik	12
Dewal	Private Hotel	Puniyal Lodge	8
Dharali	Private Hotel	Bhandari	16
Dharali	Private Hotel	Sainik Tourist	10

1	2	3	4
Dungri Pant	GMVN	F.R.P. Huts	30
Fata	Private Hotel	Renuka Lodge	28
Fata	Private Hotel	Semwal Lodge	21
Fata	Private Hotel	Shiv Lal Shah Lodge	18
Fata	Private Hotel	Meshanand Lodge	26
Dogalbitta	Forest Department	Forest Rest House	4
Garud Chatti	GMVN	F.R.P. Huts	30
Gauchar	GMVN	Tourist Bunglow	20
Gauchar	D.O.T.	Rain Basera	30
Gauchar	Dharamshala	Kali Kamli	30
Gauchar	Private Hotel	Megha Tourist Lodge	20
Gaurikund	GMVN	Tourist lodge	30
Gaurikund	PWD	Inspection House	4
Gaurikund	Private Hotel	Pankaj Lodge	10
Gaurikund	Private Hotel	Pramod Tourist Lodge	33
Gaurikund	Private Hotel	Parohit	6
Gaurikund	Private Hotel	Neel Kama Rest House	47
Gaurikund	Private Hotel	Kailash Lodge	30
Gaurikund	Private Hotel	Sunil Lodge	12
Gaurikund	Private Hotel	New Sunil Lodge	18
Gaurikund	Private Hotel	Semwal Rest House	20
Gaurikund	Private Hotel	Semwal Rest House	35
Gaurikund	Private Hotel	Vijay Hotel	40
Gaurikund	Private Hotel	Deepak Lodge	35
Gaurikund	Private Hotel	Annpurna Rest House	40
Gaurikund	Private Hotel	Goswami Rest House	40
Gaurikund	Private Hotel	Sanjay Lodge	30
Gaurikund	Private Hotel	Devlok Hotel	30
Gaurikund	Private Hotel	Hira Ram Rest House	26
Gaurikund	Private Hotel	Panjab Sindh Kshetra Dharamshala	203
Gaurikund	Private Hotel	Valley view Rest House	26
Gaurikund	Private Hotel	Raj kamal Hotel	2
Gaurikund	Private Hotel	Shiva Hotel	18
Gaurikund	Private Hotel	Satyanand Goswami Hotel	26

1	2	3	4
Gaurikund	Private Hotel	Anup Hotel	12
Gaurikund	Private Hotel	Dev Darshan Hotel	22
Gaurikund	Private Hotel	Shiv Lok	28
Gaurikund	Private Hotel	Anand Hotel	26
Gaurikund	Private Hotel	Meghdoot Hotel	36
Gaurikund	Private Hotel	Pradeep Rest House	28
Gaurikund	Private Hotel	Subash Tourist Lodge	26
Gaurikund	Private Hotel	Arti Lodge	22
Gaurikund	Private Hotel	Bahal Ashram	28
Gaurikund	Private Hotel	Temple Committee Rest House	10
Ghangharia	GMVN	Tourist Rest House	40
Ghangharia	Forest Department	Forest Rest House	4
Ghangharia	Dharamshala	Gurudwara	600
Ghangharia	Private Hotel	Harandar Hotel	6
Ghangharia	Private Hotel	Valley View	20
Ghangharia	Private Hotel	Nanda Devi	51
Ghangharia	Private Hotel	Hemkund Lodge	50
Ghangharia	Private Hotel	Kuber Lodge	42
Ghangharia	Private Hotel	Govind Hotel	6
Ghangharia	Private Hotel	Dev Bhoomi Hotel	46
Ghangharia	Private Hotel	Shivlok	30
Ghangharia	Private Hotel	Ashutosh Hotel	12
Ghangharia	Private Hotel	Pritam Lodge	7
Ghangharia	Private Hotel	Rajneesh Lodge	50
Ghangharia	Private Hotel	Deepak Lodge	20
Ghangharia	Private Hotel	Marri Cottage	18
Ghangharia	Private Hotel	Alpine Hotel	4
Ghangharia	Private Hotel	Krishna Lodge	14
Ghangharia	Private Hotel	Nanda Lodge	6
Ghangharia	Private Hotel	Priya Hotel	18
Gopeshwar	GMVN	Tourist Bunglow	24
Gopeshwar	PWD	Inspection House	6
Gopeshwar	Private Hotel	Alka	17
Gopeshwar	Private Hotel	Ashoka	26
Gopeshwar	Private Hotel	Bhandari	8

1	2	3	4
Gopeshwar	Private Hotel	Jaideep	30
Gopeshwar	Private Hotel	Janta	7
Gopeshwar	Private Hotel	Mandhate	30
Gopeshwar	Private Hotel	Meenal	18
Gopeshwar	Private Hotel	Narnarayan	14
Gopeshwar	Private Hotel	Negi	9
Gopeshwar	Private Hotel	New Star	24
Gopeshwar	Private Hotel	Yogesh	8
Gopeshwar	Private Hotel	Yogesh	24
Gopeshwar	Private Hotel	Monal	24
Gopeshwar	Private Hotel	Mahadev	16
Gopeshwar	Private Hotel	Shiva Lodge	6
Govind Ghat	Forest Department	Forest Rest House	4
Govind Ghat	PWD	Inspection House	4
Govind Ghat	Dharamshala	Gurudwara	250
Govind Ghat	Private Hotel	Hem Tourist House	33
Govind Ghat	Private Hotel	Mehata Guest Rest House	22
Govind Ghat	Private Hotel	Sapt Shring Lodge	24
Govind Ghat	Private Hotel	Him Sarover Lodge	15
Guptakashi	GMVN	Tourist Rest House	54
Guptakashi	PWD	Inspection House	4
Guptakashi	Dharamshala	Kali-Kamli	40
Guptakashi	Dharamshlaa	Temple Committee Rest House	20
Guptakashi	Private Hotel	Vinod Tourist Lodge	16
Guptakashi	Private Hotel	Kailash Tourist Lodge	15
Guptakashi	Private Hotel	Sunil Tourist Lodge	27
Guptakashi	Private Hotel	Deepak Tourist Lodge	18
Guptakashi	Private Hotel	Neel Kamal tourist Lodge	15
Guptakashi	Private Hotel	Sangam Paryatak Awas Griha	15
Guptakashi	Private Hotel	Rana Hotel	60
Guptakashi	Private Hotel	Triveni Hotel	40
Guptakashi	Private Hotel	Kamaldeep Hotel	32
Guptakashi	Private Hotel	Panwar Hotel	60
Guptakashi	Private Hotel	Nege Hotel	10
Guptakashi	Private Hotel	Abbal Singh Hotel	30

1	2	3	4
Guptakashi	Private Hotel	Geetanjali Hotal	38
Guptakashi	Private Hotel	Vivek Hotel	26
Guptakashi	Private Hotel	Sangam Hotel	12
Guptakashi	Private Hotel	Sainik Hotel	14
Guptakashi	Private Hotel	Mandakini Hotel	28
Guptakashi	Private Hotel	Neelkhant Hotel	32
Guptakashi	Private Hotel	Himalaya Hotel	28
Guptakashi	Private Hotel	Bagwari Tourist Lodge	42
Guptakashi	Private Hotel	Kailash	18
Guptakashi	Private Hotel	Kalpeshwar	20
Guptakashi	Private Hotel	Ajad	10
Guptakashi	Private Hotel	Hari Nikatan	12
Guptakashi	Private Hotel	Neel Kamal	28
Guptakashi	Private Hotel	Sumera Tourist Lodge	18
Guptakashi	Private Hotel	Vishwanath Tourist Lodge	21
Gwaldam	GMVN	Tourist Rest House	26
Gwaldam	Forest Department	Forest Rest House	6
Gwaldam	PWD	Inspection House	6
Gwaldam	Private Hotel	Hotel Trishul	32
Gwaldam	Private Hotel	Mansarovar Rest House	24
Gwaldam	Private Hotel	Vijay Rest House	14
Gwaldam	Private Hotel	Gold Star Hotel	12
Gwaldam	Private Hotel	Pramod Lodge	16
Gwaldam	Private Hotel	Rawat Lodge	8
Helang	GMVN	Fibre Glass Huts	30
Joshimath	GMVN	Tourist Rest House	74
Joshimath	GMVN	Passenger Lodge	74
Joshimath	Forest Department	Forest Rest House	8
Joshimath	Forest Department	Forest Rest House	4
Joshimath	Dharamshala	Gurudwara	200
Joshimath	Dharamshala	Kali-Kamli	160
Joshimath	Dharamshala	Shankaracharya	50
Joshimath	Dharamshala	Birla Rest House	25
Joshimath	Private Hotel	Dronagiri Hotel	32
Joshimath	Private Hotel	Durga Nivas	12

1	2	3	4
Joshimath	Private Hotel	Comet Lodge	27
Joshimath	Private Hotel	Marwari Hotel	32
Joshimath	Private Hotel	NeelKanth Hotel	38
Joshimath	Private Hotel	Barrish Tourist Lodge	9
Joshimath	Private Hotel	Shail Sikhar Hotel	32
Joshimath	Private Hotel	Pream Nivas	23
Joshimath	Private Hotel	Shivlok	24
Joshimath	Private Hotel	Nandadevi Hotel	36
Joshimath	Private Hotel	Jain Bhawan	20
Joshimath	Private Hotel	Rawat Hotel	25
Joshimath	Private Hotel	Madhuban Hotel	20
Joshimath	Private Hotel	Takhour Lodge	40
Joshimath	Private Hotel	Comet Lodge	20
Joshimath	Private Hotel	Jyoti Lodge	20
Joshimath	Private Hotel	Dronagiri Lodge	45
Joshimath	Private Hotel	Shivalik Lodge	8
Joshimath	Private Hotel	Subash Lodge	20
Joshimath	Private Hotel	Shaiya Guest House	22
Joshimath	Private Hotel	Khandoori Hotel	8
Joshimath	Private Hotel	Shail Shikhar Hotel	18
Joshimath	Private Hotel	Sudhir Hotel	22
Joshimath	Private Hotel	Bhagirathi Lodge	28
Joshimath	Private Hotel	Namboori Lodge	28
Joshimath	Private Hotel		12
Joshimath	Private Hotel	Sati Hotel	26
Joshimath	Private Hotel	Hans Dharamsala	18
Joshimath	Private Hotel	Kedar Holiday Guest House	26
Joshimath	Private Hotel	Uday Palace Hotel	42
Joshimath	Private Hotel	Shah Lodge	26
Karnaprayg	GMVN	Travellers Lodge	38
Karnaprayg	Forest Department	Forest Rest House	4
Karnaprayg	PWD	Inspection House	4
Karnaprayg	Dharamshala	Kali Kamli	30
Karnaprayg	Private Hotel	Alka	5
Karnaprayg	Private Hotel	Alaknanda	20

1	2	3	4
Karnaprayg	Private Hotel	J.K. Hotel	24
Karnaprayg	Private Hotel	Geeta Lodge	39
Karnaprayg	Private Hotel	Himalaya	43
Karnaprayg	Private Hotel	Jagdish	5
Karnaprayg	Private Hotel	Khalsa	15
Karnaprayg	Private Hotel	Maharaja & Govind Lodge	21
Karnaprayg	Private Hotel	Mahaveer	27
Karnaprayg	Private Hotel	Nanda Devi Tourist Lodge	23
Karnaprayg	Private Hotel	Sainik	5
Karnaprayg	Private Hotel	Sawgam	7
Karnaprayg	Private Hotel	Vijay	5
Karnaprayg	Private Hotel	Govind Lodge	21
Karnaprayg	Private Hotel	Pindar Lodge	30
Karnaprayg	Private Hotel	Saurabh Hotel	26
Karnaprayg	Private Hotel	Hill Queen Hotel	18
Karnaprayg	Private Hotel	Uma Lodge	36
Karnaprayg	Private Hotel	Mandakini Hotel	36
Karnaprayg	Private Hotel	Ambe Hotel	22
Karnaprayg	Private Hotel	Prayag Raj Tourist Lodge	28
Kaliyasaur	D.O.T.	Rain Basera	30
Kalimath	Dharamshala	Temple Committee	180
Kalimath	Dharamshala	Gabber Singh Rawat	20
Kalimath	Dharamshala	Hans Dharamshala	28
Kedarnath	GMVN	FRP Huts	12
Kedarnath	GMVN	Hotel Himlok	10
Kedarnath	GMVN	Tourist Lodge	36
Kedarnath	GMVN	Tourist Rest House	52
Kedarnath	PWD	Inspection House	4
Kedarnath	BKTC	Chand Cottage	8
Kedarnath	BKTC	Double Storey Bhawan	16
Kedarnath	BKTC	J.K. Singhavia	8
Kedarnath	BKTC	Modi Bhawan	8
Kedarnath	BKTC	Nepal Bhawan	100
Kedarnath	BKTC	Temple Committee Dharamshala	4
Kedarnath	BKTC	Wite Cottage	4

1	2	3	4
Kedarnath	BKTC	Sarai Cottage	4
Kedarnath	BKTC	Arati Bhawan	10
Kedarnath	BKTC	Birla Niketan	14
Kedarnath	BKTC	Janta Dharamshla	4
Kedarnath	BKTC	Vatika	8
Kedarnath	BKTC	Modi Bhawan	8
Kedarnath	BKTC	Dalmia	30
Kedarnath	BKTC	Janta	30
Kedarnath	Dharamshala	Temple Committee Rest House	10
Kedarnath	Dharamshala	Ahuti	46
Kedarnath	Dharamshala	Bhajan Ashram	24
Kedarnath	Dharamshala	Birla Guest House	46
Kedarnath	Dharamshala	Janta Dharamshala	4
Kedarnath	Dharamshala	Baba Kali Kamli	70
Kedarnath	Dharamshala	Gujrati Bhawan	40
Kedarnath	Dharamshala	J.K. House	20
Kedarnath	Dharamshala	Bhavat Sewa Ashram	103
Kedarnath	Dharamshala	Madras Bhawan	50
Kedarnath	Dharamshala	Tiwari Ashram	24
Kedarnath	Dharamshala	Jaipur House	40
Kedarnath	Dharamshala	Punjab Himachal House	32
Kedarnath	Dharamshala	Punjab Himachal House	20
Kedarnath	Dharamshala	Padam Kothi	12
Kedarnath	Dharamshala	Purohit Guest House	14
Kedarnath	Dharamshala	Sunil Guest House	31
Kedarnath	Dharamshala	Birla Mandir Niketan	14
Kedarnath	Dharamshala	Bharat Sevashram	70
Kedarnath	Private Hotel	Sonipath House	16
Kedarnath		Maharashtra Mandal	40
Kund	Private Hotel	Upkar	8
Lohajung	Forest Department.	Forest Rest House	4
Madmaheshwar	Dharamshala	Temple Committe	60
Mandal	Private Hotel	Amer Tourist Bunglow	8
Mandal	Private Hotel	Bhagat Tourist Bunglow	14
Mohankhal	Forest Department.	Forest Rest House	4

1	2	3	4
Mundoli	GMVN	Tourist Bunglow	12
Nandprayag	D.O.T.	Rainbasera	30
Nandprayag	GMVN	Tourist Rest House	30
Nandprayag	Forest Department.	Forest Rest House	4
Nandprayag	PWD	Inspection House	4
Nandprayag	Private Hotel	Uttarakhand Tourist Lodge	144
Nandprayag	Private Hotel	Shivlok Lodge	12
Nandprayag	Private Hotel	Rajendra Singh Negi Lodge	8
Nandprayag	Private Hotel	Mandakini Lodge	12
Nandprayag	Private Hotel	Vikram Singh Rotila	36
Nandprayag	Private Hotel	Ashfak Hussain Lodge	12
Nandprayag	Private Hotel	Kandari Lodge	12
Nandprayag	Private Hotel	Navia Tourist Lodge	16
Ghat	Private Hotel	Hansraj Sati Lodge	18
Nala/Narayan Koti	Private Hotel	Devlok Lodge	36
Nala/Narayan Koti	Private Hotel	Goswami Lodge	26
Narayan Bagar	Private Hotel	Sainik Hotel	10
Pakhi	GMVN	Fibre Glass Huts	30
Palta	Dharamshala	Temple Committee	30
Pana	Private Hotel	Mehar	8
Pandukeshwar	Dharamshala	Kali Kamli	100
Pipal Koti	GMVN	Tourist Bunglow	50
Pipal Koti	PWD	Inspection House	4
Pipal Koti	Dharamshala	Kali Kamli	70
Pipal Koti	Temple committee	Rest House	6
Pipal Koti	Private Hotel	Ajanta	100
Pipal Koti	Private Hotel	Anupam Lodge	28
Pipal Koti	Private Hotel	Bhawani Lodge	25
Pipal Koti	Private Hotel	Dailawar	18
Pipal Koti	Private Hotel	Madan Lal Lodge	11
Pipal Koti	Private Hotel	Pathik	6
Pipal Koti	Private Hotel	Vikrant	8
Pipal Koti	Private Hotel	Badrinath	117
Pipal Koti	Private Hotel	Alaknanda	40
Pipal Koti	Private Hotel	Atul Lodge	40

1	2	3	4
Pipal Koti	Private Hotel	Inderlok Lodge	20
Pipal Koti	Private Hotel	Kailash Lodge	28
Pipal Koti	Private Hotel	New Vikrant	42
Pipal Koti	Private Hotel	Harish Lal shah	10
Pipal Koti	Private Hotel	Yudhveer Singh	30
Pipal Koti	Private Hotel	Balram Singh	12
Pipal Koti	Private Hotel	Nayan Singh Rawat Lodge	10
Pipal Koti	Private Hotel	Deen Dayal Lodge	18
Pipal Koti	Private Hotel	Vivek Lodge	18
Pipal Koti	Private Hotel	Hement	12
Pipal Koti	Private Hotel	Ankit Lodge	8
Pipal Koti	Private Hotal	Indra Lodge	21
Pokhri	Forest Department.	Forest Rest House	4
Pokhri	PWD	Inspection House	4
Rambara	GMVN	Fibre Glass Huts	30
Rambara	Dharamshala	Baba Kali Kamli	120
Rambara	Private	Birla Rest House	4
Rambara	Private	Raja Hotel	12
Ranpur	Dharamshala	Kali Kamli	110
Ranpur	Private Hotel	Pushkar	9
Ranpur	Private Hotel	Rawat	6
Ranpur	Private Hotel	Shrine Lodge & Devlok Lodge	31
Ranpur	Private Hotel	Neelam Hotel	18
Ranpur	Private Hotel	Milan Hotel	12
Ranpur	Private Hotel	Sun Shine Lodge	36
Ranpur	Private Hotel	Devlok Lodge	38
Ranpur	Private Hotel	Mandakini Lodge	18
Ranpur	Private Hotel	Alak Nanda Hotel	22
Ranpur	Private Hotel	Kedar Hotel	18
Ranpur	Private Hotel	Uttranchal Hotel	12
Ranpur	Private Hotel	Kailash Lodge	26
Ranpur	Private Hotel	Sumero Hotel	28
Ranpur	Private Hotel	Vijay Hotel	22
Ranpur	Private Hotel	Panchwati Rest House	32
Ranpur	Private Hotel	Sikhar Hotel	12

1	2	3	4
Ranpur	Private Hotel	New Star Hotel	15
Ranpur	Private Hotel	Hari Lodge	15
Rudraprayag	GMVN	Tourist Rest House(Deluxe)	40
Rudraprayag	GMVN	Tourist Rest House	63
Rudraprayag	Dharmshala	Baba Kali Kamli	132
Rudraprayag	Dharmshala	Temple Committee Rest House	26
Rudraprayag	Private Hotel	Tourist Bunglow	63
Rudraprayag	Private Hotel	Uttrakhand Tourist Lodge	10
Rudraprayag	Private Hotel	Kala Tourist Lodge	18
Rudraprayag	Private Hotel	Rock Stone Tourist Lodge	11
Rudraprayag	Private Hotel	Badri Kedar Lodge	22
Rudraprayag	Private Hotel	Indralok Lodge	25
Rudraprayag	Private Hotel	Dev Bhumi Lodge	10
Rudraprayag	Private Hotel	Devlok Lodge	22
Rudraprayag	Private Hotel	Prayag Tourist Lodge	12
Rudraprayag	Private Hotel	Pushp Deep Hotel	58
Rudraprayag	Private Hotel	Suri Lodge	26
Rudraprayag	Private Hotel	Surya Lodge	28
Rudraprayag	Private Hotel	Pinaki Hill Resort	22
Rudraprayag	Private Hotel	Krishna Lodge	18
Rudraprayag	Private Hotel	Khanna Lodge	12
Rudraprayag	Private Hotel	Jeet Tourist Lodge	18
Siyalsaur	GMVN	Log Huts	24
Sone Prayag	GMVN	FRP Huts	30
Sone Prayag	PWD	Inspection House	4
Sone Prayag	Dhramashala	Temple Committee	30
Sone Prayag	Private Hotel	Ashok Vatika	10
Sone Prayag	Private Hotel	Apu Lodge	16
Sone Prayag	Private Hotel	Devlok	8/30
Sone Prayag	Private Hotel	Mandakini	17/30
Sone Prayag	Private Hotel	Himani Lodge	12
Sone Prayag	Private Hotel	Mansarovar Lodge	28
Sone Prayag	Private Hotel	Chauhan Hotel	18
Sone Prayag	Private Hotel	Prayag Tourist Lodge	16
Sunneet	GMVN	Fibre Glass Cottage (60/3)	20

1	2	3	4
Sunneet	GMVN	FRD Huts	48
Sunil	GMVN	Fibre Glass House	10
Sitapur	Private Hotel	Himalaya Lodge	26
Sitapur	Private Hotel	Ganesh Lodge	25
Sitapur	Private Hotel	Mahaveer Lodge	28
Sitapur	Private Hotel	Vijay Lodge	18
Sitapur	Private Hotel	Sunil Lodge	12
Sitapur	Private Hotel	Shivani Lodge	22
Sitapur	Private Hotel	Shivam Tourist Hut	28
Sitapur	Private Hotel	Hari Om Lodge	18
Trijuginarayan	Dharamshala	Kali Kamli	60
Ukimath	GMVN	Tourist Bunglow	10
Ukimath	PWD	Inspection House	6
Ukimath	Dharamshala	Temple Committee	18
Ukimath	Private Hotel	Maithani Lodge	22
Ukimath	Private Hotel	Sainik	6
Ukimath	Private Hotel	Sita Lodge	12
Ukimath	Private Hotel	Uttrakhand Tourist Lodge	12
Ukimath	Private Hotel	Upkar Tourist Lodge	8
Urgam	Dharamshala	Kali Kamli	4
Wan	GMVN	TRH	12

APPENDIX-2

DESTINATION S' DISTANCE TABLES

Table No. A.2.1
Dehradun To Yamunotri

Place (point to point)	Altitude(m) Progressive (Km.)	Distance (Km)	Distance
Dehradun	701	-	-
Mussoorie	1921	36	36
Kempty Fall	1524	12	48

1	2	3	4
Yamuna Bridge	772	16	64
Damta	1372	25	89
Naugaon	1524	28	117
Barkot	1828	11	128
Sayanachatti	1982	29	157
Hanumanchatti	2134	05	162
Phoolchatti	2561	05 Trek	167
Jannkichatti	2576	02 Trek	169
Yamunotri	3323	06 Trek	175
Dehradun to Hanumanchatti			162 Motor
Hanumanchatti to Yamunotri			13 Trek

Table A.2.2
Rishikesh to Yamunotri

Place	Altitude(m)	Distance (Km) (point to point)	Distance (Progressive) (Km)
Rishikesh	340		
Narendra Nagar	1067	16	16
Chamba	1534	46	62
Tehri	770	21	83
Dharasu	1036	37	120
Brahmakhal	1158	15	135
Barkot	1828	40	175
Sayanachatti	1982	29	204
Hanumanchatti	2134	5	209
Phoolchatti	2561	5 Trek	214
Jankichatti	2576	2 Trek	216
Yamunotri	3323	6 Trek	222

Table A.2.3
Rishikesh to Gangotri

Place	Altitude(m)	Distance (Km) (point to point)	Distance(Km) (progressive)
Rishikesh	340	-	-
Narendra Nagar	1067	16	16
Chamba	1524	46	62
Tehri	770	21	83
Dharasu	1036	37	120
Uttarkashi	1158	28	148
Gangori	1219	4	152
Maneri	1372	6	158
Bhatwari	1677	19	177
Ganganani	1982	14	191
Sukhi	2744	18	209
Jhala	2439	7	216
Harsil	2591	6	222
Lanka	2652	13	235
Gangotri	3140	10	245
Rishikesh to Gangotri		245 Km. Motor	

Table A.2.4
Gangotri To Kedarnath (By Trek)

Place	Altitude(m)	Distance (Km) (point to point)	Progressive Distance (Km)
Gangotri	3140	-	-
Bhatwari	1677	71 Motor	71
Mala	1478	2 Motor	73
Sauri ki gad	1218	5 Trek	78
Phyalu	2286	3 Trek	81
Chunachatti	1463	3 Trek	84
Belak	2439	4 Trek	88
Pangrana	2203	5 Trek	93

1	2	3	4
Jhala	2439	4 Trek	97
Agund	1981	3 Trek	100
Budakedar	1524	2 Trek	102
Tolachatti	1311	4 Trek	106
Bhaironchatti	2439	3 Trek	109
Ghuttu	1524	9 Trek	118
Panwali	3963	15 Trek	133
Maggu-Ki-Mandi	3049	7 Trek	140
Triyuginarain	1942	5 Trek	145
Sonprayag	1829	3 Trek	148
Gauri Kund	1982	5 Trek or Moter	153
Kedarnath	3583	14 Trek	167

Mala to Soneprayag = 75 Km. Trek
Sonprayag to Kedarnath = 19 Km. Trek
Gangotri to Mala = 73 Km. Moterable

Table A.2.5
Gangotri To Kedarnath (Via - Ghansali - Chirbattia)

Place	Altitude(m)	Distance (Km) (point to point)	Progressive Distance (Km)
Gangotri	3140	-	-
Dharasu	1036	125 Motor	125
Dubata	770	33	158
Tehri	770	4	162
Gadoliya	770	17	179
Ghansali	976	18	197
Chirbatia	1134	31	228
Tilwara	671	42	270
Augustmuni	762	10	280
Gaurikund	1982	51	331
Kedarnath	3583	14 Trek	345
Gangotri to Gaurikund		331 Km. Motor	
Gaurikund to Kedarnath		14 Trek	

Table A.2.6
Gangotri To Kedarnath (Via - Srinagar & Rudraprayag)

Place	Altitude(m)	Distance (Km) (point to point)	Progressive Distance (Km)
Gangotri	3140	-	-
Tehri	770	162	162
Srinagar	579	60	222
Rudraprayag	610	34	256
Gaurikund	1982	70	326
Kedarnath	3583	14 Trek	340
Gangotri to Gaurikund		326 Km. Motor	
Gaurikund to Kedarnath		14 Trek	

Table A.2.7
Rishikesh to Kedarnath - Vasukital

Place	Altitude(m)	Distance (Km) (point to point)	Progressive Distance (Km)
Rishikesh	340	-	-
Deoprayag	472	70	70
Srinagar	579	35	105
Rudraprayag	610	34	139
Tilwara	671	09	148
Agastmuni	762	10	158
Kund	976	15	173
Guptakashi	1479	05	178
Narayankoti	1500	03	181
Phata	1601	11	192
Rampur	1646	09	201
Sonprayag	1829	03	204
Gaurikund	1982	05	209
Rambara	2591	07 Trek	216

1	2	3	4
Garurchatti	3262	04 Trek	220
Sri Kedarnath	3583	03 Trek	223
Vasuki Tal	4135	06 Trek	229
Rishikesh to Gaurikund			209 Motor
Gaurikund to Kedarnath			14 Trek

Table A.2.8
Rishikesh to Badrinath

Place	Altitude(m)	Distance (Km) (point to point)	Progressive Distance (Km)
Rishikesh	340	-	-
Deoprayag	472	70	70
Srinagar	579	35	105
Rudraprayag	610	34	139
Gholtir	645	10	149
Gauchar	790	10	159
Karanprayag	795	11	170
Nandprayag	914	22	192
Chamoli	1069	10	202
Birahi	1100	8	210
Pipalkoti	1311	9	219
Garur Ganga	1372	5	224
Tangani	1677	6	230
Helang	1524	6	236
Joshimath	1890	14	250
Vishnuprayag	1372	10	260
Govindghat	1829	10	270
Pandukeshwar	1829	4	274
Hanumanchatti	2286	9	283
Dev Darshni	3101	13	296
Badrinath	3110	2	298

Table A.2.9
Kedarnath to Badrinath - Via Rudraprayag

Place	Altitude(m)	Distance (Km) (point to point)	Progressive Distance (Km)
Sri kedarnath	3583	-	
Gaurikund	1982	14 Trek	14
Rudraprayag	610	70	84
Joshimath	1890	111	195
Badrinath	3110	48	243
Kedarnath to Gaurikund		14 Trek	
Gaurikund to Badrinath		229 Motor	

Table A.2.10
Kedarnath to Badrinath-Via Ukhimath

Place	Altitude(m)	Distance (Km) (point to point)	Progressive Distance (Km)
Kedarnath	3583	-	-
Gaurikund	1982	14 Trek	14
Kund	976	36	50
Ukhimath	1311	5 "	55
Dogalbitta	2347	24 "	79
Chopta	2500	6 "	85
Mandal	1568	28 "	113
Gopeshwar	1308	11 "	124
Chamoli	1069	10 "	134
Joshimath	1890	48	182
Badrinath	3110	48	230
Kedarnath to Gaurikund			14 trek
Gaurikund to Kund			36 Motor
Kund to Badrinath			180 Motor

Table A.2.11
Mussoorie-Nagtibba Trek

Place	Altitude (m)	Distance (Km) (point to point)	Accommodation
Mussoorie	1921	-	H, TRH
Dhanaulti	2250	22 Motor	H, TRH
Morina Dhar	2350	18 Trek	T
Gnodiappa	2800	16 Trek	T
Nagtibba	3040	15 Trek	T
Panthwari	1524	8 Trek	T
Nainbagh	1115	11 Trek	T

Table A.2.12
Kalsi-Lakhamandal Trek

Place	Altitude(m)	Distance (Km) (point to point)	Accommodation
Mussoorie	1921	-	H, TRH
Kuwa	1090	69 Motor	T
Goraghati	2310	12 Trek	T
Dunagyara	1608	16 Trek	T
Churani	2180	17 Trek	T
Biratkhoi	3080	05 Trek	T
Kalsi	850	22 Trek	PWD, F
Dakpathar	790	6 Motor	TRH,PWD

Table A.2.13
Dodital Trek

Place	Altitude(m)	Distance (Km) (point to point)	Accommodation
Uttarkashi	1158	-	H, TRH
Gangori	1219	4 Motor	-
Kalyani	1829	7 Jeep	-
Agoda	2286	5 Trek	T, F
Dodital	3024	16 Trek	T, F

Table A.2.14
Har-ki-doon Trek

Place	Altitude(m)	Distance (Km) (point to point)	Accommodation
Dehradun	701	-	H, TRH
Mussoorie	1921	36 Motor	H, TRH
Purola	1524	97 Motor	TRH,F,PWD
Jarmola	1800	22 Motor	F
Naitwar	1380	28 Motor	F
Sankri	1900	12 Motor	T, TRH
Taluka	2010	12 Trek / Jeep	T, TRH
Osla	2415	12 Trek	F, TRH , PWD
Har-ki-Doon	3566	8 Trek	F

Table A.2.15
Khatling Glacier Trek

Place	Altitude(m)	Distance (Km) (point to point)	Accommodation
Tehri	770	-	H, TRH
Ghansali	976	32 Motor	H, PWD
Ghuttu	1624	31 Motor	H, TRH,PWD,F
Reeh	2134	10 Trek	T, TRH
Gangi	2591	10 Trek	T
Kalyani	2683	5 Trek	T
Kharsoli	2896	10 Trek	T
Bhelbagi	3201	3 Trek	T
Bhumka	3415	3 Trek	T
Khatling Glacier	3658	3 Trek	T
Masartar	3675	6 Trek	T

Table A.2.16
Sahastra Tal

Place	Altitude(m)	Distance (Km) (point to point)	Accommodation
Mala	1487	-	T
Kushkalyani		15 Trek	T
Kyarki	—	14 Trek	T
Parirital	—	14 Trek	T
Sahastrtal	4572	6 Trek	T
Taddiuddyar	3965	5 Trek	T
Kalyani	2683	16 Trek	T
Gangi	2589	5 Trek	T
Reeh	2132	10 Trek	T,TRH
Ghuttu	1524	10 Trek	T, TRH, PWD, F

Table A.2.17
Gangotri-Gaumukh-Nandanvan-Tapovan Trek

Place	Altitude(m)	Distance (Km) (point to point)	Accommodation
Rishikesh	340		H, TRH
Gangotri	3140	245 Motor	H, D,TRH
Chirbasa	3600	8 Trek	T
Bhojbasa	3792	4 Trek	T, TRH
Gaumukh	3892	6 Trek	-
Nandanvan	4500	6 Trek	T
Tapovan	4463	5 Trek	T

Table A.2.18
Kalindikahal Trek

Place	Altitude(m)	Distance (Km) (point to point)	Accommodation
Gangotri	3140		H, D, TRH
Nandanvan	4500	24 Trek	T
Vasukital	5300	10 Trek	T
Kharapathar	5500	8 Trek	T
Kalindibase	5590	6 Trek	T
Arwatal	3980	14 Trek	T
Ghastoli	3600	18 Trek	T
Badrinath	3110	17 Trek	H, D, TRH

Table A.2.19
Madmahshwar Trek

Place	Altitude(m)	Distance (Km) (point to point)	Accommodation
Guptkashi	1479	-	D, TRH
Kalimath	1463	6 Motor	D, T
Ransi	1765	7 Trek	T
Gaundar.	2073	6 Trek	T
Madhmaheshwar	3289	11 Trek	D, T

Table A.2.20
Rudranath Trek

Place	Altitude(m)	Distance (Km) (point to point)	Accommodation
Gopeshwar	1300	-	H, TRH
Gangolgaon	1400	3 Motor	-
Panar	2286	8 Trek	T
Naila	3354	5 Trek	T
Rudranath	3286	4 Trek	T, D
Dumak	2134	12 Trek	T
Kalgont	2073	5 Trek	T
Kimana	2074	8 Trek	T
Palla	2073	3 Trek	T
Urgam	2134	8 Trek	T, D
Helang	1524	9 Trtek	-
Joshimath	1890	14 Motor	H,TRH

Table A.2.21
Valley of Flowers Trek

Place	Altitude(m)	Distance (Km) (point to point)	Accommodation
Joshimath	1890	-	H, TRH
Govindghat	1829	20 Motor	GD, H, PWD, F
Pulna	1920	3 Trek	-
Bhyundar	2439	7 Trek	T
Ghangaria	3094	5 Trek	H, GD, TRH
Valley of Flowers	3352(lowest Point) 3658(highest point)	3 Trek	

Table A 2.22
Hemkund Sahib Trek

Place	Altitude(m)	Distance (Km) (point to point)	Accommodation
Joshimath	1890		H, TRH
Govindghat	1829	20 Motor	GD, H, PWD, F
Pulna	1920	3 Trek	-
Bhyundar	2439	7 Trek	T
Ghangaria	3049	5 Trek	H, GD, TRH
Hemkund Shahib	4329	6 Trek	T, GD

Table A 2.23(a)
Ghat, Ramni, Sanatoli to Kuari Pass Trek

Place	Altitude(m)	Distance (Km) (point to point)	Accommodation
Nandprayag	914	-	TRH
Ghat	1331	19 Motor	TRH
Ramni	1982	10 Trek	T

1	2	3	4
Sarkot	2439	4 Trek	T
Jhenjipatni	1524	9 Trek	T
Panarani	2043	12 Trek	T
Sanatoli	2439	5 Trek	T
Domabita	2286	5 Trek	T
Kuari pass	4268	5 Trek	T

Table A.2.23(b)
Joshimath, Auli and Gorson to Kuari Pass Trek

Place	Altitude(m)	Distance (Km) (point to point)	Accommodation
Joshimath	1890	-	H, TRH
Auli	2744	16 Motor	TRH, T
Gorson	3658	7 Trek	T
Tali	3506	5 Trek	T
Chitrakantha	3506	4 Trek	T
Gailgarh	3658	3 Trek	T
Kuari Pass	4268	5 Trek	T

Table A.2.23(c)
Joshimath, Mrig, Tugasi and Khaiara to Kuari PassTrek

Place	Altitude(m)	Distance (Km) (point to point)	Accommodation
Joshimath	1890	-	H, TRH
Mrig	1982	7 Motor	T
Tugasi	2012	10 Trek	T
Khulara	2896	6 Trek	T
Gailgarh	3658	6 Trek	T
Kuari Pass	4268	5 Trek	T

Table A.2.23(d)
Tapovan, Khulara to kuari Trek

Place	Altitude(m)	Distance (Km) (point to point)	Accommodation
Joshimath	1890	-	H, TRH
Tapovan	1829	15 Motor	T
Khulara	2896	10 Trek	T
Gailgarh	3658	6 Trek	T
Kuari Pass	4268	5 Trek	T

Table A.2.24(a)
Roopkund Trek (Via wan village)

Place	Altitude(m)	Distance (Km) (point to point)	Accommodation
Tharali	333	-	-
Debal	1218	12 Motor	T, TRH
Faldigaon	1354	8 Motor	-
Mundoli	2134	9 Trek	T, TRH
Wan	2439	14 Trek	T, TRH
Gairoli Patali	3049	9 Trek	T
Patar Nachauni	3658	11 Trek	T
Roopkund	5029	10 Trek	-

Table A2.24(b)
Roopkund To Homekund (Via Bedni Bugyal)

Place	Altitude(m)	Distance (Km) (point to point)	Accommodation
Tharali	333	-	
Debal	1218	12 Motor	T, TRH
Bagrigadh	1980	15 Motor	-

1	2	3		4
Mundoli	2134	2	Motor	T, TRH
Lohjung	2244	2	Trek	T, F
Bedni Bugyal	3354	10	Trek	T
Bistola	4667	8	Trek	T
Roopkund	5029	5	Trek	-
Homekund	4061	13	Trek	T
Sutola	2194	18	Trek	T
Ghat	1331	26	Trek	T

F	Forest Rest House
PWD	PWD Rest House
TRH	Tourist Rest House
H	Hotel /Lodge
D	Dharm Shala
GD	Guru Dwara

APPENDIX-3

LIST OF MAJOR MOUNTAIN PEAKS OF GARHWAL

There are more than 100 peaks, above 6000 mt. in altitude. Broadly the mountain peaks of Garhwal Himalayas are divided into three major groups.

1. **Kamet Group**
2. **Gangotri Group**
3. **Nanda Devi Group**

1. **Kamet Group**: The eastern and southern limits start from the Kiunglang La (Niti pass) and continue along the Dhauli Ganga. The western limit in the Mana Pass and Saraswati river which becomes the Alaknanda further south. Kamet group includes following peaks:

Table- A-3-1

		Height in		Location North	East
S.N.	**Peaks**	**Meter**	**Feet**	**Latitudes**	**Longitudes**
1.	Kamet	7756	25447	30°55' 13"	79°35' 37"
2.	Abi-Gamin	7355	24130	30°55' 57"	79°36' 09"
3.	Mana	7272	23860	30°52' 52"	79°36' 57"
4.	Mukut	7242	23760	30°57' 08"	79°34' 13"
5.	Mana N-West	7092	23270	30°53' 51"	79°35' 46"
6.	P 6977	6977	22890	30°52' 25"	79°38' 10"
7.	P 6940	6940	22770	31°02' 03"	79°30' 20"
8.	P 6910	6910	22670	30°59' 30"	79°31' 53"
9.	Deoban	6855	22490	30°52' 03"	79°39' 07"
10.	P 6775	6775	22230	31°01' 04"	79°30' 57"
11.	P 6760	6760	22180	30°58' 07"	79°33' 07"
12.	Hathi Parbat	6727	22070	30°41' 04"	79°42' 28"
13.	P 6684	6684	21930	30°59' 33"	79°37' 07"
14.	P 6651	6651	21815	30°57' 02"	79°37' 05"
15.	Ghori Parbat	6708	22010	30°42' 42"	79°42' 08"
16.	P 6629	6629	21750	30°42' 07"	79°41' 51"
17.	Mandir Parbat	6559	21520	30°49' 40"	79°36' 19"
18.	P 6559	6559	21520	30°56' 53"	79°35' 30"
19.	P 6541	6541	21460	30°52' 37"	79°35' 37"
20.	P 6535	6535	21440	30°57' 51"	79°40' 17"
21.	Ganesh Parbat	6532	21430	30°58' 17"	79°43' 16"
22.	P 6520	6520	21390	30°51' 53"	79°40' 51"
23.	P 6507	6507	21350	31°01' 58"	79°27' 46"
24.	Nilgiri Parbat	6474	21240	30°47' 03"	79°38' 47"
25.	Durpata	6466	21210	30°43' 02"	79°44' 27"
26.	Balbala	6416	21050	31°01' 26"	79°26' 14"
27.	Balbala West	6282	20610	31°01' 21"	79°24' 59"
28.	Rataban	6166	20230	30°45' 01"	79°42' 19"
29.	Geldhong	6163	20220	30°53' 39"	79°47' 51"

2. **Gangotri Group**: It has eastern limit in the *Mana Pass* and *Saraswati* river which becomes *Alaknanda* and the western boundary is Chorgad, the Jadh Ganga and the Bhagirathi river. Because of the size of the group the peaks are grouped into two subgroups.

(a) North-Eastern Gangotri

(b) South-Western Gangotri

Table - A-3-2

North-Eastern Gangotri Peaks (North of Bhagirathi River and North East of Gangotri Glacier).

		Height in		Location North	East
S.N.	**Peaks**	**Meter**	**Feet**	**Latitudes**	**Longitudes**
1.	Chaukhambha I	7138	23420	30°44' 59"	79°17' 28"
2.	Satopanth	7075	23212	30°50' 34"	79°12' 53"
3.	Chaukhambha II	7068	23190	30°43' 56"	79°16' 53"
4.	Chaukhambha III	6974	22880	30°43' 12"	79°16' 36"
5.	Srikailash	6932	22745	31°00' 54"	79°10' 48"
6.	Bhagirathi Pabat I	6856	22493	30°50' 49"	79°09' 05"
7.	Chaukhambha IV	6854	22487	30°43' 07"	79°15' 28"
8.	P 6805	6805	22330	30°46' 33"	79°14' 33"
9.	P 6796	6796	22297	30°57' 47"	79°12' 55"
10.	Mana Parbat I	6794	22290	30°56' 53"	79°14' 58"
11.	Vasuki Parbat	6792	22283	30°52' 15"	79°10' 40"
12.	P 6772	6772	22218	31°00' 30"	79°07' 56"
13.	Mana Parbat II	6771	22215	30°56' 56"	79°15' 20"
14.	P 6770	6770	22212	30°50' 02"	79°12' 05"
15.	Chandra ParbatI	6739	22110	30°52' 05"	79°15' 34"
16.	P 6730	6730	22080	30°56' 58"	79°13' 25"
17.	ChandraparbatII	6728	22075	30°52' 42"	79°14' 59"
18.	Matri	6721	22050	31°00' 42"	79°04' 24"

1	2	3	4	5	6
19.	P 6721	6721	22050	30°48' 27"	79°13' 36"
20.	P 6715	6715	22030	31°01' 24"	79°07' 22"
21.	P 6702	6702	21990	30°51' 23"	79°10' 37"
22.	P 6702	6702	21990	30°48' 56"	79°10' 34"
23.	P 6684	6684	21930	30°49' 16"	79°14' 33"
24.	Yogeshwar	6678	21910	30°59' 26"	79°07' 11"
25.	P 6666	6666	21870	30°50' 01"	79°14' 19"
26.	Chaturbhuj	6654	21830	30°59' 28"	79°05' 46"
27.	Nilkantha	6596	21640	30°43' 44"	79°24' 00"
28.	P 6587	6587	21610	31°00' 02"	79°11' 53"
29.	P 6587	6587	21610	30°59' 45"	79°12' 25"
30.	P 6565	6565	21540	31°00' 24"	79°05' 00"
31.	P 6565	6565	21540	30°59' 07"	79°09' 13"
32.	P 6557	6557	21513	30°51' 19"	79°15' 26"
33.	P 6557	6557	21513	30°59' 04"	-
34.	Chirbasparbat	6529	21420	31°02' 00"	79°03' 22"
35.	P 6526	6526	21410	30°50' 02"	79°16' 09"
36.	Bhagirathi II	6512	21364	30°52' 47"	79°07' 56"
37.	Sudarshanparbat	6507	21350	30°58' 24"	79°05' 43"
38.	P 6504	6504	21340	30°49' 35"	79°09' 39"
39.	Balakon	6471	21230	30°46' 00"	79°20' 40"
40.	Bhagirathi III	6454	21175	30°51' 58"	79°08' 05"
41.	Trimukhiparbat	6422	21070	31°02' 57"	79°11' 53"
42.	Chaturangi	6407	21020	30°55' 34"	79°12' 30"
43.	Kalidhung	6373	20910	31°02' 23"	79°00' 34"
44.	Swetvarn	6340	20800	30°58' 58"	79°06' 00"
45.	Avalanche peak	6190	20310	30°50' 34"	79°24' 20"
46.	Saife	6161	20215	30°57' 37"	79°06' 05"
47.	Shyamvarn	6135	20128	30°58' 21"	79°07' 45"
48.	Sarup Choti	6108	20040	31°08' 41"	79°18' 24"
49.	Kalindi	6102	20020	30°55' 10"	79°16' 53"
50.	Koteshswar I	6080	19950	30°56' 53"	79°06' 10"
51.	Tara	6069	19912	31°12' 47"	79°22' 17"
52.	Thelu	6002	19690	30°57' 47"	79°05' 00"

South Western Gangotri Group (South of Bhagirathi River and South West of Gangotri Glacier).

Table - A-3-3

		Height in		Location North	East
S.N.	**Peaks**	**Meter**	**Feet**	**Latitudes**	**Longitudes**
1.	Kedarnath	6940	22770	30°47' 42"	79°04' 10"
2.	Thalay Sagar	6904	22650	30°51' 29"	78°59' 50"
3.	Kedar Dome	6831	22410	30°48' 31"	79°04' 44"
4.	Bhrigupanth	6772	22220	30°52' 40"	79°00' 14"
5.	Gangotri I	6672	21890	30°54' 53"	78°50' 46"
6.	Meru South	6660	21850	30°51' 48"	79°02' 07"
7.	P 6638	6638	21780	30°44' 51"	79°14' 44"
8.	Jaonli	6632	21760	30°51' 04"	79°51' 19"
9.	Kharchakund	6612	21695	30°46' 43"	78°07' 51"
10.	Gangotri II	6590	21620	30°54' 06"	78°51' 31"
11.	Bharate Khunta	6578	21580	30°48' 04"	79°02' 08"
12.	Gangotri III	6577	21578	30°52' 57"	78°52' 51"
13.	Manda II	6568	21550	30°55' 52"	79°00' 00"
14.	Shivling	6543	21467	30°52' 37"	79°03' 56"
15.	Manda III	6529	21420	30°54' 06"	79°00' 09"
16.	Manda I	6510	21360	30°56' 11"	79°00' 01"
17.	Jogin I	6465	21210	30°52' 30"	78°55' 03"
18.	Meru North	6450	21162	30°52' 15"	79°01' 53"
19.	Meru West	6361	20870	30°52' 02"	79°01' 15"
20.	Jogin II	6342	20807	30°53' 41"	78°56' 00"
21.	Sumeru Parbat	6331	20770	30°46' 29"	79°07' 34"
22.	Kirti Stambh	6270	20570	30°49' 00"	79°01' 54"
23.	Mandini Parbat	6193	20320	30°43' 49"	79°12' 00"
24.	Srikantha	6133	20120	30°52' 13"	78°48' 19"
25.	Jogin III	6116	20066	30°52' 08"	78°56' 08"
26.	Brigu Parbat	6041	19820	30°57' 23"	78°59' 10"

1	2	3	4	5	6
Banderpunch Range (North and West of Bagirathi River)					
1.	Kalanag	6387	20956	31°01' 31"	78°34' 24"
2.	Bandarpunch	6316	20720	31°00' 01"	78°33' 16"
3.	Swargrohini I	6252	20512	31°05' 04"	78°30' 58"
4.	Swargrohini II	6247	20496	31°05'	78°33'
5.	SwargrohiniIII	6209	20371	31°05'	78°31'
6.	Bandarpunch West	6102	20020	31°00' 22"	78°31' 37"

Nanda Devi Group: The eastern limit starts at the Kangribingri La, goes over the Unta Dhura, through Milam and down the Ghori Ganga. The western limits are from the Kiunglang La (Niti Pass) down the Dhauliganga. It has three subgroups such as: The Eastern Nanda Devi, The Northern Nanda Devi and The Southern Nanda Devi.

Table - A-3-4

The Eastern Nanda Devi

		Height in		Location North	East
S.N.	**Peaks**	**Meter**	**Feet**	**Latitudes**	**Longitudes**
1.	Hardeol	7151	23460	30°33' 41"	80°00' 48"
2.	Tirsuli	7074	23210	30°34' 59"	80°01' 22"
3.	Tirsuli West	7035	23080	30°34' 45"	80°00' 14"
4.	Nanda Kot	6861	22510	30°16' 51"	80°04' 16"
5.	Changuch	6322	20740	30°17' 42"	80°02' 28"
6.	Kuchela	6294	20650	30°18' 27"	80°05' 26"
7.	Lohar Deo	6245	20490	30°28' 12"	80°03' 00"
8.	Nandabhanar	6236	20460	30°15' 57"	80°03' 56"
9.	Urja Tirche	6202	20350	30°39' 00"	80°01' 02"
10.	Chalab	6160	20210	30°35' 49"	80°02' 39"
11.	Kholi	6114	20060	30°35' 34"	80°04' 50"
12.	Ikualari	6059	19880	30°34' 18"	80°05' 40"
13.	Dangthal	6050	19850	30°13' 36"	80°06' 00"
14.	Nandakhani	6029	19780	30°15' 44"	80°04' 30"

1	2	3	4	5	6
The Northern Nanda Devi (North of the Rishi Ganga)					
1.	Dunagiri	7062	23184	30°31' 57"	79°50' 02"
2.	Rishi Pahar	6992	22940	30°31' 58"	79°59' 59"
3.	Kalanka	6931	22740	30°30' 01"	79°56' 36"
4.	Changabang	6864	22520	30°29' 59"	79°55' 37"
5.	P 6635	6635	21770	30°35' 13"	79°58' 53"
6.	Deo Damla	6620	21720	30°29' 42"	80°01' 16"
7.	Mangraon	6568	21550	30°28' 36"	80°00' 48"
8.	P 6547	6547	21480	30°30' 59"	79°57' 56"
9.	P 6523	6523	21400	30°31' 33"	79°53' 56"
10.	P 6504	6504	21340	30°36' 19"	79°58' 10"
11.	Purbi Dunagiri	6489	21290	30°31' 58"	79°54' 46"
12.	Latu Dhura	6392	20970	30°23' 36"	80°02' 05"
13.	Lampak I	6325	20750	30°27' 29"	79°56' 39"
14.	Bamchu	6303	20680	30°26' 56"	80°01' 25"
15.	Sakram	6254	20520	30°26' 00"	80°02' 08"
16.	Rishi Kot	6236	20407	30°27' 28"	79°53' 42"
17.	Lampak II	6181	20280	30°38' 31"	79°55' 57"
18.	Hanuman	6075	19930	30°28' 46"	79°50' 02"
19.	Barmatia	6041	19820	30°45' 17"	79°58' 10"
The Southern Nanda Devi (South of Rishi Ganga)					
1.	Nanda Devi	7816	25645	30°22' 32"	79°58' 22"
2.	Nandadevi East	7434	24390	30°21' 58"	79°59' 30"
3.	Trisul	7120	23360	30°18' 46"	79°46' 38"
4.	Mrigthuni	6855	22940	30°17' 28"	79°49' 49"
5.	Maiktoli	6803	22320	30°16' 14"	79°52' 28"
6.	Devtoli	6788	22270	30°17' 18"	79°51' 11"
7.	Trisul II	6690	21950	30°17' 37"	79°46' 36"
8.	Devistan I	6678	21910	30°20' 02"	79°52' 50"
9.	Panwali Dwar	6663	21860	30°17' 20"	79°57' 22"
10.	P 6648	6648	21810	30°18' 39"	79°52' 19"
11.	Nanda Khat	6611	21690	30°18' 07"	79°58' 47"
12.	P 6596	6596	21640	30°17' 52"	79°56' 42"
13.	P 6538	6538	21450	30°18' 44"	79°57' 02"

1	2	3	4	5	6
14.	Devistan II	6529	21420	30°20' 57"	79°53' 00"
15.	Bethartoli	6352	20840	30°22' 37"	79°47' 05"
16.	Bethartolisouth	6318	20730	30°22' 04"	79°47' 39"
17.	Nanda Ghunti	6309	20700	30°20' 56"	79°43' 09"
18.	Tharkot	6099	20010	30°14' 02"	79°49' 50"
19.	Ronti	6063	19892	30°22' 10"	79°43' 13"

Source: Indian Mountaineer 1988, Autumn, No. 22.

Bibliography

Annals of Tourism Research, Pergamon Press Ltd., USA.

Ahluwalia, H.P.S., (1985). *Himalaya A Practical Guide*, Himalaya Books, New Delhi.

Ahuja, S.P. & Saran, S.A., (Ed), (1977). *Tourism in India, A Prospective to 1990*, the Institute of Economic and Market Research, New Delhi.

Akhtar, J., (1990). *Tourism Management in India*, Ashish Pub. House, New Delhi.

Ali, Salim, (1977), *The Book of Indian Birds*, Bombay Natural History Society, Bombay.

Anand, M.M., (1976), *Tourism and Hotel Industry in India*, Prentice Hall of India, Pvt. Ltd., New Delhi.

Armington, S., (1980). *Trekking in the Himalayas*, Lonely Planet, Victoria Australia.

Amold, H. and August, G., *The Thrones of the Gods* Macmillan, New York.

Atkinson, E.T., (1973). *The Himalayan Gazetteer, Vol. I, II & III*, Cosmo Publication, Delhi.

Bagri, S.C. (Ed), (1994). *Journal of Tourism, Vol. 2*, Department of Tourism, HNB Garhwal University, Srinagar Garhwal.

Bagri, S.C., (1993). Tourism Management Education: Issues and Challenges, Navin Mathur (ed), *Tourism and Socio Economic*, Jodhpur.

Bagri, S.C. (Ed), (1998). *Journal of Tourism, Vol. 3*, Department of Tourism, HNB Garhwal University, Srinagar Garhwal.

Berryman, G.D., (1972). *Hindus of the Himalaya: Ethnography and Change*, University of California Press, California.

Bhardwaj, S.M., (1973). *Hindu Places of Pilgrimage in India,* Thomson Press Ltd., Delhi.

Bhardwaj, D.S., Kandari, O.P., (Eds), (1998). *Domestic Tourism in India,* Indus Publishing Company, New Delhi.

Bhatia, A.K., (1982). *Tourism Developemnt: Principles and Practices,* Sterling Pub. Ltd., New Delhi.

Bhattacharya, G., (1980). "Assessing Scenic Resource in Landscape for Resort Siting: A Case of Pachmarhi India", *Tourism Recreation Research*, Vol. V, No. 2.

Bisht, D.S., (1982). *Guide to Garhwal and Kumoun Hills,* Dehradun, Trishul Publication.

Bisht, Harshvanti, (1994). *Tourism in Garhwal Himalaya: With Special Reference to Mountaineering and Trekking in Uttarkashi and Chamoli Districts,* Indus Publishing Company, New Delhi.

Braham, T., (1974). *Himalayan Odyssey,* George Allen and Unwin Ltd., London.

Bruce, H.C.G., (1923). *The Assault of Mount Everest*, London.

Bryden, J.M., (1973). *Tourism and Development, A Case Study of the Common Wealth Caribbean,* Cambridge University Press.

Bond, Ruskin, (1988). *Beautiful Garhwal Heaven in Himalayas,* EBD Educational Pvt. Ltd., Dehradun.

Bose, S.C., (1968). *Land and People of the Himalaya,* Indian Publications, Calcutta.

Burkart, A.J., and Medlik, S., (1975). *The Management of Tourism,* Heinemann, London.

Burkart, A.J., (1981). *Tourism, Past, Present and Future,* Heinemann, London.

Chadha, S.K., (1988). *Himalaya's Ecology and Environment,* Mittal Publication., New Delhi.

Chamoli, S.P. (1993). *The Great Himalayan - Transverse,* Vikash Publishing House, New Delhi.

Chaube, S.K. (Ed.), (1985). *The Himalayas,* Sterling Publishers Pvt. Ltd., New Delhi.

Christopher, J., (1985). *The Business of Tourism*, Macdonald and Evans, Britain.

Cleare, J., *The World Guide to Mountain and Mountaineering,* May Flowers Book, London.

Cooper, C.P. (Ed), (1992). *Progress in Tourism, Recreation and Hospitality Management, Vol. I, II & III*, CBS Publishers, New Delhi.

Dabral, S.P., (1965). *Uttarakhand Ka Itihas, (in Hindi)*, Veer Gatha Prakashan, Dogadda Garhwal.

Datar, B.N., (1961). *Himalayan Pilgrimage,* Publication Division, Ministry of Broadcasting, New Delhi.

Darian, S.G., (1978). *The Ganges in Myth and History,* The University Press Hawaii, Honolulu.

Darman, R.F. and others, (1973), *Ecological principles for Economic Development,* John Wiley and Sons, New York.

Detwyler, T.R., (1971), *Man's Impact on Environment,* McGraw-Hill Book Company, New York.

Department of Tourism, Govt. of India, June, (1996),*Report of Working Group on Tourism for the Ninth Five Year Plan, 1997-2002.*

Dewan, M.L., (1990),*People's Participation in Himalayan Eco-System Developemnt,* Concept Pub., New Delhi.

Dosewell, R. and others, (1979), *Further Case Studies in Tourism,* Barrie and Jankins Ltd., London.

Dosewell, R. and Gamble, P.R., (1979), *Marketing and Planning Hotels and Tourism Projects,* Barrie and Jankins Ltd., London.

Dwivedi, O.P., and Tiwari, B.N., (1987), *Environmental Crisis and Hindu Religion,* Gitanjali Pub. House, New Delhi.

Eltringham, S.K., (1988), *Wildlife Resources and Economic Development,* International Book Distributors, Dehradun.

Fonia, K.S., (1998), *The Traveller's Guide To Uttarakhand,* Garuda Books, Chamoli,Garhwal.

Forster, R.R., *Planning For Man and Nature in National parks,* Morges, Switzerland.

Gautam, Ashutosh, (1990), *Ecology and Pollution of Mountain Waters,* Ashish Pub. House, New Delhi.

Gearing, C.E., (1976). *Planning for Tourism Development: Quantitative Approach,* Prager Pub., New Delhi.

Green, M. (1995). *Nature Reserves of the Himalaya and the Mountains of Central Asia (World Conservation Monitoring Centre in Collaboration with IUCN Commission of National park and Protected area).*

Gunn, C.A., (1994),*Tourism Planning: Basics, Concepts, Cases,* Washington, DC, Taylor and Francis.

Gupta, R.K., (1983). *The Living Himalaya, Vol. I,* Aspects of Environment and Resource Ecology of Garhwal, Delhi.

Hillary, E., (1979), *From the Ocean to Sky Jet Boating up the Ganges,* Holdder and Stoughton, London.

Hunt, Nigel, (1975),*Camping,* Knight Books Hodder and Stoughton, London.

IITTM Journal of Travel and Tourism, (1997). Vol. 1 & 2, IITTM, Gwalior.

IITTM, Gwalior, (1997),*Report of the Conference on Sustainable Tourism Planning and Development.*

Inskeep, Edward, (1991),*Tourism Planning: An Integrated and Sustainable Development Approach,* VNR Tourism and Commercial Recreation Series, New York, Van Nostrand Reinhold.

Iozawa, T., (1980). *Trekking in the Himalaya,* Translated by Kornhauser, M.U. and Kornhauser, D.H., Allied Pub., Bombay.

Jafari, Jafar, (1982), "The Tourism Market Basket of Goods and Services: The Components and Nature of Tourism", in Singh T.V. (Ed), Studies in Tourism, Wildlife Parks and Conservation, *Metropolitan Book Co., New Delhi.*

Jain Madhu, (1995). *The Abode of Mahashiva: Cult and Symbology in Jaunsar - Bawar in the Mid-Himalayas*, Induş Publishing Company, New Delhi.

Jones, Mike, (1979). *Canoeing Down Everst*, Hodder and Stoughton, London.

Kadt, E.d., (1979). *Tourism Passport to Developemnt*, Oxford University Press.

Kaiser, C.J. and Helber, L.E., (1978). *Tourism Planning and Development*, CBI Pub. Company, Boston, USA.

Kandari, O.P. (1984). Wildlife of Garhwal Himalaya: A recreational Resource for Tourism Promotion. *Doctoral Dissertation Submitted to University of Garhwal*, Srinagar Garhwal, (Unpublished).

Kamlesh Kumar and Nityanand, (1989),*The Holy Himalaya: A geogrphical Interpretation of Garhwal*, Daya Publishing House, Delhi.

Kapadia, H. (Ed), (1983). *Himalayan Journal*, Vol. 39 (1981-82), Oxford University Press, New Delhi.

Kapadia, H. (1997),*High Himalaya Unknown Valleys,* Indus Pub. Company, New Delhi.

Kasumov, R.M., (1974). *The Problem of Systems Theory Approach to the Question of Using the Tourist Resources of Developing Countries,* in (Ed), Matzhetter, J. Studies in Geography of Tourism, Frankfurt.

Kaul, R.N., (1985). *Dyanamics of Tourism A Triology*, Vol. 1, 2 & 3, Sterling Publishers, New Delhi.

Kaur, J., (1985). *Himalayan Pilgrimage and the New Tourism*, Himalayan Books, New Delhi.

Khachar, L.K., (1978). "The Nanda Devi Sanctuary", *Journal of Bombay natural History Society*, Vol. 75, No. 3, Bombay.

Kharakwal, S.C., (1993). *Physico-Cultural Environment and Development in U.P. Himalaya*, Nutan Publications, Kotdwar Garhwal.

Khanduri, B.M. (1994),*Archaeology of Alaknanda Valley (Central Himalaya),* Book India Publishing Co., New Delhi

Kohli, M.S., (1989). *Mountaineering in India,* Vikas Pub. House, New Delhi.

Kumar, N. and Ahluwalia, H.P.S. (Major), (1978),*Trisul Ski Expedition,* Vikas Pub. House, New Delhi.

Lal, J.S. and Moddie, A.G., (1981). *The Himalaya Aspects of Change,* I.T.C. Oxford University Press, New Delhi.

Lamba, B.S., Status Survey of Endangered and Threatened Species of Mammals and Birds at Nanda Devi National Park, *Zoological Survey (1981-84), India.*

Lickorish, L.J. and Kershaw, A.G., (1958). *The Travel Trade,* Practical Press, London.

Little, A.D., (1967). *Tourism and Recreation,* United States, Department of Commerce, Washington D.C. Govt. Printing Office.

Lloyd, E.H., "*Tourism Impact: The Need for Regional Planning*", Newzealand, Willington.

Malhotra, S.S., (1983). *Gangotri and Gaumukh - A Trek to the Holy Shrine,* Allied Publishers, New Delhi.

Malhotra, S.S.L., (1977). *At the Feet of the Badri,* Vikas Pub. House, New Delhi.

Marry, W.H., *The Scottish Himalayan Expedition,* J.M. Dent and Sons, London.

Mason, Kenneth, *Abode of Snow,* E.P. Dutton and Co., New York.

Mathieson, A., and Wall, G., (1982). *Tourism, Economic, Physical and Social Impact, Longman, London.*

Mazumdar, D.N., (1961),*Races and Cultures of India,* Asia Publishing House, Bombay.

Mcintosh, R.W., (1972), *Tourism Principles, Practices and Philosophies,* Columbus, Ohio, U.S.A.

Michael, Peters, (1969), *International Tourism,* Hutchinson, London.

Milne, L.J., Milne, M., Editors of Life, (1963). The Mountains, Life Nature Library, *Time Life International,* Netherland, N.V.

Mill, R.C. & Morrisson, A.M., (1985),*The Tourism System: An Introductory Text,* Prentice-Hall, New Jersey.

Motwani, M.C. (Ed), *Indian Mountaineer,* Nos. 1 to 25, New Delhi.

Murphy, P.E., (1985), *Tourism A Community Approach,* Methuen, New York.

Naithani, S.P. (1994),*Uttrakhand Ko Tirth and Mandir (In Hindi),* Pavetri Prakashan, Srinagar Garhwal.

Nautiyal, K.P. and Khanduri, B.M. (1977). "Ranihat and its Environs: Excavation of an early Historical site in Garhwal", *The Himalaya, Vol. I*, pp. 22-38.

Negi, J.M.S., (1982),*Tourism and Hoteliering*, Gitanjali Pub. House, New Delhi.

Negi, S.S. (1991),*Himalayan Rivers, Lakes and Glaciers*, Indus Publishing Company, New Delhi.

Negi, S.S. (1994), *Garhwal: The Land and People*, Indus Publishing Company, New Delhi.

Negi, S.S. (1995),*Handbook of National Parks, Sanctuaries and Biosphere Reserves in india*. Indus Publishing Company, New Delhi.

Negi, J.M.S. (1995),*Himalayan Heritage: A Socio-Economic, Cultural and Tourism Analysis*, Gitanjali Publishing House, New Delhi.

Norval, A.J., (1936),*The Tourist Industry*, Sir Issac Pitam and Sons, London.

O'akley, E.S., (1905),*The Holy Himalaya*, London.

O'akley,E.S.,andGairola,T.D.,(1935), *The Himalayan Folklore*, Allahabad.

Ogilvie, F.S., (1941). *The Tourist Movement*, Staple Press Ltd., London.

Owan, Oliver, (1971),*Natural Resource Conservation: An Ecological Approach*, Macmillan Pub., New York.

Painuli, P.N., *A Tourist's View of the Valley of Gods*, Vanguard Press, Dehradun.

Pallis, Marco, (1946), *Peaks and Lamas*, Jarrold and Sons Ltd., The Empire Press, Britain.

Parekh, N., (1977), *The Himalayas*, India Book House Pvt. Ltd., Bombay.

Pearce, Douglas, G., (1980), *Tourism in the South Pacific*, University of Canterbury, Newzealand.

Pilgrim,(1990),*Wandering in the Himmala (reprint)* ,Gyanodays Prakashan, Nainital.

Patiram, (1917), *Garhwal Ancient and Modern*, Army Press, Shimla.

Randhawa, M.S., (1974). *Travel in the Western Himalayas*, Thomson Press, Publication Division, India.

Raturi, H.K., (1980). *Garhwal Ka Itihas* (in Hindi) Bhagirathi Prakashan, Tehri Garhwal.

Rebuff, G., (1971). *On Ice and Snow and Rock*, Translated from French by Evans P.K. and Ward, London.

Robinson, H., (1976). *A Geography of Tourism*, Macdonald and Evans, London.

Rustamji, N.K. and Ramble, C., (1990), *Himalayan Environment and Culture*, Indus Pub. Company, New Delhi.

Sam and Beryl, E., (1965),*The First Book of Switzerland*, Edmund Ward Pub. Ltd., London.

Sankratyayan, R., (1935), *Himalaya Parichaya Part I Garhwal and Part II Kumaon*, Law Journal Press, Allahabad.

Seshadri, B., (1986), *India's Wildlife and Wildlife Reserves*, Sterling Pub., New Delhi.

Shah, Giriraj, *The Kingdom of Gods: Uttarakhand*, Abhinav Pub., New Delhi.

Shanker, Kripa, (1987). *Uttar Pradesh in Statistics*, Ashish Publishing Hosue, New Delhi.

Sharma, M.M., (1978). *Through the Valley of Gods*, Vision Books Pvt. Ltd., New Delhi.

Sherring, C.A., (1974). *Western Tibet and the Indian borderland*, Cosmo Pub., Delhi.

Shipton, E., *The Untravelled World*, Hodder and Stoughton, London.

Singh, J.S. (Ed), (1985). *Environmental Regeneration in Himalaya*, Nainital.

Singh, Karan, *Tourism in India*, Deptt. of Tourism, India.

Singh, Samer, (1986). *India's Natural Heritage*, Natraj Pub., Dehradun.

Singh, T.V., (1975). *Tourism and Tourist Industry*, New Heights, Delhi.

Singh, T.V. and Kaur J (Ed), (1982). *Studies in Tourism Wildlife Parks Conservation*, Metropolitan Book, New Delhi.

Singh, T.V. and Kaur J (Ed), (1985). *Integrated Mountain Development*, The English Book Store, New Delhi.

Singh, T.V. and Kaur, J. (Ed), (1989). *Studies in Himalayan Ecology and Development Strategies*, Himalayan Books, New Delhi.

Singh, T.V., (1989). *The Kulu Valley Impact of Tourism Development in the Mountain Areas*, Himalayan Books, New Delhi.

Skinner, T. (Captain)m (1932). *The Excursion in India* including a Walk over the Himalaya Mountains to the Source of the Jamuna and Ganga, Vol. I & II.

Smythe, F.S., (1932). *Kamet Conquered,* Victor Gollancz Ltd., London.

Smythe, F.S., *The Valley of Flowers* (reprint), Natraj Pub. Rajpur Road, Dehradun.

Swift, Hugh, (1982). *The Trekkers Guide to the Himalaya & Karakoram*, Hodder and Stoughton, London.

Tata Economic Consultancy Service, (1982). *Employment Potential of Tourism in India*, Vol. I, II & III.

Tichy, H., (1970). *Himalayas*, Pub., Delhi.

Tilman, H.W., (1937). *The Ascent of Nanda Devi*, Cambridge Press.

Unsworth, Walt, (Ed), (1982). *Peaks, Passes & Glaciers*, Penguin Books, Great Britain.

U.P. Tourism (Hills) (1997), Report on area development plan for the Char Dham Circuit in U.P. Hills, Dehradun.

Valdiya, K.S., (1980). *Geology of Kumoun, Lesser Himalaya,* Wadia Institute of Himalayan Geology.

Wadia, D.N., (1966). *Geology of India,* Macmillan, London.

Walton, H.G., (1910). *British Garhwal: A Gazetteer,* Govt. Press, Allahabad.

Weare, Gary, (1986). *Trekking in the Indian Himalaya,* Lonely Planet Pub., Victoria, Australia.

Young, George, (1973). *Tourism Blessing or Blight,* Penguin Books Ltd., England.

INDEX